DATE DUE

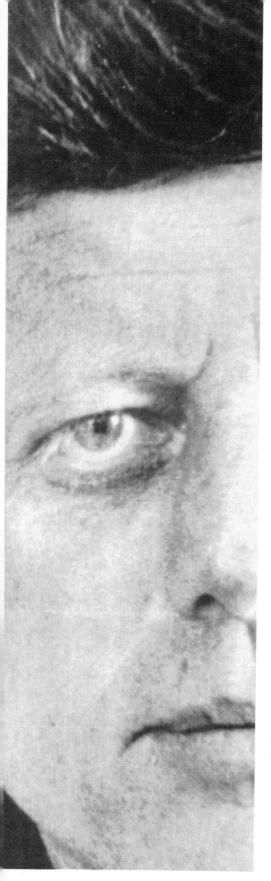

KENNEDY

University Press of Florida

Gainesville · Tallahassee · Tampa · Boca Raton

Pensacola · Orlando · Miami · Jacksonville · Ft. Myers · Sarasot

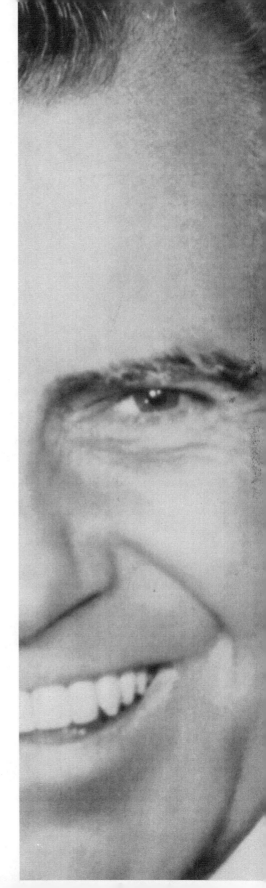

V. NIXON

The Presidential Election of 1960

Edmund F. Kallina Jr.

Copyright 2010 by Edmund F. Kallina Jr.

Printed in the United States of America. This book is printed on Glatfelter Natures Book, a paper certified under the standards of the Forestry Stewardship Council (FSC). It is a recycled stock that contains 30 percent post-consumer waste and is acid-free.

15   14   13   12   11   6   5   4   3   2

Library of Congress Cataloging-in-Publication Data

Kallina, Edmund F. (Edmund Frank), 1943–

Kennedy v. Nixon: the presidential election of 1960/Edmund F. Kallina Jr.

p. cm.

Includes bibliographical references and index.

ISBN 978–0-8130-3485-0 (alk. paper)

1. Presidents—United States—Election—1960. 2. Kennedy, John F. (John Fitzgerald), 1917–1963. 3. Nixon, Richard M. (Richard Milhous), 1913–1994.
4. United States—Politics and government—1953–1961. 5. Political campaigns —United States—History—20th century. I. Title. II. Title: Kennedy vs Nixon. III. Title: Kennedy versus Nixon. IV. Title: Presidential election of 1960.

E837.7.K35 2010   973.9219–dc22

2010015134

The University Press of Florida is the scholarly publishing agency for the State University System of Florida, comprising Florida A&M University, Florida Atlantic University, Florida Gulf Coast University, Florida International University, Florida State University, New College of Florida, University of Central Florida, University of Florida, University of North Florida, University of South Florida, and University of West Florida.

University Press of Florida
15 Northwest 15th Street
Gainesville, FL 32611-2079
http://www.upf.com

For Carol and all of our years together

Contents

Acknowledgments

The publication of this book would not have been possible without the help and support of numerous individuals. I am acutely conscious of the debt owed to so many people who helped me in this project.

The staffs at the John F. Kennedy, Dwight D. Eisenhower, Lyndon B. Johnson, and Richard M. Nixon Libraries provided invaluable assistance. These libraries are national treasures. Similarly, I am most grateful to the National Archives site at Laguna Niguel, California, and most especially Paul Wormser for his patient and knowledgeable help. Laguna Niguel until 2006 was the repository for the vice-presidential papers of Richard Nixon.

In Florida, I would like to thank the Interlibrary Loan department of the University of Central Florida Library. The Interlibrary Loan staff procured numerous books, oral history interviews, and microfilm newspapers essential to this book. They did so with unfailing courtesy and efficiency.

Also at the University of Central Florida, I am thankful for the staff in the History Department, especially Carole Gonzalez, Nancy Rauscher, and Jennifer Krolowitz, who were always ready with a helping hand. Their efficiency along with their good-humored tolerance of my eccentricities will remain with me the rest of my days.

With computers, word processors, and photocopiers, research is immeasurably easier than it was fifty years ago. What is more burdensome is the expense of extended stays away from home while doing research. I was most fortunate that Steve DeZwart, Hank Royer, Lisl Fenwick, Heather McCrae, and Larry, Arleen, and Spencer Downing were kind enough to help me find inexpensive lodging so that without great financial resources I could conduct my research. Concordia University of Austin, Texas, is due thanks for this reason as well.

I am appreciative of those who read and offered their comments on the manuscript. Connie Lester improved the manuscript with her suggestions on writing. A special tribute is due Irwin Gellman, who offered wise counsel with good humor and an unrivaled knowledge of American politics in the 1950s. It is impossible to overstate his contribution. Only he knows how much of a difference he made in the manuscript.

A final word of gratitude must go to the University Press of Florida. Meredith Morris-Babb and Jacqueline Kinghorn Brown provided critical support in guiding me through the editorial process. I am deeply indebted to my copy editor, Susan Murray, who scrutinized the manuscript with a careful eye and made numerous changes and corrections. She is a consummate professional, and it was a joy to work with her. Any mistakes that remain are my responsibility alone.

The appendix table showing the state-by-state vote for president of the United States in 1960 is from *America Votes 5: A Handbook of Contemporary American Election Statistics*, compiled and edited by Richard M. Scammon, 1964. It is reprinted by permission of the University of Pittsburgh Press.

The Oral History Collection of Columbia University granted permission to cite and quote from its extensive archives.

Cast of Characters

Acheson, Dean. Democrat. Secretary of State, 1948–1953, in the Truman administration.

Adams, Sherman. Republican. Chief of staff for Eisenhower, 1953–1958. He was forced out in 1958 because of scandal and was not politically active in 1960.

Anderson, Robert. Secretary of the Treasury and much admired by Eisenhower.

Bailey, John. Democrat. Head of the Democratic Party in Connecticut and adviser to JFK.

Baker, Bobby. Democrat. Chief aide to Lyndon Johnson.

Bowles, Chester. Democrat. Connecticut congressman and liberal activist. He was governor, 1949–1951, and ambassador to India, 1951–1953.

Brown, Edmund G. "Pat." Democrat. Governor of California.

Clifford, Clark. Democrat. Adviser to Stuart Symington.

Daley, Richard J. Democrat. Mayor of Chicago.

Dawson, Richard. Democrat. Black congressman from Chicago.

DeSapio, Carmine. Democrat. Head of Tammany Hall in New York City.

Dewey, Thomas E. Republican. Governor of New York, 1943–1955, and presidential nominee in 1944 and 1948. He was out of office in 1960, although he remained politically active.

DiSalle, Michael. Democrat. Governor of Ohio.

Eisenhower, Dwight D. Republican. President of the United States, 1953–1961.

Folger, J. Clifford. Republican. Chairman of the Republican National Finance Committee.

Goldwater, Barry M. Republican. Arizona senator.

Goodwin, Richard. Democrat. Aide to JFK.

Green, William. Democrat. Congressman from Pennsylvania and most powerful politician in Philadelphia.

Hagerty, James. Press secretary for Eisenhower.

Hall, Leonard. Republican. Former chairman of the Republican National Committee. He was a presidential campaign manager in 1960.

Harlow, Bryce. Republican. White House aide to Eisenhower.

Harris, Louis. Pollster for JFK.

Humphrey, Hubert H. Democrat. Minnesota senator.

Jackson, Henry M. "Scoop." Democrat. Washington state senator.

Johnson, Lyndon B. Democrat. Senate majority leader from Texas. He was elected to the senate in 1948 and reelected in 1954.

Kefauver, Estes. Democrat. Tennessee senator.

Kennedy, John F. Democrat. Massachusetts senator. He was elected to the Senate in 1952 and reelected in 1958.

Kennedy, Joseph P. Democrat. Father of JFK.

Kennedy, Robert F. Democrat. Brother of JFK and his campaign manager.

Kerr, Robert. Democrat. Oklahoma senator.

Klein, Herbert. Republican. Press secretary for Richard Nixon.

Knight, Goodwin. Republican. Governor of California, 1953–1959. He ran for the Senate in 1958 but was defeated and was out of office in 1960.

Knowland, William F. Republican. California senator, 1945–1959. He served as Senate majority leader and then minority leader, 1953–1959. He was defeated in the 1958 election to become governor of California. Out of office in 1960.

Lausche, Frank. Democrat. Ohio senator.

Lawrence, David. Democrat. Governor of Pennsylvania.

Lodge, Henry Cabot, Jr. Republican. Ambassador to the U.N. Former Massachusetts senator.

McCarthy, Eugene. Democrat. Minnesota senator.

McCarthy, Joseph R. Republican. Wisconsin senator, 1947–1957. He died in 1957.

Merriam, Robert. Republican. White House aide to President Eisenhower.

Meyner, Richard. Democrat. Governor of New Jersey.

Morton, Thruston. Republican. Kentucky senator and chairman of the Republican National Committee.

Nixon, Richard M. Republican. Vice president of the United States, 1953–1961.

O'Donnell, Kenneth. Aide to JFK.

O'Neill, Thomas "Tip." Democrat. Massachusetts congressman.

Patterson, John. Democrat. Governor of Alabama.

Powell, Adam Clayton, Jr. Democrat. Black congressman from New York City.

Prendergast, Michael. Democrat. Chairman of the New York State Democratic Party.

Rayburn, Sam. Democrat. Texas congressman, first elected to Congress in 1912. Speaker of the House of Representatives, 1940–1947, 1949–1953, 1955–1961.

Robinson, Claude. Pollster for Richard Nixon.

Rockefeller, Nelson A. Republican. Governor of New York, elected in 1958.

Salinger, Pierre. Democrat. Press secretary for John F. Kennedy.

Roncalio, Teno. Democrat. Chairman of Wyoming Democratic Party.

Rustin, Bayard. Civil rights activist and advocate of nonviolent resistance.

Seaton, Fred. Republican. Secretary of the Interior.

Shriver, Sargent. Democrat. Brother-in-law of JFK, he was a leading figure in the civil rights section of the campaign.

Smathers, George. Democrat. Florida senator and friend of JFK.

Smith, Stephen. Democrat. Brother-in-law of JFK, he handled campaign finances.

Sorensen, Theodore. Democrat. Aide to and chief speechwriter for JFK.

Stevenson, Adlai E. Democrat. Former governor of Illinois. Presidential nominee in 1952 and 1956. In 1960 he held no office but was a contender for the presidential nomination.

Stratton, William G. Republican. Governor of Illinois.

Symington, Stuart. Democrat. Missouri senator. He was former secretary of the U.S. Air Force.

Taft, Robert A. Republican. Ohio senator. Leader of Republican conservatives in 1940s and early 1950s. He died in 1953.

Udall, Stewart. Democrat. Arizona congressman.

Vandiver, Ernest. Democrat. Governor of Georgia.

White, Byron "Whizzer." Democrat. He headed the JFK campaign for nomination in Colorado. Later he was national director of Citizens for Kennedy–Johnson.

Whitman, Ann. Secretary to Dwight D. Eisenhower.

Wilkins, Roy. Executive director of the NAACP.

Williams, G. Mennen. Democrat. Governor of Michigan.

Wofford, Harris. Democrat. Friend of Martin Luther King Jr. and member of Kennedy campaign's civil rights section.

Introduction

Almost fifty years ago, Theodore H. White wrote perhaps the most famous book in the history of American political journalism, *The Making of the President 1960*. It won a Pulitzer Prize and made the author a wealthy celebrity. A half century later, its chronicle of the election continues to be the accepted version of the event.

White's narrative was about John F. Kennedy and his quest for the highest office in the land. The author invested his protagonist with a multitude of virtues. Although he did not know it at the time, White was writing the first installment of the story of the Kennedy presidency as Camelot. Later, in 1963, he and Jacqueline Kennedy would collaborate to fasten the label of Camelot on JFK's time in the White House. So powerful were the book's imagery and eloquence that, even today, citizens and scholars alike continue to conceive of the 1960 election in terms defined by Theodore H. White.

Nineteen sixty was a landmark election year. Three of the four candidates on the two national tickets (John F. Kennedy, Lyndon B. Johnson, and Richard M. Nixon) would eventually become president. The election took place during one of the most tense periods of the Cold War. The election year found the United States confronting a serious crisis in Berlin as well as deteriorating situations in Cuba and Indochina. Many Americans thought that the Soviet Union had achieved supremacy in intercontinental ballistic missiles. The outcome of the election, voters believed, would determine the fate of the country.

The election results were extraordinarily close in contrast to the great majority of the previous presidential contests in the twentieth century. From 1900 to 1956, the elections of 1916 and 1948 were competitive, but none of the thirteen others were. The popular-vote margin in 1960 was the thinnest of the twenty-five elections from 1900 through 1996. In the Electoral College, only 1916 and 1976 were closer.

The 1960 election was remarkable in other ways. Voter turnout was the highest in fifty years—and no voter turnout since has matched it. It was the first election to include televised presidential debates. John F. Kennedy became the first Roman Catholic president of the United States. Kennedy pioneered a new way of campaigning for the presidency that became the standard. He started immediately after the election in 1956 and worked relentlessly. The Kennedy campaign produced an innovation in media coverage as Theodore H. White attached himself to the campaign, observed it from start to finish, and published a best-selling book documenting it. In doing so, White ushered in a new era of political journalism.

For these reasons, the 1960 election looms very large in the political history of the United States as well as in the popular imagination. Yet surprisingly, it has stimulated few narratives and little analysis. Summaries of the election have appeared in Kennedy and Nixon biographies as well as in studies of the Kennedy presidency. Chris Matthews made a contribution with his examination of the Kennedy-Nixon relationship in *Kennedy & Nixon: The Rivalry That Shaped Postwar America* (1996). In these books, though, the election constitutes only a small part of the narrative. As such, none of them is comparable to Theodore H. White's work. The most recent treatments of the election offer new viewpoints, but they do not depart from what Stephen Ambrose called the "Teddy White thesis"—the idea that "Kennedy ran a brilliant campaign while Nixon committed blunder after blunder."[1]

As the fiftieth anniversary of the 1960 election (and White's book) approaches, a fresh analysis is appropriate. *The Making of the President 1960* is a marvelous piece of journalism, but it is now almost a half century old and not without defects that have become more obvious over the years. In addition, the availability of vast new archival materials and the passage of fifty years make possible insights that were not available to White.

My desire is to offer a new perspective on the 1960 presidential election. I do not intend this to be an exhaustive narrative of the campaign and election. Rather, it is an effort to provide an overview with emphasis on the most critical and controversial events and issues. It does not worship Camelot, and it does evaluate Richard M. Nixon and his campaign more highly than has been usual. Underlying this narrative is the belief that 1960 matched two outstanding candidates against each other. The men were remarkable, and so were their campaigns.

Ultimately, any rendering of the 1960 election must come to grips with the two most important questions concerning the campaign and election. First, why did Kennedy win and Nixon lose? And second, why was Kennedy's margin of victory so small? These two questions and my answers to them form the heart of this book. Because 1960 was an epic year for American politics, it deserves a detailed reconsideration that is free of Theodore White's hero worship. This book is an attempt to provide a contemporary reinterpretation and to open a new era of debate on this turning point in American history.

1

National Party Politics in the 1950s

"In his [William Knowland's] case, there seems to be no final answer to the question 'How stupid can you get?'"

—President Dwight D. Eisenhower on Republican Senate Minority Leader William F. Knowland

Inevitably, the roots of the national party politics of one decade reside in the preceding ones. The 1950s are no exception. An understanding of American politics in the 1950s, therefore, begins with the story of the 1930s and 1940s and the impact of the Great Depression, Franklin Delano Roosevelt, the New Deal, World War II, and the outbreak of the Cold War on the two national political parties.

The 1930s and 1940s were years of great turbulence. The upheaval began with the onset of the Great Depression, the greatest economic, financial, and social catastrophe ever to strike the United States. It ruined millions of lives, destroyed or severely damaged innumerable institutions, affected every aspect of American life, and produced a financial, economic, social, and political convulsion that changed the face of America.

Among the political institutions that felt its sting was the Republican Party, ascendant since the late 1890s and the great political realignment of that decade. Once established as the majority party, the GOP maintained this status through the first three decades of the twentieth century, losing just two presidential elections and controlling both houses of Congress for all but eight years between 1900 and 1930. In the elections of 1928, Republicans retained the White House with 58.2 percent of the popular vote and maintained control of Congress with majorities of 269–165 in the House of Representatives and 56–39 in the Senate. Republican gubernatorial candidates won twenty-four of thirty-five contests in that year. The GOP dominated at both state and national levels.[1]

This Republican supremacy dissipated and then crashed along with the national economy in the early 1930s. The GOP managed to maintain its congressional majorities in the midterm elections of 1930, but the depth and the duration of the Depression along with President Herbert Hoover's inability to fashion an effective response to the crisis crushed the party in 1932. In that year, Democrats won control of the White House, both branches of Congress, and an overwhelming majority of statehouses—and they did it decisively. Franklin Delano Roosevelt won 57.4 percent of the popular vote. Democratic candidates for the House of Representatives recorded 54 percent of the cumulative popular vote for the House. In the gubernatorial races, the Democratic vote reached 58.5 percent. Never before in the history of the Democratic-Republican competition that began in the 1850s had Democrats done so well or Republicans so badly.

And 1932 was just the beginning. The Democratic ascent continued through 1934; in 1936, in a referendum on his presidency and the New Deal, Franklin D. Roosevelt swept to a landslide reelection victory, losing only Vermont and Maine and achieving a victory of 523–8 in the Electoral College, the largest margin in the twentieth century. Voters confirmed their endorsement of Democratic policies in the House of Representatives and the Senate. In the House, Democrats won 335 seats and Republicans 89. In the Senate, the count was 76 Democrats and 16 Republicans. At the state level, Democrats won twenty-eight of thirty-two gubernatorial contests that year. Nineteen thirty-six was the worst election year in Republican history.[2]

Thankfully for Republicans, 1936 was the low point. After this date, a rather remarkable GOP recovery began in spite of the association of the party with the greatest financial debacle in American history. Democratic majorities in Congress and in the statehouses diminished significantly. In 1942, Republicans elected 210 members to the House of Representatives. By the early 1940s, the Democratic advantage in those who identified themselves as Democrats was down to a margin of 4–5 percent. Even FDR's overwhelming popular majorities declined in 1940 and 1944, receding from almost 61 percent in 1936 to a level of 54 to 55 percent in the two contests in the 1940s. The last Roosevelt presidential victory saw Democrats claim just 52 percent of the national vote for the House. After the 1944 elections, Republicans held as many statehouses as Democrats. Between 1937 and 1945, the GOP reestablished itself as a competitive national party.[3]

This Republican resilience surprised those doomsayers who predicted the demise of the party in the mid-1930s. The GOP would again defy the predictions of those who saw it on the verge of collapse in the mid-1960s after the Goldwater debacle and then once more in the mid-1970s following Watergate. The Republican Party of the twentieth century had enormous reservoirs of strength. It was the chief political institution representing the values of American small and medium-sized towns (outside the South), of right-wing and mainstream Protestantism (outside the South), and of

American business (both large and small). These were not inconsequential resources to be able to draw upon, and even in the darkest days of the mid-1930s, the mid-1960s, and the mid-1970s, the dangers of Republican extinction were much exaggerated.

While the Republicans began a recovery in 1938 that lasted to the end of the Roosevelt presidency, one could not hide the reality that, although the party had rebounded, the Republicans remained the minority party at every level of American politics. Between 1933 and 1940, a new majority coalition emerged from the combination of the Great Depression and Franklin D. Roosevelt and his New Deal. The Democratic Party of FDR encompassed the elements of the old Democratic Party—the white South, the northern big-city political machines, and liberal intellectuals. But it was much stronger with white ethnics, and it also included new elements, most notably organized labor and African Americans. Organized labor and black America exerted a liberalizing effect on the New Deal and the Democratic Party. The majority Democratic Party that emerged by 1940 was much more liberal than the same party had been in the 1920s.

This new Democratic majority dominated American politics during Roosevelt's presidency. It won four presidential elections and never lost control of either the House of Representatives or the Senate. When FDR died on April 12, 1945, he left the White House, Capitol Hill, and half the statehouses of the country in Democratic hands.

Despite the long list of victories for Democrats in the 1930s and the first half of the 1940s, with FDR's death, a serious question existed about the future of the Democratic majority. The party and its successes were all wrapped up in FDR. What would happen with FDR no longer at the head of the party ticket? Unlike the Republican supremacy in the first three decades of the century, when six different individuals had led the GOP to victory, the New Deal era was entirely identified with a single man. The simple arithmetic of the elections from 1932 through 1944 was there for all to see. FDR outpolled Democratic congressional candidates in all four of his runs for the presidency. There was a significant dropoff in the Democratic vote in the midterm elections of 1938 and 1942 when FDR was not on the ballot (see table 1.1). Without FDR at the top of the ticket, Democrats had to wonder how safe their margins in subsequent elections would be.

The initial answer to this question that came in the midterm elections of 1946—the first elections following the death of FDR and the end of World War II—was highly disconcerting to the majority party. Democrats lost a majority of the gubernatorial races along with fifty-four seats in the House of Representatives, thirteen in the Senate, and control of both House and

Table 1.1. Democratic Percentages of the Vote in the Roosevelt Era, 1932–1944

Year	President	House of Representatives
1932	57.4%	56.3%
1934	——	57.0
1936	60.8	58.7
1938	——	49.6
1940	54.7	53.2
1942	——	47.2
1944	53.4	52.0

Source: Rusk, ed., A Statistical History of the American Electorate, pp. 134, 220.

Senate. However, the Republican triumph was short-lived. President Harry S Truman fought back hard. Republicans overestimated their strength in 1948 and became overconfident of recapturing the White House.

In the biggest upset in presidential history, Harry S Truman defeated Thomas E. Dewey. Truman won despite the unanimous predictions of pollsters and political pundits and despite the presence of two splinter Democratic candidates (Strom Thurmond and Henry Wallace) on the ballot who presumably subtracted from his vote total. To this day, the 1948 election excites the popular imagination and provokes an ongoing debate among scholars as to how Truman managed to win.[4]

Less frequently noted is the spectacular comeback Democrats mounted in 1948 in Congress. In the House of Representatives, Democrats picked up seventy-five seats, establishing a majority of ninety-two, their largest in six years. They also regained control of the Senate, picking up nine seats there. In spite of Harry Truman's justifiably famous victory, the Democratic congressional vote was even more impressive, although one must concede that the presence of Wallace and Thurmond, with the resulting dilution of the Truman vote, makes comparisons difficult.

If the Republican victory of 1946 was short-lived, so was the Democratic triumph of 1948. President Truman achieved some remarkable successes after taking office in 1945, including formulating and establishing the Marshall Plan and laying the groundwork for the North Atlantic Treaty Organization (NATO), but after his inauguration in 1949, he encountered one reversal after another. The communist triumph on mainland China, the Alger Hiss case, revelations of scandal and corruption in Washington, the surprise North Korean attack on South Korea, and the more shattering Chinese onslaught in Korea in November 1950 left Truman extraordinarily unpopular and the administration under siege. As measured by a June 1951

Gallup Poll, 61 percent of respondents disapproved of Truman's conduct of the presidency, and only 24 percent approved. Although this number improved slightly in 1952, when he left office in 1953, Gallup showed just 31 percent approval and 56 percent disapproval.[5]

In these circumstances, once again the pendulum swung in the Republican direction. In the elections of 1950, Republicans picked up twenty-eight additional members in the House and five in the Senate and won two-thirds of the gubernatorial contests that year. Republicans could not claim control of either branch of Congress, but the political tide clearly favored them in the upcoming presidential election in 1952.

Although the GOP outlook appeared bright as 1952 began, Republicans faced a major dilemma in their selection of a presidential nominee. The eastern wing of the party and its allies, which had accommodated itself to New Deal social programs and to the new American foreign policy associated with the United Nations, the Marshall Plan, and NATO, had named the last three nominees—Wendell Wilkie in 1940 and Thomas Dewey in 1944 and 1948. All had been unsuccessful, and, in the eyes of most, the abject failure of the 1948 campaign discredited both Dewey and the accommodationist approach he represented. Hard-line conservative elements unreconciled to the New Deal domestic policies and its foreign policy manifestations were bitterly opposed to another candidate of the Wilkie-Dewey stripe.

On the other hand, conservatives had their own problems when it came to putting forward a presidential contender. Their leader, Senator Robert A. Taft of Ohio, possessed a formidable intellect, a high reputation for honesty and integrity, and a famous Republican name, but his merits as a potential winning candidate were a different matter. Taft lacked the common touch, although he had done well enough in Ohio elections; was easily caricatured as the enemy of organized labor and the working man (through his identification with the Taft-Hartley Act); and had the capacity to provoke serious defections by eastern Republicans who rejected his positions, especially on foreign policy. His ability to expand appeal beyond his conservative base was in doubt.

This time good fortune came to the GOP. Elements of the Dewey wing identified and recruited the best possible candidate, General Dwight D. Eisenhower, and managed to nominate him over the protests of the Taft opposition. Eisenhower, with his bright smile, sunny disposition, grandfatherly appearance, and optimistic demeanor, proved to be an outstanding candidate. What was not well understood then was that Eisenhower possessed a first-class intellect and was marvelously suited to the office of the presidency. Of the presidents in the twentieth century, Eisenhower came to the White House with the greatest familiarity with major world figures and the greatest insight into military affairs and their political implications.

This inner Eisenhower was not understood in the 1950s (or even the 1960s and 1970s). Instead, the conventional wisdom regarded Ike as a popular war hero who possessed a pleasant smile but no great intellect. In 1962, the historian Arthur M. Schlesinger Jr. solicited a rating of American presidents from a group of distinguished professional historians. The results of this survey put Eisenhower twenty-second of thirty-three, just behind Chester Arthur and Benjamin Harrison and just ahead of Andrew Johnson and Zachary Taylor.[6]

Others downgraded Eisenhower as well. Elite opinion in the academy, newspapers, news magazines, and other periodicals was dismissive of Eisenhower. Analysis of the presidency was much in vogue in the 1950s and the 1960s among political scientists. Their interpretations either implicitly or explicitly tended to offer an unflattering opinion of Eisenhower and his presidency. Public intellectuals like Walter Lippmann also disdained Ike.[7]

Even today, long after it became apparent that Eisenhower was a much better president than he was given credit for in the 1950s and 1960s, the standard works on the era offer a begrudging recognition of what Eisenhower wrought and little more. Typical is the comment of Charles Alexander, *Holding the Line: The Eisenhower Era, 1952–1961* (1975), who in his introduction observes that he voted against Eisenhower in both 1952 and 1956 and says that he is "in many respects in agreement" with the "conventional" interpretation of liberal historians that Eisenhower was "genial, well meaning, but indecisive and basically out of touch." The conventional wisdom to which Alexander and many others subscribe is that the administration was "standpattist in domestic affairs, unimaginative in its foreign policy, and neglectful of the nation's defenses."[8]

The opinions of academic historians are one thing, but how does one explain the disconnect between informed opinion of the time and Eisenhower's popularity and his administration's record? Several partial answers offer insights. Elite opinion in the academy and the news world enthusiastically supported Eisenhower's opponent in 1952 and 1956, Adlai E. Stevenson. Eisenhower undoubtedly suffered from the comparison between Stevenson's eloquence and his own sometimes garbled phrasing. Eisenhower made no effort to ingratiate himself with the press. With his military background, Ike was inclined to see himself as the commander and the press as underlings. He did not admire the press, did not pay attention to it, and did not know the names of most journalists. He had an especially low opinion of Walter Lippmann, Edward Murrow of radio and television fame (who he thought looked like a gangster), and Joseph Alsop. Ike simply was unwilling to ingratiate himself and play the traditional game. Early in Eisenhower's presidency, Joe Alsop stopped by to talk to an administration official and offered his support for executive policies in return for inside information. Alsop was informed that he could get his news like any other reporter, through press conferences and Press Secretary James Hagerty. This was not the response that Alsop wanted or expected. As a consequence, he turned on the administration, becoming one of its harshest critics. Eisenhower, for his part, thought Alsop "about the lowest form of animal life on earth." By the middle of the decade, Alsop was conducting an ongoing campaign against administration defense policies, and Walter Lippmann, among others, was offering advice to the 1956 Stevenson campaign.[9]

Aside from these factors, two other more intangible elements negatively affected Eisenhower's relationship with elite opinion makers. The first was Eisenhower's middle-class taste in art, literature, and music. Eisenhower was a painter of some talent, but his subjects were conventional and his rendering orthodox. In literature, he preferred Wild West stories by authors like Zane Grey. Musical favorites ran to groups like Fred Waring and the Pennsylvanians. These choices did not excite sophisticated Washington society and became a source of disdain and derision. Other aspects of his life also seemed pedestrian; he was an avid golfer and immensely enjoyed bridge.[10]

Eisenhower's conception of the presidency also differed from that of Washington insiders. The great majority of the academy and the media viewed the presidency through the lens of the administrations of Woodrow Wilson, Franklin D. Roosevelt, and Harry S Truman. In other words, they saw the White House as the command center for an activist reform program in domestic affairs. Eisenhower proved uninterested in a new wave of domestic reform, although he had no desire to attempt to roll back the New Deal. In his view, the country needed a respite from the unremitting upheaval and turmoil that had begun in 1929 and, with the Korean War still raging, continued when he took office in 1953.

Eisenhower was convinced that the greatest threat to the United States was not the Soviet Union or communism but unrestrained spending, especially military spending, that had the potential to bankrupt the country and to wreak financial and social havoc. Linked to this was his concern about the influence of the military-industrial complex and the scientific-technological elite that he warned against in his farewell address of 1961. Ike was convinced that holding the line on spending and minimizing defense spending would do more to preserve freedom and liberty than almost anything else his administration could do.[11]

Eisenhower's priorities made sense, and he pursued them faithfully, but they were not consistent with the Wilson-Roosevelt-Truman model. As a result, Eisenhower's critics automatically rejected the legitimacy of his understanding of the presidency and denounced him as passive, disinterested, and lackadaisical. Eisenhower's indirect approach to the exercise of power compounded the impression. Unlike Truman, Eisenhower avoided public confrontations if he could. The result was a presidency restrained in its use of power, conscious of its limits, and subtle and stealthy in its pursuit of goals. But it was also a presidency that could be caricatured as lethargic and unresponsive.

Whatever the attitudes of the elite opinion makers, Eisenhower never lost the support and admiration of the public. His Gallup Poll approval rating remained high, only occasionally dipping below 60 percent.[12] He won 55.1 percent of the popular vote and 442 electoral votes (against 89 for Stevenson) in 1952. He won even more decisively in 1956 with 57.4 percent of the popular vote and 457 electoral votes in 1956 against Stevenson. Among the most interesting aspects of these election results was the failure of the Republican Party more generally to profit from his name on the ticket. In 1952, the GOP reclaimed control of both House and Senate, but the margins were narrow (221–213 in the House and 49–47 in the Senate) and surprisingly small for the presidential margin. Moreover, the Republican majorities soon vanished. Democrats returned to power in both branches of Congress in 1954 (232–203 in the House and 48–47 in the Senate). In spite of the Eisenhower landslide in 1956, Democrats actually gained ground (234–201 in the lower chamber and 49–47 in the upper house). Ike became the first executive in more than a hundred years to be elected with both branches of Congress in the hands of the opposing party.

The usual explanation for the disparity between the presidential and congressional results is that Eisenhower enjoyed a personal popularity that transcended party and that his vote was not representative of support for the GOP. In this interpretation, the congressional vote in which Democrats secured 50.1 percent of the vote in 1952, 52.8 percent in 1954, and 51.5 percent in 1956 was indicative of the true balance between the parties with Democrats the majority party and Republicans the minority party.

Contemporary analysis of the 1950s election results masked a shift in electoral politics that would not become evident until later. In the history of the modern competition between Republicans and Democrats that began

Table 1.2. Democratic Percentages of the Vote after FDR, 1946–1956

Year	President	House of Representatives
1946	——	45.7%
1948	49.6%	48.0
1950	——	49.6
1952	44.1	50.1
1954	——	52.8
1956	42.0	51.5

Source: Rusk, ed., *A Statistical History of the American Electorate*, pp. 134, 220.

in the second half of the nineteenth century, a direct link existed between presidential election results and those for House and Senate. Winning the White House meant winning Capitol Hill. Beginning in the post-1945 period, this connection eroded and eventually dissolved completely in the last third of the century. Truman's victory in 1948 went hand-in-hand with renewed Democratic control of Congress; but starting with the presidential elections of the 1950s, the link between occupation of the White House and congressional majorities began to dissolve, as can be seen in table 1.2.

A new system emerged in which Democrats dominated congressional elections while Republicans were much more competitive in presidential contests. In the New Deal era, FDR outpolled Democratic congressional candidates in all four of his elections. In 1948, Truman also ran ahead of Democratic congressmen; after him, this relationship was reversed. Starting in 1952, Democratic congressional candidates ran ahead of the White House ticket and did better in the off-year elections than in presidential election years. In ten of the twelve presidential elections from 1952 through 1996, the percentage of the Democratic vote was higher in congressional elections. Admittedly, this was not easy to see in the 1950s, since 1948 was an anomaly, with Thurmond and Wallace reducing the Truman vote, and 1952 and 1956 were aberrations because of Eisenhower's popularity. In spite of these qualifications, what can be called a "two-tier system" was emerging—one in which "one set of electoral dynamics [was] operating at the presidential level, and yet another in sub-presidential contests."[13]

The hallmark of the new system was a situation, heretofore exceedingly uncommon, in which a president would be elected with the opposition party controlling both branches of Congress. As previously noted, when this happened to Eisenhower in 1956, it was the first such occasion since Zachary Taylor's election in 1848. As an indicator of the new order of things, this situation occurred another four times in the twentieth century after 1956 (in 1968, 1972, 1988, and 1996). Party preferences of voters at the presidential level did not automatically carry over to the congressional contests. The reverse was also true. Preferences for Congress did not automatically translate into votes for president.

Two other factors loomed large in the 1950s as an explanation of the failure for the Republicans to capitalize on the Eisenhower landslides of 1952 and 1956. These were Ike's attitude toward politics and government and his ambivalent relationship with the GOP. To begin with, Eisenhower did not like partisan politics (although he was very good at it), and he distrusted partisans and partisanship. During the 1952 campaign, when a friend inquired how he was getting along, Eisenhower replied, "I don't like this business; these politicians are terrible." He then went over to a corner of the room, picked up the carpet, and said "You see them crawling out from under there." He found some Republicans just as insufferable as most Democrats. In the Senate, he disapproved of William Knowland of California, John Bricker of Ohio, William Jenner of Indiana, Karl Mundt of South Dakota, and several others, including Joseph McCarthy of Wisconsin. He once observed of Knowland that in his case, "there seems to be no final answer to the question 'How stupid can you get?'" His opinion of Republican members of the House of Representatives was no more flattering. In 1960, he told his secretary, Ann Whitman, "I don't know why anyone should be a member of the Republican Party."[14]

Given these prejudices, Eisenhower did not exert himself greatly on behalf of the GOP. He had scant interest in party building. Republicans were often perplexed and dismayed by Eisenhower's approach. Texas Republicans were especially unhappy because the only two southerners in the cabinet—Texans Oveta Culp Hobby and Robert Anderson—were Democrats. National party officials occasionally found Eisenhower impossible to fathom. Len Hall, Republican National Committee (RNC) chairman, for example, was "incredulous" when Eisenhower raised the possibility of his brother Milton as the vice-presidential nominee in 1956.[15]

Aside from Eisenhower's view of himself and his policies as transcending partisan differences, a basic mismatch between the president's political philosophy and that of the Republican base further aggravated the relationship. Although a fiscal conservative and fanatical on the subject of balanced budgets, Eisenhower brought to the White House no special dislike for the New Deal and its policies. In foreign affairs, he had been an agent of the new policies of the Roosevelt and Truman administrations that the most right-wing elements of the GOP bitterly resented.

In other words, Eisenhower had serious disagreements with the part of the party that provided the most energy and enthusiasm for election campaigns. On the one hand, he could not and would not encourage them, and they, for their part, found it increasingly difficult to manufacture enthusiasm for the tepid Republicanism they associated with the president. The upshot was that, in spite of Eisenhower's popularity and his overwhelming election victories, the Republican position actually declined during the 1950s. Party morale and institutional strength were significantly greater in 1950–52 than in 1958–60.

This erosion was especially noticeable after 1956. Most two-term presidents find their second terms less productive and less pleasant, and Eisenhower was no exception. In 1957–58, Eisenhower suffered one reverse after another. Constitutionally prohibited from seeking a third term, he had less political influence. With numerous Democratic presidential prospects in the U.S. Senate, the incentive in that body to support Eisenhower declined while the rewards for opposition to and criticism of White House policies escalated. Democrats recognized Ike's popularity and generally were careful not to criticize him, but it was open season on his policies, his appointments, and anything else connected with the administration.

Eisenhower was also vexed with economic problems. His dilemma stemmed from a short but sharp recession that hit the United States in late 1957 and early 1958. Unemployment more than doubled from October 1957 to February 1958 with the East and Midwest especially hard hit. Dissatisfaction with the economy was not limited to the industrial states of the Midwest and Northeast. Farmers were also highly displeased with the agricultural policies of Secretary of Agriculture Ezra Taft Benson. The acute economic distress and its political implications could not be ignored with congressional elections approaching in November 1958 and a presidential election looming in 1960. Eisenhower and Secretary of the Treasury Robert Anderson were not impressed and refused to support increased government spending. They, along with Federal Reserve Chairman William McChesney Martin, were more worried about inflation than unemployment and recession. In spite of persuasive economic arguments in favor of a government stimulus package, Eisenhower and Anderson refused to move. The economy did begin to improve in late 1958, but not soon enough to help Republican candidates, and the economic expansion that took place was short-lived. By mid-1960, another downturn threatened Republican election chances.[16]

Democrats made a strong argument for increased spending on economic and social grounds, but what gave their demands new impetus was the perception of a growing Soviet danger. Democratic alarmists pitched in with a vengeance. Adlai Stevenson told the National Business Conference at Harvard University that the American economic system "was on trial for its life."

With Nikita Khrushchev constantly trumpeting claims of economic growth and predicting the eventual supremacy of the USSR, many Americans became convinced that the Soviet Union was on track to surpass the American economy. Even administration officials were not always helpful. The director of the Central Intelligence Agency (CIA), Allen Dulles, made a statement late in 1959 warning that the gap between the two economies would be "dangerously narrowed" by 1970 if current trends continued. The average American concluded that the United States was slipping economically.[17]

As the November 1958 midterm elections approached, the GOP was in obvious trouble. The sixth year of a two-term presidency usually produces substantial congressional losses for the incumbent party. Economic confidence was low. There was widespread discontent in farm states, and Republicans were suffering from the Sherman Adams scandal. Republican morale was low. Even Eisenhower's famous popular appeal was in decline. The Gallup Poll of late November conducted just after the elections showed approval at 52 percent and disapproval at 30 percent, the lowest approval rating of his presidency.[18]

Republicans compounded these problems with some astoundingly bad political decisions. In several states, most notably California and Ohio, they picked 1958 to launch right-to-work campaigns. These efforts infuriated organized labor and caused it to redouble efforts to turn out its voters, who were, of course, overwhelmingly Democratic. In California, the Republican Party of that state became caught up in a poisonous internecine struggle among the factions identified with Vice President Richard Nixon, Senator William Knowland, and Governor Goodwin Knight. As this Byzantine California intrigue played out, the curious result was a bizarre switch in which Knowland ran for governor and Knight ran for the Senate.[19]

Political observers predicted Republican losses, but the conventional wisdom failed to foresee the extent of the Republican debacle that took place on November 5. The *New York Times*, for example, forecast a loss of eight Senate seats and twenty in the House of Representatives.[20] In fact, Republicans lost forty-eight House seats and left the Democrats with a 283–153 majority. On the Senate side, Republicans dropped thirteen seats to produce a 62–34 Democratic advantage. Republican strength was now at its lowest ebb since the aftermath of the Democratic sweep of 1936. Pessimism in GOP circles was suffocating. Richard Nixon remembered it as "one of the most depressing election nights I have ever known." In 1978, he wrote, "The statistics still make me wince." More Republicans were in the House of Representatives in 1939 than in 1959. The 1958 elections inflicted massive damage on the Republican Party in Congress from which it would not recover for a decade.[21]

Election results at the state level were no better. After the November carnage, Republicans occupied only fourteen governorships. The situation was just as bad or worse in the state legislatures. Republicans controlled the legislatures of just seven states. Democrats held almost two-thirds of legislative seats in the country. Even outside the South, where there were *no* Republicans in seven legislatures, Democrats occupied about 55 percent of legislative positions. As an institution, the Republican Party was a crumbling edifice with little apparent reason to hope for better in the near future.[22]

Then something unusual occurred. In apparent decline and facing overwhelming opposition numbers for the last two years of his presidency, Dwight D. Eisenhower staged a major comeback. Even with the death of trusted adviser Secretary of State John Foster Dulles in May 1959, the final two years of his administration saw an Eisenhower resurgence. The president proved, as one historian has put it, "to be a lot tougher than many supposed."[23] Ike's health improved, and he found a new purpose for his presidency in both domestic and foreign arenas. On the domestic side, Eisenhower determined to stop the "spenders," as he liked to call them, and preserve what he saw as fiscal sanity. On the international front, he traveled widely in his last great effort to promote reduced tensions in the Cold War and improved relations with a variety of countries. Although his success in both areas was limited, especially on the international scene, he did manage to reassert himself as a major force who could more than hold his own against his internal and external opponents.[24]

Republican presidential prospects for 1960 and the fortunes of the leading candidate, Vice President Richard Nixon, also improved after 1958. In the immediate aftermath of the midterm election fiasco, the Gallup Poll presidential trial heat had Democratic senator John F. Kennedy leading Nixon 54 percent to 38 percent with 8 percent undecided. A year later, Gallup showed that Nixon had reversed the deficit and now led Kennedy 53 percent to 47 percent and Adlai Stevenson by an even larger margin, 56 percent to 44 percent. The GOP had been seriously weakened in 1958 in Congress and at the state level, but by the end of 1959 it was showing the capability to make a strong run in the following year's presidential contest. This was another indication of how presidential politics was becoming increasingly separated from congressional elections.[25]

As for the Democrats, the vast new majorities often proved unmanageable and difficult for Speaker of the House Sam Rayburn and Senate Majority

Leader Lyndon B. Johnson. With an influx of a new cohort of Democratic liberals, Johnson's life became more difficult. Adding to his and Rayburn's discomfort was the increased activism of the Democratic Advisory Council, a body of prominent Democrats established by Democratic National Committee Chairman Paul Butler for the purpose of giving Democratic liberals a larger voice in party policy. Rayburn and Johnson utterly detested this organization for its effort to dilute their power and because of the implied vote of no confidence in their leadership it represented. For Lyndon Johnson, 1959 was not a good year.[26]

Whatever the nature and extent of Democratic dilemmas, Eisenhower continued to face difficulties in the related issues of the missile gap and defense spending. Criticism of the administration on these subjects began in 1957, gained momentum in 1958, and carried into 1959–60, when they became central to the Democratic argument that the administration was old and tired and new leadership was necessary.

Eisenhower did his best to reduce Soviet-American antagonism and the arms race. Although there were flare-ups in his first term, the president was generally successful at keeping both tensions and the arms race in check. Eisenhower did less well after 1956. Part of the reason was the nature of the Soviet leader, Nikita Khrushchev. It was Eisenhower's misfortune to deal with this singularly difficult individual. Other Soviet leaders of the Cold War, including Joseph Stalin, tried to avoid provoking the United States. This was not the case with Khrushchev. The voluble Kremlin potentate was impulsive, given to temper tantrums, inclined to risk taking, and not very careful about thinking through the implications of his actions. With most Soviet leaders, Eisenhower could have maintained a stable relationship that might have moved toward an early version of détente. Not so with Khrushchev. For a variety of convoluted reasons, he embarked on a policy of alternating the most ferocious threats with protestations of his desire for peaceful relations. This inconsistent behavior tested the patience and perspicacity of Eisenhower and made his task of resisting pressures for greatly expanded American defense spending almost impossible.[27]

Dealing with Khrushchev was never easy, but it became increasingly difficult after 1957 and the launching of Sputnik—the first successful satellite to orbit the earth—and the test firing of a Soviet intercontinental ballistic missile (ICBM). Sputnik was a blow to American pride. The test firing of the ICBM was more ominous because it was regarded as the supreme weapon of the future. Khrushchev, quickly recognizing American anxieties, blustered about Soviet superiority in rocketry and claimed his country manufactured ICBMs like sausages.

For several decades we have known that the missile gap (that is, a Soviet superiority in numbers of ICBMs) was a gigantic deception perpetrated by Khrushchev. One of the more interesting aspects of the hoax was that it was preceded by a similar effort earlier in the 1950s—the "bomber gap." In May 1955, U.S. Air Force officers observing a rehearsal of a Soviet May Day air show overestimated the number of Soviet bombers and exaggerated their capacity. Democratic Senator Stuart Symington promptly proclaimed the strong possibility of a bomber gap and warned that the United States may have "lost control of the air." Air Force Generals Nathan Twining and Curtis LeMay told Congress in 1956 that the Soviet long-range bomber fleet might be twice the size of the Strategic Air Command (SAC) by 1959. In August 1956, the CIA predicted that the Soviets would have 470 long-range bombers within two years. In fact, within two years, U.S. intelligence managed to figure out that the alleged bomber gap did not exist and that the United States retained a decisive advantage in strategic bombing capabilities. No one learned anything from this exercise in paranoia. Instead, it was repeated—and with some of the same cast of characters.[28]

Fifty years later, the missile gap story has come into clearer focus. There never was a missile gap that favored the USSR and its forces. Instead, the United States retained strategic superiority throughout the 1950s and early 1960s. The imprecise nature of intelligence, the secrecy that enveloped the Soviet Union, and the difficulty of interpreting Soviet intentions as distinguished from Soviet capacity produced estimates of significantly larger numbers of Soviet ICBMs in place in the early 1960s than were the reality. Meanwhile, the U.S. missile buildup seemed slow because the president made the crucial decision to restrict numbers of the primitive first-generation missiles (Atlas and Titan) and wait for the second generation (Minuteman and Polaris) before committing to large force levels. The decision was a wise one because Minuteman and Polaris were less vulnerable, more reliable, and better engineered.[29]

Whatever the ambiguities of the intelligence estimates of Soviet missiles, a willing American audience accepted the most unrealistic projections of Soviet missile strength. Although undoubtedly sincere in their warnings of impending doom, U.S. Air Force generals, defense contractors, Democratic senators, and journalists had a vested interest in accepting and publicizing a worst-case scenario. In addition, a collection of think-tank strategists, upwardly mobile economists, ambitious scientists, and social reformers climbed aboard the missile gap bandwagon in their quest for funding and power. In contrast, there was no natural constituency to argue the opposing case, aside from the president and his supporters, but they were seen as blatantly self-interested. Even among Republicans there were collaborators who for their own reasons criticized what they saw as the inadequacy of administration defense efforts.[30]

Senator Stuart Symington, author of the bomber gap, led the congressional onslaught. With the right credentials (as former secretary of the air force) and presidential ambitions, the senator from Missouri had no scruples about advancing the most exaggerated and fantastic projections of Soviet missile strength. In March 1959, for example, Symington predicted that in three years the USSR would have three thousand ICBMs.[31]

Not far behind Symington was Senate Majority Leader Lyndon B. Johnson. The Texan, far abler than Symington, shared presidential ambitions and saw the missile gap as an issue that could be exploited for his benefit while also weakening the administration and the Republican nominee in 1960. As majority leader, LBJ was in a position to bring the spotlight to the subject. Leading the Senate Preparedness Subcommittee, Johnson weighted the list of witnesses in favor of the proposition that the United States was in the gravest danger and that only a much stronger response could avert the likelihood of a catastrophe for the United States. Needless to say, he had no difficulty in obtaining testimony from U.S. Air Force generals to that effect. It was easy to find defense contractors who would warn of impending doom without heroic new efforts. For example, T. G. Lanphier, vice president of the Convair Astronautic Division of General Dynamics Corporation (and maker of the Atlas ICBM), gave a speech in which he charged the president with taking "a dangerous gamble with the survival of our people" in his defense policies.[32]

Joining the chorus of Senate Cassandras were Henry Jackson of Washington, an advocate for military spending, and John F. Kennedy of Massachusetts. Kennedy, whose presidential campaign was based on the proposition of a United States in decline and consequently badly in need of renewal, found the missile gap ideal for his purposes. By November 1959, he was accusing the administration of feeding American complacency for "seven gray years" while the Soviet Union gained ground. According to JFK, in the areas of the military, the economy, education, and science and research, the USSR had either surpassed the United States or made "spectacular gains" while Americans had been encouraged to be "complacent, self-centered, easygoing." Even Senator Hubert Humphrey, who had never been considered a hardliner, decried what he called the "appalling" vulnerability of the United States and argued on behalf of an improved civil defense program.[33]

Although senators made important contributions to the propagation of the missile gap, the idea would not have had the impact that it did without the ongoing efforts of individuals in the world of journalism. The publicity afforded the claim that the United States might be in mortal peril was a natural for newspapers, the three leading news magazines (*Time, Newsweek, U.S. News & World Report*), other popular periodicals (for example, the *Saturday Evening Post, Life, Collier's*), and more elevated journals of opinion (for example, *Harper's, New Republic, The Reporter*) along with specialized magazines like *Aviation Week*. Beginning in 1959, there was an unrelenting barrage of stories and columns on the subject. Given the complexity of the subject, the lack of verifiable information, and the ambiguities of intelligence estimates, it was difficult to produce an analysis that was nuanced and not oversimplified, although the *New York Times* and a few others made a heroic effort in this cause. It was much easier to offer a sensationalized version of the looming nuclear Armageddon facing the United States.

In the realm of popular journalism, one individual stands out as the person who did more than anyone else in America to popularize and legitimize the proposition that the United States was nearing the brink of a nuclear Pearl Harbor. He was Joseph Alsop, a nationally syndicated columnist with close ties to the CIA, elite Washington society, and Senator John F. Kennedy and other prominent Democratic senators. Alsop's columns appeared in the *Washington Post*, the *New York Herald Tribune*, and many other influential newspapers.[34]

In tandem with his brother Stewart, a more restrained journalist, the two Alsops did more to popularize the missile gap and its dangers than anyone else. Stewart began the attack in late 1957 with a widely read article titled "How Can We Catch Up?" and followed with others bearing dramatic titles such as "Our Gamble with Destiny." In January 1959, Joe was cited as the source that estimated a missile gap of 100 to none in favor of the USSR in 1959 that would grow to 2,000 to 130 in 1963. Later in 1959, he wrote an article with the apocalyptic title "After Ike the Deluge" that slightly modified his estimates of January 1959 but that still showed a Soviet advantage of 100 to 30 in 1960 increasing to 1,500 to 130 in 1963. In 1959, Joe was just getting started. The following year found him going after the Eisenhower administration even more fiercely.[35]

But the national concern with what turned out to be an illusion was not simply the work of self-interested air force generals, defense contractors, politicians, and journalists. What gave vastly greater credibility to the alarm was the participation of Republicans and presumably disinterested scientists and defense experts. One of the most prominent Republicans in the country, Governor Nelson A. Rockefeller, consistently took positions through 1959 and the first half of 1960 that either explicitly or implicitly endorsed the existence of a missile gap and the necessity for billions more in defense spending. Rockefeller was not the only Republican in revolt against Eisenhower's defense priorities. Ike found himself trying and failing to convince John McCone of the Atomic Energy Commission and Secretary of Defense Thomas Gates that large new defense expenditures were unnecessary. Even Vice President Richard Nixon hinted at disagreement with the president on the subject of defense spending, although Nixon's sentiments remained private and were probably more the product of political calculations than of any belief in Soviet superiority.[36]

Secretary of Defense Neil McElroy proved ineffective at rebutting congressional criticism throughout his 1957–59 tenure. Richard Nixon called McElroy "a fine man, a very charming guy" but not nearly tough enough for the job. Even worse was Director of Central Intelligence (DCI) Allen Dulles, who contributed mightily to administration woes. His public speeches, his congressional testimony, and the National Intelligence Estimates all painted a dire portrait of a growing Soviet threat. According to Dulles, the first deployment of Soviet prototype ICBMs would occur between 1958 and 1960, and the USSR could have 100 operational ICBMs between mid-1959 and late 1960. He added that the Soviets might have 500 ICBMs in place by 1962. By 1960, he was backing away from these extreme projections, but the damage had been done. Sometimes Dulles and the CIA seemed more in league with the Democrats and their positions than the administration that he represented. In any event, congressional Democrats could draw upon Dulles and the CIA for their predictions of doom and gloom.[37]

If the simmering Republican discontent and the unreliable CIA were not bad enough, the president also had to deal with the undermining operations conducted by various experts. Eisenhower himself had established a committee of distinguished citizens to examine the role of civil defense in U.S. defense policy in 1957 before Sputnik and the clamor over the missile gap. The committee, headed by H. Rowan Gaither, became known as the Gaither Committee. It did not augur well for the administration that one of the key figures on the committee was none other than Paul Nitze. Nitze, a highly respected government official, had served in the Truman administration and was the chief author of *NSC-68*, the famous document that in 1950 urged President Truman to increase defense spending radically. He was not someone, in other words, inclined to be sympathetic to Eisenhower's approach on defense and deterrence. Nitze was not alone in his views. A number of other committee members shared his outlook on the deficiencies of Eisenhower administration defense policy. The committee made its classified report with recommendations to the president in October 1957. Eisenhower refused to declassify and have the report made public, but substantial leaks quickly developed (to Joe Alsop, among others), and the general thrust of the report quickly became public knowledge.[38]

The report proceeded from the assumption that the USSR was a major threat to the United States and that the Soviets were producing weapons at a maximum pace. On that premise, the committee concluded that the current state of civil defense was inadequate, that SAC was vulnerable to a surprise attack, that by 1959 the United States would begin to become more vulnerable because of Soviet ICBMs, and that the United States could not afford to stand by idly but needed to take strong countermeasures of its own.[39]

In short, the Gaither Committee took a position at variance with Eisenhower and one that was entirely consistent with administration critics. The significance of the committee and its report was that its bipartisan, expert makeup gave credibility to the partisan, extremist critics and their views. Most importantly, the committee report set the terms of the debate over the next three years: there was a missile gap that favored the USSR, and the United States was vulnerable. The only questions were how great was Soviet advantage, how would the USSR attempt to exploit it, and by what measures could the United States minimize its disadvantage and begin to catch up?[40]

This criticism took its toll. A popular consensus emerged that the Soviets were on the brink of military supremacy and that the Eisenhower administration was failing in its duty to provide for the common defense. A Gallup Poll in February 1960 showed that college-educated Americans by a two-to-one margin (59 percent to 30 percent) believed the Soviets were ahead of the United States. The only educational segment of the population that believed that the United States led was those with a grade-school education (by 36 percent to 33 percent). Polls of foreign public opinion demonstrated that British, French, Norwegian, and West German populations saw the Soviets as stronger militarily, and that most Europeans saw American prestige in decline. The ultimate irony was that the conventional wisdom, elite opinion, and the college-educated were wrong, and Ike and those with a grade-school education were right. The Soviets had very few intercontinental missiles, and the ones they possessed were extraordinarily difficult to operate. It took almost twenty hours to prepare to launch the Soviet R-7 missile, and the R-7 could not be kept on alert for more than a day. As Stephen Ambrose observed, Ike knew the alleged gap was "nonsense," the

Soviets were not building missiles at the rate they could have, there was no evidence that they were accelerating production, and, therefore there was no need for America to increase its defense effort.[41]

Eisenhower knew he was right because of the U-2 reconnaissance flights that showed no Soviet missile buildup. Ike was unwilling to share the U-2 intelligence results with the senators largely because he did not trust them to keep the intelligence secret. This situation thus offered an example of the weakness of Eisenhower's indirect leadership. On the one hand, he ardently desired to hold down defense spending and thereby to minimize the arms race. He also wanted to see continued Republican occupation of the White House. On the other hand, he faced a formidable array of Democratic and Republican politicians, military leaders, defense contractors, scientific experts, journalists, and others who urged a massive defense buildup. The only way the president could have prevailed in this struggle, given the strength of the opposition, would have been by playing tough, partisan politics and by revealing some of the classified intelligence and intelligence sources. Eisenhower was unwilling to engage in such sharp-edged politics. He would not lobby reporters for his policies or reveal intelligence and intelligence sources. As a result, he got everything he wished to avoid—a Democrat in the White House, increased spending with an increased deficit, and an intensified arms race.

But to have done otherwise asked Eisenhower to be someone other than who he was. Moreover, there is no guarantee that discrete revelations of U.S. intelligence would have produced an era of improved executive-legislative relations. The U-2 reconnaissance was not and could not be conclusive. There had been only thirty U-2 penetration flights, and they could take photographs just five hours a day. Seasonal conditions further limited the flights. One could not say with certainty that even the U-2 "proved" that the Soviets were not engaged in a massive missile buildup. Democratic presidential candidates and journalistic critics of the administration were so deeply invested in the missile gap it is naïve to think that they would have accepted this imperfect evidence and suddenly admitted they were wrong and Eisenhower was correct. By 1960, they could not afford to admit their mistake. To have done so would have been humiliating. Such an admission would have destroyed the centerpiece of the Democratic case against the administration and any chance that Democrats could win back the White House. If the United States was ahead of the Soviet Union in missiles, the argument that the Eisenhower administration was old and tired and the United States in decline disintegrated.

Even when satellite intelligence in early 1961 finally and definitively proved that the missile gap was nonexistent, those who had argued for it were disinclined to admit their mistake. Furthermore, leaking of intelligence data could have escalated the tensions with the USSR as Nikita Khrushchev found himself embarrassed by revelations that his blustering about Soviet missile strength was nothing more than posturing. A concerted effort from the White House in 1959–60 would have produced a contentious domestic debate and made the international situation more dangerous. It is an illusion that Eisenhower had the ability to discredit the missile gap without creating a very messy situation domestically and internationally.[42]

And so 1959 and the decade came to an end with an ambiguous and unclear political outlook for the upcoming presidential election year. The Democratic Party was in the stronger position of the two national parties by virtue of its overwhelming victory in 1958 and its domination of Congress, the governorships, and the state legislatures. It had begun to establish an idea in the national consciousness that a change was necessary in executive leadership. Eisenhower was still overwhelmingly popular, but to many, in the words of the historian Herbert Parmet, he seemed "worn, dull, unimaginative, languid, sexless, pure but antiseptic, uncreative and unprogressive."[43] Still, the Democratic Party was not without its weaknesses, and Republicans were not without their strengths. The larger Democratic majorities after 1958 pointed up divisions within the party, especially the North-South split. The Democratic Party was so successful at the congressional and state levels precisely because the party was able to stand for extraordinarily different principles from New York to Mississippi to California. But this advantage made it more difficult at the presidential level, where a single candidate somehow had to reconcile the extremes.

On the Republican side, the GOP, despite its crushing institutional disadvantage below the presidential level, still had the advantage of a very popular incumbent president. Although Republicans had demonstrated no great ability at waging successful congressional campaigns, that did not necessarily mean they were equally incompetent at the presidential level.

In other words, indicators in late 1959 pointed to a close presidential election, something with which the country was generally unfamiliar in the twentieth century. The presidential trial heats done by Gallup showed the leading Democratic and Republican candidates evenly matched. The outlook in December 1959 was for a close contest. This is exactly what the country got in 1960.

2

Kennedy and Nixon before 1960

"It was involuntary. They sank my boat."
—John F. Kennedy on how he became a war hero

*"I never drive by a vegetable stand without feeling sorry
for the guy who picks out the rotten apples."*
—Richard M. Nixon

The two men who contested the election of 1960 came from opposite ends of the country and from different socioeconomic classes, but they were close in age and shared some common values. Both men possessed personalities that stirred the interest of political observers, an interest that continues unabated today. Neither was or is easy to fathom, although for different reasons.

The easterner, John Fitzgerald Kennedy, poses monumental problems of understanding. Because of his early death, he left little behind in the form of reflections on his life and career. During his life, he was guarded in what he told people. Journalist and friend Charles Bartlett once said, "No one knew John Kennedy, not all of him" because Kennedy never revealed all of himself to anyone outside his family.[1] There were good reasons for this attitude. His family had more than its share of skeletons to conceal. JFK himself had secrets—most notably his health and his sexual behavior—that he did not wish subjected to scrutiny. The wealth, the power, the secretiveness, and the associated rumors have made it extraordinarily difficult to separate reality from hearsay.

The riddle of JFK involves far more than matters of family skeletons, health issues, and womanizing, however. The circumstances of his death and the reaction to it, and the conscious effort to construct a legend surrounding his life and presidency, complicate efforts to penetrate the mythology surrounding John F. Kennedy and understand the historical reality. Before November 22, 1963, President John Kennedy was a generally popular president with a high approval rating but not without his detractors. His assassination transformed him and his position in American history. He was enshrined in the American pantheon of national heroes and became in death a venerated figure. His youth (he was forty-six at his death), his seemingly boundless energy, his love of life, and his beautiful widow and young children added to the grief of the American people and their sense that the assassination was a cruel, irrational, and unjust act. An emotional wave engulfed the country in late 1963 and early 1964 and forever altered the perception of John F. Kennedy. Defining the historical Kennedy as opposed to the one that became enshrined in the American consciousness after November 1963 has been a challenge to historians.[2]

The concerted campaign to construct a mythology about the president that began in the immediate aftermath of his death further compounds the mists of uncertainty that swirl around him. The point of this effort was to ensure that he was remembered for his nobility rather than the unpleasant realities of his White House years. Before the end of November 1963, Jacqueline Kennedy contacted Theodore H. White, a journalist closely associated with the late president, denounced the "bitter old men" who wrote history, and pleaded with White to tell the American people that the Kennedy presidency was a great, noble moment in American history. Between them, Jacqueline Kennedy and Theodore White constructed the Camelot myth of the Kennedy White House.[3]

Although some Kennedy confidants considered Camelot romantic nonsense, a number of Kennedy court histories filled the market, not hurt by the fact that the public was more than happy to pay for and avidly devour the product. Theodore H. White's account of the 1960 presidential election, *The Making of the President 1960* (1961), was part of this corpus even before the assassination. Others quickly followed, most notably Arthur M. Schlesinger Jr.'s *A Thousand Days: John F. Kennedy in the White House* (1965) and Theodore C. Sorensen's *Kennedy* (1965). Since then the flow of books on John F. Kennedy has never ceased.

The central problem with the Kennedy court histories as represented by the works of White, Schlesinger, and Sorensen is the romantic, sanitized, and unrealistic portrayal of John F. Kennedy. With the tragic death of Robert F. Kennedy in 1968, the demand for such histories doubled as a second martyr emerged. Although the emotional response was entirely natural and understandable, the histories to which it gave rise were suspect because of their lack of realism. They did the former president no favors by portraying a man without defect. Sorensen, attempting to demonstrate that he did not consider JFK perfect, provided a list of his imperfections. They included shortcomings such as rising late and going to bed late and engaging in World Series betting pools. The court histories are useful for their depictions of the president's sophistication, wit, wisdom, eloquence, and grace as well as what they say about Kennedy's ability to inspire devotion and loyalty; but they are not convincing examinations of the complicated individual that JFK was.[4]

Even with an increasingly rich historical literature about John Fitzgerald Kennedy, the incomplete nature of his life and his presidency will continue to pose problems for those assessing him and his record. On matters of critical policy issues like civil rights and Vietnam, admirers of JFK argue that he would have been just as successful as his successor in the former area while avoiding the disastrous mistakes in the latter. To those less in thrall to Camelot, Kennedy was more style than substance, and the idea that he would have solved the racial crisis while avoiding the Vietnam disaster is fanciful. The ambiguous and incomplete records of Kennedy's life and presidency allow one to see whatever one wants.[5]

In any case, the historical literature on John F. Kennedy's life is now sufficiently extensive and reliable that we have a more unobstructed view of him, his motivations, and his strengths and weaknesses. Clearly, at the center of an understanding of John Fitzgerald Kennedy is his large Irish American family and especially his father, Joseph P. Kennedy.[6]

This was a family of enormous power and influence. Its money and power were products of the efforts of Joseph P. Kennedy. Like many founders of great wealth, he acquired his in dubious ways. Talented and ambitious from the days of his youth, he obtained a Harvard education, involved himself in a variety of business ventures, and managed to marry the daughter of the mayor of Boston. From there he proceeded into a number of business activities in banking, shipbuilding, Hollywood, and the stock market. On Wall Street in the 1920s he was a successful operator. He made a fortune and was astute enough to avoid being crushed by the crash of 1929. Joe Kennedy also made substantial amounts of money in liquor both during and after Prohibition. His activities in illegal and legal liquor gave him useful but embarrassing ties to organized crime. Meanwhile, he also established himself as a world-class philanderer without making any effort to conceal his multiple infidelities from his large family.[7]

Along with his great wealth, Joseph P. Kennedy had political ambitions. He made an astute decision in 1932 by supporting Franklin D. Roosevelt. This backing gave him entrée to the New Deal and an appointment to the Securities and Exchange Commission, where he did an excellent job. Later he became chairman of the Maritime Commission, and in 1938, FDR named him United States ambassador to Great Britain. He successfully cultivated FDR's oldest son, James. By the mid-1930s, Joe Kennedy was indulging in presidential daydreaming. FDR after 1936 was in his second term and was expected to leave office after it as had every other two-term president in American history before 1940. Joe Kennedy saw no reason why he could not succeed FDR. Unfortunately for Kennedy, FDR entertained very different visions of the future. The president distrusted his erstwhile supporter, and if he needed any additional reasons, Kennedy supplied them during his time as ambassador. Joe Kennedy thought of himself as the great operator, but he more than met his match in FDR, who manipulated Kennedy, used him for his purposes, and then, when his usefulness was at an end, discarded him.

If Joe Kennedy displayed an excellent sense of judgment in the stock market and in his support for FDR in 1932, that judgment deserted him in the late 1930s. In Great Britain, the new ambassador accumulated a sensationally bad record. He became an ardent supporter of Neville Chamberlain and his policy of appeasement, endorsed the Munich settlement of 1938, indicated his belief that fascism was the wave of the future in Europe and that it would be a big mistake for the United States to oppose it. He took a strong position that America's interest above all else was to stay out of the war that broke out in September 1939.

FDR became increasingly disenchanted with Kennedy but did not want to cut ties with him until after election day in 1940. Kennedy, unhappy with Washington, resigned as ambassador and returned to the United States in October 1940. Roosevelt temporarily soothed him, and Kennedy supported his reelection. In November 1940 and after, Joe Kennedy made a number of indiscreet, outrageous comments in newspaper interviews that destroyed what was left of his political career. As Felix Frankfurter put it: "Does anybody like Joe Sr.? Have you ever met anybody, except his family?"[8]

Still, he retained his great wealth and became even richer during the decade. By the time his second son launched his bid for the presidency in 1957, *Fortune* ranked him as one of the sixteen richest Americans and rated his worth at between $200 and $400 million.[9]

Whatever Joseph Kennedy's shortcomings as a human being, whatever his connections with stock market manipulations, bootlegging, and appeasement, whatever his infidelities, his children apparently loved, honored, and respected him. Always demanding, he pushed them to be competitive. Whatever the attitude of the outside world to him, the dominant attitude of his children was one of loyalty and devotion, although this sentiment was inevitably mixed with resentment of the unending demands and the need to obtain paternal approval. Even after the 1961 stroke that left Joseph Kennedy paralyzed, the attitude of John F. Kennedy to him was one of warmth and concern. Interestingly, the accounts we have of the family suggest that there was much greater affection for father than mother (Rose Kennedy). More than one author suggests that John and others did not much care for Rose.[10]

In spite of the affection and loyalty for Joseph P. Kennedy, a combination of historical circumstances and family machinations took a heavy toll on the Kennedy children by the end of the 1940s. The oldest son, Joseph Jr., was killed in action in World War II. Kathleen Kennedy died in an airplane crash in 1948 after becoming alienated from her mother, who refused to attend her funeral. Rosemary Kennedy, the eldest daughter, met a terrible fate. Rebelling against the family and judged mentally ill, she was subjected to a lobotomy in 1941 that destroyed her mentally and left her partially paralyzed. The family sent her to a convent in Wisconsin. Joseph P. Kennedy may have been one of the wealthiest men in the United States, but even before the terrible events of the 1960s, his family had suffered greatly.

As the second son, John Fitzgerald did not initially play a major role in his father's plans. Following the destruction of his own political ambitions, Joe Sr. shifted his aspirations to his eldest son, Joseph P. Kennedy Jr. By most accounts, Joe Jr. was an unpleasant character. Not only did he bear his father's name, but he apparently subscribed to most of his father's views. He supported the Munich agreement, justified German anti-Semitism, and seemed admiring of Hitler and the Nazis in the 1930s. However retrograde the political views of Joseph P. Kennedy Jr. and however unpleasant his personality, he was courageous. Serving in the U.S. Navy, he died in 1944 when the experimental explosive-laden airplane he was flying in blew up. He was posthumously awarded the Navy Cross, the Distinguished Flying Cross, and the Air Medal.[11]

Even if John Fitzgerald Kennedy was not at the center of the family ambitions before 1945, his father was the most important influence on his life. In retrospect, JFK's famous hypersexual activity almost certainly derived from him. From the time he was a teenager until the end of his life, John F. Kennedy seems to have been obsessed with sex.[12] It is possible, though, to make too much of JFK's sexual behavior and the reluctance of newspapers and journalists to report on it, especially before 1961. Kennedy's conduct was common among Washington politicians. Lyndon Johnson, who was never considered a great Casanova, according to his chief aide, Bobby Baker, "carried on affairs with numerous women." Among the Georgetown set of Washington in the 1950s, extramarital sex was common. As Nina Burleigh put it, "one code of behavior applied to the peasants and middle class, another to the sophisticates." In other words, JFK's activities were not unusual in his social circle before 1947 or in his social and political circles after that date. What made Kennedy different was his special combination of wealth, good looks, and prominence along with the recklessness of some of his liaisons and his willingness to talk in private about his romantic conquests. What also distinguished JFK was that after entering the White House in 1961, he did not moderate his wild sexual behavior. If anything, it became more flagrant.[13]

As for the failure of newspapers and journalists to report on this story in the 1950s or 1960s, one must remember that journalistic standards were different. Private lives of public officials, except in rare instances, were off-limits. In television news, David Brinkley recalled that he was not even allowed to use words such as "rape" or "abortion" and had to resort to code words. Social and political pressures worked against, not in favor of, reporting on John Kennedy's sexual behavior. This was especially true when one took into consideration the wealth and power of the Kennedy family.[14]

Beyond his sexual drive and the exploitative attitude toward women that came with it, Joseph P. Kennedy passed on to Jack his competitiveness, his admiration for and cultivation of toughness, and an acceptance of inequality, among other characteristics. John F. Kennedy seemed to sympathize with the downtrodden and was capable of individual acts of personal kindness. Like his father, though, he did not believe that blacks were equal to whites or that women were equal to men. He did not revel in such inequalities, but neither did he think much could be done about them. JFK had seen life: it was unfair, and nothing could change that.[15]

The second son was not an uncritical admirer. He loved, respected, and admired his father, but he had his own mind and did not slavishly follow his father's lead. If John Kennedy held relatively conservative viewpoints like his father in the 1930s, the 1940s, and the early 1950s, his political trajectory moved toward more liberal positions in the later 1950s. Jack saw no contradiction between love of father and disagreement with many of his viewpoints. To his credit, the patriarch did not allow the disagreements to ruin the relationship. Perhaps Joe did not understand his second son, but he was proud of JFK's growing success in the 1940s and 1950s and never stopped encouraging him.

If the example and influence of Joseph P. Kennedy was one of the two greatest shaping forces in the life of John Fitzgerald Kennedy, the other was his health. In his youth, JFK was perpetually ill—with back problems, scarlet fever, diphtheria, asthma, colitis, various allergies, and more. The family joke was that if a mosquito bit JFK, the mosquito was bound to die. Although Kennedy outgrew some of these afflictions, the back problems remained constant and caused him considerable difficulty and pain to the end of his life. He also acquired new maladies including Addison's disease, diagnosed in 1947. Fortunately for Kennedy, doctors had discovered the use of cortisone as a treatment for Addison's, but the regular injections of cortisone produced other health problems.[16]

The consequences were profound. John F. Kennedy lived with serious pain for most of his life. He was vulnerable to medical complications. His back pain was so severe that in October 1954 and again in February 1955 he underwent operations rather than continue to live with the discomfort, even though doctors and his father advised against the procedure. He nearly died, and the back problems did not end, although after 1955 his health generally improved. Even so, between May 1955 and October 1957, he secretly underwent hospitalization nine times for a total of forty-four days. As president, he had to be careful about lifting his young children because of his back.[17]

If chronic pain and discomfort were one obvious result of Kennedy's poor health, a second important consequence was the courage he developed and manifested in coping with these disabilities. Facing great physical challenges, Jack Kennedy did not surrender but developed resources of strength, courage, stoicism, and tenacity that served him well. His ability to respond in this fashion was a tribute not only to JFK but to the success of his father in instilling the qualities necessary to overcome the overwhelming physical problems the son confronted.

Kennedy put aside his problems, acted as much as possible like a healthy individual, and never asked for sympathy. One story, told by friend Paul Fay, is revealing. Once watching JFK get ready to inject himself in his thigh, Fay remarked to Kennedy, "[T]he way you take that jab, it looks like it doesn't even hurt." Kennedy sprang at Fay, jabbed him in the thigh with the needle, provoking a scream from Fay. Kennedy commented to him, "It feels the same way to me."[18]

With the pain and courage came concealment, deception, and a search for relief. As Joe Kennedy's plans and JFK's ambitions advanced, public knowledge about his physical condition became a major threat. Any revelation, admission, or leak of the true state of Kennedy's health, especially of the Addison's, might have doomed his presidential ambitions. There was enough knowledge in the public sphere for many politicians and journalists to have an idea of the situation. And so there were denials, subterfuges, equivocations, and whatever else was needed to avoid a full explication of John F. Kennedy's physical condition. The evasions carried through the 1950s and the presidential campaign of 1960, into the early 1960s, and even beyond Kennedy's death.

Kennedy and his political aides knew that it was impossible to explain his condition in a way that would satisfy the public. Therefore, they resolved to ignore the issue as much as possible and say nothing "because it would be misunderstood." When pressed on the issue, the standard response was to deny any connection with the disease or to obfuscate. In July 1959, Kennedy told Arthur Schlesinger Jr. he did not have Addison's "and have never had it." He even told Schlesinger that he no longer took cortisone. On other occasions, he or his aides denied that he had "classic" Addison's, or admitted that he had it and was now over it, or asserted that it was under control and no hindrance to a normal life. Equally noteworthy are Kennedy's deceptions about his health and his raw courage in overcoming his physical disabilities.[19]

In spite of his health, John F. Kennedy was determined to join the military as war loomed in 1941. The U.S. Army rejected him because of his physical problems, but in September 1941 he managed to secure a naval commission through the influence of his father. Although Joseph P. Kennedy strongly opposed the war, he saw military service as a necessity for the political future of his two eldest sons. The trick, as far as he was concerned, was for them to perform military service without getting killed. Joe just wanted Jack sent somewhere that "wasn't too deadly." JFK's eagerness to serve was much to his credit and much in contrast to later years in which individuals commonly used political influence to avoid military service. John F. Kennedy, who was physically unfit for military service, joined the U.S. Navy. To what extent he and his older brother may have been using military service to attempt to redeem the family name after his father's disgrace is not clear. This may well have been a motivating factor, but so undoubtedly were JFK's daring, his love of adventure, and his desire to escape the family confines.[20]

His World War II service, while not lengthy, did not lack excitement. After shore duty in the Office of Naval Intelligence, John F. Kennedy found himself in the Southwest Pacific Theater as captain of a patrol torpedo (PT) boat, one of the most dangerous vessels in the U.S. Navy. On the night of August 1, 1943, a Japanese destroyer rammed and sank Kennedy's boat, the *PT-109*, in the waters off the Solomon Islands. After the sinking and the loss of two sailors, JFK led the survival effort, and eventually he and the remaining crewmen were rescued. He returned to the United States as a war hero and was discharged in March 1945.[21]

Characteristically, John F. Kennedy, while enormously proud of his naval service, did not boast about it. In 1946, he told one newspaperman that he did not wish to be portrayed as a war hero. Kennedy, like most World War

II veterans, thought being a "hero" was just being in the right place at the right time with someone to witness your action and write the appropriate recommendation. JFK did not add that it helped to have a father like his with the wealth and promotional abilities to make sure the deed did not go unrecognized. When campaigning in Wisconsin in 1959 and asked about how he became a hero, he responded: "It was involuntary. They sank my boat."[22]

John F. Kennedy spent much of 1945 in California as a journalist but returned later in the year to make his first political bid for the House of Representatives. With the death of Joe Jr., the second son now became the first and with that change in status came all the pressures and expectations that went with it. But John F. Kennedy's character had been forged as a younger son, not the eldest. He had grown up something of a maverick questioning authority and refusing to accept conventional orthodoxies. His experiences with doctors and the military left him a skeptic of those in power. Still, he was a Kennedy and his father's son. Joseph P. Kennedy was deadly serious about making him president of the United States. In 1946, the great enterprise began with JFK's bid for a seat in the House of Representatives. With the massive support of his father, he easily won the Democratic nomination and then the general election.

John Fitzgerald Kennedy arrived in Washington in 1947, having overcome great obstacles in both war and peace. As suggested by Nigel Hamilton, JFK had enjoyed an extraordinary early life but was now embarking on an even more extraordinary political career.[23] He brought to Washington a personality and manner well suited to the presidential politics that would develop in the second half of the twentieth century. He possessed a vast amount of charm that he combined with self-assurance and a sense of humor to good effect. That the charm, self-assurance, and humor came with great wealth and good looks made them more potent. These qualities and the wealth came with an absence of self-promotion. Instead, as Florida congressman (later senator) and friend George Smathers observed: "[H]e never kidded himself or had any delusions about himself. He saw himself candidly and accurately and frankly."[24]

As one of his interpreters has noted, Kennedy "projected an indescribable grace" that combined "Harvard intellectualism and an Irish cultural heritage" and made him "perhaps the first Irish Brahmin in American politics." He loved luxury, enjoyed caviar, and ate it by the spoonful. He was used to wealth and power. The Great Depression had had almost no effect upon him. He had never had to work in his life and almost never carried money with him, relying on others to pay for any daily expenses that arose.[25]

With the love of luxury came an intellectualism that JFK could apparently summon on command. Kennedy, who had great admiration for the English style of politics, laced his speeches and observations with literary and historical allusions. Late in the 1950s, the *New York Times* reported that "Senator Kennedy was at his best before university audiences, raining upon them historical allusions, quoting from Bismarck, Shakespeare, and Queen Victoria. He has a sharp historical sense but it is that of a cum laude Harvard graduate who writes books."[26] Numerous observers remarked on Kennedy's quick, inquiring mind that seemed ever in search of new theories to explore. He created in many the impression of an intellectual in politics.

With his grace and elegance along with his wealth, John F. Kennedy was a much sought after companion. He did not have to seek out friends and associates; they flocked to him, and he had his choice of friendships and social events. There emerged something of a competition for his attention. He set the tone for his circle, and those who did not conform to his tastes were eliminated. Kennedy did not like pretense and self-importance. He had no patience with pieties, and flattery was not effective with him. He distrusted emotional individuals.[27]

Kennedy was detached, restless, and easily bored. As Richard Reeves observed, he was "very impatient, addicted to excitement, living his life as if it were a race against boredom." Some of his friends lived in terror of the possibility that he might become tired of them. They had the sense that they were disposable, like his girlfriends. Associates, female friends, the press, and many others found themselves under his spell. His relaxed and sardonic humor, his sense of irony, his inquiring mind, his openness to new ideas offered a bright new political light and captivated a growing audience in Washington beginning in the late 1940s and throughout the succeeding decade.[28]

Kennedy not only charmed people, he manipulated them. Polly Kraft, the wife of one of his speechwriters, observed that he [JFK] was "an artist who paints with other people's lives." Richard Reeves concluded that Kennedy's life "was sequential seduction and there were few complaints from the seduced." When Kennedy became displeased with someone, even a close friend, he had no difficulty in retaliating against that individual. After JFK became president, Ben Bradlee, one of his closest journalist friends, wrote a story to which Kennedy objected. Bradlee, for his efforts, found himself ostracized for more than a month.[29]

Nor was Kennedy's record in Washington so scintillating that everyone became an admirer. Felix Frankfurter said he was "totally disbelieving" in Kennedy's "alleged great knowledge of history." Sam Rayburn, Speaker of the House of Representatives, said that in the House, JFK was "one of the laziest men I ever talked to" and "just . . . another seat-warmer." Later, during the presidential campaign of 1960, Rayburn changed his mind. Then he was "amazed at the depth of Kennedy's knowledge."[30]

Even Kennedy admirers concede that JFK's performance in the House of Representatives, from 1947 to 1953, was uninspired and uninspiring. There were obvious reasons. His health continued to be poor. He found congressional duties unimportant and unexciting. According to a close friend, the House "began to look like a Three-I League job to a major league ball player." Kennedy was frequently absent, often appeared in casual clothes (including sneakers), and was bored with constituent services. Still, the new representative could and did show occasional flashes of brilliance. John F. Kennedy may not have made a record as a serious and important member of the House, but he did display an intelligence and political talent far above that of the typical first-term congressman.[31]

The new Massachusetts representative had no intention of remaining in the House any longer than necessary and soon began plotting his rise to the U.S. Senate. This meant challenging Henry Cabot Lodge Jr. in 1952. Lodge was in a very strong position, and 1952 shaped up as a Republican year. Joseph P. Kennedy thought a race against Lodge was a big mistake with the potential to ruin his son's political career. JFK was determined; he had had his fill of the House. He believed if he was going to get ahead he had to take the risk. Kennedy was something of a fatalist: either he was destined for higher office or not, and he might as well find out. His poor health seemed to have led him to think that his life expectancy was short. In the late 1940s, he told Joseph Alsop that he had "some kind of slow-motion-leukemia." He had seen too many premature deaths in his family and in the war to believe there was any point in putting off his bid to rise. Kennedy's willingness to take political risks, to plunge into unknown waters, and to not second-guess himself was one of his political strengths. Without this quality, he might have fallen short in the presidential sweepstakes. With Kennedy, there were no regrets and no looking back.[32]

Kennedy confronted enormous obstacles in 1952 as he faced an incumbent senator from an old and honored Massachusetts family, a powerful Republican presidential candidate at the top of the GOP ticket, and an election year that generally favored Republicans. However, Henry Cabot Lodge Jr. proved to be a less formidable campaigner than expected, and Joseph P. Kennedy mobilized his massive resources for the campaign. Robert F. Kennedy for the first time made his mark as campaign manager. In a crucial showdown, JFK bested Lodge in a debate. In it, JFK was "cool and offhand," his performance a matter of "effortless grace," while Lodge "sweated and his hands shook." John F. Kennedy narrowly won the election in spite of Eisenhower's massive victory in the state. Kennedy became only the third Democrat ever elected to the Senate from Massachusetts.[33]

Although JFK was happy to be out of the House and into the more exclusive Senate, his early years in the upper chamber were undistinguished. He married Jacqueline Bouvier in 1953, but his health continued to be a serious problem, especially in 1954–55. After that, although the back pain remained and he was never completely well, there was some improvement in his condition.

With better health, JFK developed a new zest for politics and for his father's grand project to make him president. Four years into his first term in the Senate, John F. Kennedy experienced a political epiphany. In 1956, the Democratic presidential nomination went for a second time to Adlai E. Stevenson, who made the unexpected decision to throw open the nomination of the vice-presidential candidate to the national convention. JFK had been angling for the vice-presidential nomination, but there could be no planning for this eventuality. John and Robert Kennedy immediately took up the challenge. They launched an impromptu campaign to secure the nomination for vice president against the advice of their father, who thought this an exceedingly stupid idea. The battle between Senator Estes Kefauver of Tennessee and Kennedy was hard fought. At one point, Kennedy was within forty votes of the nomination. In the end, Kefauver narrowly won. The Massachusetts senator made an excellent showing, received much favorable publicity, and elicited support from Democratic delegations across America, perhaps most surprisingly from the South.[34]

Subsequently, Robert F. Kennedy traveled with the Stevenson presidential campaign to observe its operations. Stevenson lost, but the Kennedy brothers learned much from the 1956 campaign. First was the realization that even with no preparation and no organization, JFK had almost won the vice-presidential nomination. (Since Kefauver had been Stevenson's main opponent, he already had an organization in place for the vice-presidential fight.) Second, Bobby Kennedy discovered that Stevenson was incompetent and neither to be feared nor respected. According to Bobby, the former Illinois governor lacked decisiveness and refused to delegate authority, while his campaign was disorganized. Bobby, who did not conceal his contempt, was "sullen and withdrawn" and "hard bitten and sour" during the campaign. He made no effort to pretend that he admired the candidate. At one point, he called JFK to tell him that he thought "Adlai's a faggot." After quitting the campaign, he called Larry O'Brien and told him: "I feel as if I'm alive again. . . . That asshole was absolutely killing me."[35]

The third great revelation centered on the location of real power in the Democratic convention delegations. Ken O'Donnell and Robert Kennedy went to see Senator John McLellan of Arkansas to ask for his state's votes for JFK for vice president. McLellan responded that they were talking to the wrong person—the real power rested with Governor Orval Faubus. It occurred to O'Donnell and Robert and John Kennedy that members of the House or Senate did *not* control state delegations, and they set out to determine on a state-by-state basis who did.[36]

In short, John and Robert Kennedy came away from Chicago in 1956 unimpressed with Democratic leaders and convinced that they could capture the presidential nomination in 1960 if they organized and worked hard. Before 1956, JFK thought he would have to work toward the vice presidency first and then move on to the presidential nomination. Now, he was convinced the presidential nomination was attainable without going through the vice presidency.

In 1957, Massachusetts senator John F. Kennedy began to focus his considerable talents on this effort. He possessed many assets but also a few serious liabilities. His youth was against him as the great political bosses of the Democratic Party tended to see him as a young, rich upstart without the qualifications to be president. He also had a serious problem with liberals. The Kennedy family had befriended, supported, and never renounced Senator Joseph R. McCarthy, an association that marked the Massachusetts senator as suspect. John Kennedy supported basic liberal economic and social programs, but he disdained the liberal label and disliked sentimental, emotional appeals. Whatever his progressive inclinations, John F. Kennedy was not a liberal in 1957. As journalist friend Rowland Evans tried to explain: "Kennedy didn't like the word liberal. He thought the liberals often posed and postured. . . . [H]e had scorn for the professional liberals." For their part, self-proclaimed liberals were naturally suspicious of the Massachusetts senator. One such individual recalled what he saw as Kennedy's "coldness." "He smiled, he was charming, but there was no outgoing affection or warmth, or even indignation."[37]

Liberals were not JFK's only problem. He was suspect among African Americans and white southerners. Beginning in 1957, he attempted to steer a middle course trying to figure out how to appeal to both groups without irrevocably alienating either of them. With memories of southern support in Chicago, he first made overtures toward the South. His votes on the civil rights bill of 1957 marked him as a moderate. He cultivated Alabama governor John Patterson. In 1957–58, southerners saw John F. Kennedy as someone who understood their problems.[38]

The southern tilt aggravated Kennedy's problems with liberals. He and his campaign managers came to see the candidate's southern associations as more of a liability than an asset. By 1959, the Massachusetts senator was backtracking from the South and trying to demonstrate his liberal *bona fides*. He invested time and effort to recruit Chester Bowles as a foreign policy adviser because, he said, he and Bowles shared similar views. When Bowles endorsed Kennedy in late 1959, it was a breakthrough on the liberal front. Kennedy's true views about Bowles and party liberals like him were revealed in a later comment: "Chet tells me there are six revolutions going on in the world. One is the revolution of rising expectations. I lost track of the other five." In truth, Kennedy was a centrist and a realist. He lacked the emotional commitment to liberal ideals, and he found men like Bowles, Stevenson, and Humphrey pedantic and boring.[39]

In 1957, the Kennedy presidential campaign accelerated. The candidate received some 2,500 invitations for speaking appearances and fulfilled hundreds of them. He was on the cover of *Time*. He won the Pulitzer Prize for his book *Profiles in Courage* as well as a coveted seat on the Senate Foreign Relations Committee. Ironically, the latter was the handiwork of Senate Majority Leader Lyndon B. Johnson, who denied the seat to Estes Kefauver, considering the Tennessee senator a greater threat to his (LBJ's) presidential ambitions than the Massachusetts senator. John F. Kennedy's campaign was serious. There were no more of the halfhearted, languid efforts that characterized his first ten years in Washington. His opponents failed to take the new Kennedy seriously.

If John F. Kennedy's life up to 1947 was "extraordinary," as Nigel Hamilton maintains, not even the most dedicated admirers of Kennedy's Republican opponent in 1960 would make a similar claim in his behalf. Yet, Richard Milhous Nixon is just as interesting an individual as Kennedy, and his political career between 1946 and 1959 involved higher stakes.

The difficulties in understanding Nixon and getting at the core of his personality are equal to those posed by Kennedy, though for different reasons. Any attempt to describe Nixon, his thinking, and his actions in the 1940s and 1950s runs hard into the perceptions of Nixon from his presidency and especially the Watergate scandal. As with Kennedy, the great challenge is to understand Nixon as he was in the 1950s.[40]

Nixon fascinated observers then and now because of his unusual mixture of characteristics. Those who worked with him very quickly recognized his powerful intelligence and his remarkable memory. One individual said that Nixon possessed "the most retentive memory I've ever encountered." Another person who knew him from the Eisenhower administration said Nixon impressed him with his ability for summarizing succinctly and effectively both sides of an argument at congressional leadership or cabinet meetings. Bryce Harlow, an especially astute observer of Congress and presidents, maintained that the "intellectual competence of this man [Nixon] is probably the highest of any person ever to serve in the Oval office—the finest intelligence, the most disciplined at any rate." By 1960, he also possessed an unparalleled knowledge of American state and local politics.[41]

With this ability came a virtually impenetrable personality. Over the years, there has been no shortage of politicians, journalists, and historians who have undertaken the task of trying to understand Richard M. Nixon without a great deal of success. Theodore H. White remarked to Hugh Sidey of *Time* and *Life*, "Do you realize . . . that I have spent the greatest portion of my adult life writing about Richard Nixon and I still don't understand him?" Economic adviser Arthur Burns said he would never completely understand Nixon. A Soviet diplomat in 1972 said that the Soviets found Nixon "so impenetrable that we had no idea what would please him." Close associates of Nixon such as Robert Finch and H. R. Haldeman contended that they had no personal relationship. Haldeman, for example, asserted that Nixon did not know how many children his chief aide had or their ages.[42]

The sources of this problem are obvious. Richard M. Nixon was an introvert, a loner who kept to himself as much as possible. He almost never relaxed and had few close friends outside his family. He was socially awkward, not very dexterous, and mechanically inept, attributes that reinforced his loner tendencies. Nixon said to H. R. Haldeman, his lead advance man in 1960 and later his chief of staff, "I'm an introvert in an extrovert's profession." Nixon had difficulty dealing with people. He struggled with small talk as a social lubricant and took none of the pleasure that someone like Lyndon Johnson did in the conviviality and backslapping that characterized politics at every level. In 1972, when speaking to a policeman who had suffered a minor injury after having been accidentally hit by a vehicle in the presidential motorcade, Nixon asked him, "How do you like your job?" Nixon's trip to talk to the protestors at the Lincoln Memorial at the time of the American invasion of Cambodia in 1970 is well known for the president's difficulty in trying to strike up a conversation. According to Haldeman and others, Nixon could not relax with people outside his family. In social contacts, he was "stiff" and "artificial," but with groups he was "superb," and in situations in which the matter was strictly business, Nixon was "usually excellent" with individuals, but he hated to see anyone who had to be persuaded or threatened. He disliked any situation that meant personal confrontation and did his best to avoid them. He found it almost impossible to fire someone himself.[43]

Haldeman attributed much of Nixon's attitude and behavior to his rigid self-discipline. From his youth, Nixon had worked exceptionally hard. His focus and self-discipline were extraordinary. This approach to life meant that he was always self-conscious of what he did and what he said. Newsman Edward P. Morgan observed that it was "impossible for him [Nixon] to relax. It's impossible for him to just sit down and say something without posturing." Many interpreted this as artificiality, deviousness, manipulation, or Nixon calculating his statements and actions for effect rather than stating his true beliefs. Nixon seemed unable to be spontaneous. When his public relations people tried to get him to appear in a relaxed setting on a beach at San Clemente, he appeared in a white shirt and tie and walked along the beach in his wing tip shoes. This self-discipline was also noticeable in his diet. He paid careful attention to what he ate, opting for healthy food before that became common. He drank sparingly (although he occasionally did become inebriated). He exercised regularly. His weight changed very little over the last fifty years of his life. Haldeman thought Nixon's self-discipline so encompassing as to be "unnatural."[44]

One of his very few close personal friends was Bebe Rebozo. Rebozo's successful relationship with Nixon was instructive. He succeeded because he was completely loyal, did not gossip, never made requests of Nixon, and tolerated endless Nixon monologues or hours of Nixon writing on his yellow legal pad in silence. Bebe was a "genial, discrete sponge" who asked nothing of Nixon. He was the one person outside his family with whom Nixon enjoyed effortless companionship.[45]

Most people found Nixon's persona strange and baffling. His straining efforts at congeniality seemed manufactured and synthetic. His political, journalistic, and other critics considered it a manifestation of his insincerity. In a famous comment, Ann Whitman, Dwight D. Eisenhower's secretary and no Nixon admirer, remarked that the vice president "sometimes seems like a man who is acting like a nice man rather than being one." A typical reaction of those who met Nixon and took a dislike to him was that of Ben Bradlee of *Newsweek* and a friend of Jack Kennedy's. Bradlee said that he met the vice president when he covered him in the 1960 election but he "never got behind that staged, programmed exterior to anything like an inner man that I could understand or laugh with." Richard Rovere developed an "instinctive dislike and distrust" for Nixon and considered him a "transparent demagogue and fraud."[46]

Others critics viewed Nixon with a combination of pity and disdain. Theodore White, the great friend of the Kennedy presidential campaign, wrote pityingly of Nixon that "rather than being the hard, cruel, vengeful man as constantly described in the liberal press, Nixon was above all a friend seeker, almost pathetic in his eagerness to be liked."[47]

Nixon grew up in a modest Quaker family. The future vice president and president possessed a spiritual dimension that remained with him his entire life, although he was less interested in theological issues. He was a sentimentalist and someone who took pride in making small, kind gestures to the less powerful. This practice began in his youth when he convinced his mother not to have a shoplifter arrested because of the effect on her two children of having their mother labeled a thief, continued at Duke Law School, and followed him as vice president. He befriended Senate janitor Robert Collins, sent him flowers when his wife had a stroke, gave him a cane for a neighbor, and wrote him a letter of thanks as Nixon prepared to leave Washington in January 1961. At about the same time, he penned another letter to Herb Kaplow of NBC television reporting to him that two hostesses on the press plane that followed Nikita Khrushchev around the country in 1959 had told him that Kaplow was "the most considerate of the whole press crowd." In Nixon's view, this was a genuine compliment to a member of the media, most of whom the vice president disliked and distrusted. Later, when he became president, he read a story about Billy Corbett, a karate expert who attempted to set a world record by breaking 2,056 bricks with his hand. He hoped people would give one dollar a brick for children with kidney diseases. Unfortunately, Corbett broke his hand in the effort and raised less than $300. Nixon sent Corbett a check for $100. Nixon sincerely empathized with the middle and working classes and was scornful of those of the elite who treated such people callously.[48]

Exactly how and why Richard M. Nixon became what he was has been a matter of considerable debate. H. R. Haldeman's analysis with emphasis on Nixon's obsessive self-discipline and its consequences is probably the best explanation. But it is not the only one. Henry Kissinger, in a famous comment to Hugh Sidey at the end of the Watergate debacle, remarked: "Can you imagine what this man [Nixon] would have been had somebody loved him? I don't think anybody ever did, not his parents, not his peers. He would have been a great, great man had somebody loved him." Bryce Harlow offered a similar interpretation. Harlow said he guessed that sometime in his youth Nixon "got badly hurt by someone he cared for very deeply or trusted totally. . . . [A]nd from that experience and from then on he could not trust people."[49] According to this theory, Nixon suffered some traumatic event in his youth from which he did not recover. For his part, Nixon despised psychological explanations of his behavior.

Nixon's early life was not one of great hardship or suffering, and his parents were decent, ordinary people. The Nixon family was stable and loving. Life was not easy, but the family was middle class in the context of the early twentieth century. Frank and Hannah Nixon had four other sons in addition to Richard. From what is known, Frank and Hannah were good, loving parents, and their family was a close one. Like many families, though, in the harsh world of the early twentieth century, they were forced to confront their share of adversity and suffering. One son (Arthur) died suddenly in his childhood of uncertain causes (probably encephalitis or meningitis), and another (Harold) passed away in his early adulthood from tuberculosis after a lengthy illness. These personal tragedies undoubtedly affected Richard and his family, but such events were not uncommon in the America of the first third of the century.[50]

Like most other families in the 1920s and 1930s, the Nixons enjoyed only a narrow economic margin, and the Great Depression battered them in the 1930s. Nevertheless, the economic and other setbacks they endured were not enough to prevent Richard from beginning his college education at Whittier College in 1930 or moving on to law school at Duke in 1934. In short, what one saw in Richard M. Nixon was a very unusual and very talented individual who emerged from ordinary circumstances.

If Richard M. Nixon possessed great ability, he also capitalized on it by working long, hard hours at whatever he undertook. At age fifteen, he was responsible for the vegetables in the family store. He would arise at 4:00 A.M., drive to a Los Angeles vegetable market, buy the produce, bring it back, and then wash and display it. After that effort, he would go off to school. This regimen forced him to give up football and orchestra, but he had no difficulty in maintaining his status as one of the best students in the school. The significance of the work in the grocery store, which he continued even after he entered college, was multifaceted. It conditioned him to work hard, to organize himself and his time, and to develop self-discipline. It contributed to his serious nature and his view of life as a very serious business. It also gave him firsthand experience with the realities of the life that most Americans faced, which helped him to understand and empathize with their outlook. Nixon would say later that he never drove by a vegetable stand "without feeling sorry for the guy who picks out the rotten apples."[51]

With the completion of his studies at Duke Law School in 1937, Nixon tried but failed to secure jobs with a New York City law firm and the FBI. He returned to Whittier. If peacetime did not allow Nixon to escape Whittier, World War II did. With his new wife, Pat, whom he married in 1940, he obtained a job in the Office of Price Administration (OPA) in Washington in early 1942. The job gave him his first bad taste of the federal bureaucracy. Richard Nixon had already decided years earlier to become a politician, and any aspiring politician knew that wartime service, if not an absolute necessity, would be a major asset. So, in 1942, he joined the U.S. Navy, and in 1943 he shipped out for the South Pacific, where he served as a logistical officer.

Nixon's naval service was hardly as eventful as John F. Kennedy's, but it was of considerable significance for the Californian. In the navy, Nixon discovered an unknown side of himself. He fit in well in the male setting. He played poker extremely well, held his own in profanity, and operated a trading post, all the while doing an excellent job of providing for his men. Perhaps most importantly, he discovered a rapport with working-class men. He was well known and well liked. His ability to understand the working-class perspective, its wants and needs, and its resentments proved invaluable in his subsequent political career. Accounts of his navy service indicate none of the social awkwardness usually associated with him. Instead, he seems to have been a version of the character made famous by Henry Fonda in the movie *Mr. Roberts*, as difficult as it may be for many to reconcile Nixon with the movie character. Apparently, for one time in his life, Nixon was able to relax, be himself, and temporarily put aside the striving that was so ingrained in him. Over the years, many of his critics, often members of the social, media, and academic elites, would confound themselves in attempting to explain Nixon's popular appeal. They would have done well to have studied his navy years as well as his time at the family grocery store.[52]

Back in the United States in 1945, Nixon initially returned to his law practice—but with his eye on a political career. In 1946, he became the Republican nominee for the House of Representatives in the Twelfth Congressional District of California, a seat held by Democrat Jerry Voorhis. This marked the beginning of a remarkable and meteoric political rise for Nixon. His initial victory in 1946 was quickly followed by reelection in 1948, a victorious campaign for the United States Senate in 1950, and election as vice president of the United States in 1952 at age thirty-nine.[53]

His rise was swifter than that of John F. Kennedy, despite Kennedy's advantages of wealth and fame. Without these, Nixon had advantages of his own. He benefited from the fact that, in three of the four years he ran (1946, 1950, 1952), the political tide favored Republicans. Only in 1948 did he have to run in a year that turned out to be unfavorable, and in that year he had only a minority-party opponent in the general election. He seized upon and made highly effective use of the anticommunism issue. He ran a huge risk with the Alger Hiss case—one that could have ruined him politically—but he made the right call and reaped great rewards. Nixon's anticommunism was usually reasonable and benefited from the numerous irresponsible practitioners whose wild excesses made Nixon appear moderate by comparison. He also did well to position himself as a centrist in the great internal clash in the Republican Party.

In the late 1940s and early 1950s, the Republican Party was badly divided. The eastern Dewey wing of the party, which accommodated itself to the New Deal and supported the new departures in American foreign policy, battled the Taft wing, which generally remained opposed to the New Deal and the new foreign policy of the late 1940s. The choice of Nixon as vice president in 1952 rested in large part on his acceptability to both sides of the party. He had supported the Marshall Plan and NATO, thereby aligning himself with the eastern Republican establishment on the one hand, while his hard-line anticommunism and his role in the Hiss case made him look good to more conservative Republicans. Nixon's ability to maintain his credentials with both wings of the party was crucial to his political career from the late 1940s until his election in 1968. In that year, he managed to beat back the challenge of New York governor Nelson Rockefeller while simultaneously warding off the rising California governor, Ronald Reagan.

His rapid advance was not without liabilities. The politics that Nixon practiced had very sharp edges. His efforts in the Hiss case made enemies. Alger Hiss was a symbol of New Deal liberalism and Ivy League elitism. Nixon took delight in discrediting Hiss and what he stood for. New Dealers, Hiss loyalists, and the journalistic and academic elite despised Nixon's work.

The campaigns of 1952 and 1954 were clearly characterized by an unusual level of antagonism. There is a question of whether those of 1946 (against Jerry Voorhis) and 1950 (against Helen Gahagan Douglas) were as bad as they were later portrayed to be or whether it was more of a case of Democrats rendering an ex post facto judgment on them. The conventional wisdom has been to see 1946 and 1950 as exceptionally dirty campaigns in which Nixon with his ignoble character overwhelmed the naiveté and idealism of his opponents. The heterodox view is that Nixon won because 1946 and 1950 were Republican years and because Voorhis and Douglas ran exceedingly poor campaigns, not because Nixon played unfairly. According to this theory, Nixon's campaigns were not especially rough in the context of 1946 and 1950, and many of the complaints against Nixon were manufactured after Nixon reached the national stage as the vice-presidential candidate in 1952. There is no debate about the nature of the 1952 campaign, which turned into one of the nastiest of the century. Both Democrats and Republicans delivered numerous low blows, and Richard Nixon was one of the most prominent figures in the fray. Nixon supporters argued he was under as much attack as anyone because of the liberal dislike for him growing out of the Hiss case. His detractors saw Nixon as one of the major perpetrators of the poisonous politics of the late 1940s and the first half of the 1950s.[54]

Richard Nixon accumulated a very large number of political enemies. These included not only militant liberals but Harry Truman, Adlai Stevenson, and Sam Rayburn. Nixon brought much of this dislike on himself with his incendiary rhetoric. In 1952, he accused Truman, Stevenson, and Secretary of State Dean Acheson of being "traitors to the high principles in which many of the nation's Democrats believe." He accused Stevenson of "having a Ph.D. degree from Acheson's College of Cowardly Communist Containment." In the 1954 campaign, he mentioned Secretary of State John Foster Dulles and then said, "[I]sn't it wonderful finally to have a Secretary of State who isn't taken in by the Communists?" Democrats such as Truman, Rayburn, Stevenson, and Acheson interpreted Nixon's remarks to mean that he was accusing them of disloyalty. They did not forget, and Stevenson, for one, never forgave.[55]

As far as Truman was concerned, Nixon had called him a traitor, and he would have nothing to do with the vice president even when Nixon tried to make amends in 1958. Rayburn said Nixon had "the cruelest face he'd ever looked into" but denied hating him. Rayburn went on to add: "I don't hate anybody. But there are a few I loathe." Adlai Stevenson regarded him with passionate contempt. One associate of the former Illinois governor said that Nixon was the only individual he ever heard Stevenson refer to as "a son of a bitch."[56]

Nixon did not hold a grudge—at least against Acheson, Rayburn, and Truman. In his memoirs, one of his few expressions of regret concerned his attacks on Acheson in 1952. On Rayburn's death, he wrote an undoubtedly sincere tribute to the Speaker's sister, calling him "one of the greatest leaders our nation has ever produced" and attributing to him "never-failing courage." Nixon belatedly paid tribute to Truman—first in 1958 and later in the 1990s—when, among other things, he attributed "great leadership" to Truman, noting that Truman "had some of the best gut instincts I have ever seen" and that he was "the architect of our winning position in the cold war." These comments summarized one of many Nixonian paradoxes. He could lambaste men like Truman and Acheson in unmerciful terms and still express admiration for them. In the case of Rayburn, he could absorb the wrath and disdain that he undoubtedly felt from the Texan, yet still respect and admire him. These were obvious inconsistencies, even contradictions, and there may be no way to reconcile them. In Nixon's mind, politics was a tough business, one in which one had to be able to take it as well as give it out, and there is a gulf between what he said in political campaigns and his historical assessment of individuals.[57]

Although a good deal of the dislike for Richard Nixon was reasonable and understandable, there was also an irrational element. There were the conspiracy theorists, then and now. There were those who believed that Alger Hiss was innocent and that Nixon helped to frame him. Stewart Alsop, in 1959, reported that a little old California lady told him: "I know it's against religion to hate anybody, but I just can't help hating Nixon. He's just like that Hitler." The idea that Nixon was Nazi-like was common among his critics. Walter Cronkite told Tom Dewey that a great many people said that Nixon reminded them of Max Schmeling, Rudolf Hess, and Joe McCarthy in his physical appearance. Other Democrats entertained fantasies of Nixon as a Nazi storm trooper. What one is supposed to make of all this is uncertain. Nixon had no connections with fascist or Nazi political fronts, had never supported appeasement, and had served in the U.S. Navy.[58]

Some of Nixon's unsavory reputation was the product of his role in the Eisenhower administration. Ike relied on the vice president to conduct the necessary partisan attacks. So, Nixon was the Republican point man in 1952 and 1954, and the president was able to stay above the battle as he preferred.[59]

Nixon soldiered on, loyal to the administration and accumulating more than his share of political scars and resentments. Within the administration during the first term, he was "a political Mr. Fix It." However, he handled himself very well at the time of the president's heart attack in 1955 and won new respect as a consequence of his circumspect behavior. Nixon's problem by the end of the first Eisenhower term was twofold. First, in the service of the president and the party he had made himself widely disliked among Democrats and some independents. Second, his signature issue of domestic anticommunism was in decline. As he entered 1956, Nixon faced the prospect of becoming an obsolete political product—too controversial and too partisan to continue as vice president. He was especially vulnerable because, although Eisenhower had no hesitation in sending Nixon out to lead the attack on the Democrats, he seemed to dislike the specific means that entailed and blamed the vice president for the resulting messy situation.[60]

For Nixon as well as Kennedy, 1956 was a turning point. Nixon's accomplishment was to survive the undermining efforts of his Republican enemies. Led by Harold Stassen, elements in the party and the White House did their best to convince Eisenhower that Nixon would be a drag on the ticket and should be replaced. Eisenhower, for his part, appeared to be willing to consider someone else as his running mate. Whether Ike was serious or merely attempting to stimulate interest in the Republican convention is open to question. In April 1956, after several months of uncertainty, the announcement that Nixon was Ike's choice to continue as vice president was made. Nixon survived, although the experience was an unpleasant one. Everyone knew that with Eisenhower unable to run again in 1960, the 1956 decision put Nixon in the forefront to succeed Eisenhower.[61]

Nixon was smart enough to see his problems and know his vulnerabilities. Beginning in 1956, he set out to redefine himself. This would be the first of several "new" Nixons to surface over the years. He was milder and less combative in his campaign speeches in 1956. After November, with Eisenhower's support and assistance, he began to focus his attention on foreign affairs. Eisenhower sent him on several international trips to represent the United States in 1957, 1958, and 1959, and Nixon made good impressions. The trip to the Soviet Union in 1959 proved to be a publicity coup as he engaged Nikita Khrushchev in the famous "kitchen debate." By the second half of 1959, Richard Nixon had managed the successful transition from the partisan zealot and the political "Mr. Fix It" of the early and mid-1950s to a more respected statesmanlike figure. Although not without liabilities, he was in an excellent position to pursue the presidency in 1960.

As John F. Kennedy and Richard M. Nixon planned their paths to their respective party nominations, they established a cordial relationship with each other. They had much in common. They were about the same age, with Nixon four years older, and they came to Washington in the same year, 1947, after both had won election to the House of Representatives in 1946. They reflected different constituencies, but both were political realists and their positions on foreign policy were similar.

Despite the party differences, the two men had a high regard for each other. Joseph P. Kennedy contributed to Nixon's Senate bid in 1950, and

JFK told people he was pleased that the Republican had won. He also sent Nixon a letter in 1952 saying he was "tremendously pleased" by the Californian's nomination as vice president. The New Englander added, "You were an ideal selection." Kennedy's Senate office was directly across the hall from Nixon's vice-presidential office in the mid-1950s. Nixon was greatly troubled by Kennedy's near-death in 1954 and was a frequent visitor to Kennedy's office after his return from back surgery. He sent word that, in the narrowly divided Senate, he would not allow Republicans to take advantage of the Kennedy absence to take over the upper house. Nixon sent a letter supporting Kennedy's admission to membership in the exclusive Burning Tree Club in Washington. As late as May 1958, Kennedy described Nixon as "a man of really enormous ability who was consistently underestimated" and stated he would be a "formidable man to beat in 1960."[62]

The Kennedy-Nixon relationship was a cordial one, but Nixon liked and admired Kennedy more than the reverse. Although JFK respected Nixon's political skills, he was hardly the kind of individual Kennedy sought out for social companionship. And Nixon's speeches with their sentimentality and appeal to middle-class pieties were emphatically not Kennedy's style. Given the very different natures of the two men, it was inevitable that once they were locked in their great contest, John F. Kennedy developed a distaste for his Republican opponent. Nixon, however, remained admiring of John F. Kennedy and fascinated with the Kennedy family into the 1980s and even beyond. The unequal nature of the Kennedy-Nixon relationship gave JFK a psychological advantage over Richard Nixon when the two men became rivals for the highest office in the land in 1960. The vice president never unleashed the attack he could have on the Massachusetts senator. Kennedy, in contrast, had no difficulty in rhetorically assaulting his opponent in the harshest terms.[63]

3

John F. Kennedy and
the Democratic Nomination

"Kennedy outsmarted all the pros. . . . But if he had ever stumbled just once, the wolves would have closed in on him."

—Carmine DeSapio

After the 1958 congressional sweep and with Eisenhower constitutionally prohibited from running, Democratic spirits soared. Under these circumstances, there was no shortage of available candidates to make the run at the head of the Democratic ticket. By the end of 1959, five leading presidential contenders were identifiable—Senators Hubert Humphrey, Lyndon Johnson, John Kennedy, and Stuart Symington and former governor and presidential nominee Adlai E. Stevenson. All but Stevenson were actively soliciting support. Other possibilities such as former New York governor Averell Harriman, Michigan governor G. Mennen "Soapy" Williams, and Chester Bowles lurked in the background.[1]

All four of John F. Kennedy's major opponents were limited men with flawed strategies. Humphrey lacked money and organization and had a reputation for being too liberal and talking too much. Johnson's southern background and segregationist votes made him unacceptable in most of the North, and he refused to declare his candidacy for the presidency until July 1960. Stuart Symington possessed an impressive appearance but no great brain. One columnist wrote of him that he was "known as the candidate who looked most formidable until he opened his mouth." Another said Symington would be "the worst possible candidate of all parties, including the Communist Party."[2] Adlai Stevenson was a two-time loser with a reputation for indecisiveness

Although it is easy to second-guess nomination strategies with the benefit of fifty years, there was a historical reason for Symington, Stevenson, and Johnson to hold back from the primaries and set their sights on the national convention. The 1960 convention was only the second contested one for Democrats since the old convention rule requiring a two-thirds majority for the nomination had been lifted in 1936. There was no nomination fight in that year or 1940, 1944, and 1948 with a Democratic incumbent president.

Thus, the Democratic Party's experience with contested nominations boiled down to 1952 and 1956. In both years, Senator Estes Kefauver emerged as an insurgent candidate, defying the party establishment, which detested him. With no chance of winning the nomination based on support from the party leaders, Kefauver launched himself into the primaries. In 1952, beginning with New Hampshire, he was spectacularly successful, winning twelve of fifteen primaries that year and receiving 64.3 percent of the total primary vote. The presidential nomination, however, went to Adlai E. Stevenson, who appeared in none of the primaries. In 1956, something similar happened.[3]

The history of these two campaigns left an identification of Kefauver with the strategy of winning the presidential nomination through primaries. Because Kefauver attracted so much animosity, the dislike of him spilled over onto his primary strategy. In late 1959, the consensus was that primaries were a dead end and that the nomination would be decided by the party leaders at the national convention as it always had. In November 1959, DNC chairman Paul Butler predicted that the nomination would be decided on the fifth ballot. The *New York Times* reported that most Democratic politicians expected a strong Kennedy showing on the first ballot, putting him in a position to try to win on the second or third. Party elders convinced themselves that primaries would be just as meaningless in 1960 as they had been in the two previous presidential campaigns.[4]

Their analysis ignored Kefauver's lack of a regional base and financial resources. He had no effective campaign organization and therefore no ability to exert pressure on the party bosses of the large states. What was remarkable was not Kefauver's failure to win the nomination in 1952 and 1956; rather, it was that he came as close as he did given his liabilities.

In 1960, John F. Kennedy was a candidate unacceptable to most party leaders. Like Kefauver, he proposed to use the primaries as a vehicle to stake a claim on the nomination. Unlike the Tennessee senator, Kennedy had a regional base, massive financial resources, and a strong campaign organization. It would be far more difficult to stop the Massachusetts senator than the Tennessee maverick, as the great party barons discovered.

Kennedy entered 1960 with determination to succeed, with excellent preparation, and with a well-thought-out strategic plan. Kennedy had been an undistinguished representative and senator, but after his awakening in 1956 and with the prodding of his father, he worked with resolution toward the great prize of the presidential nomination. The Kennedy publicity machine that had been churning out favorable material on JFK since 1940 moved into high gear. Kennedy won the Pulitzer Prize for his book *Profiles in Courage* in 1957. In better health, he took his Senate duties more seriously. He moved to make his policy positions more acceptable to liberals while also attempting to court the South. This was not easy, and Kennedy found himself suspect in both liberal and southern circles. Even so, the Massachusetts senator did well in the Gallup Polls of 1959, which placed him either first or second (to Stevenson) in all the presidential trial heats conducted in that year. These polls showed both Kennedy and Stevenson with about 25 percent of the Democratic vote and the remaining 50 percent fragmented among Johnson, Kefauver, Humphrey, and Symington. By February 1960, Kennedy was ahead of Stevenson by double digits and could claim to be the leading Democratic candidate.[5]

John Kennedy had a highly impressive operation. The Massachusetts senator traveled widely throughout the country, giving speeches and meeting and greeting as many local Democrats as possible. Travel became immensely easier when Joseph P. Kennedy contracted for the use of an aircraft specifically to accommodate his son. When JFK met someone for the first time, that individual invariably received a personalized note. An unofficial campaign office opened in Washington. It focused on identifying potential delegates to the 1960 convention, compiling information on them and their preferences, trying to assess their attitude to JFK, and determining what would be required to shift uncommitted delegates to his cause.[6]

Meanwhile, the Kennedy campaign contracted with pollster Lou Harris to undertake an unprecedented effort on behalf of the Massachusetts senator. Eventually, Harris conducted more polls for JFK than any other presidential candidate had ever used. The Harris polls were invariably overly optimistic (one had Kennedy ahead of Nixon in Nebraska in 1959), but they provided important information for the Massachusetts senator. They also served as a public relations device to publicize favorable results and argue that JFK had emerged as the choice of Democrats and the strongest possible candidate against the likely Republican nominee Nixon. The Harris polls were just one more weapon in the Kennedy arsenal that no other candidate could match.[7]

The Kennedy campaign was fueled by far more than money. It was also bolstered by the recruitment of hundreds of volunteers, the participation of the seemingly innumerable Kennedy clan in primary states, and the rallying to the cause of old friends, especially from JFK's days in the U.S.

Navy. In brief, the Kennedy campaign had it all—money, resources, family, friends, volunteers, advanced technology (for 1960), and a handsome and appealing candidate.

The campaign also had strategic vision. It began with the premise that JFK could not sit back and expect the nomination to fall into his lap. There was too much concern about the religious issue and too much resentment at the New Englander's youth, wealth, and inexperience. Starting with New Hampshire, primaries served to demonstrate the Kennedy appeal and to influence other states and the political bosses. However, primaries determined only a small fraction of convention delegates. Political bosses and favorite sons controlled the majority. Dealing successfully with these powerbrokers was crucial to a successful presidential bid.

JFK, campaign manager Robert Kennedy, and associated campaign officials therefore spent large amounts of time cajoling, flattering, and, if necessary, intimidating the host of political bosses and favorite sons that would be holding their states' votes in the hopes of obtaining fame or material gain. The six most important—because their states controlled the largest numbers of delegates—were Governor Michael DiSalle of Ohio (64 delegates), Governor Edmund "Pat" Brown of California (81), Chicago mayor Richard J. Daley (69 Illinois delegates), Governor G. Mennen Williams of Michigan (51), Governor David Lawrence of Pennsylvania (81), and Governor Robert Meyner of New Jersey (41).

In addition, there was the largest bloc—the New York delegation with 114 votes. The situation in New York was a bizarre mess, with no single leader in a position to determine the disposition of the state's delegates. Carmine DeSapio headed the venerable Tammany Hall machine, but his power was in decline. Other bosses such as state chairman Michael Prendergast, Charles Buckley in the Bronx, Joseph Sharkey in Brooklyn, Daniel O'Connell in Albany, and Peter Crotty in Buffalo exerted a significant degree of influence. A strong New York reform faction identified with former senator Herbert Lehman and Eleanor Roosevelt further complicated the situation.

A delegate mining expedition in the Great Plains and Mountain West states provided another key element for the campaign. The northeastern quadrant of the country was either Kennedy territory or staked out by a favorite son. The southeastern quarter was in the hands of state organizations largely loyal to Lyndon Johnson. That left the Pacific Coast, the Great Plains, and the Mountain West as the best locations to prospect for delegates. Among the Pacific Coast states, Oregon had a primary, and California governor Pat Brown was determined to go to the national convention as favorite son, leaving Washington as the only state in play. The Great Plains and Mountain West should have been LBJ territory, but a hardworking Kennedy grassroots campaign turned these areas into promising ground for JFK. The combination of demonstrated strength in primaries, the successful courting of favorite sons and political bosses, and a grassroots campaign in the West reflected a Kennedy strategic vision far superior to the plan of any of his rivals.

John F. Kennedy formally announced his candidacy on January 2, 1960, but the effective launching of his campaign occurred much earlier. Meanwhile, the New Englander's two most formidable foes found it extraordinarily difficult to bring themselves to declare their candidacies. Lyndon B. Johnson would not announce until July 5, and Adlai E. Stevenson would never formally take that step.

In spite of the theory that the primaries were crucial for influencing the bosses, the initial Kennedy focus was on a boss—Governor Michael DiSalle of Ohio. This was because Ohio had an early primary and Kennedy had to make a choice whether to enter it. A decision to enter Ohio would have kept Kennedy out of Wisconsin since the two primaries were close together. In fact, Kennedy preferred to make a deal with DiSalle whereby the Ohio governor could run as a favorite son in the Ohio primary with a public commitment to deliver Ohio and its sixty-four convention delegates to JFK. Such an arrangement would be a bloodless victory, give Kennedy a large number of delegates without the necessity of spending the time and the money involved in a primary, and allow him to enter the Wisconsin contest.

However, the Kennedy campaign distrusted DiSalle. The Ohio governor had thrown his support to Kefauver in the 1956 battle for the vice presidency and was flirting with Symington in 1959. The good news for the Kennedy camp was that DiSalle was vulnerable to pressure. He had a large number of enemies including Cuyahoga County (Cleveland) party leader Ray Miller and Congressman Wayne Hays. Maverick Ohio senator Frank Lausche was no admirer of the governor, either. In addition, DiSalle's popularity in the state was slipping thanks to rising taxes. Lou Harris reported a commonly heard sentiment that "Mike has gone tax crazy." The Harris polling showed that Kennedy was the strongest Democratic candidate for November 1960 and that he could defeat DiSalle if the Massachusetts senator entered the Ohio primary.[8]

JFK, Robert Kennedy, and various Kennedy political operatives spent much of 1959 cajoling Michael DiSalle into a formal announcement that he would back the New Englander. The attempts to pressure the governor involved several meetings with him but also meetings with his Ohio

Democratic enemies, who welcomed an opportunity to ally themselves with Kennedy in an attack on DiSalle. Meanwhile, the governor received telephone calls from anti-Kennedy forces in Washington, telling him that if he opposed JFK in the Ohio primary, he would not have to be concerned about campaign funds.[9]

In September 1959, with DiSalle still waffling despite the attention, JFK indicated his intention to enter the 1960 Ohio primary. The announcement produced another flurry of activity culminating in a showdown in late 1959, featuring DiSalle against John Bailey and Robert F. Kennedy. It was no match. Bailey, a tough old politician, was startled at the browbeating RFK gave DiSalle. The Connecticut leader told Ken O'Donnell that "Bobby was all over DiSalle like a fly on shit." The rough treatment had its desired effect. The governor capitulated, and by January 1, 1960, DiSalle and Ohio were in the Kennedy camp. In early January, the Ohio governor announced his support for Kennedy and pledged all sixty-four Ohio delegates to him. Oregon senator Wayne Morse, unhappy with DiSalle's surrender, said: "Ohio doesn't have a Favorite Son. It has a Favorite Stooge."[10]

Ohio was a big win for the Kennedy campaign. In one swift stroke, it picked up more delegates than were available in any primary, while reinforcing its growing reputation as an efficient and ruthless operation. An internal campaign memorandum noted that Ohio was "a marvelous psychological stroke." It cracked the favorite son movement, badly damaged the big state holdout bloc, and provided momentum for the Massachusetts senator. It also demonstrated that the campaign could and would exert excruciating pressure if that was needed to get results. Other bosses with large delegations who thought they could fob off the Kennedy campaign with delay and vague promises were put on notice.[11]

With Ohio decided, Kennedy moved on to Wisconsin. The New Hampshire primary was first, but the Granite State was a sure thing given its proximity to Massachusetts. There was some debate in the Kennedy camp over the merits of entering the Wisconsin primary. Reports from Wisconsin, however, were highly positive. Governor Patrick Lucey saw the opposition Humphrey campaign without newspaper or television coverage and without crowds, going nowhere. He advised in December 1959 that Humphrey's supporters were "demoralized" and that they had "a bleak outlook of what lies ahead." The Wisconsin governor strongly urged Kennedy to enter.[12]

In many respects, Wisconsin, with its large Catholic population, presented a favorable outlook for the Massachusetts senator. Richard Nixon's pollster Claude Robinson estimated in 1960 that 35 percent of Wisconsin voters were Catholic. Since it was an open primary (that is, all voters, re-gardless of political affiliation, had the right to vote in the Democratic pri-mary), Kennedy could expect to attract thousands of Republican Catholic crossover votes. Kennedy had visited the state on numerous occasions from 1956 through 1959. The Lou Harris polling showed him ahead of Humphrey and in excellent shape in the Badger State. On January 21, 1960, John F. Kennedy announced that he would enter the Wisconsin primary as well as the one in Nebraska.[13]

The rosy Wisconsin outlook had its share of thorns. Humphrey was from the neighboring state of Minnesota and well regarded. He was especially strong in the three Wisconsin congressional districts (the Third, Ninth, and Tenth) bordering Minnesota that were overwhelmingly agricultural and Protestant. The newspapers, radio, and television in these border districts were more oriented to the Land of 10,000 Lakes than to Wisconsin. One observer remarked that anybody who thought Kennedy could carry those three districts was "out of their head."[14]

Although Kennedy enjoyed considerable support in Wisconsin, the lead-ing party officials were divided. Governor Lucey, who was also the state chairman, was in Kennedy's camp, as were Senator William Proxmire and Attorney General John Reynolds. But the lieutenant governor supported Humphrey, as did the chairman of the Milwaukee County Democratic Party. Senator Gaylord Nelson officially proclaimed himself neutral but, behind the scenes, worked for Humphrey in the hope of stopping Kennedy and seeing Adlai Stevenson get the nomination. Representatives Robert Kas-tenmeier, Henry Reuss, and Lester Johnson maintained an official neutral-ity that was unhelpful to Kennedy.[15]

Another Kennedy disadvantage was the liberal tradition in Wisconsin. The state had been a hotbed of progressivism, and it spawned a militant liberalism that was suspicious of John F. Kennedy and his liberal creden-tials. As one Wisconsinite put it, "there were a lot of liberals who felt that Senator Kennedy was not liberal enough." The center of this liberal purism was the state capital, Madison, the home of the University of Wisconsin and the *Capital Times*. The publisher and editor of the newspaper, William Evjue, and its political columnist, Miles McMillin, were no Kennedy admir-ers. In fact, they had a distaste for him largely based on their perception of Kennedy's support for Senator Joseph McCarthy. In April 1959, Evjue referred to Kennedy as Senator McCarthy. The editor and publisher later said it was a slip of the tongue. Slip or not, the coverage of the *Capital Times* was unsympathetic to the Massachusetts senator. At one point, Kennedy became so upset with the newspaper that he sat down with Evjue to try to convince him that the newspaper's treatment was unfair. JFK laid a series of stories in front of Evjue and told him that on the basis of these clippings, the senator would not vote for himself. It did no good. The Madison newspaper continued its unfriendly treatment of Kennedy through the Wisconsin primary and beyond. For example, it ran a headline on March 31 about the endorsement of Kennedy by Alabama governor John Patterson under the headline "Bama Governor, Negro Hater in Kennedy Camp." It did not help matters that the leading Milwaukee newspaper, the *Milwaukee Journal*, did not provide friendly coverage, either.[16]

Campaigning in Wisconsin in winter was a tough test, and the winter of 1960 was a harsh one. By March 24, Milwaukee had accumulated 90.3 inches of snow, the fourth-heaviest on record. The zero-degree temperature reading in Milwaukee on March 25 was the latest date in history for a temperature that low.[17] Even with these problems, the Kennedy campaign moved ahead. The campaign swept over Wisconsin with victory seemingly inevitable.[18]

Meanwhile, Hubert Humphrey and his loyalists became frustrated. They lacked money and organization. The Humphrey political operatives were ineffective. Perhaps nothing better symbolized the difference between the two campaigns than the means of travel. Jack Kennedy flew in his Convair aircraft. The Minnesota senator rode in a rented bus—old, slow, and cold. Because there was no place to rest in it, one of the Humphrey campaign staff finally bought an army cot for the back of the bus, where Humphrey stretched out and tried to rest while reporters talked to him. When the company arrived at their destination, in the words of Humphrey, "we were zombies, almost always late, rumpled, bleary-eyed."[19]

The Minnesota senator saw Jackie and Rose Kennedy as "queen and queen mother" moving "among the commoners extracting obeisance, awe, and respect. They lacked only tiaras and you knew if crowns were needed Joe Kennedy would buy them. I felt like an independent merchant competing against a chain store." Humphrey's mood was not helped by the ruthlessness he perceived in the Kennedy campaign. Kennedy refused to debate the Minnesota senator because, according to the New Englander, they were in general agreement and there would be nothing to debate. Meanwhile, RFK put out a story that Teamsters boss Jimmy Hoffa was backing Humphrey.[20]

Until late March, everything went spectacularly well for Kennedy. Lou Harris's polling showed a good chance of carrying nine of the ten congressional districts. Ed Bayley, press secretary for Senator Gaylord Nelson, told newsmen that he expected JFK would win nine to one in the congressional districts. *Time* reported that one of Wisconsin's political insiders said it would not surprise him if Kennedy "swept the state" and by that, he said, he did not mean "just the popular vote and six or seven districts." He meant "all ten districts." *Newsweek* reported that the capital correspondent of the Green Bay and Appleton newspapers said that it was "easily conceivable that he [JFK] will carry all the districts." Kennedy himself predicted that he would win nine of the ten.[21]

In late March, the victory parade suddenly ran into trouble. A furor developed over religion that, until this time, had largely remained beneath the surface. Increasingly, the issue began to dominate headlines. The newspapers and other media seized on the subject and launched intense and sensational analysis. Reporters loved the subject because it provoked controversy, gained attention, and sold newspapers.

The proximate cause of the uproar was the mailing of anti-Catholic leaflets to a large, but unknown, number of Wisconsin voters. Interestingly enough, some evidence suggested that many of the recipients were Catholics. Gerald Heaney of Duluth, a Catholic, a Humphrey supporter, and a national committeeman, demanded an investigation. An incident at the end of March followed in which a Milwaukee man and vice president of the Wisconsin AFL-CIO placed an advertisement in some 250 Wisconsin weekly papers sponsored by the Square Deal for Humphrey Committee. The controversial ad cited the solidarity of the Catholic vote for Kennedy, suggested that Humphrey was not getting a square deal, and implicitly encouraged Protestants to get behind the Minnesotan.[22]

The inflammatory advertisement provoked a wave of outraged protests. Humphrey and his supporters immediately repudiated it. Even the titular head of the Square Deal for Humphrey Committee criticized the ad and the committee. John Kennedy tried to link the advertisement to Jimmy Hoffa and the Teamsters. Meanwhile, suspicion arose in the Humphrey camp and elsewhere that rogue elements from the Kennedy side had financed the mailing of anonymous anti-Catholic tracts to Roman Catholics to incite them to vote for the Massachusetts senator. Whatever the source of the scurrilous literature, the newspapers had a field day as they printed one story after another on the subject of religion and the primary and began a serious examination of the potential of religious affiliation to influence the Wisconsin primary vote.[23]

On April 3, the *Milwaukee Journal* published an analysis in which it showed the breakdown of religious affiliation congressional district by congressional district. The newspaper then posed three key questions: "Will Catholic Democrats go top heavy for Kennedy? Will a substantial number of Catholic Republicans cross over into the Democratic primary and for whom will they vote? Will Protestant Republicans cross over, remain loyal to Nixon, or stay home?" The combination of the mailings and the media attention made the religious issue central. This was not good news for Kennedy for several reasons. As the front runner, he did not welcome anything that upset the status quo and threatened his lead. The Catholic vote for him in Wisconsin was already solid. Any disturbance was bound to work to his disadvantage. Perhaps most seriously, the religious issue scared many Democratic leaders outside Wisconsin and any signs of its resurfacing could erode their willingness to support him.

As the religious issue exploded, Hubert Humphrey began to make some progress in his appeals by emphasizing the differences between him and Kennedy on agricultural issues. Kennedy was an urban politician and had trouble appealing to rural populations. Humphrey, on the other hand, was in his element talking about agriculture. The overconfident Kennedy campaign in Wisconsin peaked too soon. The Humphrey campaign hit Kennedy hard on agriculture and took advantage of its underdog status.[24]

The primary and its results produced even more controversy.[25] On the surface, John Fitzgerald Kennedy won a decisive victory. He attracted more than 56 percent of the primary vote on the Democratic side and carried six of ten congressional districts, losing the three on the Minnesota border and the second district that included Madison (Dane County) and the *Capital Times*. He did this in a state that was a neighbor of his opponent and in which his opponent was well known and well liked. It should have been a triumph that a New England candidate campaigning far from home relished.

It was not, for two reasons. First, the Kennedy camp had anticipated a much larger victory, believing it would carry nine congressional districts, not six. Second, the postprimary analysis focused on the religious issue and Kennedy's success in winning the Catholic but not the Protestant vote.

Lou Harris and his polls provided another source of unhappiness in the Kennedy camp. Harris's predictions left much to be desired. He was off by ten or more points in five of ten congressional districts.[26] Kennedy's overconfidence was largely a product of Harris's projections. Late in the campaign, Harris told Kennedy to focus his attention on the Third and Ninth Congressional Districts instead of the Second. In retrospect, Kennedy had had no chance in the Third and Ninth. On the other hand, more effort in the last two weeks in the Second almost certainly would have produced a Kennedy victory there. The bad advice left Kennedy "bitter . . . for quite a while."[27]

The controversy surrounding the Wisconsin results spilled over on primary night. On a CBS-TV election-night program with Walter Cronkite, guest analyst pollster Elmo Roper said that "religion is playing a rather large role in this election" and called religious affiliation "the single most important issue in the election there today." He went on to say that "every Republican Catholic" who crossed over to vote in the Democratic primary intended to vote for Kennedy while Republican Protestants who crossed over split fifty-fifty between the New Englander and the Minnesotan. In a primary-night interview, Cronkite asked Kennedy about the perceived religious coloration of the vote. The Kennedys were furious. Bobby stormed into the studio after the interview and ranted and raved at Cronkite. Later he called Columbia University president Grayson Kirk and IBM president Thomas Watson to demand that they suppress the IBM-CBS statistical analysis of ethnic-religious voting patterns in Wisconsin. The next day, CBS and IBM ordered the Columbia researchers to justify their methodology and prove that their analysis was not politically motivated. Meanwhile, JFK telephoned CBS president Frank Stanton and reminded him that if elected, he would be naming members to the Federal Communications Commission.[28]

The following day's headlines reinforced the primary-night emphases. A *New York Times* story appeared under the headline "Religion Big Factor in Kennedy Victory," while the *Washington Post* ran its story under the banner "Triumph for Kennedy Not Up to Expectations."[29] The analysis and editorials in the leading national papers, Wisconsin papers, and the national news weeklies reinforced the twin messages of a religious vote and a disappointing Kennedy showing. The *Capital Times* proclaimed: "U.S. Senator John Kennedy of Massachusetts, a Catholic, defeated his Protestant opponent, U.S. Senator Hubert Humphrey of Minnesota overwhelmingly in Catholic areas, and in reverse, Humphrey piled up substantial votes in Protestant areas." The *New York Times* editorial "Result: Negative" commented that Senator Kennedy "did not have the magical popular appeal that his friends and most political prognosticators expected of him. . . . His victory was not precisely a defeat; but it was no victory either, of the kind to put the nomination within his grasp." The *Times* added that the primary "did something else that was also negative. It showed that many Catholic voters—Republicans included—cast their votes for Senator Kennedy as a Catholic." James Reston observed that Wisconsin "demonstrated there is indeed a 'Catholic vote' in America." *Time* contributed the opinion that the Catholic vote for JFK "almost amounted to a bloc vote."[30]

This interpretation of the primary was very bad news for Kennedy because it suggested that he did well in Wisconsin because of its large Catholic population. It hinted that when he got to states with a smaller percentage of Catholics, the outcome would be unfavorable to him. Furthermore, the reports implied that since the United States in 1960 still had a heavy majority of the population identifying themselves as Protestants, Kennedy's chances of winning the general election in November were slim. The Kennedy campaign resisted this analysis and the obsession of the media with religion.

The Kennedy unhappiness with the media frenzy was justified. A later, more sober analysis made the elementary but profound point that people "did not simply vote their rosaries or their hymnals" and that it was "a mistake to believe that Roman Catholics voted for John F. Kennedy just because he was Roman Catholic." According to this assessment, the Sixth District went for JFK because he was more conservative than Humphrey, plus the Minnesotan was anti–Joe McCarthy in an area that was distinctly pro-McCarthy. In the Third, Ninth, and Tenth Districts, Humphrey received greater support because he was identified with progressivism and agriculture. In short, religion was "only one of many factors, and not necessarily the most important one" in determining the choices of voters. Newspapers and television were either unable to grasp these complexities or incapable of explaining them. The media discovered, much to their amazement, that people of similar ethnic and religious backgrounds and common economic interests tended to vote for candidates with the same backgrounds and interests. In a deterministic style, they oversimplified this discovery to mean that Catholics could be counted on to vote only for Catholics and Protestants for Protestants.[31]

Despite winning almost 57 percent of the Democratic primary vote and six of ten congressional districts, the Kennedy campaign was on the defensive. Minnesota governor Orville Freeman, a staunch Humphrey supporter, proclaimed that his fellow Minnesotan had "won a victory in Wisconsin." Although galling to the Kennedy camp, the alleged "defeat" was more appearance than reality. Kennedy gained far more than he lost in Wisconsin. He won a key primary far from his New England base. He learned valuable lessons. Most importantly, the illusion of a strong Humphrey showing enticed the Minnesota senator to persist in his campaign and go onto the West Virginia primary, where he played an indispensable role in the decisive moment in the Kennedy march to the nomination.[32]

In April, however, there was little joy. From the Kennedy perspective,

Humphrey had lost in Wisconsin, but he refused to accept the decision. He was now nothing more than a spoiler, a stalking horse for the Johnson and Stevenson campaigns whose strategy was to stop the Kennedy candidacy, deadlock the convention, and win the nomination without ever contesting the primaries. Adding to Kennedy disgruntlement, in late January, the Wisconsin State Democratic Party Administrative Committee voted to alter the formula by which the Wisconsin delegates were allocated. The shift increased the votes allotted to each congressional district and decreased the delegates selected on the basis of the overall state primary vote. It was a transparent and successful effort on the part of the Humphrey camp to establish rules to its own benefit.[33]

For its part, the Humphrey campaign was no happier with its rival. Humphrey thought Kennedy had won only because of Republican Catholic crossover votes, especially in the Sixth and Eighth Congressional Districts. He was angry about some of the calls on him to withdraw. Some forms of the pressure, according to Theodore White's account, were "so vile as to amount to little short of blackmail." The Wisconsin primary produced great bitterness between Humphrey and Kennedy and between their staffs and their supporters in Wisconsin. The antagonism did not dissipate. Even after his withdrawal as a candidate in the spring, Humphrey refused to back Kennedy, and at the national convention the Minnesotan's forces were part of the stop-Kennedy movement. The unpleasantness in Wisconsin divided the two factions, prevented them from effective cooperation in the general election, and played a significant role in Kennedy's failure to carry Wisconsin in November.[34]

On the night of the Wisconsin primary, one of the Kennedy sisters watched her brother scrutinizing the primary returns and asked him, "What does it mean?" Kennedy's sardonic but obviously displeased reply was: "It means that we have to do it all over again. We have to go through every one and win every one of them [the primaries]." Although the future president almost certainly did not realize it at the time, Hubert Humphrey had done him a huge favor. By remaining in the race, Kennedy's rival helped create the circumstances for the greatest Kennedy triumph of the primary season.[35]

The next primary was in West Virginia, five weeks after Wisconsin. West Virginia, as it turned out, proved to be even more controversial. Its narrative is clear and simple. The Kennedy forces came into the state shaken and discouraged from their Wisconsin experience. They quickly regrouped, conducted a highly effective campaign that overcame the indications of an early Humphrey lead in the state, and came away with an overwhelming victory that gave the New Englander an unstoppable momentum toward the nomination.[36]

If the overall narrative is straightforward, aspects of the West Virginia story remain murky. One uncertain element is the state of the race in early and mid-April. How did the Kennedy campaign assess its position? Did it believe that Humphrey was ahead? If it did, was this perception accurate? A second key issue is the means of the Kennedy triumph. Was his decisive win the product of lessons learned in Wisconsin combined with superior resources and a highly efficient campaign? Or was the success more the result of underhanded tactics including bribery, smears, and the aid of organized crime?

A third conundrum for historians is the abject failure of the national press corps to anticipate the outcome of the West Virginia primary. Almost unanimously, the leading national reporters covering the primary and the most prestigious newspapers forecast a Humphrey win. Given Kennedy's overwhelming margin, how does one explain the failure of presumably astute political observers to predict this outcome? Why could they not see the likelihood of a close contest, with Kennedy a possible winner?

As the two rivals moved into West Virginia in April 1960, the state of the race was uncertain. The confusion derived from two conflicting Lou Harris polls combined with the unpredictable effects of the religious issue. Harris conducted a West Virginia survey between mid-December 1959 and early January 1960. The results portrayed West Virginia as an easy win for Kennedy against Humphrey. According to Harris, the New Englander was in the lead 54 percent to 23 percent, with 23 percent undecided. With the undecided out, the Kennedy lead became 70 percent to 30 percent. In Harris's view, West Virginia was a guaranteed win.[37]

Then in mid-April, Harris conducted another poll—this one covering just Kanawha County (Charleston). The results were radically different— almost the reverse of those from three months before. The new Harris numbers showed Humphrey ahead by the astounding margin of 60 percent to 40 percent or 64 percent to 36 percent, depending which part of Theodore White's chronicle of 1960 one is reading.[38]

From one perspective, as dismal as the early Harris polls were, they did serve a purpose. The Kennedy campaign committed itself to a deliberate strategy of consciously underrating its strength while overstating the strength of the opposing forces. No one on the Kennedy side publicly predicted the sweeping victory of May 10. There is every indication that the Kennedy campaign genuinely believed it was behind during the campaign and, even at the end, could not believe that it had forged into a decisive lead.

The Kennedy campaign did many things right. It had an attractive candidate who mixed with the people of West Virginia and won them over. The campaign made good choices in the West Virginians they trusted with important roles, men like Robert McDonough and Sid Christie. As always, the campaign had overwhelming resources and money to deploy. The Kennedy effort effectively utilized Franklin Delano Roosevelt Jr., son of the most revered American of the twentieth century. FDR Jr. came to the state and campaigned extensively on behalf of the Massachusetts senator.

Money was especially important in West Virginia. The state was depressed, and its politics revolved around a slating process in which candidates competed for positions on the strongest slate possible. With the governorship in Republican hands, no single Democrat could shape the outcome in the state. Candidates had to go into the counties and establish good relationships with the leading county politicians to improve their chances in the slating process. Getting slated inevitably required a willingness to hand over larger or smaller sums of money, depending on the county and its size. Theodore White, among others, found West Virginia politics "sordid" for its focus on money—"hot money, under-the-table money, open money." He traced this characteristic to the state's poverty, but, in his view, everything—including political offices—was up for sale. In this situation, Kennedy had a tremendous advantage and Humphrey an equally great disadvantage.[39]

The Kennedy campaign also benefited from the lessons learned in Wisconsin. In that state, the campaign made two major mistakes. First, it badly mishandled election projections. The campaign anticipated a sweeping victory and allowed the public and press to expect such a triumph. When the Kennedy victory did not live up to expectations, the Humphrey campaign proclaimed the Minnesota senator the winner. In West Virginia, the Kennedy campaign behaved very differently. It consciously "talked poor mouth" and consistently provided low numbers for what would represent a Kennedy win. According to John Bailey, the Kennedy side put out that 40 percent of the popular vote would be "great," 45 percent "a tactical victory," and 50 percent or more "a tremendous victory." Less than a week before the primary, JFK said he would be lucky to get 40 percent of the vote.[40]

The second great lesson from Wisconsin was how *not* to deal with the religious issue. In the Badger State, Kennedy did his best to say as little as possible until late in that primary because religious preferences were working in his favor. But the issue exploded in the last three weeks of the campaign, and at that point there was nothing the Massachusetts senator could do to manage the eruption and its consequences. Kennedy learned he had to take the initiative on the issue, set the terms of the discussion, and shape the subject to his advantage. That is exactly what he did in West Virginia.

Most observers saw religion as the issue that would defeat Kennedy in West Virginia. With few Catholics in the state and with the assumption that voters would make their primary decision on religious grounds, Kennedy appeared doomed. Closer study could have and should have produced a more sophisticated interpretation. The appearance of a militantly Protestant population was an illusion; only 5 percent of the West Virginia population was Catholic, but it was also true that only 35 percent of the population was Protestant, and 59 percent had no affiliation at all.

This is precisely what West Virginians told Robert Kennedy on April 8 when he asked them to give him "a cold-blooded appraisal" of the situations in various counties of the state. In only five counties was there any suggestion of trouble. One reporter later reflected that the press "was considerably conned" and that the state "was less Protestant . . . than it was atheist or non-religious." One could make the case that Kennedy faced much more religious opposition in Wisconsin. The large Catholic population—with its potential as a bloc vote—excited an antagonism that did not exist in West Virginia. The conflict between German and Scandinavian Lutherans and German, Irish, and Polish Roman Catholics in Wisconsin had a long and sometimes bitter history. There was nothing comparable in West Virginia. In short, religion was a much smaller factor in West Virginia than in Wisconsin.[41]

Even so, the Kennedy campaign ran scared after what happened in Wisconsin. It did not quite know what to make of the initial reaction to JFK's campaigning in the state and continually worried about a Protestant backlash. The Kennedy campaign moved swiftly and efficiently to confront the subject on its terms. From his first appearance in April, JFK attacked the issue. He said his religion would not determine his decisions as president and invoked the name of his elder brother, who had died in the armed forces of the country. JFK declared: "Nobody asked me if I was a Catholic when I joined the United States Navy." He added: "Nobody asked my brother if he was a Catholic or a Protestant before he climbed into an American bomber plane to fly his last mission." Kennedy quickly gained the advantage. By the end of the West Virginia contest, some of his supporters were arguing that the real issue was not the Roman Catholic Church and its influence, but Protestants who would not vote for Kennedy. Such individuals, it was suggested, were either bigots or at least voting for bigoted reasons. Chief advocate for this idea was Joe Alsop, who wrote that the majority of Humphrey's support were "people who were influenced by religious prejudice" and that "if Humphrey wins, no matter what he himself may say on the stump, his victory will be a triumph for prejudice." Now the burden of proof shifted to Protestant voters to demonstrate that they were not bigots. Voting for Kennedy was the only way to accomplish this.[42]

In spite of the clear Kennedy superiority, there remained a suspicion with Humphrey and others that the outcome of the primary was tainted by underhanded tactics. There were charges of vote buying. There was a messy campaign smear. Later, it developed that elements of organized crime had actively supported the Kennedy candidacy. From almost the beginning of the contest, rumors circulated that Kennedy bagmen roamed through the state, handing out money to politicians willing to sell themselves and their organizations to Kennedy. According to Humphrey, Joseph P. Kennedy, through Cardinal Cushing in Boston, sent financial contributions to Protestant churches, especially small black ones. Frustrated by the wealthy New Englander's success in making connections with people Humphrey considered his natural supporters, the Minnesota senator became unhappier. His language became tougher, as did his indictments of the Kennedy campaign. In late April, he proclaimed, "I don't think elections should be bought," and then, "I can't afford to run through this state with a little black bag and check book." Humphrey's attacks on JFK and his father were harsher than anything Richard Nixon would say in the general election campaign.[43]

Humphrey's continuing charges aggravated Kennedy. In JFK's view, the Minnesotan could not win the nomination. There was evidence that Humphrey was playing the front man for the Johnson and Stevenson campaigns. One of most outspoken advocates of a vote for Humphrey was Senator Robert Byrd, who was a staunch supporter of LBJ. As the campaign moved toward its conclusion, Franklin Delano Roosevelt Jr. delivered the lowest blow of the primary. He charged that during World War II, Humphrey had sought a draft deferment in order to manage a political campaign. Although FDR Jr. made the allegation, almost everyone outside the Kennedy camp thought that the command to launch the smear came from Bobby Kennedy. Eugene McCarthy later recalled that JFK asked to see him and when he went over to Kennedy's office, the Massachusetts senator told him, "Tell Hubert to lay off in West Virginia or we will unload on him." Not long afterward the draft-dodging charge surfaced.[44]

In the final analysis, West Virginia was a paradox. There were Kennedy bagmen running around the state buying as much support and as many politicians as possible. Bobby Kennedy was behind the attack on Humphrey's lack of military service. But there is no evidence that the Kennedy skullduggery, such as it was, determined the outcome or affected the margin of victory. John F. Kennedy won a decisive victory because he was the superior candidate with a superior campaign. To Humphrey's credit, he recognized this. He wrote: "Jack Kennedy was at his best in West Virginia, and his best was without equal."[45]

As the primary approached, opinion held Humphrey to be in the lead. Not much had changed since a New York Herald Tribune story had declared two weeks before the primary that "gloom" gripped the Kennedy campaign. According to the newspaper, Kennedy could lose the primary by twenty points or more. The Wall Street Journal agreed. It saw Humphrey getting as much as 60 percent of the vote. The Washington Post followed suit, noting that with just one or two exceptions, every West Virginia politician or journalist the writer had interviewed predicted a victory for the Minnesotan. The New York Times completed the chorus with its judgment that "every surface political sign" pointed "to a 'victory' for Senator Hubert H. Humphrey of Minnesota."[46]

Even the Kennedy camp was not overly optimistic. Joe Alsop, an avid Kennedy enthusiast, said JFK's position was improving and that he had "a narrow chance to defeat Sen. Hubert H. Humphrey." That was small praise indeed from the usually hyperbolic Alsop. On the weekend before the vote, Theodore Sorensen told Michigan politicians, "we don't know what's going to happen." Pierre Salinger believed the outcome would favor Kennedy but by a 51–49 or 52–48 margin. Lou Harris had Kennedy slightly behind on the Saturday before the primary and then slightly ahead on the eve of the primary. Ken O'Donnell recalled that "our supposedly peerless pollster" was "in a dither" and "seemed to be changing his figures every hour." Even John F. Kennedy himself showed no great confidence in a positive outcome. He and Larry O'Brien hoped to finish within 2–4 percent of Humphrey and claim a moral victory. As usual, JFK handled the anxiety and tension with graceful aplomb.[47]

Thus, the question remains as to how so many analysts could be so terribly wrong. The answer is simple and comes in two parts. First, journalists became victims of their own sensationalism and propaganda about the importance of the religious issue as the determining factor in West Virginia. Second, the Kennedy campaign fooled the newsmen, some of whom were personal friends of JFK, into believing that the Massachusetts senator was the underdog.

The central mistake was the exaggeration of the religious issue. Religion was not decisive for the great majority of West Virginia voters; economic matters were. While one could argue that this factor should have favored Humphrey, it did not. There was no significant agricultural sector in West Virginia, a natural constituency for Humphrey. Kennedy, despite his great wealth, convinced West Virginians that he had their interests at heart and would do something to advance them. The voters knew that Humphrey had no chance to be president, while Kennedy did. The latter might actually be able to do something for them while the former could not. The importation of FDR Jr. was brilliant. To many in West Virginia, he was "almost God's son coming down and saying that it was all right to vote for this Catholic." In the end, the surprising thing is not that JFK won a landslide victory in West Virginia, but that virtually no one, including those inside his campaign, could see it coming.[48]

West Virginia was the last chance to stop John Kennedy before the national convention. The state gave him only fifteen votes in Los Angeles, but the primary convinced politicians that his religion was not an insuperable barrier and that he could win in overwhelmingly Protestant states. Breaking this psychological barrier was crucial. The same day he won in West Virginia he also carried Nebraska with 89 percent of the vote, albeit against no organized opposition. Two more primary victories followed in Maryland on May 17 and in Oregon on May 20. With these, the primary season concluded and the Kennedy campaign claimed victory in the ten primaries he had entered (New Hampshire, Wisconsin, Illinois, Massachusetts, Pennsylvania, Indiana, West Virginia, Nebraska, Maryland, and Oregon). None was more important than West Virginia.

Political bosses, especially those in states with large Catholic populations, now came to an obvious conclusion. JFK could win in Protestant states. More than any other candidate, he would help state and local tickets, at least in the East and Middle West. JFK was the Democrat who had the best chance of winning the White House. Most bosses did not believe that on January 1, but by May 15, they were largely convinced. To argue after West Virginia that Kennedy could not win because of his religion was no longer persuasive. Even for those who would have preferred to hold out against the Kennedy tide—and there were some—such an action no longer made sense. Throughout the East and Midwest, getting on the Kennedy bandwagon was a matter of self-interest.

Before West Virginia, Kennedy had locked up just one of the seven big state delegations (Ohio), although he did have positive signals from Illinois.

That left five states (New York, New Jersey, Michigan, Pennsylvania, and California) with a total of more than 350 delegates still uncommitted. By the end of May, large majorities of delegates from New York and Michigan committed to JFK with Illinois all but signed, sealed, and delivered. That left the holdouts of New Jersey, Pennsylvania, and California, where a combination of the reluctance of favorite son governors and residual support for Adlai Stevenson prevented additional breakthroughs at that time. The Kennedy effort in the states with the most delegates had triumphed.

Meanwhile, the campaign quietly accumulated delegates in the Great Plains and the Mountain West. The situations in the Great Plains (North and South Dakota, Nebraska, Kansas, and Oklahoma) and the Mountain West (Idaho, Montana, Utah, Wyoming, Colorado, Nevada, Arizona, and New Mexico) were very different than in the East or Midwest. The Great Plains and Mountain West were not good hunting grounds for the Massachusetts senator. These states should have been natural supporters of Lyndon B. Johnson. New Englander Kennedy had no ties to these states, no interest in agriculture or other relevant economic issues, and no affinity for the West or western culture. The Texan Johnson, in contrast, was well versed in the pertinent economic issues and understood western culture. In Los Angeles, however, the New Englander came away with more than twice the number of delegates from these states than the Texan.

How does one explain this? The answer is straightforward. The Johnson campaign relied on the Texan's fellow U.S. senators, did not work hard, and made almost no effort to go into the states early and organize them. When it did move in its typically halfhearted fashion, it was too little and too late.

Energy was plentiful on the Kennedy side. Young, ambitious politicians, sometimes acquaintances of John F. Kennedy, sometimes self-recruited, led the fight for the Massachusetts senator. In Arizona, it was Stewart Udall; in Colorado, Byron "Whizzer" White; in Wyoming, Teno Roncalio. Comparable individuals, familiar with their states, undertook the tough, tedious task of building support and securing delegates.

On the Johnson side, what was happening did not sink in until it was too late. In Montana, one of LBJ's top campaign aides, James Rowe, met Mike Mansfield on the eve of the state convention and told him: "It's too late, Mike. They've already did [sic] the job." In an internal memorandum about the situation in Wyoming in early May, a Johnson operative reported: "Our pre-tour intelligence was very bad. We were led to believe that Senator Johnson was the front-runner in Wyoming and that Senator Gale McGee was in his corner. Actually, we found Kennedy with a virtual stranglehold on the state. . . . We also found that no one knew where Senator McGee stood. . . . We found, also, that the Kennedy and Symington groups had us badly beaten in organization and prior contacts."[49]

A Johnson campaign memo from March 1960 plaintively summarized the bleak western picture. In Montana, "We have no State leader; very few contacts and none of significance." In Colorado, "We have had no report of any kind from Jerry Van Dyke or Big Ed Johnson. We do not know what they are doing or what their plans are." In Idaho, "We have no State Chairman. A. W. Bill Brunt . . . showed some interest at one time, but has produced no names or work. A newspaper acquaintance of mine reported to me that he thought Brunt was for Kennedy." In Nevada, "We really have nothing started." In Oregon, "We have no State Chairman. We have had only one man that has outlined and sent us information from Oregon, and he does not really know what he is doing."[50]

The night the Democratic Party chose its presidential nominee, Lyndon Johnson received sixty votes from the states of the Great Plains and the Mountain West, with two-thirds of them coming from Oklahoma and New Mexico. In the case of Oklahoma, the large and powerful presence of Senator Robert Kerr intimidated any Kennedy poaching or any delegate who contemplated straying. Outside Oklahoma, JFK did very well, receiving 126 votes from the western states, more than twice the number that went to LBJ. They provided his margin of victory.

The combination of John F. Kennedy's primary victories, the successful wooing and intimidation of favorite sons and party bosses, and the western delegate operation produced a situation in which John Fitzgerald Kennedy had the delegates to claim the party nomination. On May 25, 1960, Robert F. Kennedy provided Steve Smith with a delegate count. RFK, who counted convention delegates as well as anyone in American history, showed his brother with 777 votes. That was sixteen more than he needed to be nominated. Bobby Kennedy did not indulge in speculation, so his figure was a cautious one. He noted that in addition to the 777, "we should be able to pick some up from Delaware, Kentucky, possibly some from Minnesota, Alabama, South and North Carolina, Tennessee. So, I think this is almost a conservative count."[51]

Some delegate votes shifted between late May and mid-July, but RFK's count was remarkably accurate. The only significant instance in which he overestimated delegate support for his brother was in New Jersey, where he estimated thirty. JFK received no votes from New Jersey as Governor Robert Meyner held on to his favorite son status until the bitter end. There was a less serious error with California. There Robert Kennedy estimated forty votes, and his brother received 33.5. Some cautious figures offset these overestimates. RFK counted on no votes from Kentucky, Alabama, North Carolina, Montana, or Alaska. JFK received thirty-two votes from these states. In addition, Robert Kennedy anticipated just thirty votes from Pennsylvania, and the Massachusetts senator realized sixty-eight. The combination of these underestimates more than canceled out the overestimates. In late May, Robert and John Kennedy knew they had the votes to win the nomination on the first ballot.

The period between mid-May and the start of the convention was one of consolidation and expansion. The chief task was to make sure that the delegates they had counted remained committed to the candidate. The campaign had to continue to work on Michigan. New York and Illinois required attention as well. At the same time, the campaign relentlessly sought out more delegates. The more convention votes it accumulated, the less the temptation for a delegate to stray, since as the Kennedy victory became more certain, the likelihood of anyone abandoning the winning side would diminish.

Although campaign manager Bobby Kennedy was willing to go anywhere to recruit new delegates, he wrote off almost the entire South, exerting little effort there. The more natural targets were the big state holdouts—California, New Jersey, and Pennsylvania. All three Democratic governors—Brown, Meyner, and Lawrence—were capable of seeing that Kennedy was on the verge of victory. For a variety of reasons, though, none of the three was willing to move. In the case of Meyner, he thought that the convention would go to a second ballot or that he could put Kennedy over the top by changing the New Jersey vote after the first ballot. He also longed for the publicity associated with a favorite son. As for Lawrence, although Catholic himself, he remained concerned about the impact of Kennedy's religion on the state ticket in Pennsylvania. In addition, he retained a strong loyalty to Stevenson.[52]

With California and Brown, the situation was extraordinarily complicated because of the Byzantine character of California politics. Kennedy considered entering the California primary against Brown, who ran as a favorite son. Eventually, JFK decided not to challenge Brown, partly because of the time, effort, and money that would be required and partly because the governor reassured him that he would support the Massachusetts senator if Kennedy was victorious in the primaries. The Kennedy-Brown relationship was never a comfortable one. The first time they met, the California governor began the conversation by asking JFK about Addison's disease. Relations never got a great deal better. Eventually, JFK managed to make a deal with Brown whereby the Californian agreed to endorse him if Kennedy did well in the primaries, but this arrangement did not work out well for the Massachusetts senator.[53]

After the agreement with Brown, the situation in California deteriorated. The Golden State was a hotbed of Stevenson support, and LBJ's operatives were active in the state. The delegate-selection process played out disadvantageously for Kennedy. Delegates were named before the spring primaries and Kennedy's strong showing. Furthermore, the allocation of delegates revolved around the strength of various party factions and not the commitment of the delegates to particular presidential candidates. With the convention set for Los Angeles, the number of Democrats wanting to serve as delegates expanded radically, with personal expense for travel no longer a prohibitive factor. As a result, as one observer put it, "everybody in Los Angeles County wants to get into the act this year, and there are more screwballs per square mile down there than any place in the country." The closer the convention, the less committed Brown seemed to be to Kennedy.[54]

In addition, Brown was not a political boss like David Lawrence or Richard J. Daley or even Michael DiSalle. California, with its progressive heritage, was a state in which amateurs, volunteers, and activists dominated the political landscape. In this political environment was a large force of Stevenson admirers who were determined to make their voices heard. Brown was limited in his ability to command delegates to vote for Kennedy, even if he had wanted to (which he did not).

Brown's indecisiveness furnished more fuel for the California turmoil. As one observer replied when asked which individual had the most influence with the governor—"the elevator man is most influential—he sees him last." The deal Kennedy thought he had with Pat Brown was worthless. The governor lacked both the will and the power to carry it out. The California Democratic Party, not for the first time and not for the last, was in chaos by June 1960. There was virtually no chance to put the pieces back together by the time the national convention assembled in July.[55]

As Democrats descended on Los Angeles in early July, they did so with a perception that John F. Kennedy was the front runner but with some doubt as to whether the nomination fight was over. Clearly, there remained substantial opposition to Kennedy, but whether that opposition had the means and the resources to block Kennedy was doubtful. Mirroring this uncertainty were the two leading news weeklies, *Time* and *Newsweek*. The former put LBJ on its cover while the latter's choice was JFK. The Kennedy camp understood that they stood on the brink of victory, but one that could be lost if the campaign became complacent or made mistakes.[56]

The stunning energy, efficiency, and youth of the Kennedy campaign, the spontaneous outburst in the convention for Adlai Stevenson, Eugene McCarthy's eloquent nominating speech for Stevenson, John F. Kennedy's triumph on the first ballot, and the nominee's bold and controversial selection of Lyndon B. Johnson as his running mate are familiar tales. So are the bitter, last-ditch efforts of John F. Kennedy's opponents. Adlai Stevenson's supporters launched a passionate effort to convince delegates that their hero deserved the nomination. Lyndon Johnson hurled harsh accusations against the Massachusetts senator and his father. LBJ insulted the latter as pro-Nazi, saying: "I wasn't any Chamberlain—umbrella policy man. I never thought Hitler was right." Meanwhile, an LBJ campaign aide charged that JFK had Addison's disease and would not be alive without cortisone. All this was too little and too late.[57]

As familiar as the convention is, two subjects invite further attention. The first is the question of how close the opponents of Kennedy came to denying him the nomination. The second is the matter of the decision-making process in Kennedy's selection of Lyndon Johnson as his running mate.

In the days prior to the start of the convention, Robert Kennedy had reason to feel confident. On Friday, July 8, the campaign manager met with Pennsylvania governor David Lawrence, who informed him that he would do what his delegation wanted and support JFK. Lawrence had held out a long time out of loyalty to Adlai Stevenson and because he feared that a Catholic candidate for president would hurt the state ticket. Other Pennsylvania leaders, most notably Congressman William Green, wanted John Kennedy. They exerted increasing pressure and eventually prevailed. Elated, Robert Kennedy went away from the meeting thinking, "That's the ballgame." Pennsylvania caucused on Monday, announced its decision then, and supplied sixty-eight votes on the first ballot to John F. Kennedy.[58]

Between July 8 and July 13, the day of balloting for president, Kennedy gained in states beyond Pennsylvania. Mayor Richard J. Daley formally threw his support along with his large bloc of delegates behind the front runner. Favorite sons George Docking of Kansas and Herschel Loveless of Iowa announced their intention to abandon their candidacies and support the Massachusetts senator. Governor Pat Brown declared the end of his candidacy, released his delegates, and stated he would vote for John F. Kennedy. The only negative notes were the continuing holdout of Robert Meyner and the disintegration of the California delegation.

Still, Robert Kennedy refused to be overconfident. On the morning of Wednesday, July 13, he told his forces: "We can't miss a trick in the next twelve hours. If we don't win tonight, we're dead." But the Kennedy campaign did not make many mistakes. As the roll call of the states proceeded that night, there were few surprises. California disappointed with just 33.5 votes. The Kennedy coordinator in Delaware miscalculated, and JFK received nothing from that state, although the cost was probably only five votes. Kansas cast its twenty-one votes for favorite son Governor George Docking rather than Kennedy, though it switched to the winner at the end of the first ballot. Meyner kept his monopoly on the forty-one New Jersey delegates. Even these were disappointments rather than surprises. Robert F. Kennedy's state projections were extraordinarily accurate. Most importantly, the small variations did not derail the opportunity for the first-ballot victory. That hope became reality when Wyoming cast its entire complement of fifteen votes to give John Fitzgerald Kennedy 765 delegates and make him the Democratic Party's nominee for president.[59]

One of the best delegate-hunting and -counting operations in American political history triumphed. Still, two questions linger. Could Kennedy's opponents have prevented his first-ballot victory? If they had stopped JFK on the first ballot, could they then have thwarted his nomination? Since these are speculative issues, the answers are matters of opinion and cannot be conclusive. The final Kennedy count on the first ballot was 806. After Wyoming, Kennedy received no votes from the Canal Zone, nine from the District of Columbia, seven from Puerto Rico, four from the Virgin Islands, and twenty-one from the Kansas switch.[60] This was forty-five more than the 761 he needed. To have denied Kennedy the nomination would have required holding him significantly under 761 delegates. If the first roll call had ended with Kennedy needing a small number of additional votes, those were readily available from delegations that would have been happy to cash in on the opportunity to help put JFK over the top and reap the presumed rewards for having done so. Even without a switch at this point, Kennedy, with 710 or more delegates on the first ballot, would almost certainly have been unstoppable on the second ballot.[61]

It is true that there were Kennedy delegates bound to him on the first ballot who would have deserted him on the second. The most likely defectors were in Indiana, where Senator Vance Hartke would have taken perhaps twenty delegates to Lyndon Johnson, and Ohio, where, as the rumors had it, there were approximately another twenty delegates ready to bolt. In addition, the Kennedy delegate positions in California, Iowa, Oregon, Maryland, and North Dakota were tenuous. Once in a second ballot, anything could have happened. In retrospect, one reporter saw the Kennedy bandwagon as being "of a fairly fragile variety." It was like a jet aircraft in that "it had to keep moving to keep from crashing." Stewart Udall hypothesized that the convention could have even gone to a third, fourth, or fifth ballot with Lyndon Johnson making a bid and falling short, Kennedy having a second shot, and then a choice between Adlai Stevenson and Stuart Symington emerging. Carmine DeSapio opined: Kennedy "outsmarted all the pros. . . . But if he had ever stumbled just once, the wolves would have closed in on him."[62]

Even if there had been no Kennedy victory on the first ballot, the candidate was not necessarily doomed. There were more potential Kennedy delegates out there. Governor John Patterson of Alabama had more votes at his disposal. He provided just 3.5 on the first ballot, in part because both John and Robert were beginning to find Patterson an embarrassment and did not wish to be identified with him. On the second ballot, another ten Alabama votes might have materialized. There were at least thirty pro-Kennedy delegates in New Jersey. Meyner had promised to free them after the first ballot so they likely would have become available. Some Kennedy confidants claimed as many as an additional one hundred votes on the second ballot. In the final analysis, the stop-Kennedy movement needed mistakes from the Kennedy camp. They were not forthcoming, and therefore the stop-Kennedy forces failed on July 13.[63]

With the nomination in hand, John F. Kennedy turned to the question of his running mate. What transpired in Los Angeles, beginning late Wednesday night and continuing Thursday morning and afternoon, provides the most controversial subject of the 1960 Democratic convention. The decision to choose Lyndon Johnson, his acceptance, and the prolonged and confused negotiations between the Kennedy and Johnson camps provide large doses of confusion and contradiction. To this day, no one has managed to provide a fully satisfying account.

Two issues are especially in dispute. The first centers on the decision-making process in the Kennedy camp and, specifically, what caused JFK to change his mind and move away from a conventional, safe choice like Stuart Symington with whom he apparently had a tentative agreement? The second concerns the maneuvering over the vice presidency between John and Robert Kennedy, on one hand, and Lyndon Johnson and his allies on the other.[64]

Both John F. Kennedy and Lyndon B. Johnson had to move very carefully. They never completely revealed their motivations and intentions even to their closest confidants. This behavior was necessary because of the extraordinary antagonism that existed between the two camps. On the Kennedy side, the nominee and his father had a favorable opinion of LBJ. With his detachment, JFK could admire the Senate majority leader's talents. Johnson could be annoying with his histrionics, but Kennedy viewed him as a man of ability who except for his southern background might have easily captured the Democratic nomination. On more than one occasion in the period just before the convention, the prospective nominee suggested his interest in LBJ as vice president. For his part, the Kennedy patriarch spoke the same language of power that Johnson did. In spite of their clashes, they were men of similar minds.[65]

Aside from these two men, almost everyone else on the Kennedy side despised Johnson and his crude, overbearing manner. Jackie referred to LBJ and Lady Bird Johnson as "Colonel Cornpone" and "Little Porkchop." The greatest hater, of course, was Robert F. Kennedy. RFK's acquaintance with Johnson began in the mid-1950s. Johnson invariably addressed Robert as "sonny." At the Los Angeles convention, Johnson's attacks on Joseph Kennedy and the stories put out about JFK and Addison's disease further inflamed Robert Kennedy. On the occasion of the joint appearance of Kennedy and Johnson before the Texas delegation, RFK sipped and tasted the water before passing the glass on to his brother. Bobby's attitude toward LBJ was neatly summed up in his famous comment about the Texan. Johnson, he said, "is incapable of telling the truth. . . . [H]e lies all the time. I'm telling you, he just lies continuously about everything. In every conversation, I have with him, he lies. As I've said, he lies even when he doesn't have to." JFK knew that he would have to proceed indirectly and discreetly to convince his brother and his supporters to accept Johnson as his running mate.[66]

On the Johnson side, despite his protestations, the Texan welcomed and wanted the vice-presidential nod. He did not look forward to continuing as Senate majority leader under either Kennedy or Nixon. The vice presidency offered him the opportunity to break the constraints imposed by Texas. He thought he would be able to exert considerable influence in the new administration since his knowledge and experience in legislative affairs far exceeded that of JFK. It also undoubtedly occurred to Johnson, who had said many disparaging things about Kennedy's health, that Kennedy could expire while in the White House.[67]

LBJ was favorably disposed to the Massachusetts senator, although he had not taken him seriously. Most of his closest friends and advisers, however, possessed a disdain for the Kennedy clan. House Speaker Sam Rayburn was dismissive of the Kennedys and lukewarm to the idea of the vice presidency. Senator Robert Kerr of Oklahoma utterly despised them. Lady

Bird was unenthusiastic. Johnson knew that if he wanted the vice presidency, he would have to make it appear that he was accepting the nomination reluctantly.

Thus, both JFK and LBJ wanted Lyndon B. Johnson as vice president. The problem was that neither could be certain of the other, but they could count on overwhelming disapproval from friends and family. Both men needed to proceed with the utmost caution. Each man had to pretend that the nomination of LBJ as vice president was something they agreed to only reluctantly. Neither could afford to admit that LBJ became the vice-presidential choice as the result of conscious, intentional decisions by both men. So successful were the two in covering their tracks that even today many continue to believe that John F. Kennedy did not desire LBJ as his running mate and that Johnson went along with the nomination grudgingly.

In the course of his quest for the nomination, John Kennedy dangled the vice presidency before numerous individuals and flattered them with the idea that each would make a fine vice president. As Hubert Humphrey put it, "there were more vice-presidential commitments around than a mangy dog had fleas." Kennedy's behavior was nothing new. He, like other presidential nominees before him, used the vice presidency to keep various delegations on his bandwagon. Before the convention, Theodore Sorensen provided JFK with a list of vice-presidential possibilities, including LBJ. But Kennedy, at this point, apparently thought that LBJ would not accept. There were, however, numerous signs of LBJ's availability. In June, Bobby Baker told Sorensen, "Don't be too sure," when the latter stated his doubts about Johnson's willingness to accept the number-two position. On July 3–4, LBJ refused to rule out taking the vice presidency. On July 11–12, a series of important and influential individuals including Joseph Alsop, Philip Graham, David Lawrence, Richard J. Daley, Carmine DeSapio, and Tommy Corcoran lobbied JFK on behalf of naming Johnson. On July 12, the *Washington Post* ran a story proclaiming that Kennedy would offer the vice presidency to LBJ. The evidence suggests that John Kennedy was giving consideration to Johnson as a possible choice well before Wednesday, July 13.[68]

Apparently, John Kennedy pursued a two-track approach—a first track where safe, noncontroversial vice-presidential choices were explored and a second track where he tried to determine the availability of Lyndon Johnson. On the first track, the choice seems to have come down to Washington senator Henry "Scoop" Jackson, Missouri senator Stuart Symington, and Minnesota governor Orville Freeman. The winner was Symington. With Clark Clifford negotiating for him, an offer was in hand on Wednesday evening. Clifford, among the most adroit powerbrokers in Washington, said, "We had a deal signed, sealed and delivered."[69]

The next morning the deal had vanished. Kennedy regretfully informed Clifford that he could not honor the agreement and that he was moving in a different direction. Something had happened Wednesday night. Kennedy had become convinced that Lyndon Johnson would accept a vice-presidential offer. Conversations and telephone calls involving Tip O'Neill, Tommy Corcoran, Sam Rayburn, and Sargent Shriver, among others, did the job. In the early-morning hours of Thursday, a telephone call from Johnson headquarters stated that he would accept the offer of the vice presidency if Kennedy extended it to him.[70]

The other individual who may have contributed to this development was Joseph P. Kennedy. There is no direct evidence that he was consulted, but some role and perhaps a decisive one is consistent with events. LBJ's last desperate attacks in Los Angeles were directed as much at Joseph Kennedy as John Kennedy. JFK must have resented the verbal assaults, and he knew that his brother despised Johnson. But what did his father think? The Kennedy patriarch most likely supported Johnson in spite of the personal attacks. John Kennedy's thinking on the vice-presidential choice shifted Wednesday night. The positive signals emanating from the Johnson camp were the most important element in effecting this change, but there is an excellent chance that a conversation between father and son, in which the former gave his approval and encouragement to the Johnson selection, also played a role.[71]

The second part of the vice-presidential melodrama played out Thursday morning and afternoon. It began with a meeting between Johnson and Kennedy, an offer of the vice presidency, and an expression of definite interest from the Texan. Although Kennedy and Johnson were ready to deal with each other, their allies were unprepared. Once word of Kennedy's choice of Johnson leaked out, outraged howls of anger, resentment, and betrayal erupted from both camps. On the Texas side, Senator Robert Kerr, a large and forceful man, made his unhappiness felt. When Bobby Baker gave him the news, he slapped Baker across the face. He then stormed into Johnson's quarters and shouted: "Get me my .38. . . . I'm gonna kill every damn one of you. I can't believe my three best friends [LBJ, Lady Bird, Bobby Baker] would betray me." Neither Lady Bird nor Sam Rayburn initially favored the offer. Others, not immediately attached to Johnson, made their displeasure known. After the convention, Georgia senator Herman Talmadge told LBJ that he hated to see him take the vice presidency because most vice presidents ended up "very unhappy people and political eunuchs." Barry

Goldwater sent LBJ a two-word note that read: "I'm nauseated." Johnson possessed great manipulative talents, and although he never convinced everyone, Sam Rayburn and others did become converts. It took much of Thursday morning to accomplish this.[72]

On the Kennedy side, the reaction, if anything, was even more negative. Bobby, to whom JFK had broken the news on Wednesday night, was appalled and depressed. Ken O'Donnell and others who gave delegates specific guarantees that Johnson would *not* be the vice-presidential choice were furious. Arthur M. Schlesinger Jr. came close to physically attacking Phil Graham, whom he blamed for promoting the idea of Johnson for vice president. Friend Charles Bartlett went to dinner with the Kennedys on Thursday night. He found Jackie in "a very low state of mind" and Robert "in near despair." Bobby commented: "Yesterday was the best day of my life, and today is the worst day of my life."[73]

Opposition in the convention quickly materialized with the Michigan delegation leading the way. Organized labor represented by Arthur Goldberg, Alex Rose, and Walter Reuther made strong objections. Johnson did have considerable support among the northern bosses—Lawrence, Wagner, DeSapio, Prendergast, Green, DiSalle, Bailey, and Sharkey thought him a good choice. As the furor mounted, the presidential nominee apparently began to have second thoughts. His brother encouraged such reconsideration. Between 2:00 P.M. and 4:00 P.M., Robert F. Kennedy twice went to talk to LBJ about the extent of the Texan's interest in the vice presidency and the building opposition. In the second visit, RFK suggested that LBJ might want to withdraw. This behavior reinforced the unfavorable Texan view of the Kennedys and brought the relationship between the two camps to a crisis almost before it had been established. This is where the second great dispute concerning the behavior, motivations, and intentions of JFK and RFK arises. The latter insisted everything he did and said was done and said on the direction of his brother. Yet, the episode ended with John Kennedy repudiating the proposal that Johnson should withdraw with the offhand comment that Bobby was out of touch with recent developments.[74]

The key question is whether JFK desired, at any time, to see Johnson withdraw or whether he was simply allowing his brother to vent his anger and have his opportunity at trying to undo what may very well have been a fait accompli as far as the nominee was concerned. The nominee had serious second thoughts about Johnson. Yet, he had to understand that to oust Johnson would have been a political disaster. Forcing Johnson off the ticket would have lost the election twice over. First, Johnson's withdrawal would have produced a southern backlash that would have doomed Kennedy in the South. Second, the act of selecting Johnson and then reversing the decision in less than twenty-four hours would have been irrefutable proof that John F. Kennedy was too young and too inexperienced to lead the United States. Robert Kennedy, because of his blind hatred of Johnson, did not understand this, but his brother did. Exactly what was going on in the mind of John F. Kennedy on the morning and afternoon of July 14 is unknown and unknowable.[75]

We do know two things. First is that John and Robert Kennedy handled the vice-presidential choice very badly. They were exhausted and operating under great pressure, but their behavior was an example of the kind of indecisiveness the Kennedys continually ridiculed in Adlai Stevenson. It was decision making that suggested they were not ready for the White House. The great majority of Democrats, both supporters and opponents of Johnson, came away from the incident in a sour mood.

Second, we know that on the verge of political catastrophe, John F. Kennedy recovered and made the right decision to stay with LBJ. Kennedy recruited David Lawrence to give the nominating speech and Congressman William Dawson, the leading black politician in Chicago, to give a seconding speech for Johnson. Behind the scenes, Adam Clayton Powell Jr. of Harlem and Roy Wilkins of the NAACP indicated their willingness to go along with Johnson. So did David Dubinsky, a powerful labor leader. The Texan helped matters by agreeing to support the liberal platform and especially the civil rights provisions. The flare-up was intense but brief. Once the nominee took a strong stand, Johnson's nomination was never truly in danger. The only real threat to Johnson's nomination was the Kennedy overreaction to the opposition and the ensuing temporary panic on their part.[76]

In the end, John Kenneth Galbraith and Joseph Kennedy offered the most perceptive judgments on the vice-presidential imbroglio. Galbraith observed: "This is the sort of cynical Machiavellian thing that nobody would have thought of or done except maybe Franklin D. Roosevelt in 1932!" Joe Kennedy opined: "Don't worry about it. In one week everyone will think you're a genius."[77]

If the vice-presidential selection process did not win accolades, neither did John F. Kennedy's acceptance speech on Friday, July 15, at the Los Angeles Coliseum. In the succeeding decades, JFK won a deserved reputation as a highly effective speaker. What many do not realize is that Kennedy was not a great orator in 1960. His acceptance speech of July 15, though it coined the term "New Frontier," was not a great success. Even Kennedy admirers conceded that he was not at his best. The nominee was close to exhaustion. The Los Angeles Coliseum was a poor location for such an address. The crowd was too small in a huge facility, it was too scattered, and it was too far away from the Massachusetts senator. With only about half the seats filled, with Kennedy facing the sun, and with helicopters flying overhead, the speech did not go well. Kennedy addressed the crowd with what some considered a "grating, erratic staccato voice." It was a somewhat disappointing end to a dramatic week.[78]

In the aftermath of the national convention, the great majority of northern liberals, white southerners, party elders, civil rights advocates, and some members of the Johnson camp were disgruntled. Eleanor Roosevelt left the convention in tears. Senator Richard Russell said that the party platform was "the worst platform that has ever been suggested by a major political party." Roosevelt, Truman, and Russell did not even bother to attend JFK's acceptance speech.[79]

For many in the Democratic Party, the convention ended with serious doubts about the nominee. For the Kennedys, the week was a triumph. Obviously, neither the vice-presidential selection process nor the acceptance speech went as well as they wished, but they had the presidential nomination and they also had the vice-presidential candidate that they needed to win the general election. Moreover, they had defied the odds, outmaneuvered the bosses, and demonstrated that they could play the political game better than anyone in the party. They had every confidence that despite the complaints they could defy the conventional political wisdom once again and capture the White House. Others might doubt, but the talents that surfaced in the campaign for the nomination would serve the Kennedy campaign very well in the general election contest. John F. Kennedy, Joseph P. Kennedy, and Robert F. Kennedy were now on the crest of a wave of destiny that they had long imagined.

4

Richard M. Nixon and
the Republican Nomination

*"If you ever let them [the Democrats] campaign only on domestic issues,
they'll beat us—our only hope is to keep it on foreign policy."*

—Richard M. Nixon on the reason he chose Henry Cabot Lodge as his running mate

For the Republican Party, 1957 and 1958 were not good years. In November 1958, the GOP suffered its worst defeat since 1936 and came out of the midterm elections badly wounded. In 1959, the party began to rebound. As it entered the presidential election year in 1960, it did so with a popular incumbent president, albeit one who was constitutionally prohibited from running in 1960, and two formidable presidential candidates, Vice President Richard M. Nixon and New York governor Nelson A. Rockefeller.

The Republican Party in 1960 had three centers of power: the old guard right, the center right, and the center left, insofar as one can speak of a left in the 1960 GOP. On the right, there was a power vacuum. Its natural and much-revered leader, Senator Robert A. Taft of Ohio, had died in 1953. For the remainder of the decade, none of the pretenders to his mantle proved remotely worthy. Senator Joseph R. McCarthy ended his bid in disgrace and alcoholism and died in 1957. Taft's successor as Senate majority leader, William Knowland of California, did not measure up. As Republicans became a minority in the Senate, the Democratic majority leader, Lyndon Johnson, outmaneuvered Knowland. The Californian embarked on a course of self-destructive personal behavior and in 1958 suffered a humiliating defeat when he ran for the governorship of California. The death of Taft and the failure of McCarthy and Knowland left the Republican right without a dynamic, effective leader. Only in 1960, when Arizona senator Barry Goldwater began his remarkable ascent, did a new Republican right once again constitute a powerful force. In this year, though, Goldwater was at the very beginning of his national career.

The power vacuum in conservative leadership was a benefit to Vice President Richard Nixon, who occupied a position on the center right. Nixon, a staunch domestic anticommunist, made his mark with the Alger Hiss case.

He established himself as a strong opponent of international communism and a firm ally of Secretary of State John Foster Dulles. On the other hand, Nixon supported U.S. engagement abroad and was never sympathetic to attempts to roll back New Deal social programs. The combination of a strong anticommunism linked to moderate domestic policies gave Nixon the ability to appeal to both the Republican right, as well as the more moderate and progressive elements in the GOP.

Finally, Nelson A. Rockefeller, governor of New York, on the center left, was the leading GOP advocate of more domestic social welfare programs, expanding government both in Albany and Washington D.C., and increasing taxes to pay for these policies. At the national level, he stood for increased spending on national defense. Rockefeller was never happy working under Eisenhower. He had little power, was unable to accomplish much, and felt stifled. He entered the administration as undersecretary of Health, Education, and Welfare (1953–54), and then became special assistant to the president for foreign affairs (1954–55). During these years, he also advised Eisenhower on government reorganization. Further advancement and real influence in the administration, though, were not forthcoming. Secretary of Defense Charles Wilson liked Rockefeller and wanted to make him deputy secretary with a view to Rocky taking over when Wilson stepped down. Tight-fisted Secretary of the Treasury George Humphrey, though, was in no mood to see a spender like Rockefeller in a position where he could be counted upon to bombard the administration with requests for more programs and more money. Humphrey persuaded the president to kill the idea. A frustrated Rockefeller left the administration in 1956 and returned to New York to enter state politics. In the dismal Republican performance of 1958, Rockefeller was one of the bright lights, winning the New York governorship by more than 500,000 votes against Democratic incumbent Averell Harriman. Rockefeller's initial electoral performance was a brilliant one and portended greater things to come.[1]

In the aftermath of November 1958, political observers believed that Rockefeller was not satisfied with being governor of New York. Overnight, he became a de facto presidential candidate and maintained that appearance through 1959. In some ways, the Rockefeller campaign resembled John F. Kennedy's. Fueled by immense amounts of money and an attractive and energetic personality, Rockefeller hoped to use concern over the American future, especially in matters of national defense, combined with his popularity to convince Republican leaders that he was more electable than Richard Nixon.

To this end, Rockefeller conducted an extensive speaking tour in the fall of 1959. He traveled to California and Washington state and then to Missouri, Indiana, Minnesota, Wisconsin, Oklahoma, Texas, and Florida, seeking support from the public and from party regulars who would either be delegates or control the delegations to the national convention. He advertised his competition with Nixon as "the pros against the people," portraying his campaign as a spontaneous citizens' effort and Nixon's as the handiwork of professional politicians. Rockefeller obtained a good deal of favorable publicity for his efforts as journalists speculated about the impending announcement of his candidacy. By mid-December, the *New York Times* was predicting an announcement within two weeks and gushing over the "fabulous" and "fantastic" Rockefeller organization.[2]

Richard Nixon was certainly concerned. Facing Rockefeller's unlimited bank account and the power and influence it exerted, he had to be. What was worrisome was that Rockefeller, as an alumnus of Dartmouth College, had numerous political contacts in New Hampshire, the first important primary state of 1960. With his New Hampshire connections, the New Yorker seemed to be well positioned to get off to an excellent start and to obtain the early momentum in the race for the nomination. According to reports, Rockefeller was also considering entry into the California primary and "going for the jugular." Rockefeller's strategy was clear. He would attempt to reprise 1952 and paint Richard Nixon as Robert Taft, with the New York governor assuming the Eisenhower role. Nixon, according to this scenario, was a party regular loved by the old guard and party officials, but one who could not win the general election.[3]

Rockefeller's drive came out of his great personal ambition, a general dissatisfaction with the Eisenhower administration, and his dislike of Richard Nixon. Rocky, like the Democratic critics of Ike, saw Eisenhower's presidency as overly passive and insufficiently activist in confronting the great national issues of the day, especially national defense. Moreover, the governor did not like the vice president. In October 1958, Nixon visited New York, and Rockefeller informed him that he did not want the vice president campaigning for him. On one occasion, he said, "I hate the idea of Dick Nixon being president." He was convinced that the vice president had "the wrong ideas, the wrong friends, the wrong reasons for seeking power."[4]

The vice president was well aware of the developing situation and did not sit idly by and allow Rockefeller to bring his plan to reality. He dispatched agents to trail Rockefeller and report on his efforts to woo support. In New Hampshire, Meade Alcorn, Fred Scribner, and Len Hall led an anti-Rockefeller opposition group. Alcorn and Scribner were prominent GOP officials and classmates of Rockefeller at Dartmouth. Hall was a New Yorker, a former chairman of the Republican National Committee, and a bitter opponent of Rockefeller. While the Rockefeller campaign contemplated the favorable New Hampshire scenery, Nixon's people moved. They nailed down delegates, developed a statewide organization headed by the governor, and booked town halls for rallies.[5]

Despite the grand buildup and the magnificent appearance, the 1959 Rockefeller effort fizzled. Part of the failure was the consequence of Rockefeller mistakes. More of it was a result of the loyalties Richard Nixon had forged with local party officials. In his tour of the West and Midwest, Rockefeller found some interest, but little support and encouragement, from local and state Republican officials. The vice president, through his assiduous courting of them for seven or more years, had their loyalty and their commitment. As a *New York Times* reporter observed, they "have seen him come into their districts and work like a stevedore for their chosen candidate for Congress or Governor or even sheriff. They have seen him raise money for their party treasury, heal wounds among the party disaffected, pump enthusiasm into dispirited party workers. They have called him 'Dick' and been honored that he remembered their first names. . . . What counts is that he is somebody—a big somebody—whom they know as a human being and not just a name in a newspaper." Rockefeller never understood the attitudes and loyalties of party officials. He could not believe the nomination was based on "who had attended the most Lincoln Day dinners, who had been most solicitous about the Yates County chairman's hernia operation, or whose agents had captured control of an obscure town committee." Richard Nixon understood this, and so did John F. Kennedy. If Rockefeller had been up against the opponents that Kennedy faced in 1960, he might have won. Against Nixon he had no chance. As the vice president's pollster noted: "Rocky is an amateur; a Johnny-come-lately. He has a painfully exaggerated conception of his place in the sun, and he looks like a Little League ballplayer against the Yankees when he takes you [Nixon] on."[6]

If Rockefeller did not have a particularly good year in 1959, Nixon did. In late November 1958, President Eisenhower dispatched Nixon to London to dedicate a chapel at St. Paul's Cathedral, honoring American dead in World War II. The vice president gave a well-received speech. Then, in July 1959, Nixon went on a trip to the Soviet Union and Poland. This excursion produced a gold mine of favorable publicity for the vice president, most notably in his famous confrontation with Nikita Khrushchev. This episode showed Nixon standing up to the Soviet leader and greatly increased his popularity in the United States. Nixon's foreign trips did wonders for popular perception of him while Rockefeller was tied down in the routine of state government that included raising taxes.[7]

Rockefeller's argument that he was more electable than Nixon was not credible. Even in early 1959, Gallup showed Nixon favored 56 percent to 27 percent among Republicans. Rockefeller was essentially even with independents, trailing only 32 percent to 31 percent, but this figure did not hold up as the year moved on. The last Gallup Poll for 1959 had Nixon with a lead of 66 to 19 among Republicans and one of 49 to 22 among independents. Presidential trial heats indicated Nixon was stronger than Rockefeller against specific Democratic candidates. Even Rocky's popularity in New York seemed on the wane. By early 1960, increased state taxes had made him less popular than he had been in 1958.[8]

The Rockefeller campaign, in spite of its money, its highly favorable publicity, and the energetic personality of the candidate, stalled. Rockefeller recognized the reality. In a surprise statement on December 26, 1959, just as political analysts awaited his entry into the nomination race, he instead announced his withdrawal, saying that it was "definite and final." He added that he wished to avoid a "massive struggle" within the party.[9]

Rockefeller's renunciation of his candidacy was neither definite nor final, but his December declaration effectively ended any chance he had to provide a credible challenge to Nixon for the presidential nomination. The Nixon camp breathed a sigh of relief, not quite believing their good fortune and wondering about Rockefeller's thought processes. Rockefeller's action "dumbfounded" Robert Finch. The New Yorker lost his best opportunity to achieve a breakthrough and destroy the belief that Nixon's nomination was inevitable.[10]

The other major menace to the Nixon candidacy was the attitude of President Dwight D. Eisenhower and the possibility that he might support another candidate. In the worst-case scenario, Eisenhower would endorse the New York governor. That possibility was remote, given Ike's decidedly negative opinion of Rocky and his fitness to be president. The president considered most career politicians suspect. He often offered succinct and sarcastic commentary on various national politicians, and Rockefeller did not escape his displeasure. Of Rockefeller, Ike remarked that he was "too used to borrowing brains instead of using his own" and that the New York governor "did not have the brains or the character to be President." The New Yorker's sniping at the administration's social and defense policies irritated Ike, but so did his double-dealing ways. For example, on one occasion, he called Eisenhower to inform him that he would take a position that morning against the administration's proposal on medical care for the aged and in favor of a Democratic alternative. Later, it developed that even before the telephone call, Rocky had held a press conference to make the announcement. Rockefeller infuriated Eisenhower, and there was no way that the president would have supported him against the vice president.[11]

Just because Ike disdained Rocky did not mean that he would endorse Nixon. In truth, the Eisenhower-Nixon association was complicated, tangled, and difficult to decipher. The relationship was not a close one. In 1960, Eisenhower's friend Tex McCrary, who was trying to promote an article about Ike and Nixon to *Look*, wrote a letter to the president telling him that it was very difficult to find good photographs of the president and vice president "working, talking, planning or even laughing together." Plaintively, he asked Eisenhower, "Can't you let a *candid* photograph capture the relationship between you two?"[12]

The president had reservations about the vice president and his fitness to succeed him. The complications in the relationship derived from two circumstances. For one thing, Eisenhower thought Nixon too narrow. The vice president did not seem to grow—to become more mature, to develop a broader point of view. In Ike's opinion, the only considerations that crossed Nixon's mind or moved the vice president were political ones. For this reason, Eisenhower thought that Nixon was not quite ready to be president. This view carried with it some irony since it was precisely for this reason that Eisenhower brought Nixon in as vice president. It was also the role Eisenhower assigned him in 1952, 1954, 1956, and 1958. Nixon, as nothing more than a political partisan, became a self-fulfilling prophecy. Whatever unhappiness Ike had with Nixon, he was careful to avoid open criticism of the vice president. One can find none of the pungent barbs aimed at Nixon that Eisenhower directed at Knowland, Stevenson, Rockefeller, JFK, or LBJ.[13]

The second element that shaped the Eisenhower-Nixon relationship was the generational divide. Nixon was young enough to be Eisenhower's son. While Eisenhower was the supreme Allied commander in World War II, Nixon and Kennedy were lower-level officers, and that is how Ike continued to see them in the 1950s. When Senator John Kennedy first met Eisenhower, the president kept calling him "Kennedy." JFK thought this a peculiar form of address, as if he were "a junior officer or something." That was exactly how Ike viewed someone like Kennedy—as a junior officer. The men who won Eisenhower's respect and whom he thought deserving of presidential consideration were invariably older individuals who were not career politicians. Such men included Eisenhower's brother Milton (b.

1899), Al Gruenther (b. 1899), and Secretary of the Treasury Robert Anderson (b. 1910), who was close to Nixon's age but whose career had been not in politics but in banking and then as secretary of the navy, deputy secretary of defense, and finally as secretary of the treasury. This was the kind of man Eisenhower admired and thought of as qualified to be president.[14]

Finally, one must be aware that if Eisenhower did not socialize with Nixon, he was not singling out the vice president. The president compartmentalized his life; his job was one thing, and his relaxation another. He kept the two separate, and this principle applied across the board. John Foster Dulles once informed the *Chicago Tribune* columnist Walter Trohan that he had never been invited to a family dinner at the White House. Dulles told Trohan that this omission hurt him. Trohan told him not to take offense because Eisenhower divided social and business life so that when he "was through with business he was also through with his Secretary." Attorney General Herbert Brownell noted that Eisenhower chose his inner circle of personal friends almost entirely from outside government. Brownell thought that a World War II analogy was appropriate. Officials in the administration were like the generals he commanded in the war: "They were comrades in arms but not cronies." In short, there was nothing in Eisenhower's treatment of Nixon that suggested any personal dislike.[15]

Still, the prevailing consensus held that all was not right between Ike and his vice president. The president appeared to welcome the possibility of a different running mate in 1956 and a different nominee in 1960. In 1956, Eisenhower suggested to Nixon that in order to prepare for the presidency, he would be well advised to leave the vice presidency and take a cabinet post in a second Eisenhower term. There is no reason to doubt Eisenhower's sincerity in this proposal, but it was politically impossible for Nixon because it would have been interpreted as a sign of weakness and would have instantly created a powerful competitor for the 1960 nomination. In 1959, Eisenhower refused to endorse Nixon openly. In early 1960, he urged Robert Anderson and Al Gruenther to become candidates.[16]

No doubt the vice president agonized over these Eisenhower initiatives, but there is no documented criticism of Eisenhower by Nixon. The vice president had to have resented some of his treatment in the administration, but Nixon always spoke of Ike with admiration and respect. A Nixon watcher at the end of his life noted that Ike's vice president "simultaneously venerated and resented" Eisenhower. Nixon observed that Ike was "very charming and warm socially" but also a "hard-ass" and "a tough son of a bitch" and not loyal enough for his taste.[17]

To understand Eisenhower's reluctance to endorse Nixon, one must grasp his personal identification with the presidency. In Ike's mind, he was the standard, and therefore he tended to evaluate individuals based on how they compared to his own qualifications and abilities. Not surprisingly, no one measured up. Stephen Ambrose thinks that Eisenhower was convinced that the country would have been best served by a third term for him, but the Twenty-second Amendment made this impossible. Eisenhower worried about the future of the country because he would no longer be in the White House. He had his doubts about Nixon, but the vice president was far and away the best man in the race. He was not Kennedy ("an incompetent") or Lyndon Johnson ("a small man"). Ike's problem was that the kind of candidate he wanted was someone who was apolitical (like Milton Eisenhower or Robert Anderson) and therefore someone who could never be nominated.[18]

Eisenhower's desire to liven up the Republican nominating process, as well as his wish to keep the nomination open to an outsider, persisted into 1960. As late as May, he suggested to Oveta Culp Hobby that the Texas delegation ought to name Robert Anderson as a favorite son candidate in order to "get some Republican interest started up in Texas." If Anderson declined, Eisenhower proposed, "we ought to be the first to name a lady as the 'favorite son.'"[19]

After his definite and final withdrawal from the nomination contest, Nelson Rockefeller resurfaced as a presidential candidate in the spring of 1960. In April and May, Rockefeller floated the possibility of a draft and then said he would definitely accept a draft but would not encourage it. In June, he coupled the declaration of his renewed candidacy with a stinging attack on the domestic and foreign policies of the Eisenhower administration. Having insulted Ike, Rocky, in typical fashion, then called him asking his advice on how to proceed with his candidacy. Rockefeller avowed his desire to do what was in the best interests of the Republican Party and told the president that his recent statement was not a criticism of the administration, but of the lack of leadership coming from the vice president. Rockefeller exasperated Eisenhower. The situation did not improve over the next month, as the New York governor pressed his de facto campaign, calling for the passage of a bill that would provide federal medical care for the aged, as well as an increase of $3 billion in defense spending and $500 million on civil defense.[20]

Aside from Rockefeller and Eisenhower, Nixon had three other concerns in the spring of 1960. First, he and the administration found themselves under fire from Democrats and their journalistic allies over the alleged inferiority of the United States in ballistic missiles. Joe Alsop led the assault. He began 1960 with a column on New Year's Day titled "The Year of Decision" and proclaimed the upcoming presidential election the most important peacetime presidential election in American history, except for 1860. In the last week of January 1960, Alsop published a series of six stories, asserting, among other hysterical judgments, that the president was "playing a vast game of Russian roulette with the national future" and that Eisenhower as president acted "as a kind of super-tranquilizer."[21]

Symington and other Democrats quickly chimed in, and the Missouri senator even charged that the administration had intentionally misled the American public about the seriousness of the situation. This allegation produced a white fury in Eisenhower, who, in a February press conference, called the charge "despicable" and with anger in his voice stated that he would "like to tell him to his face what I think about him." John F. Kennedy offered the opinion that although there might be a dispute about missile numbers, "the point is that we are facing a gap on which we are gambling with our survival."[22]

Other developments in the international arena raised questions about the administration's competence and credibility in the first half of 1960. Events seemed to be drifting out of control, and the administration appeared incapable of coping with them. The most sensational occurrences were the U-2 affair and the collapse of the Paris summit conference. Eisenhower and the administration mishandled the U-2 incident and emerged from it appearing incompetent. Rioting in Turkey nearly overthrew that pro-American government. More rioting in South Korea produced the overthrow of Syngman Rhee, and Eisenhower was forced to cancel a trip to Japan when anti-American rioting there broke out.[23]

The political impact of this chain of events is difficult to gauge. On the one hand, these incidents gave credibility to the Democratic charges that the administration was too passive and lacked the ability to shape international affairs. On the other hand, the foreign crises increased the importance of foreign policy issues and therefore reduced the weight of domestic policy in the equation that determined voter decisions. This shift tended to benefit the GOP and Nixon because of their general strength in this area and because the chief argument against Kennedy was one that emphasized his youth and inexperience. As Nikita Khrushchev ranted and raved and continued his odd and threatening behavior, this was not necessarily bad news for Republicans. At worst, they gained as much as they lost.

What was not helpful to Nixon or the Republican cause in the spring of 1960 was the administration's response to the country's economic situation. After a major recession in 1957–58, the economy had done reasonably well in 1959, but in March 1960, the economist Arthur Burns warned of a coming downturn unless lower interest rates and increased spending offset the inadequate demand in the economy. Nixon, worried by the political implications of Burns's projections, pushed for the economist's proposed solution. The vice president ran into the united opposition of the president, the secretary of the treasury, the chairman of the Federal Reserve Board, and the majority of the Council of Economic Advisers. They were more worried about inflation and the budget deficit.

In this case, Nixon and Burns were right, and Eisenhower and Anderson were wrong. The expansionary cycle that started in mid-1958 was the shortest of the post-1945 period, and the economy settled into decline in mid-1960. In the words of one economic historian, the decision to focus on a balanced budget in the immediate aftermath of the 1957–58 recession was "the greatest fiscal policy mistake committed by any administration between 1945 and the Americanization of the Vietnam War." The ironic result was that Eisenhower, who worked so hard to defeat the Democratic "spenders," adopted a fiscal policy that contributed mightily to their victory in 1960 and helped them to gain control of the White House, where they could do what Eisenhower abhorred.[24]

This economic decision making was symbolic of Nixon's dilemma. He could suggest, but he had no control over decisions that affected his destiny. As the administration found itself beleaguered with bad news through the first half of 1960, it could not help but adversely affect the Nixon campaign. By early 1960, the symbol of *Sputnik*, combined with the repeated assertions of a missile gap aided and abetted by various Democratic politicians, Nelson Rockefeller, and journalists such as Joseph Alsop and Walter Lippmann, had produced a sense of decline that pervaded informed opinion and the national public debate. As Lippmann proclaimed the existence of "a dangerous complacency" and warned ominously that "the influence of the United States as a world power is declining," the critical self-examination picked up momentum. During the same period, John F. Kennedy attracted accolades from the press as his presidential drive moved from one success to another. His youth and energy provided a positive contrast to the alleged passivity and smugness of the administration. A week before the Republican National Convention, Nixon's pollster, Claude Robinson, placed Kennedy ahead of any Republican ticket 55 percent to 45 percent.[25]

The Republican convention offered Nixon the opportunity to regain the initiative and reverse the negative tide. However, the convention also provided Nelson Rockefeller another opportunity to cause trouble. There was a distinct possibility that Rocky might ruin Richard Nixon's moment of triumph and rob the nominee of the momentum that he badly needed from the convention. By this time, Rockefeller had no chance of being the nominee, but he did have the ability to cause Nixon serious trouble, and he knew that. His leverage derived from the Democratic convention and John F. Kennedy's success in snaring Lyndon B. Johnson as his running mate. With such formidable opposition, and in light of Claude Robinson's recent poll, Nixon needed Rockefeller and his support or, at least, his willingness to accommodate himself to the party platform and the vice president's nomination. Rockefeller needed nothing from Nixon and wanted nothing from him. The New Yorker held the advantage. Either Nixon would appease Rockefeller, or he could watch his presidential dreams fall apart even before the general election campaign began.

In the month before the convention, Rockefeller stepped up his attacks on administration defense policy. He embraced the missile gap idea as completely as any Democrat with the possible exception of Stuart Symington. In late June, Rockefeller asserted that the United States was seriously vulnerable to a missile attack and declared the "relative military power of the United States as compared with the Soviet Union has steadily and drastically declined over the past 15 years." In early July 1960, Charles Percy, the future Illinois senator and head of the platform committee, went to New York to discuss the platform with Rockefeller. The governor lodged several objections, especially on the defense plank. Percy discussed these objections with Nixon and produced a compromise that Rockefeller rejected. With less than a week to go before the start of the convention, Rockefeller threatened a fight on the convention floor over the platform.[26]

Convinced of the necessity of dealing with Rockefeller, Nixon called Herbert Brownell, who in turn contacted Rocky. Knowing they held the upper hand, Rockefeller and his aides imposed a number of humiliating conditions for agreeing to a meeting. They demanded that Nixon personally call the governor and request it, that it be held at a location of Rockefeller's choosing, and that the governor's office would issue the press release. Without consulting anyone, Nixon accepted these terms, flew to New York City, went immediately to Rockefeller's apartment and commenced negotiations that lasted from Friday evening through the early-morning hours of Saturday. Nixon made a snap decision that caught the Secret Service short-handed and left the Nixon staff as well as Percy and the platform committee uninformed.

Late that Friday night, Charles Percy received a telephone call from the vice president, who then brought the Illinoisan into the discussion of the changes being made in the platform. Percy was not being consulted; he was being told what was being done and what he, as chairman of the platform committee, would have to accede to. The vice president and the governor, with assistance from their aides, managed to reach agreement on a text that Rockefeller released early Saturday morning. What emerged was a fourteen-point compact that promptly became known as the Treaty of Fifth Avenue. Rockefeller professed himself satisfied with the agreement.[27]

If Rockefeller was pleased with the results of the late-night negotiations, others were not. At the top of the list was the president, already no great admirer of the New York governor. What especially infuriated Eisenhower was the phrase in the defense plank that proclaimed, "there must be no price ceiling on America's security." Nixon tried to explain to the president that he was just trying to find the necessary language so that "Nelson can be with us and not against us." Eisenhower signaled his displeasure to Nixon. Ike also hinted that his support in the general election campaign was dependent on the avoidance of any language that was critical of the administration or repudiated administration policies. Eventually, the offending language in the defense plank was removed and the president pacified.[28]

Eisenhower was not the only disgruntled Republican. Members of the platform committee were upset as was Barry Goldwater and the majority of Republican conservatives. They had never liked Rockefeller and the apparent surrender to him rankled. So did the secretive manner in which it occurred. One anonymous Republican official said of Nixon's meeting with Rockefeller, "He didn't fly, he crawled all the way on his hands and knees." On Sunday, July 24, according to Theodore White, the convention was "thoroughly out of control." Nixon had placated Rockefeller, but he now risked losing support among the party regulars who had been most loyal to him.[29]

Understanding the crisis that he faced, Nixon arrived in Chicago on Monday, July 25, and promptly set about trying to repair the damage. He held a press conference in which he emphasized the concessions that Rockefeller had made. He talked to members of the platform committee in groups of two or three and individually. He then shook hands and had photographs taken with all 2,600 delegates and alternates. With this massive effort undoubtedly helped by the goodwill he had built up over the years, Richard Nixon managed to extinguish the minor rebellion that burned in Chicago. He restored peace and harmony, and, although some grumbling continued, a spirit of good humor and goodwill took hold and dominated the convention week.[30]

The conventional wisdom then and now is that Nixon's agreement with Rockefeller was a sellout and a mistake. In fact, the vice president had little choice. Although the agreement with Rocky caused momentary party indigestion, it passed fairly quickly. Nixon's concessions were more apparent than real, and in some cases the vice president agreed with Rockefeller's positions. He managed to eliminate the one part of the defense plank that was unacceptable to Eisenhower. He came away with a placated Rockefeller. With the anti-Rockefeller crowd subsequently mollified, Nixon took a major step toward achieving party unity for the general election campaign. After the Treaty of Fifth Avenue, Rockefeller ceased to be a problem. Nixon had paid a price, but he had obtained what he needed.[31]

Then Richard Nixon came into some good luck. In 1960, Senator Barry Goldwater emerged as the new face of the reawakening Republican right. The Arizonan, elected to the Senate in 1952, was in the process of becoming the new conservative messiah. His book, *Conscience of a Conservative*, that appeared in the spring of 1960 was a smashing success. By November, it had sold 500,000 copies. Unlike Rockefeller, Goldwater wanted to help Nixon. Just before the convention, Goldwater assured Nixon that he would not be a candidate. The Arizonan allowed his name to be placed in nomination, at which point the convention staged its most spontaneously enthusiastic demonstration of the week. It was the Republican version of the emotional explosion in favor of Adlai Stevenson at the Democratic convention. Goldwater then arose, asked that his name be withdrawn, and proceeded to give a short but brilliant speech, one of the best of his career. He aimed his remarks at conservatives. He reminded them that the Republican Party was their historic home. He urged them to put their differences with the platform behind them and not allow those differences to deter them from exerting themselves in the general election campaign. He implored conservatives with the plea to "put our shoulders to the wheel for Dick Nixon and push him across the line." He concluded with the thought that conservatives needed to grow up. If they wanted to win control of the party, he told them, they needed to get to work. Nixon received as enthusiastic an endorsement from the rising leader of Republican conservatives as he possibly could have asked for—and he paid nothing for it.[32]

The most controversial moment of the week, the brouhaha over the Treaty of Fifth Avenue, was over even before the convention commenced. After the furor over the concessions to Rockefeller subsided, the convention proceeded as smoothly and harmoniously as the nominee could have wanted. Goldwater's speech was an unexpected treasure. Eisenhower's address was a powerful performance. Ike provided a ringing defense of the administration's defense policies while comparing his critics to Job's boils. He received rapturous applause for his effort.

In Chicago, unlike Los Angeles, there was no excitement or anticipation at the roll call of the states that made the nomination of Richard M. Nixon official. But, as in Los Angeles, a critical choice rested with the nominee on the matter of his running mate. The pressure on Nixon was even greater because of John F. Kennedy's coup in convincing Lyndon B. Johnson to run with him. The only way in which Nixon could have equaled Kennedy would have been to add Nelson Rockefeller to the GOP ticket. Nixon had polls showing that the New York governor was far and away his strongest possible partner. One poll indicated that in California the presence of Rockefeller would increase the Republican vote 4 percent among Democrats, 6 percent among political independents, 5 percent among nonwhites, and 4 percent among Catholics.[33]

But the Nixon-Rockefeller ticket was not to be. Nixon indirectly raised the possibility in the conference between the two men on July 23. The New Yorker reiterated his long-stated position of disinterest. Earlier the vice president asked Eisenhower to help persuade Rockefeller to accept the second position on the ticket. So had Gabriel Hauge. Ike was cold to the idea. He told both Nixon and Hauge that he had talked to Rockefeller two or three times, and the New Yorker had made it clear that he would not take the vice-presidential nomination even at the president's request. As far as Ike was concerned, Rocky was "no philosophical genius" and he had "a personal ambition that is overwhelming." In any event, Eisenhower had no intention of begging the New Yorker to accept.[34]

From Nixon's viewpoint, Rockefeller's refusal was neither surprising nor entirely unwelcome. Nixon would lose votes without Rockefeller, but the New Yorker was a difficult individual who would have caused numerous headaches for the presidential nominee. Nixon knew he would need all his energy and all his concentration for the race of his life against John F. Kennedy.[35]

With Rocky out of the vice-presidential picture, Nixon turned to the available alternatives. In the Californian's version of events, there were six possibilities—Senator Thruston Morton (Kentucky), Congressman Walter Judd (Minnesota), Congressman Gerald Ford (Michigan), Secretary of the Interior Fred Seaton (Nebraska), Secretary of Labor James Mitchell (New Jersey), and UN Ambassador Henry Cabot Lodge Jr. (Massachusetts). Late that night, in the aftermath of his nomination, Nixon convened a meeting of twenty party leaders. According to the vice president, by this time the choice was down to three—Morton, Judd, and Lodge. Judd asked to be removed from consideration on the basis of his age and his belief that he could not hold up to the rigors of an intense national campaign. Morton would have liked the nomination but recommended Lodge, as did Eisenhower. Henry Cabot Lodge Jr. was the choice for vice president.[36]

Although the new nominee conveyed the impression that the choice was still open at the time of this meeting, the evidence points to the conclusion that he had already decided for Lodge. When Governor William Stratton of Illinois argued for a candidate that would help with the farm vote, Nixon's response was, "If you ever let them [the Democrats] campaign only on domestic issues, they'll beat us—our only hope is to keep it on foreign policy." From Nixon's perspective, Lodge was the best available candidate because, as the UN ambassador who had been on television numerous times, he was both well known and could maintain a foreign policy focus for the campaign. In addition, he was potentially helpful with the white ethnic vote in the big cities because of his attacks on Soviet oppression of Eastern European countries. Finally, he was acceptable to both party conservatives and liberals, and Eisenhower liked him.[37]

Later, the choice of Lodge came in for a great deal of criticism. To many political observers, the UN ambassador was an ineffective candidate who especially suffered in comparison to Lyndon Johnson. But the torrent of criticism came later during the campaign and especially after the narrow loss to Kennedy-Johnson. At the time of the convention, most Republicans were happy with Henry Cabot Lodge Jr. The UN ambassador won applause at the time of his selection and received overwhelmingly favorable coverage through the first part of the general election campaign. He served the function of keeping the focus on foreign policy, and he posed minimal internal problems to the campaign. He was not as effective as LBJ, but the Texan was the most influential vice-presidential candidate of the twentieth century.

With the vice-presidential selection set, all that remained was the acceptance speech. In this instance, Richard M. Nixon rose to the occasion, delivering one of the best speeches of his political career. It conveyed a personal modesty but carried with it strength and conviction. The nominee was in top form, and his delivery was polished and persuasive. Supporters were exhilarated. Even critics grudgingly admitted that Nixon had done well.[38]

Richard Nixon and the GOP had a good week in Chicago. They came into the Windy City facing a significant amount of discontent. The Californian managed to pacify the malcontents, and Barry Goldwater supplied a most helpful boost of support. The convention witnessed three inspiring speeches from Goldwater, Eisenhower, and Nixon that outshone the addresses from Los Angeles except for Eugene McCarthy's brilliant effort. Republicans left

Chicago in a united frame of mind, confident in their nominee, and highly motivated for the tough contest that was about to take place.

The Gallup Poll was the best indicator of the success of the convention. In the matchup before Chicago (and even before Los Angeles), JFK led Richard Nixon 50 percent to 46 percent, with 4 percent undecided. In the first poll after the Republican convention, Nixon forged ahead of Kennedy 50 percent to 44 percent. It would be the largest lead Nixon would have after the naming of the two nominees. The poll result was a tribute to Nixon, Eisenhower, Goldwater, and their marvelous effort in Chicago. Their dilemma was that to win they needed as good a performance in the general election campaign as they had managed in Chicago. That would not be easy.[39]

5

The General Election Campaign, July 28–September 25

"Sure Teddy [White] sucked up to the Kennedys. . . . We all did."
—Ben Bradlee

"Nixon did everything but sweep out the plane."
—Robert Finch

As he stood before the Republican National Convention on July 28, 1960, Richard M. Nixon noted that he had been asked when his presidential campaign would begin. That night, Nixon proclaimed: "This campaign begins tonight, here and now, and it goes on. And this campaign will continue from now until November eighth without any letup."[1] With this declaration, Nixon unleashed one of the hardest-fought general election campaigns in American history. With a combined age of ninety (Kennedy was forty-three and Nixon forty-seven), the two men represented the youngest pairing of presidential contestants the country had ever seen. Both men were supremely talented, full of energy, and willing to drive themselves to the point of exhaustion in their quest for the White House. After the careful preparation and the necessary supplications of the previous years, the campaign was a liberating experience, sending them out on their own to seek the biggest political prize.

The Kennedy-Nixon contest falls into three phases. The first ran from the end of the Republican convention to the eve of the first presidential debate, July 28–September 25. The second encompassed the period of the four presidential debates, September 26–October 21. The final stage was the last two and a half weeks of the campaign, October 22–November 7. Kennedy prevailed in the first two rounds, but Nixon closed with a rush and almost pulled off a political upset that, if he had managed it, would have ranked second only to Harry Truman's comeback victory in 1948.

In the first period, the two campaigns organized themselves, set their strategies, and began to implement them. The two months were marked by a number of important developments, including the August lame-duck session of Congress, JFK's reconciliation with the elder statesmen of the Democratic Party, an inadvertent remark by Dwight D. Eisenhower in a presidential press conference, Nixon's preliminary foray into the South, and John F. Kennedy's spectacularly successful performance before the Houston Ministerial Association.

The first order of business, a rump session of Congress, Lyndon Johnson designed to strengthen his hand at the national convention. Almost everyone but Johnson considered it an extremely bad idea, including Sam Rayburn, who expressed a vehement desire to adjourn Congress before going to Los Angeles. Johnson persisted. The session turned into a fiasco. In spite of their overwhelming congressional majorities, Democrats passed no significant legislation. Eisenhower, rounding into fighting form, continually derided them or vetoed their bills, while observing how remarkable it was that with their huge majorities, Democrats could accomplish nothing. *Time*, in a story titled "Democratic Debacle," characterized it as a "disastrous post-convention session," "a defeat," the "collapse of [Kennedy's] . . . high political hopes," and "an utter rout." *Time* asserted that Kennedy had been "thoroughly trounced."[2]

August was a low point for Kennedy with the ongoing embarrassment in Washington and a Gallup Poll that showed Nixon ahead. There was petty infighting with the Democratic National Committee people and brewing conflicts between Kennedy volunteers and state party organizations. Even so, Kennedy did make some positive inroads during the month. He shored up his relations with Truman, Stevenson, and Eleanor Roosevelt. Perhaps, given the dislike these three worthies had for the Republican nominee, the reconciliation was inevitable, but Kennedy carried it off with his usual grace. Even if the three had their reservations about the Massachusetts senator, they campaigned enthusiastically for him. Truman made twenty-seven speeches on behalf of Kennedy, while Stevenson gave more than eighty.[3]

Meanwhile, the Kennedy campaign took shape. Following the Los Angeles convention, Kennedy returned to Hyannis Port for an extended round of strategy sessions as well as rest and recuperation. He was exhausted, and his voice was gone. The rest and relaxation at Cape Cod was time well spent. A national plan emerged along with a delegation of responsibilities. JFK and his strategists agreed that the campaign would concentrate on the nine states with the largest numbers of electoral votes—Massachusetts, New York, New Jersey, Pennsylvania, Ohio, Michigan, Illinois, Texas, and California—along with the other southern states and targets of opportunity as they presented themselves. The nine big states had 237 of the 269 electoral votes needed for the White House. In none of the nine states was Kennedy worse than a slight underdog, and in the majority he was a clear favorite. Kennedy himself would focus on the first seven on the list, while LBJ would be responsible for Texas and the South, and Adlai Stevenson would make California his emphasis. Lou Harris was already churning out polls that showed Kennedy with double-digit leads in many of these states.[4]

The Kennedys also established the structure of the campaign. Robert F. Kennedy acted as campaign manager. From the beginning, he infused the campaign with unparalleled energy and commitment. To these qualities he added a ruthlessness that was not endearing. As he remarked to New York party officials: "I don't give a damn if the state and county organizations survive after November, and I don't care if you survive. I want to elect John F. Kennedy." Beyond RFK, Lawrence O'Brien went to Washington, D.C., and worked out of the Democratic National Committee. Kenneth O'Donnell served as the chief schedule coordinator. John Bailey supervised contacts with the state organizations and the professional politicians. Stephen Smith, Kennedy's brother-in-law, oversaw campaign money. Pierre Salinger served as press secretary. The campaign command staff was extraordinarily young—Robert Kennedy was thirty-four; Sorensen, thirty-two; O'Donnell, thirty-six; and Salinger, thirty-five. They were all Kennedy confidants who were deeply attached to him and had been for years. Of these, only Salinger was relatively new. Few newcomers exerted any true authority in the campaign. Leonard Reinsch, who planned television and radio strategy for Democrats, and James Rowe, who had done scheduling for Adlai Stevenson, were two important exceptions. John F. Kennedy trusted his veterans implicitly and had no difficulty in extending to them the authority necessary to get their jobs done.[5]

Lyndon Johnson and some of his staff were present at these initial strategy sessions, and his position in the campaign quickly became clear. Although John Kennedy had considerable respect for his running mate and his talents, almost no one else in the presidential nominee's staff did, and some, most notably Bobby Kennedy, despised LBJ. The Kennedy staff looked on the Johnson staff as "a bunch of country yokels." LBJ further aggravated the situation with his tendency to talk too much. By the end of the discussions, the Kennedys and their aides wanted to have as little to do as possible with LBJ and his Texans. They preferred to run the presidential effort and have Johnson and his gang remain south of the Mason-Dixon Line, doing whatever was necessary to win Texas, the other former Confederate states, and any border states the Senate majority leader could manage.

Later, during the campaign, in a frame of mind dominated by self-pity, LBJ pleaded with one journalist to tell the Kennedys what a great job he was doing or at least how hard he was trying.[6]

The other figure who exerted influence in the campaign was Joseph P. Kennedy. In 1960 and after, journalists displayed no interest in probing his role, nor did the various Kennedy court historians ever bother to examine the subject. Thus, a half century after the event, there is still no adequate assessment of Joseph Kennedy and his part in the general election campaign. Some specific details have emerged. For example, we do know that Joe Kennedy called the president of Notre Dame University to obtain the university's consent for Harris Wofford to join the campaign. Wofford was a crucial individual in the successful quest for African-American votes. We also know that Kennedy intervened with his acquaintances in organized crime to secure their support for his son in 1960. He engaged in many other activities on behalf of John Kennedy in the presidential election year, but what they were remains unknown to this day. Clearly, he was the great silent backer for the campaign. There is no indication that he attempted to influence policy positions or campaign strategy, but there is every reason to believe that he willingly utilized his connections and the vast resources at his command to do whatever was necessary to achieve the election of his son as president of the United States.[7]

The Kennedy presidential campaign got under way in early September with the nominee's opening rally in the traditional Democratic Labor Day event in Detroit. The Kennedy organization had many strengths and few weaknesses. The greatest strength was the candidate. In the words of Herbert Parmet: "He was young. He was elegant. Maturity and improved health had filled out his face and he had never looked better."[8] He was well suited to a politics in which television was an increasingly important factor. He was photogenic and had the ability to appeal to the inhabitants of the great American cities, but he was also able to reach suburbanites and the liberal intellectual community that was initially suspicious of him. He had the ability to touch the imagination and the heart, especially of younger voters, and to elicit their idealism. Among white ethnic Americans, especially Roman Catholics, the Kennedy appeal was especially potent. Here was an engaging, eloquent representative of immigrant America of whom everyone could be proud. John F. Kennedy personified a coming-of-age story that immigrants could take great pride in. As his campaign proceeded, he attracted larger and larger crowds that were increasingly demonstrative. He and his brother had endless resources of energy that they poured into the campaign as they drove themselves relentlessly. The contrast with the leisurely Stevenson campaigns of 1952 and 1956 that failed to fire the enthusiasm of Democrats, except for the liberal intellectuals, could not have been greater.

Along with the candidate came another great asset, the most positive press relations imaginable. There were two main sources of the adoring press coverage that Kennedy began receiving in the 1950s, became even more blatant in 1960, and then reached Olympian heights during his presidency. The first was that John F. Kennedy and his family were glamorous and a natural subject not only for serious news, but also for general-interest readers who were not necessarily interested in politics. Newspapers, news magazines, and other publications did endless stories about JFK and the Kennedy family, not simply because they liked them (which they did) but because stories about the Kennedys excited reader interest and sold copies. In other words, Kennedy stories were very much in the financial self-interest of those who published them. The writing on JFK and family was positive and even gushing. For example, on the eve of the Democratic convention, *Time* described Jackie as "a limpid beauty who would have excited Goya," referred to the "tawny-haired Eunice Kennedy Shriver" and the "leggy Patricia Kennedy Lawford," and characterized Jean Kennedy Smith as "the slim, tanned baby sister of the family." Two weeks later, *Time* published a story in which it attempted to analyze the favorable press coverage. It observed that JFK was getting "undoubtedly the best press of any presidential candidate in modern history" and then concluded that this treatment was deserved.[9]

There was a second and more important reason for the extraordinarily positive coverage. John F. Kennedy liked the company of reporters, and they reciprocated. Their relationship with Kennedy was in stark contrast to the ones with Eisenhower and Nixon. The former ignored them, and the latter disliked them. In Kennedy's case, journalists basked in their association with him and outdid themselves with flattery and glowing tributes to the candidate. As Ben Bradlee put it: "Sure Teddy [White] sucked up to the Kennedys. . . . We all did." JFK was at ease with reporters, enjoyed the conversational give-and-take with them, and understood their needs. He had worked briefly as a journalist and understood the mechanics of the job. After entering the White House, he did his best to assure them of transcripts of speeches and press conferences almost as soon as possible. Kennedy and aides such as Lawrence O'Brien, Kenneth O'Donnell, Theodore Sorensen, and RFK were easily accessible during the campaign.[10]

The relationship was one of openness, availability, and familiarity. Journalists enjoyed Kennedy immensely, especially after the Eisenhower presidency, relishing JFK's wit and humor. He could poke fun at himself, and he avoided pretension. Covering him was fun. Some of Kennedy's closest social friends were journalists—Ben Bradlee, Charles Bartlett, and Rowland Evans. JFK was candid and direct with them, although not always honest, and managed to create a sense of closeness and shared secrets that won over the newsmen. The reporters reciprocated with highly favorable coverage, avoiding his statements that would have embarrassed him. In effect, Kennedy was using the press, but they did not mind. Like the women that Kennedy seduced, the reporters willingly participated. They liked to pretend that they were maintaining their journalistic professionalism and may have even believed that they were doing so. In the 1970s, Ben Bradlee made an unctuous statement that "one of the penalties of being a reporter and a friend of someone in high office" was that one had "to explore potentially derogatory information with even a greater zeal than would be devoted to similar information about a non-friend." Bradlee and others displayed precious little such zeal from 1959 through 1963. Only much later did any of them have second thoughts or regrets, and even then they were few.[11]

One later incident after he became president indicated how far Kennedy managed to take in journalists and manipulate them for his purposes. The episode involved Hugh Sidey, a *Time-Life* correspondent who wrote on the presidency. In a dinner conversation with Henry Luce, JFK's sister Eunice Shriver told the media potentate how her brother was a speed reader who could read entire books in one sitting. Luce instructed Sidey to explore the matter. The journalist checked with an institute where Kennedy had enrolled but had not completed the course. An expert source there had no records on him but indicated that he probably read at seven hundred to eight hundred words per minute, or twice the average for men his age. When Sidey mentioned this figure to the president, he disputed it. He stated that John Kenneth Galbraith had timed him reading a twenty-six-page memorandum in ten minutes. That exercise gave him a speed of about one thousand words per minute. But JFK did not like that figure either. Sidey then suggested 1,200 words per minute, and Kennedy agreed to it. *Life* printed that number in an effusive article entitled "The President's Voracious Reading Habits" with a subtitle of "He Eats up Notes, Books at 1,200 Words a Minute." Thus, thanks to *Life*, the story of John F. Kennedy's prolific reading speed of 1,200 words per minute became part of the Kennedy legend. It was the handiwork of the president and his journalistic accomplice.[12]

Even after his death, the spell JFK cast over newsmen continued. In the mid-1960s, former presidential mistress Mary Meyer was murdered. In her diary was the story of her affair with JFK. Ben Bradlee, perhaps Kennedy's closest journalist friend, made certain that the diary and its tale were suppressed. Such was Kennedy's hold on Bradlee and others that they continued covering up for him after his death. Whatever the journalistic ethics of these and many other incidents of questionable behavior on the part of Kennedy's friends and allies, the relationship he had with the media was an immense asset in 1960.[13]

With its ample assets, the Kennedy campaign had its flaws, especially in the early weeks. No one in the campaign had any experience in running a national effort. The race for the nomination had been national, but the only two contested primaries, those in Wisconsin and West Virginia, were in states with a combined total of twenty electoral votes against a badly overmatched opponent. In the general election campaign, there was a need to coordinate efforts with state political organizations and bosses, many of whom were not well disposed to the candidate or his campaign manager. According to one veteran Democrat, Robert F. Kennedy refused to remain in Washington, D.C., and make decisions, and he also refused to delegate authority. Hard feelings remaining with supporters of Johnson, Stevenson, and Humphrey further complicated the situation. The Kennedy campaign never resolved many of these antagonisms and never achieved effective co-ordination in many states.[14]

Despite its reputation, largely the creation of Theodore White, the Kennedy campaign was not a well-oiled machine or a model of efficiency. As Arthur Schlesinger Jr. noted, the real strength of JFK and RFK rested in their improvisational abilities. The truth was that the organizational aspects of the Democratic presidential operation left a great deal to be desired. Press secretary Pierre Salinger was "not quite prepared" at times. Chicago newspaper man Peter Lisagor recalled: "You never knew whether your bags were going to be at the hotel or whether they'd catch up with you. It was a kind of amiable sloppiness." Kathleen Jamieson compared the Democratic media advertising effort to "an Edsel kept on the road by mechanics frantically redesigning spare parts."[15]

The initial trip to the West Coast in early September did not go well. Even Kennedy's admirers admitted that the advance work in Oregon and Washington was "atrocious" and resulted in "humiliation" for the candidate. Bad scheduling and bad advice turned the first foray into the key state of California into a "failure," according to Theodore White. His first speeches were poorly delivered. Effective speaking was a chronic problem for Kennedy. Through the primary season, he had struggled with pace. By the end of the convention, he was hoarse. In August, he recovered from the hoarseness but still had problems with delivery that continued into the first month of the general election campaign. He hired speech coaches, who educated him how to eliminate the strain on his voice. Improvement did not occur immediately, but by the halfway point in the campaign, he had become much better. He relaxed, began to use his voice more naturally, developed a better rhythm, and became generally more confident.[16]

In spite of these rough spots, Kennedy's position in the Gallup Poll actually improved from early August to mid-September. In the aftermath of the Republican convention, Kennedy trailed Nixon by six points, 50 percent to 44 percent in a poll taken between July 31 and August 4. The two surveys taken in late August and then in mid-September showed Kennedy ahead by one point and then behind by one point. In other words, after Nixon came down from his convention bounce, the presidential contest was essentially tied. Despite Kennedy's less than stellar performance through August and the first third of September, he was running even with the vice president.[17]

Whatever the shortcomings of the first weeks of the Kennedy campaign, it executed a dramatic turnabout in the last two-thirds of September that propelled it into the lead, a lead that it never would relinquish. Two events gave John F. Kennedy the great momentum that carried him through September and most of October. The first of these was JFK's magnificent performance before Protestant ministers at the Houston Ministerial Conference on September 12. The second, to be discussed in the next chapter, was his equally brilliant effort in the first televised presidential debate on September 26. The combination of the two altered the course of the presidential contest.

The decision for Kennedy to appear before the Houston ministers emerged out of a growing concern in the Democratic camp over the religious issue. Kennedy had confronted and overcome the religious issue in his bid for the Democratic nomination, but everyone knew that was not the end of it. By September 1, the Kennedy campaign was in possession of a blunt analysis of religion and the campaign, and a recommendation for a course of action. This report came from the Simulactics Corporation, which was under contract to the Democratic Party in 1960. It took public opinion polling data and used it to formulate campaign strategy. It furnished John F. Kennedy with a report that contained important conclusions about the religious issue that shaped the course of the campaign.

What Simulactics found was that as of late August, John F. Kennedy had already lost the "bulk of the votes he would lose if the election campaign were to be embittered by the issue of anti-Catholicism." Kennedy stood to lose a "few more" Protestants, but these losses would be more than offset by gains among Catholics and "minority group votes." It concluded that

Kennedy had "already suffered the disadvantages of the issue even though it is not embittered now—and without receiving the compensating advantages inherent in it." In other words, the Democratic nominee stood to benefit from public displays of anti-Catholic prejudice. They would win votes for him from outraged Catholics, minority groups, and those disposed to "resent overt prejudice." According to this analysis, what JFK and the Democratic Party needed was more, not less, discussion of religion—and the more inflamed, the better. The Democratic Party stood to gain by stimulating anti-Catholicism in all its repulsive forms because such vitriol would bring more votes to the Democratic ticket.[18]

It is impossible to prove that John F. Kennedy ever read this report or acted on its recommendations, but given the affinity of the candidate and the campaign for polling data, it is likely that he and some of his top aides did peruse it. Whether they did or not, after September 1, 1960, the Democratic candidate and his campaign acted as if they had. Their subsequent actions were almost perfectly consistent with the Simulactics recommendations. The Kennedy campaign knew that it was to its advantage to stir up the religious issue and to welcome the rants of radical anti-Catholics. All the expressed dismay about the deplorable outbursts of anti-Catholicism was ceremonial. The underlying reality was that the more the anti-Catholic zealots could be provoked, the better off were JFK and the Democratic campaign.

In September, the campaign abandoned its passive approach to religion and embarked on a course to seize the initiative, set the agenda, and define the subject in terms favorable to the Massachusetts senator. The precipitating event was the newspaper story of September 7 about the National Conference of Citizens for Religious Freedom (NCCRF); its best-known member, Norman Vincent Peale; and its statement to the effect that John F. Kennedy's religion was a legitimate topic of discussion. Among other things, the NCCRF declared that a Catholic president "would be under extreme pressure from the hierarchy of his church" to bring American foreign policy into line with Vatican objectives. The Kennedy campaign felt that it had to act, but if it had not been Norman Vincent Peale and the NCCRF, there were any number of other provocations that could have been cited.[19]

The Kennedy team came up with an immediate reply and a long-term response. The immediate reply was the quickly planned Kennedy appearance at the Houston Ministerial Conference on September 12. JFK's appearance in Houston was one of the great turning points in the campaign. Carefully staged in one of the most prominent locations in the city, the Crystal Ballroom of the Rice Hotel, the program was designed to portray JFK as the good guy and his interrogators as the bad guys. The Kennedy advance man picked the "'meanest, nastiest-looking ministers' to put in the front row." Kennedy went before the hostile audience, made an eloquent statement on behalf of his belief in religious freedom and the separation of church and state, and then gracefully and effectively took on a series of antagonistic questions from the ministers in the audience. The questions were almost all unfriendly in nature. Many were based on elaborate quotations from papal encyclicals and the *Catholic Encyclopedia*. They conveyed the clear impression of a group of inquisitors attempting to trap their subject, rather than engaging in an honest attempt to explore differences. It was one of the moments in which JFK's campaign could have imploded. Instead, he performed magnificently and ended the evening as the clear victor in the encounter.[20]

This was a reprise of the Kennedy strategy that had worked so well in the nomination fight. Houston served the purpose of putting Kennedy on record asserting his belief in the basic American principles of freedom of religion and separation of church and state. It also began the second phase of turning the issue into one of religious freedom versus religious prejudice, with Kennedy and the Democrats representatives of the former and Nixon and the Republicans the agents of the latter. Richard Nixon now found himself the target as the Kennedy campaign began its adroit effort to link the Republican candidate with the nasty-looking ministers and their sectarian views.[21]

As this massive Democratic offensive proceeded, the response of Nixon was curiously passive. In mid-August, he put out an edict that contained three main points. First, it directed that no individual or group that based their support on religious grounds would be recognized. Second, there would be no discussion of the religious issue in any party literature, and no literature from any source on this subject would be distributed or available at party headquarters. Third, all staff and volunteers should avoid any discussion, even casual discussion, of the topic. The edict concluded that the "vice president has made it clear he wants these directives pursued with the most careful and specific adherence." In early September, he proposed that both campaigns cut off all discussion of religion. From the very beginning of the contest, Richard Nixon worked to avoid any discussion of the religious question.[22]

While the Kennedy campaign first sputtered and then began to catch fire in the second third of September, the Nixon effort began well but then encountered difficulties on the religious issue and in other areas. The Republican nominee enjoyed an excellent national convention, a better one than his Democratic rival. The boost he received from it was reflected in the Gallup Poll and his first campaign swing.

Nixon carried many assets into the general election campaign. He was in top physical condition. He had participated in two presidential campaigns (1952 and 1956), honed his campaign style, and knew what he had to do. From the beginning, he was sharp. One reporter wrote, "He [Nixon] plays his crowd like a pipe organ virtuoso, telling them things they like to hear, making small but effective adjustments from city to city and in the first few days . . . he hasn't hit a sour note." Nixon was an accomplished speaker. He adapted well to his environment. His deep baritone voice allowed him to vary his tone from conversational to one of strong advocacy, and he could adapt it to suit the occasion. At the outset of the campaign, Nixon was a more effective speaker than John Kennedy.[23]

Nixon was blessed with a highly competent and experienced campaign staff. There was no single campaign manager; rather three men theoretically shared the responsibility. Campaign chairman Len Hall was in charge of managing affairs in Washington. Campaign director Robert Finch traveled with the candidate and was supposed to preside over the day-to-day effort. Meanwhile, Senator Thruston Morton had the responsibility of coordinating the activities of the Republican National Committee (of which he was chairman) with the presidential campaign. Other key figures were planning director James Bassett, RNC publicity director L. Richard Guylay, director of television operations Carroll Newton, and White House liaison Robert Merriam. Nixon's chief media consultant was Ted Rogers, who had worked with the vice president since 1952 and had advised him on the Checkers speech of that year. The individual who supervised the advance work and exercised a growing influence was H. R. Haldeman, a man of great organizational ability but one whom many found unpleasant. Nixon's chief pollster, whom he trusted implicitly, was Claude Robinson. Also close to him were his longtime secretary, Rose Mary Woods, and his military aide, Don Hughes. The final, though hardly the least valuable, asset was Pat Nixon. Although not necessarily enamored of politics and the demands that came with it, she was a highly effective campaigner. These were men and women of exceptional ability who were familiar with Nixon and he with them. With this experience and familiarity, the Republican campaign got off to a strong start. From the beginning, the Nixon effort ran at peak efficiency. As one campaign observer remarked: "Nixon's first day was a killer. . . . But he was on time almost to the minute for every scheduled appearance."[24]

Still, the vice president's campaign was not without its problems. Nixon faced a more difficult path to the White House in assembling the needed electoral votes than Kennedy did. Nixon needed at least four of the nine states with the largest numbers of electoral votes to win. Massachusetts, as Kennedy's home state, was not in play. The Californian faced a great obstacle in Texas because of Lyndon Johnson, his potent political machine, and the Democratic domination of the state. The Republican state organization in the Lone Star State was nonexistent outside of a few large metropolitan areas like Ft. Worth, Dallas, and Houston. New York was problematic with its heavily Roman Catholic vote and the Rockefeller machine, which had scant interest in a Nixon victory. Beyond Massachusetts, Texas, and New York, Nixon faced a decided disadvantage in New Jersey, Pennsylvania, and Michigan, where Republican state organizations were weaker than their Democratic counterparts. In Illinois, the GOP state organization was strong, but there was an unpopular Republican governor trying for an unprecedented third term and a weak U.S. Senate candidate. Ohio and California offered the best chances for success in November, but they were not sure things. In the end, Nixon never solved his Electoral College dilemma. He focused on the big seven (the above nine minus Massachusetts and New Jersey) but had difficulty in deciding where among these seven his resources should be concentrated.

The other strategic dilemma facing Nixon was the question of whether to concentrate on the black vote or the white southern vote. Since the days of the New Deal, Democrats had managed to carry both, and the 1960 Democratic ticket was designed to perpetuate that legacy. JFK—with the strong civil rights plank in the platform and the support of the big-city Democratic machines and their black allies—appealed to the African-American vote in the North, while Lyndon Johnson traveled around the South reassuring white southerners that he and the new administration would look after their interests.

This concurrent appeal to blacks and southern whites, of which FDR was the master, had become increasingly difficult. Blacks were increasingly disinclined to tolerate their place of inferiority, and support of the civil rights position meant alienating powerful white southern interests. In 1956, Eisenhower captured almost 40 percent of the black vote along with five former Confederate states. Although Nixon was no Ike, there were Republican opportunities in exploiting the split over civil rights. The question was whether the Republican effort should be directed at white southern votes or black votes? Democrats had the luxury of being able to appeal simultaneously to both groups because of their control of southern courthouses and big-city machines, and because they had one candidate (Kennedy) to work on black votes in the North and another candidate (Johnson) to cultivate white votes in the South. Without such advantages, the GOP and its candi-date had to make a choice. This riddle bedeviled the party and the candidate throughout the fall. They never devised a consistent, coherent plan that made electoral sense.

With difficulty fashioning a workable Electoral College strategy, Nixon made a pledge to appear in every state. This promise was an attempt to por-tray his campaign as a national one and contrast it to a Democratic ticket of two regional candidates with the presidential nominee focusing on the North and his running mate on the South. Nixon hoped that his approach would cast him as the one genuine national leader while reducing his op-ponents in stature and credibility. It also derived from his belief that the election would be a close one in which smaller states could provide valu-able electoral votes. Since Nixon was strongest in the smaller states of the Midwest and West, he was hopeful that domination of these electoral votes added to just enough big states would produce a winning combination.[25]

In excellent health and spirits, Nixon anticipated a narrow outcome and was determined to outwork his opponent. (Kennedy, of course, intended to do the same thing.) Unlike his Democratic rival, whose campaign geared up as quickly as it could and then ran as hard as it could as long as it could, Nixon constructed his campaign to build to a climax in the last two weeks. In his view, a presidential campaign was one of peaks and valleys, with the last few weeks crucial. The vice president traveled nationwide, fulfilling his fifty-state pledge, but the campaign also concentrated its resources for one last great offensive in the final weeks. The GOP made large purchases of television time in order to dominate the airwaves in this period. President Eisenhower would make his major effort at this point. Nixon, who worked hard all along, would redouble his efforts for the last great push.[26]

If the fifty-state program was questionable, especially after illness put Nixon in the hospital for two weeks, his theory about saving resources for a final campaign offensive was astute and almost won him the election. In such a hard-fought and close contest, the outcome would be in doubt at the end. The Kennedy campaign failed to plan for this eventuality and ef-fectively ran out of gas in the last week or ten days. Meanwhile, the massive Republican effort almost allowed the GOP to snatch the election away. This aspect of Republican campaign planning was right on target.

The Republican campaign was better organized and more efficient than the Democratic effort but not necessarily better run or more harmonious. In fact, it may have been too organized. The campaign mounted a massive effort to produce ideas, position papers, and programs, but few of these saw the light of day. Here the quirks of the vice president's personality were a mismatch with his formidable operation. Nixon had a wealth of talent and experience at his disposal—men and women who were willing to exert themselves unstintingly on his behalf. The vice president, however, was a loner and someone who could not leave campaign details alone. He found it almost impossible to entrust his talented staff with the management of the campaign. Aggravating this tendency was his reluctance to consult or confide. This was not something new. In his 1946 and 1950 campaigns, Nixon was open to advice. In 1952, though, he began to go his own way, and by 1960, he tried to control as many details as he could. The problem was obvious. Stewart Alsop wrote, "Nixon is, and always has been, his own Jim Farley" and "his own public relations expert." Alsop added, "He is even, astonishingly, his own ghost writer." Nixon's friend Earl "Red" Blaik, the renowned football coach at West Point, wrote the candidate a long letter warning him about the problems of "physical attrition" and urging him to get "sufficient rest" during the campaign.[27]

The upshot was that Nixon did too much. He barraged Haldeman with complaints about the schedule and other logistics and drove himself ragged rewriting speeches. As Robert Finch declared: "Nixon did everything but sweep out the plane." The consequences for the campaign were damaging. The campaign structure meant nothing; Nixon made key decisions alone. This approach frustrated and infuriated his advisers, who had increasing difficulty gaining access to him. Complaints that no one could get through to the candidate mounted as the campaign proceeded. Some told Theodore White that the RNC might as well shut down. Nixon was a master political tactician, but anyone close to the campaign and even those at a distance could see that he was overextended. This adversely affected morale among his advisers and exhausted the candidate. Toward the end of the campaign, he was increasingly irritable. Occasionally, this condition had its humorous side, such as when the candidate proclaimed to Haldeman that he "didn't want to land at anymore airports." At a purely intellectual level, Nixon probably understood the drawbacks of his method, but temperamentally he seemed unable to do it any other way. As Eisenhower aide William Ewald put it: "There's no question but that he [Nixon] ran things out of his own mind. Always has and always did."[28]

For once, Nixon's famous self-discipline failed him. He could not leave the minutiae of the campaign alone. The two men who were supposed to be responsible for the direction and management of the campaign, Len Hall and Robert Finch, had little power. In late 1961, when Hall saw Nixon getting ready to make a bid for the governorship of California, he wrote him a letter warning against trying to be his own campaign manager, saying, "I am going to repeat for the hundredth time that you just can't do everything yourself."[29]

The other great liability the campaign carried was Richard Nixon's press relations. If John F. Kennedy liked reporters and reporters liked him, the reverse was true of the Republican candidate. Richard Nixon most emphatically did not admire reporters, and reporters most decidedly detested Richard Nixon. Of course, the press was not monolithic. There were reporters whom John F. Kennedy disliked, including Richard Wilson of Cowles Publications, Roscoe Drummond and Earl Mazo of the *New York Herald Tribune*, Arthur Krock of the *New York Times*, and Lyle Wilson of United Press, among others. There were members of the press who favored Nixon, including Mazo, Krock, and Drummond and Willard Edwards of the *Chicago Tribune*. Moreover, Nixon had the overwhelming support of the editors and publishers of American newspapers, something that provoked Democratic complaints. In fact, Nixon owed his rise in American politics in part to the *Los Angeles Times*, publisher Norman Chandler, and reporter Kyle Palmer. The *Times*, Chandler, and Palmer had been invaluable allies in his campaigns of 1946 and 1950. If anyone could claim press bias in those years, it was Jerry Voorhis and Helen Gahagan Douglas. Even in 1960, Nixon enjoyed a press advantage in some areas of the country. In Chicago, for example, all four daily newspapers endorsed him, and two of the four (the *Tribune* and the *Daily News*) did much to help him in their news coverage.[30]

Whatever the qualifications, the generalization remains accurate: Nixon had an enormous press problem. It manifested itself in open hostility to him. Bryce Harlow, who was aware of the problem in the abstract, traveled with the vice president in the spring of 1960 to Illinois. There he "could hardly believe what I heard and saw . . . it was frightening. Nixon was in a snake pit, not in a press conference. . . . He would respond to a question, and they would climb all over him, shout at him, snarl at him, interrupt and insult him. . . . I was aghast over the viciousness of it, the malice, the open hatred. Saliva was running. Fangs were bared. . . . It was scary. . . . You could see the bile, the poison. The press was hooked on an anti-Nixon drug and could never break the addiction." Later Nixon told Harlow that this was the least contentious press conference he had had in a long time.[31]

There were some perfectly reasonable explanations as to why the press so much preferred Kennedy. The Democrat was far more open, gregarious, humorous, and relaxed than the Republican. Nixon was more close-mouthed, a loner, highly serious with little sense of humor, and he never relaxed. John Ehrlichman observed that Nixon had good impulses, but in the presence of the press he lost spontaneity. According to Ehrlichman, Nixon's press people "were not unlike florists who were trying to sell a flower that would bloom only in absolute darkness."[32]

Urbane and witty, Kennedy espoused the cosmopolitan, liberal values in vogue with the elite power brokers of the northeastern journalistic elite. In contrast, Nixon was painfully serious and a self-proclaimed advocate of the middle-class values of the suburbs, small towns, and countryside of America. In addition, Nixon was a sentimental individual who told emotional stories about his parents and his family and the hardships and deprivations they had endured. These tales about the toy train the candidate never got or the pony his brother wanted for a Christmas present and could not have might have moved his midwestern audiences, but they alienated the news correspondents. These stories struck them as contrived, maudlin, and full of self-pity. The press felt vastly more comfortable and preferred to associate with JFK. There was nothing wrong with their pro-Kennedy inclinations as long as they understood the favoritism and did what was necessary not to allow the preference to infect their coverage. Of course, they exercised no such restraint and through 1960 generally indulged themselves in an orgy of Kennedy-worshiping and Nixon-bashing. There was almost no effort to examine or offset these prejudices; instead, they wallowed in them. In the aftermath, there was little remorse and no sense of that their behavior had been unprofessional.[33]

Many individual reporters openly supported and rooted for Kennedy and Johnson against Nixon. Theodore White joined the Nixon campaign wearing a "Kennedy for President" button and then wondered why the Californian would not talk to him. Sarah McClendon wrote to Lyndon Johnson, telling him, "We pray and believe you are winning." Tom Wicker passed along criticism of Henry Cabot Lodge Jr. to Johnson staff and then recommended that LBJ hit Nixon because "the press does not like him [Nixon]." He suggested that if the Texan became a Nixon antagonist, he would get "good press play." Earl Behrens of the *San Francisco Chronicle* said 80 percent of the California reporters were for the Democratic ticket, and Bill Becker of the *New York Times* looked forward to the Johnson campaign sending him more anti-Nixon material of the kind that he used in his recent story. Mary McGrory observed, "He [Nixon] was just so icky, so yucky—humorless, self-righteous and smarmy." Harrison Salisbury contributed the observation that in the Nixon campaign there was "a terrible sleazy quality that crept into many of his appearances."[34]

Some reporters were worse than others. William Lawrence of the *New York Times* and Phil Potter of the *Baltimore Sun* possessed the worst reputations.

At one point Rose Mary Woods became so infuriated at Lawrence that she poured a drink over his head. Hugh Sidey recollected that Potter "hated his [Nixon's] guts" and would go around "telling us all what an awful man he was and we generally believed it." According to press secretary Herb Klein, Lawrence and Potter, along with Sander Vanocur of NBC and Arthur Sylvester of the *Newark Times,* acted in concert, asking coordinated questions designed to embarrass the Republican candidate. Perhaps the ultimate indication of press favoritism for Kennedy was the Republican discovery that one member of the media contacted Kennedy headquarters before the first debate with a tip on the questions that were likely to be asked. Later, Hugh Sidey summed up the press attitude on the Nixon presidency, which had not changed from 1960—"We didn't like the way Nixon looked; we didn't like the way he acted; we didn't like the way he talked." The dislike and the hatred for Nixon were pathological. Bryce Harlow was right. It was as if a significant minority, if not a majority, of the press had been injected with some potent narcotic that sent them into an anti-Nixon frenzy.[35]

The credit for this unfortunate condition did not rest entirely with the press. The Republican candidate and his campaign were partly responsible. They did little to ameliorate the situation and much to worsen it. They seemed to prefer to wallow in the distrust, suspicion, and hatred that developed between the two parties than to do something about it. Richard Nixon was nothing if not a realist, and there were two great realities that his campaign needed to address. The first was that the majority of the reporters from the national press were Democrats. This was true in 1952 and 1956 and remained true for the rest of the twentieth century. Second, John F. Kennedy was a more attractive candidate who was more at ease with the press and someone whom it was inevitably going to favor. The real question was how to deal with these realities and mitigate the damage of press attitudes. The Nixon campaign never came to grips with this fundamental issue.

Perhaps a longer perspective would have helped. The press had favored Stevenson over Eisenhower. Barry Goldwater received worse treatment in 1964 than Nixon had four years earlier. Neither was Ronald Reagan, later in the century, a great press favorite. One might wonder, if press attitudes were a major factor in election outcomes, how the Republicans managed to win a majority of the presidential contests in the second half of the century? Dwight D. Eisenhower had the best response in his last press conference when asked if the press had been fair to him. Ike's answer was, "[W]hen you come right down to it, I don't see how a reporter could do much to a president, do you?" Eisenhower, and later Reagan, downplayed the importance and influence of the press and thereby minimized its impact. Nixon would have done well to have followed Ike's example.[36]

But it was Eisenhower who was responsible for the biggest press flap of the campaign. The incident occurred at the end of a press conference on August 24 in response to a question from Charles Mohr of *Time* concerning Richard Nixon's role in the administration and in what specific decisions he had participated. Eisenhower's famous reply that resounded through the remainder of 1960, and still resonates today, was: "If you give me a week, I might think of one." The answer was embarrassing to Nixon and immediately seized upon by Democrats. The humorous aspect of it made it even more memorable than it otherwise would have been. Many saw it as another indication of Eisenhower's latent dislike of the vice president. Whatever the reason for the response, Ike's statement was a heavy blow to the Republican claim that Nixon was better qualified for the office by virtue of his experience.

There was much more to Eisenhower's comment than met the eye. There was a long history behind it that reflected the press's baiting of the president and their attempt to drive a wedge between Eisenhower and Nixon. Reporters picked at Ike about Nixon's claims of experience and his role in the administration. The issue came up several times. Eisenhower was sensitive because of allegations that he was not fully in control of his administration. This sensitivity became especially acute after the badly managed U-2 affair. On August 24, Sarah McClendon asked, "Sir, will you tell us some of the big decisions that Mr. Nixon has participated in since you have been in the White House, and he as Vice President has been helping you?" As White House aide Robert Merriam observed, McClendon was someone "who was always asking stupid questions, and he [Eisenhower] really hated her with a purple passion. . . . She was really stupid." In the president's view, she had just asked another typically stupid question. Eisenhower responded with a long philosophical answer in which he said that he as president made the decision. He noted that he had numerous advisers, that Nixon was a principal one, and that he kept Nixon well informed because of his position as vice president. He also observed that as an army officer he was accustomed to using his staff, but the commander made the decisions. In his reply, he said, not for the first time, "I don't see why people can't understand this." He added, "When you talk about other people sharing a decision, how can they?"[37]

Apparently, neither McClendon nor others could grasp Eisenhower's logic. So, at the end of the news conference, Mohr returned to the same question accompanied by a dismissive thrust at Nixon: "I wonder whether it would be fair to assume that what you meant is that he has been primarily an observer and not a participant in the Executive Branch of the Government? . . . Many people have been trying to get at the degree that he has . . . acted in important decisions, and it is hard to pin down." The president's immediate answer began well enough, explaining that all leaders consult subordinates and advisers, but "there is no voting." He added that the vice president had taken "full part in every principal discussion" in the administration. The follow-up question did Ike in. Unwilling to give up, Mohr pressed for a specific example of a major idea of Nixon's that the president had adopted. Eisenhower, exasperated at the inability of the press to understand his point, snapped back to give him a week to think about it. Ike immediately knew he had made a mistake, but it was too late. The damage was done, and he had given the Democrats a quotation they could utilize for the balance of the campaign.[38]

This remark came early in the campaign, two and a half months before election day, by which time most people probably had forgotten about the episode. It had little effect on the election. It is more significant for what it reveals about press attitudes, especially the delight in baiting Eisenhower and denigrating Nixon. After the election, Eisenhower expressed his heartfelt regrets about this and other incidents. What Nixon thought of them he kept to himself.

The other major event of the first phase of the general election campaign was Nixon's invasion of the South. In August, he conducted two forays into former Confederate territory, the first to North Carolina and the second to Alabama and Georgia. The second trip culminated in a huge crowd in Atlanta. On the surface, these ventures were great successes. The Republican candidate encountered wildly enthusiastic audiences in a region of the country that was supposed to be solidly Democratic. Newspaper stories followed that Republicans could carry most southern states and, at the very least, Democrats would have to worry about the South.[39]

In fact, these southern excursions hurt Nixon in two ways. In Greensboro, North Carolina, in his initial journey, he banged his knee against a car door. His knee became infected and eventually he was forced to submit to hospitalization. He went into the hospital on August 29 and did not come out until September 9. Upon release, he immediately attempted to return to his campaign routine, but within a week he was sick again with a fever of 103 degrees. The chance accident in Greensboro threw his schedule off. It cost him several weeks of campaigning as well as his normally excellent health. It was also the source of his poor appearance on September 26, the night of the first television debate. One of the many ironies of the fall of 1960 was that the congenitally well Nixon spent it in poorer health than the congenitally ill Kennedy.

The second negative result of the two southern trips in August was that they fed the illusion that the Deep South could be competitive in November. They caused Nixon to invest more time, effort, and energy in the South than were warranted. As Theodore White noted, it was one of the puzzles of 1960 that Georgia, which produced such an outpouring of support for the vice president in August, gave John F. Kennedy the second-highest percentage of votes of any state in the country. The outer South (that is, Florida, Virginia, Texas, and Tennessee) was vulnerable to a Republican appeal as Eisenhower had vividly demonstrated in the previous two elections. Other southern states were long shots, although Nixon came close in the Carolinas. Any campaigning that took away from the big electoral vote states was questionable, especially because Kennedy did not have to spend comparable time. With Lyndon Johnson commanding the southern front, JFK was not distracted from the big states.

The first stage of the general election campaign came to an end. In this phase, Kennedy began poorly but ended well, while Nixon made a highly successful beginning only to encounter later setbacks. The one element that remained constant was the closeness of the race. Once the initial impression of Nixon's triumph in Chicago wore off, the Gallup Poll showed the two men deadlocked. On September 25, 1960, the eve of the first debate, Gallup released a poll showing Nixon with 47 percent, Kennedy with 46 percent, and 7 percent of the vote undecided. The candidates and the country were looking at a dead heat as John F. Kennedy and Richard M. Nixon prepared to confront each other in the first televised presidential debates in American history.[40]

6

The General Election Campaign, September 26–October 21

"Accept at once without any qualifications. Agree to meet Nixon any time, anywhere."
—J. Leonard Reinsch to JFK on how he should reply to an invitation
to participate in televised presidential debates

"The TV joint appearances will take you into practically every home in America and millions of voters will be exposed to the idea that you talk and act more like a President than Kennedy."
—Claude Robinson to Richard Nixon

In 1960, most intellectuals favored John F. Kennedy. The intellectual, though, who might have been the most influential in getting JFK elected was Charles Van Doren, a lowly Columbia University instructor of English. He assisted Kennedy by unleashing the great television quiz show scandal of the late 1950s. Van Doren was first a popular hero who captivated people with the range of his knowledge and his appealing personality on the hit TV program *Twenty-One*. He then became a villain when *Twenty-One* and other game shows were exposed for fixing their outcomes. Not for the last time, commercial television was revealed to be a sleazy enterprise that cared only about larger audiences and more advertising profits. Grand jury investigations, newspaper stories, and tearful confessions followed. So did a tidal wave of bad publicity. Television executives were desperate for ways to show themselves and their networks in a better light. Thus, sponsorship of televised debates between the presidential nominees emerged as a way to display the true civic-mindedness of the industry.[1]

There was a problem. The Federal Communications Commission interpreted section 315 of the federal communications law to require equal time for all candidates, including those of minor parties. In 1960 there were fourteen such candidates, and televised debates were a practical impossibility unless Congress agreed to do something about section 315. On June 27, 1960, Congress temporarily suspended it, freeing television moguls to exhibit their good citizenship. With John F. Kennedy and Richard M. Nixon agreeing to participate in this great experiment, American politics entered a new age, one in which election outcomes turned on what transpired on television. American politics would never be the same.[2]

Although there have been numerous other televised presidential debates (every election from 1976 to the present), none has ever matched the initial series, perhaps because they were the first and perhaps because the Kennedy and Nixon duo was more interesting than any subsequent pair of rivals. The Kennedy-Nixon encounters became the signature event of the 1960 election and dominated the campaign for almost a month. Fifty years later they remain a subject of interest and controversy.

The first important question is why Richard Nixon agreed to debate. Almost everyone on the Republican side at the time thought it would be a mistake. Eisenhower argued that the candidate representing the "ins" should never take on an "out" in a debate. In the president's opinion, "the latter is free to say anything he wants since there is no test of responsibility or ability to make good on proposals." There were other powerful arguments against it. On the most practical level, Nixon's biggest advantage over his rival was his position as vice president, the experience it represented, and the greater public familiarity that derived from it. Simply by appearing on the same stage with John F. Kennedy, the Republican nominee would diminish these advantages while giving the Massachusetts senator the opportunity to establish himself as the equal of the vice president. Kennedy did not have to outperform Nixon. He just had to appear equal. From this standpoint alone, the decision made no sense.[3]

As the representative of the incumbent administration, the vice president would inevitably be on the defensive as the challenger criticized the administration and its policies. On the domestic front, the defensive position the vice president would be forced into might be annoying, but it posed no special dangers. On foreign policy issues, there were serious problems. Kennedy could attack freely, saying almost anything that was politically advantageous to him. In contrast, as a member of the administration, Nixon's statements could and would prejudice existing policy positions. In addition, Nixon possessed knowledge that he could not reveal for national security reasons. On these grounds as well, the vice president would have been well advised to have sidestepped the debates. Herb Klein recalled that Nixon had made this very argument; when Klein heard that Nixon had reversed himself, he "almost fell over."[4]

Analysts of 1960 have advanced two theories of Nixon's apparently inexplicable decision. The first is that Nixon believed in his own debating superiority, underestimated his Democratic opponent, and agreed to the debates out of overconfidence. Theodore White related a story of Richard

Nixon at home, with two unnamed friends, watching Kennedy's Los Angeles acceptance speech on television. According to White, the vice president was unimpressed with Kennedy's delivery, with the content of the speech, and with various technical flaws. In the course of the viewing, Nixon remarked that he "could take this man on TV." Whether Nixon ever made this comment is open to question, although there is little reason to doubt that he was confident of his debating abilities.[5]

The other explanation for the Nixon decision is a psychological one. According to this theory, the vice president wanted to demonstrate that he was his own man, and he could not avoid the debates without making himself appear afraid to face JFK. In addition, Nixon resented the confinement the vice presidency represented. The presidential nomination liberated him from having to take orders from Eisenhower and the president's staff. He could make his own decisions and rely on himself. Thus, the decision to debate Kennedy was part of Nixon's declaration of independence. One aide recalled, "There was a very definite feeling in my mind that Nixon wanted to win on his own."[6]

These explanations are not mutually exclusive; there is some truth in both. Nixon was proud of his record as a debater and of the great success of the 1952 televised Checkers speech. He considered Kennedy the strongest possible Democratic nominee, but he did not foresee how formidable an opponent the Massachusetts senator would be. The Californian was convinced that he had to establish his own independent identity beyond that of Eisenhower's vice president. He knew that Kennedy would attack him mercilessly if he ducked the Democratic nominee.

There were other considerations as well. Nixon was correct in recognizing that once Congress suspended section 315 and brought the possibility of televised presidential debates to the verge of reality, he was in an impossible situation. To debate Kennedy was a mistake. To refuse to engage him gave Kennedy an issue on which he could attack Nixon. Moreover, it would undercut Nixon's argument that he was the better of the two to represent the United States in foreign affairs. Inevitably, the Kennedy campaign would argue that if Nixon was not willing to confront John Kennedy, he could not stand up to dangerous foreign leaders.

The obvious solution to this quandary was to derail the presidential debates before they became a real possibility. White House aide Robert Merriam recalled a legislative leaders' meeting in late 1959 or early 1960 that included Eisenhower and Nixon as well as the congressional leadership of the GOP. According to Merriam, GOP House minority leader Charles Halleck suggested that there was "an obscure bill" in the House Rules Committee that Republicans could and should kill. This was the legislation to suspend section 315 and allow televised debates between the principal candidates. Eisenhower's reaction was to turn to Nixon and say, "Well, Dick . . . It's going to be your campaign, what do you think?" In Merriam's account, Nixon, "without batting an eyelash," said, "Let the bill go through."[7] If Republicans had killed the bill at this point, there would have been no possibility of televised debates and no blame could have attached itself to Nixon. But the vice president did not act to kill the possibility of televised debates. There is every indication that he welcomed the opportunity to debate.

Why Nixon welcomed the debates is best understood through his exchanges with his pollster, Claude Robinson, a man who enjoyed Nixon's trust and confidence and with whom he worked closely. Their thinking on election strategy and tactics was almost identical. Significantly, Robinson was the one man on the GOP side who actually welcomed the prospect of debates. Writing after the decision for debates had been made, Robinson told the vice president, in his opinion, the television encounters "despite their hazards, are likely to benefit you."[8]

Robinson based his belief that the debates would work to Nixon's advantage on his analysis of Nixon's fundamental strategic problem. In 1960, Democrats outnumbered Republicans nationwide. When combined with public preferences for Democratic control of Congress and the Democratic majorities in the House, the Senate, and the governorships, the GOP appeared to be so institutionally weak that Nixon was bound to lose unless he broadened his appeal to attract large numbers of Democrats and independents. With lingering partisan antagonisms from the 1950s compounded by unfavorable press and television coverage, the vice president's chances of winning sufficient numbers of such voters were dim, indeed.[9]

From the perspective of Nixon and Robinson, the televised debates offered the vice president the forum to appeal directly to the two voter groups, without having his views filtered and distorted by intermediaries. According to Robinson, "The TV joint appearances will take you into practically every home in America and millions of voters will be exposed to the idea that you talk and act more like a President than Kennedy."[10] Whatever advantages the debates offered his Democratic rival, Nixon felt that he could not pass up this one great opportunity to reach the voters he needed to win the election. The political arithmetic dictated his actions. Nixon was willing to give Kennedy the exposure he wanted in order to obtain the audience he believed he needed.

The problem with this rationale was that Nixon gave up far more than he obtained. Ironically, as the vice president worried about his standing with

Democrats and independents, a Democratic survey, taken in early 1960, downgraded his problem. The Democratic analysis noted that Nixon's vulnerability rested "primarily in his identification with the Republican Party." The survey went on to say: "the public's awareness of the McCarthyite activities of Nixon (Voorhis campaign, Douglas campaign, attacks on Truman and Stevenson) has been small. The image of Nixon as a ruthless opportunist has been held only by a very small per cent of the people, almost all of them Democrats. . . . All in all, Nixon had a reasonably good reputation with the people, and is currently about as popular as our two best-known candidates." In other words, Nixon's and Robinson's fears about his low standing with Democrats and independents were exaggerated.[11]

In any event, the Nixon camp should have sensed how badly JFK wanted the debates and driven a harder bargain. After the Democratic nominee received a telephone call from the president of NBC extending an invitation to participate in TV debates, Kennedy called his chief television adviser, J. Leonard Reinsch, who would negotiate the terms of the debates, and asked him what to do. Reinsch replied: "Accept at once without any qualifications. Agree to meet Nixon any time, anywhere." Reinsch wanted as many debates as he could get. In his view, every time Kennedy and Nixon appeared together, Kennedy won. Fewer debates would have been better for Nixon. The two sides settled eventually at four—a Kennedy victory. In the end, none of the ground rules were especially favorable to the Republican candidate.[12]

The Nixon headquarters had one last opportunity to wage psychological warfare on the debates. With the Republican candidate in poor physical condition after his hospitalization, the GOP could have, and should have, insisted on a week's delay. Instead, Nixon and Republican leaders proceeded as if nothing was amiss. They did nothing to try to throw the Democrats off their timing as the big day approached.

There are many accounts of the first debate, and all agree that the event was a triumph for John F. Kennedy. On the Republican side, just about everything that could go wrong did go wrong. The outcome was more than mere coincidence. Kennedy took the occasion more seriously, prepared for it better, and had a better plan going into the debate. He rested and devoted considerable time to prepare for the encounter. JFK arrived at the television studio cool, calm, confident, and relaxed. He looked like "a young Adonis." In contrast, Nixon got to his Chicago hotel late on Sunday, spent Monday morning campaigning, and rushed through debate preparations in the afternoon. When he arrived at the TV studio, he cracked his knee in getting out of the car. Nixon was tired and still showing the effects of his illness and hospitalization. To his friends and neutral observers, Nixon's appearance was troubling. Television adviser Ted Rogers, who had not seen him recently, was stunned by his "gray and ashen" face and his shirt that "hung loosely around his neck like that of a dying man." Howard K. Smith, who moderated the debate, thought that Nixon looked "depressed" and like a man "who knew he'd made a mistake." Edward Folliard of the *Washington Post* recalled that "he looked ghastly." Nixon's enemies in the press and the Kennedy camp were less kind. Ben Bradlee thought the vice president looked like "an awkward cadaver." Richard Goodwin believed that the Republican appeared "more like a losing football coach summoned before the board of trustees than a leader of the free world" and professed to believe that "What we saw on Nixon's face that night was the panic in his soul."[13]

Whether Kennedy's tanned, confident appearance bothered Nixon is a matter of dispute. He recalled that his impression of Kennedy was that he "had never seen him look more fit" and commented on the Democrat's deep tan. On the other hand, Nixon also maintained that he felt he was "as thoroughly prepared for this appearance" as he "had ever been in my political life up to that time." What cannot be doubted is that Nixon's bearing and demeanor could have done nothing but increase the Democrat's confidence. There followed the famous makeup incident in which Kennedy rejected the use of makeup (although Ted Rogers later claimed that he utilized something), and Nixon, apparently in response, also refused. The result, as is well known, was to make Nixon look even worse.[14]

Nixon's cavalier approach to this event is difficult to explain. A few partial answers suggest themselves. In Nixon's greatest television triumph, the Checkers speech, he had proceeded as he did in Chicago in September 1960. There had been a stand-in substitute for lighting and sound adjustments, and no studio rehearsals. He had arrived and spoken. That became his way of doing things, and he was not open to advice. It is also true that Nixon was focused on what he would say and how he would respond. To him, it was a debate, and he would win or lose based on his remarks, not his physical appearance and not the technical details of the television production. He underestimated Kennedy, but he also probably calculated that his superior debating and political experience would compensate for any shortcomings in preparation and allow him to prevail.[15]

The debate itself did not go a great deal better than the preliminaries for the Republican candidate. John F. Kennedy performed brilliantly. He succeeded on the basis of two great understandings. The first was that on television, appearance did count—and Kennedy was at his cool, calm best. Televised presidential debates were not an intellectual contest. True debating and substantive argument were tangential to the central elements of the television extravaganza. In the most important qualities, John F. Kennedy started with an inherent advantage. As Ted Rogers, Nixon's television adviser noted, "it is almost impossible to take a bad picture of JFK," while "It is very easy to take a bad picture of RN." Second, Kennedy understood that, although advertised as a debate, he would not win or lose on the basis of scoring points, but on how effectively he came into people's homes and reassured them of his competence and his ability. In other words, Kennedy's most important audience was the American public in their living rooms rather than his debating partner, the media panel posing the questions, or the audience in the TV studio. He also demonstrated his quick intelligence and his wide-ranging knowledge. JFK had a good day.[16]

In spite of the later perceptions, the newspaper reaction to the debate was not overwhelming, and Kennedy did not immediately emerge in the press as the big winner. In fact, the debate was not even the top story in the *Washington Post* on September 27. The initial response was generally favorable, although the tabloid *New York Daily News* ran an editorial "Lincoln and Douglas Did Better," and the *Los Angeles Times* described what it called "the great electronic experiment" as a "dud." News stories and columnists treated the debate cautiously. The most common tendency was to congratulate both men and proclaim the outcome a draw. The *Washington Post* headline read, "Big Debate Viewed as Dead Heat." Joseph Alsop, the Kennedy admirer, declared that both JFK and Nixon "were in fact enormously impressive." Later, of course, as analysts and the public decided that John F. Kennedy had won decisively, that became the agreed-upon version of the story, although it took time for it to emerge.[17]

Interestingly enough, most people who had listened to the debate on the radio concluded that Nixon won by a narrow margin. Lyndon Johnson was one of those. As he took in the exchange, he kept score, recording "one for Nixon" or "one for the boy." At the end, LBJ had the Republican as winner. Even most of those who had seen the encounter in the television studio, such as Joseph Alsop or Howard K. Smith, tended to see the outcome as a draw or a small win for Nixon. What really mattered, though, were the tens of millions who absorbed the debate on television, and the verdict from them gradually, but unambiguously, favored John F. Kennedy.[18]

There was no delay in the political reaction to the Monday night event. Enthusiasm, exhilaration, and relief immediately gripped Democratic politicians. The day before the debate, Ohio senator Frank Lausche indicated that he would not appear with Kennedy at a scheduled appearance in Cleveland on Tuesday, September 27, the day following the first debate. The morning after the debate, Lausche presented himself at 7:30 A.M., demanding to join the motorcade through Ohio. Ten of eleven southern governors (Ross Barnett of Mississippi being the exception) issued a public endorsement of JFK. Theodore White wrote that one of his most striking memories from 1960 was "the quantum jump in the size of crowds that greeted the campaign Senator from the morrow of the first debate to the morning of Tuesday, September 27th, when he began to campaign in northern Ohio." According to White, they now "seethed with enthusiasm and multiplied in numbers, as if the sight of him, in their homes on the video box, had given him a 'star quality' reserved only for television and movie idols."[19]

The invigoration of the Kennedy campaign was the most significant result of the first television debate and, indeed, of the debates as a whole. Although Democrats never admitted it, vast numbers of the party faithful, from the rank-and-file to the top officeholders, entertained profound doubts about John F. Kennedy, his qualifications, his experience, and his readiness to lead the country. Because of their obsession with the sinister image of Richard Nixon exemplified by the political cartoons of Herblock, Democrats feared that the vice president might demolish him in a televised confrontation. In short, there was widespread apprehension that Kennedy v. Nixon could turn into a Democratic debacle.

When the debate proved not to be a disaster, feelings of relief and exhilaration washed over Democrats, party officials, as well as casual voters. In a curious way, although it was hardly planned, Kennedy benefited from the lower expectations. When his performance far exceeded Democratic hopes, the result was a decisive public relations victory. Democratic officeholders, at least those outside the South, rushed to associate themselves with him while his crowds became much larger and more enthusiastic. The reaction was a tribute both to JFK and to the power of television.

On the Republican side, it was mostly doom and gloom. If Kennedy exceeded expectations, Nixon failed to rise to the occasion. Republican complaints fell into two categories. The first revolved around the vice president's appearance. The parents of Rose Mary Woods called Nixon's secretary to ask if he was sick because he looked ill and tired on television. Eisenhower, television consultant Robert Montgomery, and press secretary Jim Hagerty viewed a tape recording and "didn't like it." To them, Nixon "looked bad. . . . He had a shirt on that was his normal size, and it was hanging down around his neck." Nixon heard these and similar comments often enough that he was forced to agree, although he continued to maintain he "had never felt better mentally before any important appearance than . . . before the first debate."[20]

The other predominant criticism was that the vice president had been too passive, had agreed with Kennedy too much, and had taken it too easy and not hit back. Nixon friend Julius Klein wrote him to say he and his associates were "disappointed." Klein declared that, in his view, the vice president was "one of the toughest, most plain spoken campaigners who ever came down the pike in American politics," but "That didn't show up last night." Eisenhower and Hagerty concurred that Nixon's first comment that he agreed with Kennedy in his first set of remarks was a mistake. Running mate Henry Cabot Lodge Jr. stated that the nominee "gave the appearance of allowing Kennedy to take the initiative away from him. He [Nixon] appeared on the defensive."[21]

Just as Kennedy profited from exceeding expectations that were too low, Nixon suffered from failing to live up to excessively high ones. In fact, the first debate was not a total disaster for Nixon. Kennedy reaped the rewards of September 26. But those rewards focused largely on Democratic voters. There was little indication that the first debate exerted any real influence on Republicans or independents.

Furthermore, Nixon accomplished certain objectives in the first debate. Before the debate he told Eisenhower that he was "going to play it low key. He was going to be gentlemanly." Nixon avoided shrill, partisan sloganeering and made a statesmanlike appeal to voters, including Democrats and independents, that belied his reputation. With the debate on domestic policy, he did his best to sound progressive on social questions. If the major motivation of the debates for Nixon was the opportunity to speak directly to millions of Democrats and independents and present himself as a serious, reasonable candidate who had their interests at heart, he accomplished that objective. Unfortunately for him, Kennedy's performance was so scintillating that it tended to eclipse everything else.[22]

On the Republican side, Claude Robinson agreed with the vice president's approach in the first debate. Robinson argued that "Voters judged the debate through the glasses of their partisanship." Kennedy's greatest achievement was to strengthen his position with Democrats. Nixon's problem was that the GOP was the minority party and therefore to win "must draw some Democratic and a good many Independent votes." For Robinson, the idea that Nixon needed to get tough and start hitting Kennedy hard was a prescription for disaster. By his polling, the vice president already had 93 percent of the Republican vote. Nixon could not gain the Democratic and independent votes he needed by making partisan Republican appeals. As far as Robinson was concerned, he could not "for the life of me figure out any different strategy than RN is following right now." Robinson worried that what he called the "'raw meat' fellows" would prevail and Nixon would drastically escalate the partisan rhetoric—a sure road to defeat in November.[23]

The top levels of the GOP concluded that the first debate was "a setback—but not a disaster," as Nixon himself put it in 1962. Lodge concurred, and so did Eisenhower. The three subsequent debates (October 7, 13, and 21) provided the Kennedy campaign with additional momentum. Nixon's appearance and performance improved, but the central reality of the debates did not change. John F. Kennedy was more telegenic than Richard M. Nixon. Kennedy projected an image of a candidate who was cool and collected, yet energetic and dynamic. Nixon was not bad on television, but Kennedy was one of the two or three American politicians of the second half of the twentieth century best suited to the medium. As NBC television producer Reuven Frank observed, "The cameras loved him [JFK], and it was not unrequited." No matter how much Nixon improved, he could not match Kennedy.[24]

The last three debates never matched the interest or audience size of the first one, although the infighting between the two candidates became tougher. Nixon did better, and, after the second debate, James Reston reported that Nixon's supporters "were pleased and even delighted." Claude Robinson subsequently told Nixon that his survey indicated that the vice president had "won." Interestingly enough, the Kennedy camp was also happy with the outcome, and Lou Harris informed Kennedy he had "won."[25]

Nixon did better because foreign policy—Nixon's strong suit—dominated the second and third debates. The issue of Quemoy and Matsu appeared at the end of the second debate and continued into the third, in which it was the most discussed subject. Quemoy and Matsu were two very small islands off the Chinese coast that Chiang Kai-shek's government controlled. The military forces of the Chinese People's Republic periodically threatened to attack them and thereby to exert pressure on the United States. There were two crises over these islands in the 1950s in which President Eisenhower and Secretary of State Dulles played a high-stakes game of brinksmanship with the government in Beijing, but without ever conclusively stating that the United States would use its military forces to defend the islands.

When Quemoy and Matsu arose as a point of dispute in the presidential campaign, Nixon seized on it to bludgeon his Democratic opponent. From Nixon's perspective, it was an excellent issue with which to attack Kennedy's foreign policy. He put Kennedy at a disadvantage by portraying him as the advocate of withdrawal and retreat. Kennedy attempted to turn the matter to his advantage by raising the question of risking war over flyspeck islands. Each side exaggerated the other's position. More experts agreed with Kennedy, but, in political terms, Nixon had the better of the argument. By the end of the third debate, members of the Kennedy camp were imploring Secretary of State Christian Herter to get Nixon to agree to terminate the discussion. As they presented it, Kennedy did not want to give the Chinese the impression that the United States was not in agreement on the issue. JFK was prepared to modify his position so as not to appear in conflict with the administration if Nixon would just drop the subject. Nixon did so, after pointing out the Democratic nominee's handling of it reflected his inexperience.[26]

An even more dangerous intrusion into American foreign policy by the debates and presidential politics occurred in the fourth debate. This time the subject was Cuba, Fidel Castro, his increasingly anti-American orientation, and the correct response to it. The underlying issues were Kennedy's need to show toughness and the possibility of military action against Castro and Cuba before the November election. The Kennedy campaign was clearly worried. Nixon had successfully bested Kennedy on foreign policy issues, most recently in the exchange over Quemoy and Matsu. Cuba offered Kennedy an opportunity to strike back. It was a Republican vulnerability, and Kennedy made much of it during 1960. During the discussion of the Chinese offshore islands, he emphasized more than once the incongruity of Nixon's desire to stand firm there, while simultaneously doing nothing about the growing menace ninety miles from the United States. Kennedy attempted to exploit Cuba to offset his apparent weakness on Quemoy and Matsu.

But the Pearl of the Antilles posed a potential danger as well as an opportunity for JFK. Rumors of possible military action against Castro swirled around the campaign. Any such action before the election would undercut Kennedy's criticism, rally voters around the president, and almost certainly provide an immense boost to Nixon's candidacy. For all these reasons, Cuba was of great concern to JFK. Kennedy talked tough on Cuba, so tough that he began to provoke criticism from his liberal supporters. After one speech in late September, Harvard academician David Riesman wrote to Louis Harris saying that he and the Kennedy supporters were "horrified" by JFK's "extravagantly bellicose speech." Riesman suggested that in comparison to Theodore Roosevelt's famous maxim, Kennedy "wants to carry five big sticks and speak savagely." The Massachusetts senator was not worried about the Harvard vote. What concerned him was the possibility that the Eisenhower administration might launch a military effort to overthrow Fidel Castro just before election day. He and other Democrats harbored vivid memories of 1956, when twin crises over Suez and Hungary had hit in October and destroyed what was left of the Stevenson campaign.[27]

In fact, not only Kennedy, but also Castro and Khrushchev worried that an invasion would occur before the election. But it was not to be. The United States was indeed training a large number of Cuban exiles in Central America with the intention of launching them against Castro. The original target date for the operation was September 1960 and then October. Eisenhower, however, proved unwilling to proceed until a Cuban government-in-exile was established. When he decided the original concept of relying primarily on anti-Castro forces in Cuba would not work and insufficient progress on the establishment of the government-in-exile had been made, he refused to go ahead with any attack before the end of his administration. Planning then shifted to the landing of a military force. Richard Nixon urged action, but he was not making the decisions.[28]

On the eve of the fourth debate, the Cuban issue exploded when the Kennedy campaign issued a statement charging the administration with "doing nothing for 6 years" and "standing helplessly by" in an "incredible history of blunder, inaction, retreat and failure." JFK called for overt support for anti-Castro rebels: "we must attempt to strengthen the non-Batista democratic anti-Castro forces in exile, and in Cuba itself, who offer eventual hope of overthrowing Castro. Thus far these fighters for freedom have had virtually no support from our government." The language of the press release, while ambiguous, suggested that Kennedy wanted military action against Castro. The story dominated newspaper headlines and the following night's debate. The Kennedy press release enraged Nixon because he knew Kennedy had received briefings from Director of Central Intelligence Allen Dulles. The vice president assumed from these briefings that his opponent had to be aware of the administration's military preparations.[29]

There were two distinct points of contention over the Cuban brouhaha of October. The first was over the statement itself and whether Kennedy actually saw and approved it. Richard Goodwin later took responsibility, saying that he rephrased the standard Kennedy position and issued the press release without the candidate's review to meet newspaper deadlines. He did this, Goodwin said, because the candidate was asleep and he did not want to awake him. Goodwin maintained that "It was the only public statement the candidate made in the entire campaign that he had not personally reviewed." If accurate, Goodwin's explanation exculpated Kennedy from direct responsibility for the declaration. However, the most thorough examination of the chronology by Herbert Parmet concludes that the Kennedy aide's account was untrue and manufactured to try and absolve JFK of responsibility.[30]

The more serious question was whether Kennedy made his declaration with full knowledge that the Eisenhower administration was proceeding with a plan to overthrow Castro. This is what Nixon believed, and it infuriated him. As he asserted: "For the first and only time in the campaign, I got mad at Kennedy—personally."[31]

The Kennedy court historians have consigned this event to the memory hole. It reflects badly on the Democratic candidate and his willingness to misrepresent a critical issue for political gain. The evidence is overwhelming that Kennedy knew that the Eisenhower administration was engaged in developing a military operation against Castro, although the Democrat could accurately claim that no one had briefed him on "invasion plans" since no specific plan had existed when Dulles talked to Kennedy in 1960.[32]

This affair increased Nixon's suspicions of the CIA. The intelligence agency was a creature of the Ivy League and the social elite. Many prominent journalists, including the Alsops, Phil Graham, James Reston, and Ben Bradlee, had a cozy relationship with the agency and its members. The culture of the CIA was quite comfortable with the idea of John F. Kennedy as president and even favored his election. Richard Bissell, the number-two man at the CIA, sent messages via Adlai Stevenson to Kennedy that he would be willing to take a leave of absence in order to work in his presidential campaign. About a month before the election, Bissell received a call from an intermediary, telling him that the Democratic candidate wanted to talk to him. In the course of the conversation, Kennedy raised a number of topics on which Bissell commented. The CIA man maintained that since he was still in government he could do "nothing of an active nature for him," but he also asserted that he "agreed with most of his philosophy." Bissell contended that he was "sure" that he had informed Allen Dulles of the contact and "probably" had reported to him after the meeting.[33]

There are other reasons to think that Kennedy was aware that the administration planned to act against Cuba. JFK's favorite southern governor, John Patterson of Alabama, told the candidate sometime in mid-October before the fourth debate that an invasion was imminent. Patterson could speak with authority because the Alabama Air National Guard was involved in training anticommunist Cuban forces. The head of the state's air national guard, who commuted between Alabama and Central America, told the governor, "Any morning now you're going to read in the morning newspaper when you wake up where we've invaded Cuba." This statement prompted Patterson to request an immediate meeting with Kennedy.[34]

There were two additional tantalizing indications of the Kennedy camp's knowledge of an anti-Castro military operation, although both came after the fourth debate. On October 25, Robert F. Kennedy received a telephone call reporting "invasion fever" in Guatemala and hinting that some military action could be in the offing. Then, in early November, J. Edgar Hoover reported to the vice president on an October 31 conversation between French ambassador Hervé Alphand and George Ball, a close associate of Adlai Stevenson. The FBI report on the conversation indicated that Ball was worried about the situation in Cuba, thought an invasion could come that week, and feared the impact on the election would be similar to what had occurred in 1956. In Ball's opinion, an invasion would produce a "terrible atmosphere for the election." Ball's information was good enough to say that the invasion would come from a Cuban force in Central America. If George Ball possessed this kind of intelligence, so did John F. Kennedy. With the warnings from Patterson and Ball, with Kennedy's close association with Florida senator George Smathers, and with the loose talk and poor security in Florida, it exceeds the bounds of credulity to believe that Kennedy's statements on Cuba in October were not calculated in their intent. His chief motivation was probably defensive in nature. Knowing that a military strike before the election was a distinct possibility, Kennedy performed preemptive damage control. His aggressive statements put him in a position to claim that he had been first to advocate a military solution.[35]

When the subject of Cuba arose in the fourth debate, Nixon launched into a lengthy and devastating criticism of the Kennedy position. The vice president explained in great detail the disadvantages of what Kennedy proposed and predicted the undesirable repercussions that would come from it. It was a brilliant explication of why such action was undesirable. The only trouble was, as Stephen Ambrose suggested, that Nixon "did not believe a word of what he said."[36]

In retrospect, the spectacle of Kennedy's advocacy of military intervention against Castro and Nixon's probing critique of it gave the final debate its surrealistic character. Kennedy's position presented the vice president with a golden opportunity. He could have stated that the Eisenhower administration was addressing the issue and had a number of plans under consideration. He then could have added that Kennedy had received briefings on the subject and knew that he was endangering national security with his reckless statements. It could have been the decisive moment in the debates, but, for whatever reasons, Nixon passed up this grand chance. In his memoirs, Nixon observed that he doubted that "they [televised debates] can ever serve a responsible role in defining the issues of a presidential campaign." He was right, but he was also someone who had welcomed the debates in the first place.[37]

Whether the debates were more showmanship than statesmanship, as Nixon believed, they did have an effect on voter perceptions, largely to the advantage of John F. Kennedy. The debates, especially the first one, sparked enthusiasm in Kennedy's crowds and produced a sense of optimism and momentum that was reflected in newspaper and television coverage. The favorable media notices generated more crowds and more crowd enthusiasm. The debates proved a perpetual source of energy for the Kennedy campaign. Perhaps even without the debates, the Kennedy effort would have taken off, but there can be little doubt that the debates and the reaction to them gave the Democratic candidate momentum.

This Kennedy surge coincided with the debates and carried through the third week of October. In Arthur Schlesinger Jr.'s recollection, by mid-September, JFK's "intelligence and intensity were beginning to command the attention of the electorate." By mid-October, one began to feel "the real Kennedy was coming over." Kennedy's speaking improved while he continued to lace his addresses with allusions to Charles Dickens, Otto von Bismarck, Rudyard Kipling, Winston Churchill, Ralph Waldo Emerson, T. S. Eliot, and Robert Frost, among others. Joe Alsop reported that, in what he called "the Kennedy campaign safari," "the buoyancy, the optimism, the sense of being on a rising curve, are now so strong, they are all but tangible." He added that one could not doubt that the candidate "has somehow captured the imagination of enormous numbers of the American people." In early October, Alsop saw Kennedy on the verge of "a major break-through." As Kennedy campaigned, there were increasing numbers of "jumpers," usually young girls, who leaped at the candidate, and "touchers," also young girls or women, who would yell: "I can't get near enough. I'll touch you and you touch him for me." In upper New York State, one observer witnessed a Kennedy tide unseen since the days of FDR.[38]

Meanwhile, Lyndon Johnson was proving his worth in the South. Early national reaction to LBJ was not positive. Various surveys showed that of the four candidates for president and vice president, Johnson was the least respected. This may have been true, but Kennedy did not need Johnson in the North. Where he needed him was the South, and there Johnson went to work. The initial reports in the wake of Nixon's two trips south in August suggested the possibility of a strong Republican showing. By mid-September, this sense had waned, and in the next month Johnson conducted his famous "Cornpone Special," a railroad whistle-stop that traversed eight states, welcomed more than 1,200 state and local officials and almost two hundred media people on the train, took more than one thousand pictures, and featured forty-nine stops and fifty-seven LBJ speeches. One of the first stops was Culpeper, Virginia, where LBJ gave a stemwinder and then, as the train was pulling out, yelled, "I ask you what has Dick Nixon ever done for Culpeper?" The crowd applauded, but one old farmer piped up, "Hell, I'll ask you what anybody ever did for Culpeper!" At every whistle-stop, the local bands played "The Yellow Rose of Texas" so that everyone on the train got sick and tired of it. LBJ finished a speech at one location with, "Now God bless you . . . and remember to vote Democratic," and then, thinking the microphone was off, yelled at Bobby Baker, "And Bobby, turn off that goddamned 'Yellow Rose of Texas.'" LBJ's exhortation to Baker came right out over the speaker for all to hear.[39]

LBJ press secretary George Reedy remembered the 1960 campaign as "a nightmare for the staff—a weird collage of beratings, occasional drunken prowls up and down hotel corridors, and frantic efforts to sober him up in the mornings." Johnson was unhappy much of the time and made periodic threats to leave the campaign. In spite of this behavior, LBJ was effective. He reached the Democratic courthouse politicians of the South with his message that Kennedy was better than Nixon, and that nothing would come out of Washington that would threaten southern political interests. He also helped defuse the independent elector movement that threatened the Democratic ticket in a number of southern states.[40]

On the Republican side, the dynamics for the September 26–October 21 period were just the opposite. The perception grew, fed by the debates and the news reports coming out of the campaign, that Nixon was losing ground. News reports portrayed a sullen and withdrawn candidate, and a campaign characterized by discontent and a growing defeatism. Part of the problem was that the news coming out of New York was almost all bad. The Empire State had the most electoral votes in the country. It was the nation's media and financial center. Whatever happened in New York was amplified throughout the entire nation, and the outlook there was "grim." The situation in New York undoubtedly increased GOP apprehensions.[41]

Morale in the Nixon campaign seemed low. Speechwriters came and went because Nixon insisted on rewriting their efforts. Chief scheduler James Bassett increasingly felt ignored. The already antagonistic press picked up on the discontent in the ranks and emphasized it in their reporting. Nixon drove himself relentlessly to the point of exhaustion on a daily basis. H. R. Haldeman recalled that Nixon often disappeared in the middle of the night during campaign trips with only the Secret Service following him. He could be found looking "haggard and wan" in "a flea-bitten coffee shop." His military aide, Major Don Hughes, reminisced about one night in Fresno, California, when Nixon was asleep on his feet and Hughes had to put him to bed.[42]

The low point for Nixon came in mid-October. With Kennedy riding the crest of a wave of popularity based on the first two debates, there was a general sense that the Democrat nominee was establishing a significant lead and the Republican candidate was being left in the wake. A certain amount of the bandwagon mentality that dominated the second half of October was the product of the prodigious Kennedy publicity machine, but even Nixon loyalists were dismayed and convinced that something had to change to get the Republican campaign back on the right track. Henry Cabot Lodge Jr. made an embarrassing statement promising that Nixon would name an African American to his cabinet. This displeased the South, but even among African Americans, the pledge was viewed unsympathetically as a crude attempt to buy black votes. Lodge, after a good start, turned into a disappointment with his leisurely campaign style and his inability to match Lyndon Johnson.[43]

Obviously, some things had gone poorly for Nixon, but there is a legitimate question as to whether the situation in October was as bad as it seemed from the perspective of the New York–Washington axis or as it subsequently appeared in the accounts of Camelot. Claude Robinson's polling painted a more optimistic picture. Robinson's figures indicated some decline for Nixon, largely concentrated in the East. According to the pollster, Kennedy's greatest achievement in the debates had been to bring back doubtful Democrats but without making much headway with independents. In early and mid-October, Robinson showed Nixon at 50 percent in the popular vote and in a favorable position for getting the 269 electoral votes he needed to become president. In his evaluation of the campaign in mid-October, Robinson had Nixon above 50 percent in states with 259 electoral votes. Robinson portrayed Nixon leading in Ohio, Illinois, Texas, and California. The Gallup Poll presented a less favorable outlook for the

GOP candidate, but it still showed a very close race. It had Nixon behind 49 to 46 percent in one poll released on October 12 and 49 to 45 percent in another survey published on October 26. Neither indicated a great Kennedy wave.[44]

Nixon was not as glum as the press thought he should have been, presumably because of Robinson's polls. Even if the vice president was correct and the situation not so dire, he had to welcome the end of the debates on October 21, 1960. Kennedy had gained ground in the four weeks since the first joint appearance. It was no coincidence that, freed of having to contest Kennedy face-to-face in the electronic medium, Nixon soon mounted a comeback.[45]

7

Civil Rights and the General Election Campaign

"I've got a suitcase of votes and I'm going to take them to Mr. Kennedy and dump them in his lap."

—Martin Luther King Sr. after JFK assisted in Martin Luther King Jr.'s release from a Georgia prison

As the presidential debates ended in rancor over Cuba, another event that attracted relatively little attention at the time influenced the presidential race and symbolized a rising issue that would loom large in American politics in the 1960s. The event was the jailing of Martin Luther King Jr. The subsequent turmoil over it injected King and civil rights into the presidential campaign and offered a portent of things to come.

When John F. Kennedy formally announced his candidacy on January 2, 1960, he did not know who Louis Martin was. In fact, according to one observer, JFK was not aware of the Congress of Racial Equality (CORE). Ten months later, Louis Martin was one of the individuals responsible for John Kennedy's victory in the general election. Although it would be an exaggeration to portray civil rights at the center of the Kennedy campaign or the presidential race, it was becoming a major social and political issue. One of the important stories of 1960 is how John F. Kennedy and Richard M. Nixon dealt with the race issue, of which the celebrated Martin Luther King Jr. incident was the most visible manifestation.[1]

In the world in which John F. Kennedy grew up, there was little contact with African Americans.[2] Even as late as 1960, America remained to a large extent a collection of island communities, as the historian Robert Wiebe has phrased it. Outside the South and a few other areas, one could live and have little or no day-to-day contact with African Americans. The United States of 1960 was a country where long-distance telephone calls were still an adventure, where telephone exchanges still bore names, and where jet travel was new. Blacks simply were not a factor in the everyday life of John F. Kennedy or Richard M. Nixon. The Californian probably had marginally more exposure to blacks and other minorities in his years before coming to Washington. The only African American Kennedy spent any time with was his valet George Thomas, who, according to Richard Reeves, had "literally been a gift from Arthur Krock, who had repaid past favors from Joe Kennedy by sending Thomas over to take care of Congressman Jack Kennedy."[3]

Although both men possessed a sense of fair play and equal treatment, until they came to Washington in 1947, race was not a matter that impinged on their lives and thought. Even after 1947, it had minimal impact. Both Kennedy and Nixon were much more interested in foreign policy issues and Nixon in communist subversion. From their appearance in Washington in 1947 until 1960, civil rights was at best a secondary or tertiary concern for them.

If John F. Kennedy had no particular associations with African Americans, he did possess a natural antipathy for discrimination, since Irish Americans had been the target of ethnic prejudice for more than a century in Massachusetts. When the future president ran his first race for Congress in 1946, he made a statement on behalf of civil rights. His pro–civil rights position was also part of his Senate campaign of 1952 against Henry Cabot Lodge Jr. First as representative and then as senator, JFK took consistent stands in favor of civil rights. By nature and temperament, though, Kennedy was not a natural advocate. His celebrated detachment and lack of emotion created a gulf between him and both blacks and whites who felt moral outrage over segregation and discrimination. Harris Wofford reflected that Kennedy found the racial situation in the United States "appalling" and "irrational" but evaluated any action of his on its political consequences.[4]

In 1956, JFK's pro–civil rights position wavered. In Chicago, the Massachusetts senator came close to winning the vice-presidential nomination. In the convention vote, Kennedy received significant support from the South. This southern endorsement had relatively little to do with JFK and much more to do with the hostility to Kennedy's opponent, Estes Kefauver, who was widely despised in southern political circles. Nevertheless, with Kennedy working toward the presidential nomination after 1956, the memories of the convention offered strong possibilities for winning southern votes. That required moderating his earlier positions and making himself acceptable to the South. Beginning in 1956, John F. Kennedy positioned himself so that he could win both northern and southern votes and attract backing from both white southerners and civil rights advocates. For Kennedy, positions on racial issues were a matter both of political calculation and political philosophy, but the former clearly predominated over the latter.[5]

After the Chicago convention, John F. Kennedy found himself increasingly suspect by the civil rights movement because of two developments. The first was his vote in favor of the jury trial amendment to the Civil Rights Act of 1957. This piece of legislation, the handiwork of Lyndon Johnson, was a part of the Texan's attempt to enhance his presidential credentials by showing northern liberals that he would embrace civil rights. Simultaneously, he sold the legislation to the South on the grounds that with blacks becoming more militant and northern pressure building for civil rights, the best option was to pass a mild bill and thereby avoid a more extreme measure. As part of his effort to make the bill palatable to the South and to maintain his position as someone who would protect southern interests, LBJ inserted a concession. He supported a provision by which, in contempt cases, defendants charged with denying blacks their right to vote would be entitled to a trial by jury. Since white southern juries were certain not to convict, the civil rights political establishment, including the NAACP, strongly opposed the jury trial amendment. So did the Eisenhower administration and Vice President Nixon. When John F. Kennedy chose to vote in favor of the jury trial provision, he enhanced his standing with the South, but he damaged it with the civil rights movement. Clarence Mitchell, director of the Washington, D.C., branch of the NAACP, considered the Kennedy vote on the jury trial amendment an "outright double cross."[6]

The vote on the jury trial amendment was not an easy one. The choice was between accepting this stipulation or sacrificing the chance of passing any civil rights legislation. Kennedy defended his vote with opinions from legal experts at Harvard who assured him that the amendment would not weaken the bill. Some liberal Democrats both inside and outside the Senate favored the compromise. Still, it was difficult to escape the sense that the major considerations for the Massachusetts senator were the political implications of his vote for his presidential campaign.[7]

The other symbol of Kennedy's courting of southern support and increasing estrangement from civil rights leaders was his relationship with Alabama governor John Patterson, a strong segregationist. In the late 1950s, JFK courted Patterson. In July 1959, Kennedy entertained the governor along with the president of the Alabama White Citizens Council at a secret breakfast meeting. When word of the meeting leaked out, Patterson provided an overenthusiastic endorsement for Kennedy. The support from the Alabama governor immediately became a problem since he was engaged in an ongoing campaign to harass and destroy civil rights organizations, most notably the NAACP, in his state. He also supported the state prosecution of Martin Luther King Jr. on grounds of perjury in a tax statement. After King's acquittal, Patterson ordered the president of Alabama State University, a black school, to fire dozens of King's friends and supporters.[8]

Even Kennedy's Pulitzer Prize–winning *Profiles in Courage* can be seen as part of his southern strategy. *Profiles* examined courageous and politically costly decisions made by senators from John Quincy Adams to Robert A. Taft. Among those whom Kennedy praised were Edmund Ross, who cast the key vote that acquitted President Andrew Johnson in his impeachment trial, and John Calhoun. Meanwhile, he characterized Reconstruction as "a black nightmare the South never could forget." *Profiles* was history distinctly sympathetic to the white South and almost completely devoid of any empathy for African Americans. This was history that stamped Kennedy as a friend of the white South.[9]

Beginning with Kennedy's votes on the civil rights legislation in 1957, the Massachusetts senator came under increasing criticism. In 1958, Roy Wilkins, executive secretary of the NAACP, launched a bitter attack on Kennedy in the senator's state. Kennedy resented Wilkins's assault, which he considered unfair on a number of accounts. He accused the NAACP leader of cozying up to Richard Nixon.[10]

Kennedy's choice of advisers compounded his difficulties. Like any coalition of organizations and individuals, the civil rights movement had its share of rivalries and conflicts. The NAACP tended to be highly critical of Martin Luther King Jr. and the Southern Christian Leadership Conference. Powerful congressmen like Adam Clayton Powell Jr. of New York and William Dawson of Chicago had their own agendas. With a limited knowledge of black America, John F. Kennedy recruited two Washington attorneys, Belford and Marjorie McKenzie Lawson, as liaisons and charged them with the responsibility of repairing his relationship with the civil rights movement and African Americans.

The Lawsons were an attractive and well-connected couple. He had graduated from Harvard Law School and she from Columbia. He was the president of the country's largest black fraternity, and she was legal counsel for the National Council of Negro Women. Both were large, influential African-American organizations. Marjorie Lawson especially appears to have committed herself to the Kennedy cause. From the perspective of a half century, the Lawsons were in over their heads. Roy Wilkins and the NAACP, Martin Luther King Jr. and the SCLC, and various members of the Kennedy camp including Robert Kennedy, Sargent Shriver, and Harris Wofford concluded that the Lawsons were unequal to the task before them. Eventually, the campaign managed to correct the problem, but the Lawsons did not improve the situation, although they were hardly the source of Kennedy's trouble.[11]

As Kennedy entered 1960, his relations with African Americans were poor. Roy Wilkins and the NAACP distrusted him. Jackie Robinson blasted him over his association with Governor Patterson. The former baseball star campaigned for Humphrey in Wisconsin, where Kennedy did little to appeal to the black vote. In November 1959, Kennedy wrote to Martin Luther King Jr. Thinking JFK a political playboy and friend of segregationists with a poor record in the Senate, King did not reply.

To Kennedy's credit, he made a major and sustained effort to improve the situation. Genuinely curious about the views of others, he sought out black entertainer and activist Harry Belafonte in an attempt to understand African-American dissatisfaction. Belafonte explained that the key to his success in attracting black support rested with the civil rights groups—especially the Southern Christian Leadership Conference (SCLC) and the Student Non-Violent Coordinating Committee (SNCC), and most especially Martin Luther King Jr. Belafonte predicted that if Kennedy could win over King, he "would have an alliance that would make the difference." To this point, JFK had viewed King simply as the minister who led the Montgomery bus boycott and who was now in tax trouble in Alabama.[12]

The Democratic candidate took Belafonte's advice and arranged a meeting with King. The two met for the first time on June 23, 1960, in New York City. Kennedy told King that he had come to understand the moral force of the civil rights movement. King came away more impressed with the Massachusetts senator. In 1964, King would say that Kennedy "had a long intellectual commitment but . . . he didn't quite have the emotional commitment." As far as he was concerned, Kennedy had not been involved with the civil rights movement and did not know many blacks. If the Kennedy-King relationship improved over the course of 1960, the same could not be said of King and RFK. Through 1960 and much of 1961, Bobby Kennedy continued to hold a negative view of the civil rights leader.[13]

As John F. Kennedy approached the Los Angeles convention, he was still trying to improve his standing with liberals and civil rights activists. He made a good impression on the Michigan delegates, perhaps the most ardent pro–civil rights state delegation, in a no-holds-barred question-and-answer session before the convention. To bolster their civil rights position, JFK and RFK decided to support the strongest possible civil rights plank in the platform. With southerners, at least partially at LBJ's direction, offering little or no resistance, the convention voted the strongest civil rights plank in Democratic Party history into the platform. Among other things, it called for the elimination of literacy tests and the poll tax, an executive order prohibiting discrimination in federal housing, the establishment of a Fair Employment Practices Commission, and a requirement for southern school districts to submit a plan for school desegregation.[14]

The civil rights plank improved the atmosphere with civil rights organizations, although many remained unconvinced. The instincts of the skeptics were sound. While the Kennedy forces pushed a strong civil rights plank, their operatives reassured southerners that JFK was a gradualist who would not necessarily feel bound by the promises of the platform. When Harris Wofford and others approached Robert Kennedy concerning a response to LBJ's stand on civil rights, RFK retorted: "I'm busy as hell. What do you think we're running a campaign for? Negroes alone?"[15]

The doubters multiplied when John F. Kennedy named Lyndon B. Johnson as his running mate. The reaction against LBJ was vitriolic, and the most steadfast advocates of civil rights led it. One of the many ironies of 1960 was that the most militant champions of civil rights vented their wrath on the man who proved to be the greatest civil rights president of the twentieth century. In the aftermath of the convention, the hostility to both JFK and LBJ was thick. When Kennedy met with black delegates the morning after the convention, they were "cold as fish" toward him. At a civil rights rally in Los Angeles shortly after the conclusion of the convention, Kennedy received "perfunctory applause mingled with boos" when he was introduced. But this was nothing compared to the antagonistic reception that met Lyndon Johnson's representative. The venomous unhappiness of the crowd drowned out his words. NAACP Washington Bureau Director Mitchell twice had to lecture the crowd on its behavior. LBJ's spokesman was unable to complete his remarks. JFK plainly had a good deal of fence mending and repair work to do before he could expect to rally African-American voters to his candidacy.[16]

JFK's opponent also wrestled with his approach to race and civil rights. Nixon had some of the same background on the subject that Kennedy did and shared some of his attitudes. Like the Democrat, Nixon had grown up in an overwhelmingly white environment, although his years at Duke Law School exposed him to some degree to racial issues. With JFK, Nixon shared a distaste for discrimination and segregation, as well as a tendency to calculate actions on the basis of political advantage. As astute politicians and centrists, Kennedy and Nixon did their best to placate both northerners and southerners and to avoid any actions or statements that would irrevocably alienate one group or the other. Similar to Kennedy, Nixon possessed a moral understanding of the wrongness of discrimination and segregation.

As with JFK, there was a serious question about his emotional commitment and his willingness to expend political capital to eradicate racial inequities. For both, the costs seemed too high and the likelihood of success too small. Like the Massachusetts senator, the Californian was most interested in and concerned with foreign policy. Both men saw civil rights and other domestic issues as secondary to the paramount issue of the day—the great struggle with the USSR—to which everything else was subordinate.

Although these similarities were important, there were important differences between the vice president's situation and approach and those of Senator Kennedy. The chief problem for the latter was how to navigate between powerful northern and southern Democratic political interests without destroying his presidential chances. Nixon paid less attention to southern Republican forces because they were weak. He did, however, have to operate within an administration whose attitudes were mixed.

President Dwight D. Eisenhower epitomized the problem. Ike possessed a genuine belief in the dignity of all citizens and believed he had an obligation to represent everyone. At the same time, he was of a generation and background that saw African Americans as subordinate. His career in the army reinforced this belief. Comfortable with his many close southern friends, he would not condemn the social system from which they came. In addition, Ike seems to have been ill at ease with African Americans in social settings.[17]

Other characteristics disinclined Eisenhower to undertake anything more than limited action. The president had a sincere distaste for grandstanding or what he saw as meaningless symbolism. Hence, he was opposed to doing or saying things simply for the sake of signaling his support for equality. He was skeptical of the belief that big, activist government was the solution to every problem.

Eisenhower much preferred to work anonymously behind the scenes. He was willing to act in areas where his authority was clear, and he did. He moved to end segregation in the District of Columbia and the armed forces. When Ike took office in 1953, Washington was still a segregated city. There was no place for blacks to get coffee in the downtown area aside from Union Station. Eisenhower called in merchants and hotel owners and told them to open up their establishments to African Americans. He ordered public facilities in the capital desegregated, and the attorney general argued to the Supreme Court that discrimination by restaurants was unconstitutional. Eisenhower brought pressure on Washington theater managers to end Jim Crow seating in their theaters. Hotels began accepting blacks. The fire department and other municipal agencies ended segregation. Secretary of the

Navy Robert Anderson, without publicity, accomplished the desegregation of naval bases at Norfolk and Charleston.[18]

Beyond these measures, Eisenhower was reluctant to act. He refused to make a strong public statement endorsing the decision of *Brown v. Board of Education* and the desegregation of schools. He rejected pleas to denounce the brutal murder of Emmett Till. During his first term of office, he did not have an organized public meeting with civil rights leaders. Eisenhower made no real attempt to understand the black perspective or the terrible hardships that African Americans encountered in their daily lives.

In 1955, Eisenhower did appoint the first black to serve on the White House senior staff. The appointee was E. Frederic Morrow, a graduate of Bowdoin College and Rutgers Law School, a World War II veteran, former field secretary for the NAACP, and employee at CBS. Morrow encountered astounding difficulties that were representative of the state of American society. Several White House aides would not eat with him, and he experienced great difficulty in obtaining a secretary. Women were under instructions to enter Morrow's office only in pairs. In 1960, Morrow made a brief but historic speech at the Chicago convention, but the television networks cut away in order not to offend southern stations and audiences. When Morrow departed the administration in 1961, no executive job awaited him.[19]

Few other blacks in the White House had access to the president. When the position of civil rights liaison fell vacant in 1958, no one was appointed to fill the slot. There were individuals in the administration who pushed a civil rights agenda, most notably Attorney General Herbert Brownell. Some like chief of staff Sherman Adams were supportive, while others were less inclined to move on this subject.[20]

Richard Nixon was squarely in the pro–civil rights camp. Nixon's attitudes toward blacks in general were not flattering. He doubted black equality, but he also strongly believed in the right for all to compete for the good things in American life. With the influence of his Quaker background, Nixon was a sincere civil rights advocate during his years as vice president under Eisenhower. According to biographer Stephen Ambrose, Nixon's record as vice president on racial relations was "excellent." He consistently denounced Jim Crow and worked to advance the cause of civil rights even when the political benefits were absent or negligible.[21]

In August 1953, Eisenhower appointed Nixon to head the President's Committee on Government Contracts (PCGC). This was Ike's alternative to the Fair Employment Practices Commission (FEPC) that FDR and Truman had initiated. In making the appointment, Eisenhower declared: "On no level of our national government can inequality be justified. Within the Federal Government itself, however, tolerance of inequality would be odious." Nixon threw himself into this enterprise with enthusiasm, holding numerous meetings across the country, and appearing on both radio and television to argue on behalf of breaking down job barriers to blacks. Some success followed, especially in Washington. The Chesapeake & Potomac Telephone Company and the Capital Transit Company both opened jobs that previously had been closed to blacks. Progress elsewhere was more limited and less noticeable, in part because of the administration's emphasis on quiet negotiation. Critics did not think enough had been accomplished, but there is no reason to question Nixon's efforts. Eisenhower offered limited support, and the administration faced great resistance in the South and among private businessmen.[22]

Nixon enhanced his reputation with his performance in the battle over the Civil Rights Act of 1957. As presiding officer of the U.S. Senate, he issued one procedural ruling that benefited supporters of the bill. He also vigorously opposed the jury trial amendment. When that provision passed, Nixon was visibly upset by the vote, as were the great majority of civil rights leaders.

As one of the most prominent civil rights advocates in the administration, the vice president established and maintained cordial relations with major black newspapers and civil rights leaders, especially after their alliance over the 1957 legislation. The *Chicago Defender* published an editorial praising Nixon for his stand on the jury trial amendment and commenting positively on his recent African trip. Clarence Mitchell wrote the vice president to wish him well in 1959 as he prepared for his trip to the USSR. Mitchell noted that "the country knows that whatever may arise you will meet it with courage and dignity." As late as mid-1960, Roy Wilkins praised Nixon for his "good record on civil rights." From the mid-1950s into the general election campaign of 1960, Richard Nixon had a good reputation on civil rights and a positive and friendly relationship with civil rights organizations.[23]

In February 1957, the vice president made a trip to Africa that took him to Ghana and seven other African countries. In Ghana, where he represented the United States at the nation's independence ceremonies, he met Martin Luther King Jr. and invited him to meet with him in Washington about civil rights issues in America. King, accompanied by Ralph Abernathy, met with Nixon in mid-June. Nixon listened carefully and took detailed notes on what King had to say about the flagrant disfranchisement of blacks, the need for federal action, and the inability to get southern school officials to discuss integration. For his part, Nixon urged the need for cooperation with the administration against both segregationist southern Democrats and wildly unrealistic northern liberal Democrats. In Nixon's view, the latter with their extreme proposals were almost as guilty as the former at preventing passage of meaningful civil rights legislation. Later Nixon invited King to speak before a conference on racial discrimination in employment. At that event, Nixon declared that there was a need for Americans to recognize that the issue was "basically a moral problem."[24]

Between 1957 and November 1960, the Nixon-King relationship was a good one. King had reservations, especially that the vice president's "relish and conviction seemed so evenly applied to all subjects as to mask his interior substance." King told Bayard Rustin that, in his view, Nixon was a mixture of enthusiasm and pragmatism and would help civil rights if it did not hurt him politically. In August 1957, King wrote to the vice president and praised him for his "assiduous labor and dauntless courage in seeking to make the Civil Rights Bill a reality." King added, "You have my prayers and best wishes for the great work that you are doing in making our democracy a living reality." As late as 1959, King viewed Nixon as the leading presidential candidate with an interest in civil rights. He saw Nixon as "very personable" and "one of the most magnetic personalities that I have ever confronted." He believed that Nixon as president would do more for civil rights than Eisenhower.[25]

The other black leader that Richard Nixon courted with energy and success was baseball great Jackie Robinson. Robinson was a historic figure who had desegregated major league baseball in 1947. He was a well-educated athlete with decided opinions on political matters. His role in the desegregation of baseball made Robinson a true hero to black America, and his opinions carried considerable influence. The vice president's association with Robinson went back to the Republican National Convention of 1952, when the two men first met. Robinson was impressed by Nixon's "warmth" and "evident admiration" for the black baseball player. Nixon's reaction was genuine and consistent with his love of sports and his respect for professional athletes. Nixon's detailed recollection of seeing him playing for UCLA in a football game against the University of Oregon won over Robinson. In his discussion with the Brooklyn Dodger, the vice president provided a detailed description of a complicated play that Robinson had executed in the game. Robinson was "charmed" and "dazzled." He probably never met any politician before or after who could repeat what Nixon had told him.[26]

By the late 1950s, Robinson had retired from baseball and made the transition into business and other pursuits. He worked for Chock Full O' Nuts, wrote a column for the *New York Post* (beginning in 1959), and hosted a radio show once a week on WRCA in New York. Robinson did not hesitate to tell people what he thought, especially on the subject of the upcoming presidential election. Although he was a strong advocate of the civil rights movement, his other attitudes placed him in a Republican orbit. One biographer described him as "a Republican at heart." Robinson liked the strong anticommunism, the moral austerity, and the pro-business philosophy of the GOP. In early 1960, he jumped into the nominating contests on both sides. He said his favorite was Hubert Humphrey followed by Richard Nixon. Few other people in the country had a first choice of the Minnesota senator and a second choice of the vice president.[27]

Robinson also developed a decided distaste for John and Robert Kennedy. He was critical of the former for his votes on the 1957 Civil Rights Bill and his cozy relationship with Governor Patterson. On the Patterson-Kennedy meeting, Robinson noted that the president of the Alabama White Citizens Council accompanied the governor. Robinson went to Wisconsin and campaigned for Humphrey, asserting that he was "a Humphrey man." He then declared that he had "no doubts at all concerning Nixon" but criticized Eisenhower. He said Ike "is more interested in breaking 90 [at golf] than seeing to it Negroes and other minorities get civil rights." Robinson's relationship with the Kennedys was not helped by Bobby, who sniped at him with charges that Humphrey paid for Robinson's trip to Wisconsin and criticized him for opposing unionization at Chock Full O' Nuts. He called Bobby's comment on his Wisconsin trip a "smear" and observed that RFK "will not hesitate to use lies, innuendos and personal attacks on those who disagree with him."[28]

With Humphrey out of the race after the West Virginia primary, Robinson shifted to Nixon. He attended an NAACP dinner with JFK in the spring of 1960 and refused to have his picture taken with the Massachusetts senator. The hostility of Robinson and Roy Wilkins puzzled Kennedy. He did manage to get Robinson to agree to a meeting in early July 1960, but that turned into a disaster. Kennedy tried to explain himself by admitting, according to Robinson, "I don't know much about the problems of colored people since I come from New England." Robinson said that Kennedy "couldn't or wouldn't look me straight in the eye," and he left the meeting "even less than an admirer" than previously. Robinson later softened his opposition to the Kennedys, but for the 1960 campaign, he loomed as their most formidable black opponent.[29]

Entering July 1960, Richard Nixon had a fighting chance to obtain the African-American votes he needed to win the White House. With the sizable numbers of black voters concentrated in key states like New York, Pennsylvania, Michigan, and Illinois, their decisions would help determine the outcome of the national contest. Nixon did not have to win a majority of black votes, but he did need to come close to Eisenhower's number in 1956 that Gallup put at 39 percent.

Kennedy started the general election campaign with some disadvantages when it came to appealing for African-American votes. An internal study of the situation found that black leaders as well as the common citizen had "little feeling of identification" with Kennedy. According to the memorandum, "many are distrustful, some are suspicious, some are bitterly opposed, few are enthusiastic." The bases of these sentiments were numerous, some obvious, others "subtle" and "elusive." JFK had a reputation of avoiding African-American meetings, and some asked the question, "When did he ever speak in Harlem?" The campaign had major obstacles to overcome.[30]

On the other side, the Republican candidate possessed certain advantages. Overall, his civil rights record was better than that of the Massachusetts senator. He had contacts in the civil rights movement. He had the enthusiastic and powerful support of the outspoken Jackie Robinson. Beneath the surface, though, the Republican campaign had serious weaknesses that became apparent as the presidential contest unfolded. First, there was no one in the Republican high command who would be a fierce advocate for civil rights. Given the controversial nature of the subject, only someone with the strongest commitment and access to the candidate could make civil rights a priority, even a limited one. In contrast, on the Democratic side, Sargent Shriver and his compatriot Harris Wofford could and did make the strongest possible arguments in behalf of civil rights. Second, the GOP simply did not have the necessary infrastructure at the precinct level in the great cities of the country to make its case and to recruit and turn out black voters. For example, in Chicago, there were six black wards—the Second, Third, Fourth, Sixth, Twentieth, and Twenty-fourth—under the thumb of the Chicago Democratic machine. In November, these six wards produced a margin of more than 100,000 votes for the Democratic ticket. The GOP simply did not possess the resources, the infrastructure, or the desire to compete for the black vote in the big cities of the Northeast and Midwest.[31]

The verdict of the African-American vote depended upon the quality of the Kennedy campaign; success was not guaranteed. In 1956, the Stevenson campaign badly botched its approach to civil rights and black America and saw about 40 percent of the vote go to Eisenhower. As late as August

1960, the Kennedy campaign appeared ready to duplicate the Stevenson performance.[32]

To their credit, John and Robert Kennedy understood that a serious problem existed, and they moved to do something about it. From the convention, they emerged with the strongest civil rights plank in the history of the Democratic Party. The commitment embodied in the platform made a positive impression on many individuals, including Martin Luther King Jr. The campaign then implemented a highly effective "strategy of association" for appealing to the black vote. Its essence was a carefully calibrated appeal in which Kennedy associated himself with African-American concerns and grievances without advancing specific proposals to deal with them. Kennedy's approach was "powerful rhetorically but vague politically."[33]

Through the fall, Kennedy expanded upon this plan. In August, the campaign established a Civil Rights Section (CRS) that was responsible for making sure that Kennedy appeared in a favorable light. Marjorie McKenzie Lawson was appointed director. Other prominent members included Sargent Shriver, Harris Wofford, William Dawson, Frank Reeves, and Louis Martin. The CRS portrayed his Republican opponent as weak and inadequate in his efforts on behalf of civil rights. The Democratic candidate took care to ensure that he would speak to and greet integrated audiences, that there would be an African American in his campaign party, and that news photographs would portray an integrated look. Sargent Shriver, acting on behalf of the Kennedy Foundation, offered $100,000 to bring 240 African students to study in the United States after the State Department turned down a request for support. In mid-October, the Civil Rights Section staged its grand event, the National Conference on Constitutional Rights, in New York. The two-day conference was a rousing success in convincing participants of JFK's commitment to civil rights. At its conclusion, Kennedy gave his longest speech on civil rights in the campaign and then went to an enthusiastic rally at the Hotel Theresa in Harlem. By November, most of the Kennedy doubters entertained much-improved attitudes about the Democratic nominee. They had no difficulty in voting for him and urging others to do the same. The strategy of association along with the favorable references to Africa succeeded magnificently.[34]

Meanwhile, Lyndon Johnson barnstormed around the South, denouncing Richard Nixon as an enemy of the region and criticizing the vice president's support for civil rights. The Democratic campaign made much of Eisenhower's intervention in the Little Rock School Crisis of 1957 and linked Nixon to the event. On October 6, LBJ, through press secretary

George Reedy, issued a statement declaring that "the present Republican administration has certainly racked up a record which is dangerously close to the evils of Reconstruction times." It demanded to know whether Nixon favored "the bayonets and paratroopers in Little Rock" and whether he believed that "white southerners accused of violating civil rights statutes should be deprived of the ancient Anglo-Saxon right of the jury trial." Waving the Confederate flag, the Johnson campaign emphasized Nixon's honorary membership in the NAACP, a badge of dishonor in the white South, while painting John F. Kennedy as a much more reasonable and moderate northerner. Johnson evoked his heritage as the grandson of a Confederate solider, and assured the courthouse politicians of the South that they would have nothing to worry about on civil rights with JFK in the White House. As vice president, he would be well positioned to protect southern interests. While the CRS succeeded in the North in condemning Nixon for being insufficiently strong and effective on civil rights, the Johnson campaign in the South had as much success condemning the vice president for supporting civil rights.[35]

Although the strategy of association was highly effective, it did not address the basic organizational problems that the Kennedys faced. From the outset, the relationship between campaign manager Robert Kennedy and the CRS was less than amicable. Although the husband of Eunice Kennedy, Shriver was not considered a "real" Kennedy. From the beginning, Shriver was suspect and out of favor with Bobby, Ted Sorensen, and Ken O'Donnell, among others. For their tastes, Sarge was too soft and too idealistic. Sorensen warned Wofford upon his arrival not to get too close to Shriver because insiders saw him as the "house communist." The campaign high command saw the CRS as a source of trouble and preferred that it remain as invisible as possible to American whites. Even the title was controversial. Byron "Whizzer" White, director of Citizens for Kennedy, wanted a different name since in his view the term "civil rights" was inherently inflammatory to undecided white voters. In the end, the CRS kept its title, but its office was separate from the national headquarters, and its major campaign event, the National Conference on Constitutional Rights, intentionally omitted the dreaded term "civil rights."[36]

Meanwhile, the CRS itself was badly divided. There were continual conflicts among Marjorie McKenzie Lawson, Frank Reeves (who traveled with JFK as the campaign's representative African American), Congressman Dawson, and Shriver, Wofford, and Martin, who worked in concert. Whether her fault or not, Lawson irritated the others and quickly alienated them. In due course, she lost out in the power struggle and Louis Martin assumed command.[37]

The Martin takeover was a most fortuitous development for the Kennedy candidacy in the black community. More than anyone else, Louis Martin was responsible for the high black turnout and the heavy vote for John F. Kennedy. Unlike others in the campaign, he understood the subtleties of black politics and knew what needed to be done and how to get it done. Martin was in his late forties, a graduate of the University of Michigan, and someone with long experience in business and journalism. He had been a reporter for the *Chicago Defender* and helped establish the *Michigan Chronicle*. He had worked in the Democratic presidential campaign of 1944 and had numerous contacts in the world of black newspapers. In 1960, he had just returned from Nigeria and, in the aftermath of the convention, was trying to decide whether to go back into business or pursue his journalistic interests. Wofford and Frank Reeves brought him to Washington, and very quickly he identified the key problems and attacked them.[38]

With the support of Wofford and Shriver, Martin became "chief counselor, colleague, and co-conspirator." He was tough and acerbic. His favorite slogan was, "Let's get all the horses on the track." By that, he meant he wanted coordination among the NAACP, the newspapers, black churches, Adam Clayton Powell Jr., and black celebrities like Harry Belafonte. He insisted, as a condition for his work, that the Democratic National Committee pay all outstanding debts to black newspapers and magazines dating back to the 1956 campaign. With that issue resolved, he moved to ensure good relations with the premier black newspapers and magazines, including the *Amsterdam News*, the *Pittsburgh Courier*, the *Chicago Defender*, and *Jet*. Among its many failures, the Stevenson campaigns allowed Republicans to garner the support of black newspapers in 1952 and 1956. In the first election, Republicans convinced some newspapers to blast Stevenson's running mate, Senator John Sparkman of Alabama, as a racist. In 1956, the Republicans won the endorsement of several black publications, including the *Pittsburgh Courier* and the *Amsterdam News*. Martin made sure that this would not happen in 1960. He talked with the editors about the qualifications and positions of Lyndon B. Johnson to convince them not to do to him what had been done to Sparkman. In due course, glowing endorsements for JFK and LBJ appeared in the key black newspapers of the country.[39]

Martin went to work on key black politicians. One of them was Congressman William Dawson, the titular head of the CRS. Dawson, who had his own agenda, was not an easy individual to deal with. He resisted the title

"Civil Rights Section," preferring the designation from previous campaigns, "Minorities Division." Dawson was a machine politician who maintained good relations with white southern Democrats, and he had no desire for what struck him as radical new departures. He wanted an operation run by him and his black allies without the interference of whites like Shriver and Wofford. He objected to the open physical setting of the CRS that did not include an office for him. Shriver and Wofford did not have the authority or the ability to control Dawson. Bobby Kennedy, who despised machine politicians like Dawson, had no interest in mediating such disputes. Martin took charge of the situation and told RFK to his face that while he might prefer not to deal with people like Dawson, he would have to "do business" with him and Adam Clayton Powell Jr. of New York. Martin gave Dawson what he wanted—an office of his own. Then, outside of ceremonial occasions, Martin ignored him. At Martin's direction, the CRS built what became known as "Uncle Tom's Cabin," and William Dawson was left to his own devices, which included turning out more than 113,000 votes on November 8 for John F. Kennedy, while the CRS pursued its own agenda.[40]

Adam Clayton Powell Jr., the best-known black member of Congress, was as important to the Kennedy campaign as Dawson. Powell, a flamboyant character who wheeled and dealed to advance civil rights and to aggrandize himself, had defected from Democratic ranks and endorsed Eisenhower in 1956. The inability to keep Powell satisfied, along with the cavalier treatment of the black newspapers, symbolized the ineptitude and incompetence of the Stevenson campaign. Martin was determined to avoid a repetition of this performance in 1960. The only question was how much it would take to guarantee Powell's loyalty.

Earlier in the year, when Martin Luther King Jr. and A. Phillip Randolph proposed to hold civil rights demonstrations at both national conventions, Powell warned them against that and threatened to charge King with a homosexual relationship with Bayard Rustin if he proceeded. Meanwhile, Powell negotiated with Sam Rayburn and Lyndon Johnson to support LBJ as the Democratic nominee, in return for a committee chairmanship in the new Congress. At the same time, he leaked word that he would entertain overtures from the Kennedy camp. Through Harlem leader Ray Jones, Powell demanded $300,000 for his endorsement and support. Martin, who was accustomed to dealing with men like Powell, bargained him down to $50,000 for a series of speeches with payment to be made in installments through middleman Robert Wagner. In this fashion, John F. Kennedy was able to retain the loyalty and the voice of Adam Clayton Powell Jr. in 1960.[41]

Money was not a problem for black Democrats in 1960. Thanks to Joe Kennedy, big-city politicians with thousands of votes to offer had little difficulty obtaining cash, and neither did black preachers. Len Hall recalled 1960 with some amazement: "My God, I've never seen anything like it. I've paid these fellows more than they ever got before and Joe Kennedy's come in there and raised me every time. We didn't get one of 'em."[42]

With John Kennedy and Robert Kennedy unable to understand African-American politics, and wishing to focus on other matters in any case, they gave Louis Martin wide latitude to organize the Democratic appeal to blacks. Martin delivered. He was highly successful in lining up support from black publications and key black politicians. He associated JFK with FDR in campaign advertising. With the support of Eleanor Roosevelt, Martin underlined the link between the 1960 Democratic nominee and FDR.[43]

With the rousing success of the National Conference on Constitutional Rights only three weeks before the election, the Democratic campaign positioned itself to win a heavy majority of black votes. While Democrats were busy, the Republican effort languished. In part, this was because there were no comparable figures to Wofford and Shriver in the Nixon campaign and no internal pressures in the Republican Party to develop a strong stand on civil rights. The Republican strategy focused on foreign policy issues; civil rights turned the national attention back to domestic affairs, which is precisely what Nixon wanted to avoid. The vice president did not have the luxury of running a dual campaign—one in the North that was pro–civil rights and another in the South that suggested the opposite. Nixon thought his record on civil rights was good enough to speak for itself. Republican strategists calculated that they had an opportunity to win large numbers of white southern votes if Nixon avoided pushing too hard on civil rights. All these elements combined to deemphasize a Republican thrust on civil rights.[44]

Finally, a Republican fatalism about the black vote prevented effective action. Republicans convinced themselves that they had done all they could and that African Americans were irrevocably tied to the Democratic Party for economic reasons. This judgment was accurate, at least in part. Black leaders disliked the Eisenhower administration's opposition to raising the minimum wage, to federal aid to education, and to a government program to provide medical care for the aged. As the election approached, they increasingly leaned toward JFK because he offered "a better deal on civil rights and economic benefits." After the election, Eisenhower lamented, "we have made civil rights a main part of our effort these past eight years but have lost Negro support instead of increasing it." Claude Robinson's pre-election assessment was: "The Negro reacts a good deal as economic man; less as civil rights man. Kennedy looks more like an economic friend than Nixon to these voters." The trouble with this analysis, aside from the fact that civil rights had not been an Eisenhower priority, was that it became a self-ful-filling prophecy. Republicans believed that there was little hope for attracting significant African-American support so they made minimal effort and were rewarded with few black votes. The Republican failure to make a push for the black vote reflected a neglect of the African-American community that spoke persuasively to its voters and produced a massive majority for John F. Kennedy on November 8.[45]

By mid-October, John F. Kennedy had sold himself as the preferable presidential candidate to American blacks and was in position to capture a large majority of the African-American vote.[46] One last event, however, tipped the balance even more in his favor—the famous incident involving the arrest of Martin Luther King Jr.

In 1960, Martin Luther King Jr. felt conflicting pressures. Black students in Atlanta pressed him to join the sit-ins that the Student Non-Violent Co-ordinating Committee (SNCC) was organizing. His father and other Atlanta leaders wanted him to endorse Richard Nixon. Harris Wofford, Louis Martin, and others were urging him to endorse JFK. King seemed more favorably inclined toward Kennedy as a result of their June meeting, the strong civil rights plank in the Democratic platform, and the presence of Wofford and Chester Bowles in the Kennedy camp. He did not see comparable individuals on the Republican side. Nevertheless, he had no intention of issuing any endorsement. However, he did tell the Kennedy campaign he might say something favorable about the Democratic candidate's commitment to civil rights if the Massachusetts senator would demonstrate his commitment by meeting him publicly in a southern city. The Kennedy campaign very much wanted to maneuver King into an expression of support for the nominee, but was fearful of the repercussions of a meeting in the South. The Kennedy camp rejected Atlanta and proposed alternatives. The two sides finally reached agreement on Miami, but Kennedy abandoned the project when King said he had to invite Nixon to the meeting.[47]

With the Kennedy-King meeting off, King had no excuse for not participating in the Atlanta sit-ins. He did and was duly arrested on October 19. He went to jail, but his incarceration did not make news outside of Atlanta. It worried Harris Wofford, who interjected himself into King's situation. Without the knowledge or approval of campaign headquarters, Wofford called Morris Abram, a personal friend. Abram told him that Mayor William Hartsfield of Atlanta was already maneuvering behind the scenes to get

King released. Hartsfield managed to broker an agreement to get King out of jail and, in his ensuing discussion with reporters, invented a story about JFK intervening in the affair and credited him for bringing about King's release. From the Kennedy camp's perspective, it was fortunate that this story broke on Saturday, a slow news day as well as the day after the fourth television debate. The Hartsfield story was troubling enough that it set in motion a series of telephone conversations with Pierre Salinger, Kenneth O'Donnell, and John F. Kennedy to determine how to handle JFK's alleged involvement in King's release.[48]

But King was not free. Since he was on parole as the consequence of an outstanding traffic ticket, he was brought before Judge Oscar Mitchell on Monday, October 24, sentenced to four months of hard labor, and transferred to the state penitentiary in Reidsville. This event precipitated a greater crisis because of the disproportionate nature of the sentence and the possibility that serious harm could befall the civil rights leader in backwoods Georgia. King finally escaped from the clutches of Georgia justice on October 27, when Judge Mitchell ordered his release.

The story of King's release was one filled with intrigue—and numerous telephone calls. The latter included John F. Kennedy's famous call to Coretta Scott King, Robert F. Kennedy's call to Oscar Mitchell, JFK's and RFK's assorted calls to various Georgia politicians, Adlai Stevenson's refusal to talk to Coretta Scott King, and the exchanges among Georgia politicians.[49]

The most famous telephone call was the one by John F. Kennedy to Coretta Scott King. About it there is less debate than any of the others. Sargent Shriver and Louis Martin originated the idea. Knowing that Bobby Kennedy, Ted Sorensen, and others never would agree to it, they made an end run around the high command. Shriver cornered JFK alone and stated the argument for the call. Kennedy responded favorably to the proposition. Shriver placed the call, Mrs. King came on the line, and John Kennedy spoke to her briefly, but eloquently, assuring her of his concern for the welfare of her and her husband. JFK's action was generous and gracious, and he deserves credit for his decision.[50]

The aftermath of JFK's call is less edifying and more controversial. Once Robert F. Kennedy found out about it, apparently from Pierre Salinger, he "exploded." In a white fury about the potential political consequences and Shriver's end run, he reached out to his brother-in-law and in no uncertain terms "scorched" Shriver's "ass on long distance telephone." According to Shriver, Bobby Kennedy "landed on me like a ton of bricks and claimed that we had lost the election." Bobby reiterated his point, saying that Shriver had "screwed the whole election up and Jack Kennedy was going to get defeated because of the stupid call to Martin Luther King." Later, RFK confronted Wofford and Shriver, "his fists tight and his blue eyes cold." Telling them that three southern governors had promised to throw their states to Nixon if John F. Kennedy supported Martin Luther King Jr., RFK proclaimed, "Do you know that this election may be razor close and you have probably lost it for us?"[51]

After reprimanding Shriver, Robert Kennedy shifted his righteous indignation to another target—Judge Oscar Mitchell, who had sentenced King to the state penitentiary. According to the Camelot narrative, Bobby, infuriated by the injustice perpetrated in Georgia, proceeded to make his own telephone call to Judge Mitchell. The judge, apparently overcome by Kennedy eloquence, succumbed and quickly ordered the release of the prisoner. In the Kennedy hagiography, the two telephone calls stand as monuments to Kennedy passion and brilliance, and as a symbolic prelude to their later embrace of the civil rights crusade.

Omitted until recently were the discussions between the two Kennedys and Governor Ernest Vandiver. In August 1960, Kennedy had conferred with Vandiver in Washington. In their meeting, the Georgian had promised to support the nominee in exchange for a promise never to send federal troops to Georgia. Now JFK called Vandiver with a plea for help in getting King out of jail. The governor proceeded to talk to his brother-in-law Robert Russell (a nephew of U.S. senator Richard Russell), who in turn reached George B. Stewart (secretary of the Georgia Democratic Party), who made contact with Judge Mitchell. Mitchell indicated his willingness to order the release of King but wanted assurances that the governor had talked to John F. Kennedy about the situation. Vandiver was now able to telephone Robert Kennedy and assure him that if he called Judge Mitchell, Martin Luther King Jr. would be freed. RFK made the call, and King was released.

Upon King's release, Vandiver opined that it was a sad day "when the Democratic nominee makes a phone call to the home of the foremost racial agitator in the country." At the time, neither Vandiver, nor RFK, nor Mitchell could afford to tell the truth. Instead, Robert Kennedy developed a convenient fiction that Theodore White, Arthur Schlesinger Jr., and others enchanted with Camelot engraved in the historical record.[52]

The discharge of Martin Luther King Jr. did not end the story. Not only did the Kennedy campaign avert a potential disaster, it now managed to turn it into a success. Dr. King quickly spoke of his gratitude to Kennedy. He stated he would not publicly endorse a candidate because he headed a nonpartisan organization, but his associate Ralph Abernathy made clear that Senator Kennedy would get his vote. Martin Luther King Sr., who had backed Nixon up to this point, announced his support for John Kennedy and promised to bring black voters with him: "I've got a suitcase of votes, and I'm going to take them to Mr. Kennedy and dump them in his lap." He condemned Eisenhower and Nixon for "not saying a mumbling word."[53]

The main dilemma for Democrats was how to publicize the event to the black masses without alerting southern whites to what they were doing. Shriver, Wofford, and Martin solved the riddle by printing tens of thousands of leaflets on blue paper with the title "'No Comment,' Nixon versus a Candidate with a Heart, Senator Kennedy: The Case of Martin Luther King" and distributing the "blue bombs" in areas inhabited by African Americans. The leaflets—purportedly printed by the "Freedom Crusade Committee," a nonexistent organization invented to avoid their association with the Democratic National Committee—were handed out by volunteers in black neighborhoods in the days just before the election. Sargent Shriver himself dispensed them in front of the Ebenezer Baptist Church in Chicago. The "blue bomb" was a coup for the CRS and Shriver, Wofford, and Martin, and a great source of satisfaction after the abuse they had taken from higher-ups throughout the campaign.[54]

While JFK handled the King incident well, the same cannot be said for Richard Nixon. It is surprising that Nixon did not respond effectively. The Republican nominee was good at making personal gestures, and a telephone call, telegram, or personal note to Mrs. King, Dr. King, or Dr. King's father should have come easily. There were some obvious reasons for the failure. As with the Democrats, Nixon and GOP strategists worried about the reaction of white southern voters. Unlike the Democrats, however, there was no Republican version of Shriver and Wofford to make a strong argument for action, and civil rights was less of a priority to the GOP than to Democrats.

There were individuals who attempted to reach the vice president and convince him that he needed to do something. E. Frederic Morrow, the leading black official in the Eisenhower administration, urged action. Morrow recommended sending a letter or telegram to Mrs. King. This idea was rejected by the campaign staff, who called his proposal "a stupid move," adding, "you're always thinking up things to get us into difficulty, so forget it." Morrow persisted and attempted to reach the candidate himself, but he ran into a stone wall. He could not get access to Nixon. Fed up and disgusted, Morrow claimed he got off the campaign train and returned to Washington. He blamed the advisers more than Nixon. Jackie Robinson also made a heroic attempt to get through to Nixon and persuade him to take some action, but he had no more success. Like Morrow, Robinson ended the campaign disenchanted and despondent.[55]

There is good reason to believe that Nixon was aware of mounting pressure on behalf of King. He received a barrage of telegrams from NAACP leaders and chapters, as well as from ordinary citizens, that would have been difficult to miss. There is evidence that, with the vice president's support, the Department of Justice prepared a draft statement of a "friend of the court" brief to support the release of King. Copies went to the White House and to the Nixon campaign for approval, but no action was forthcoming. It is likely that President Eisenhower offered no support for the idea. Certainly, chief of staff Jerry Persons did not. Nixon claimed that he took up the issue with Attorney General William Rogers. Rogers strongly recommended that Jim Hagerty issue a statement from the White House indicating that the Justice Department had been instructed to look into the matter. According to Nixon, "Rogers was unable to get approval from the White House for such a statement." Who refused, the vice president did not say. In any event, by the time the administration had energized itself to do something, the news of the Kennedy call to Mrs. King had broken, and Nixon felt that anything he might do or say after that would be interpreted as politically inspired and nothing more than a reaction to JFK. In his view, any statement by him would do more to alienate blacks than to win their support.[56]

It does not follow that had Nixon beaten Kennedy to the punch with telephone calls, telegrams, and White House action, this incident would have played out in his political favor. Imagine the following counterfactual for a moment. Suppose Richard M. Nixon had immediately contacted Mrs. King and various Georgia politicians. What would have followed? The sad answer is obvious. The vice president would have earned the gratitude of the King family. There is no indication that northern politicians who controlled vast black voting blocs like William Dawson or Adam Clayton Powell Jr. would have been impressed. Georgia politicians would not have been grateful to Nixon. Governor Vandiver, who referred to Martin Luther King Jr. as "that son-of-a-bitch," would hardly have been in the mood to come to the rescue of the civil rights leader. Neither would have Hartsfield, Russell, Stewart, or any other state or local Georgia officials. Any call to Judge Mitchell would not have found a friendly audience. These men were partisan Democrats. They had no love for King, but they wanted Kennedy to win the election. If they could help Kennedy by freeing King, they would do so, but only for that reason. In fact, Nixon's intervention probably would have prolonged

King's imprisonment. Georgia Democrats would have calculated that they could embarrass the Republican candidate by not releasing King.

Meanwhile, a Nixon intervention would have produced a strong reaction from southern Democrats outside Georgia. Lyndon B. Johnson and his southern supporters would have led the Confederate charge against the vice president, denouncing Nixon, reminding southerners of Little Rock, and warning them that Nixon's election would mean the return of the dark days of Reconstruction, that most evil of times.

Richard Nixon was in an impossible situation. He lost by failing to make the telephone calls, but he also would have lost had he made them. He probably would have been an even bigger loser with the calls. Democrats would have broadcast his actions across the breadth of the former Confederacy, but Nixon would not have offset these losses with votes from northern blacks. Nixon could have and should have made the telephone call to Coretta Scott King, but this action would not have benefited him as it did John F. Kennedy. Democrats had fixed the outcome. Nixon had his choice of how he would lose, but he would lose no matter what he did.

In the end, John F. Kennedy outmaneuvered Richard M. Nixon on the Martin Luther King Jr. incident and on the civil rights issue in general. There were many reasons why he managed to do so. Kennedy possessed a number of advantages, but his victory was not foreordained. He needed to maintain a balance between his appeal to southern whites and African Americans. In a close election like 1960, a centrist position on a controversial issue like civil rights was essential for Kennedy to win. With Lyndon Johnson's help, he found that balance. He appealed to blacks effectively without greatly alienating white southerners. Kennedy might not embrace civil rights as Shriver, Wofford, and his critics wanted him to, but he demonstrated respect and sympathy for black political interests. His actions in the Martin Luther King Jr. incident were both a symbol and the culmination of his successful effort. In contrast, Richard Nixon never managed to signal his respect and sympathy for black interests in the 1960 campaign. Nixon had amassed a good record on civil rights in the 1950s. He faced serious disadvantages in competing for the black vote, but after all the excuses have been made, Nixon never convincingly demonstrated his commitment with actions in 1960. The King episode exemplified Nixon's unsuccessful attempt to win over the black vote.

8

The Final Days of the General Election Campaign, October 22–November 7

"With every word he [Eisenhower] utters, I can feel the votes leaving me. It's standing on a mound of sand with the tide running out. I tell you he is knocking our block off. . . . If the election was tomorrow I'd win easily but six days from now it's up for grabs."

—John F. Kennedy on the impact of Eisenhower's campaigning in the last week of the campaign

When Robert F. Kennedy scorched Sargent Shriver for instigating his brother's telephone call to Coretta Scott King, he was motivated by a belief that the call was dangerous because the presidential contest was so tight. But most observers believed that John F. Kennedy was in a position to win decisively, and there was growing optimism within the Kennedy camp. According to Theodore White, "confidence had swollen to overpowering certainty." Those who traveled with JFK "became dazzled, then blinded, with the radiance of approaching victory." Pollster Lou Harris placed Kennedy ahead in each of the nine states with the largest number of electoral votes. Among Democrats, only occasional doubters like Lawrence O'Brien thought the outcome was still in question. For most, the only issue was the margin of victory.[1]

This view was not restricted to Democrats. A late October Gallup Poll showed Kennedy ahead 51 percent to 45 percent, his largest lead of the campaign. A *New York Herald Tribune* survey gave Kennedy 187 secure electoral votes and another 160 leaning his way. (The winning number was 269.) The *New York Daily News*, another newspaper sympathetic to the Republican candidate, placed Kennedy ahead in states with almost 400 electoral votes. It put JFK ahead of Nixon in California by 200,000 votes. Within Republican circles, gloom was the predominant mood. Theodore White claimed that there were individuals in Nixon's entourage speculating about the names of individuals Kennedy would appoint to his cabinet.[2]

Then, sometime in the last ten days of October, the Kennedy tide began to recede, and a Nixon surge took place. Exactly how and why this shift occurred is uncertain. By November 7, although a number of Kennedy aides remained oblivious to what was happening around them, John F. Kennedy was trying to avoid becoming the Democratic version of Thomas E. Dewey. The story of the final phase of the general election campaign on the Democratic side was one of overconfidence and miscalculation, offset by enough fortuitous events to allow the Democratic nominee to hold on and win by an excruciatingly small margin.

What happened to the unstoppable Kennedy wave? The lack of any more debates was part of the answer. For the previous month, the Democratic campaign had been capitalizing on them. They provided the oxygen for the campaign. Without the debates to provide free television exposure, free publicity, and fresh enthusiasm, the campaign had to find new sources of energy. With its candidate approaching a state of exhaustion and with a poorly planned and coordinated television schedule, the campaign struggled.

Beginning October 30, the last nine days of the campaign had Kennedy spending two days in the Philadelphia suburbs, two days in California, a two-day whirlwind trip through Arizona, New Mexico, Texas, and Oklahoma to Virginia, Ohio, and Chicago. The Saturday before election day had the Democratic nominee in a motorcade in New York City, followed by a trip to New England, where he spent Sunday and Monday. John F. Kennedy, ever the realist, sensed that something was wrong. On Saturday, as his motorcade got lost and spent the afternoon driving around the Bronx searching for crowds, JFK became infuriated. He asked, "What am I doing here?" He knew New York was his. He also knew he should have been in California, which was still in doubt. Kennedy lashed out, blaming Carmine DeSapio, blaming Mike Prendergast, blaming Kenneth O'Donnell (his scheduler), and blaming the "son-of-a-bitch" who was driving him. Kennedy, who was the master of television, now found himself assaulted by a Republican television blitz that Democrats were poorly prepared to offset. They lacked the funds for a counterattack, and the shows they aired were badly done. One of his advisers later admitted, "our election eve shows in Boston were not nearly as good as they could have been, and even hurt us."[3]

John F. Kennedy understood that he was losing ground. As Arthur Schlesinger Jr. declared, "It was a strange, impalpable ebbing away." A few others had the same sense. Mildred Jeffrey in Michigan got "the uneasy feeling" that Kennedy "had peaked too early." So did Richard Goodwin, who "never doubted that Kennedy would win. Not until election day."[4]

These Kennedy loyalists were in the minority. The overwhelming majority of informed Democrats were unaware of the growing danger. Adlai Stevenson wrote in a letter, "the windup looks like an easy victory for Kennedy." Chester Bowles believed that Kennedy would win "by a large majority." Joe

Alsop wrote on November 2 that voting surveys showed "a gradual but consistent movement of voters away from Vice-President Nixon." An internal campaign memorandum declared that Nixon strength was declining, Kennedy strength was rising, and "clearly this electorate today is getting ready to break heavily into the Kennedy column." A late Lou Harris poll, according to *Newsweek*, had JFK at 49 percent, Nixon at 41 percent, and 10 percent undecided. Kennedy aides conducted an election pool in which they estimated the popular and electoral vote. Participants predicted between 53 percent and 57 percent of the popular vote. Ted Sorensen predicted 408 electoral votes, a figure that was lower than some others.[5]

Meanwhile, the Nixon campaign picked up momentum. Theodore White saw a change in the candidate as he crossed into Ohio on October 25 and began speaking to a midwestern audience. According to White, Nixon "sensed these people with him" in a way the eastern voters were not. The vice president came to life. His attacks on JFK became more pointed, and he bombarded the electorate with a series of plans and promises. From Nixon's perspective, he was now on the offensive and felt the current running in his favor. He later reminisced that "far from being downhearted and pessimistic, I thought our campaign was going well and was confident about the outcome."[6]

The Kennedy decline and the Nixon ascension occurred for three basic reasons. First, the Nixon campaign planned for a final big push. In contrast, campaign manager Robert F. Kennedy professed not to believe in peaks and valleys in a presidential race and embraced an approach of running as hard as possible for the entirety of the campaign from late August until election day. According to Theodore White, RFK considered the idea of campaign ups and downs "nonsense." Therefore, on the Democratic side, there was no provision for an intensified effort in late October and early November. In this calculation, Bobby Kennedy was wrong and Richard Nixon was right. The last weeks of a close contest are critical. In 1960, the GOP anticipated this and the Democratic high command did not. Nixon ratcheted up his rhetorical attacks on the Democratic nominee and dominated the last two weeks. Nixon gained on Kennedy, and the Democrats had neither the plans nor the resources to counter the Republican surge.[7]

Second and most importantly, the GOP finally unleashed President Dwight D. Eisenhower, the most popular figure in the country. His entry attracted the largest crowds of the season. His infectious smile and hard-hitting speeches infused the Republican campaign with an energy and enthusiasm it had not previously possessed. Even Theodore White, who openly rooted for Kennedy, commented that Eisenhower possessed "a magic in American politics that is peculiarly his: he makes people happy. No cavalcade I have followed in the entourage of any other political figure in this country has ever left so many smiling, glowing people behind as an Eisenhower tour." Eisenhower's intervention was enough to change the race and almost enough to win it for his vice president.[8]

Ike's participation provided the last chapter in the melodrama that was the Nixon-Eisenhower partnership. The story of the president and the Republican presidential campaign began with the meeting in July in Newport, Rhode Island, between the two men in the immediate aftermath of the Republican convention. They agreed that the president would maintain a low profile and confine himself to nonpolitical speeches until late in the contest. Then Eisenhower would embark on a series of partisan speeches to lift the campaign in its closing days. Eisenhower made it very plain that he would do anything requested of him but that the vice president must ask. From the outset, the basis of his participation in the campaign was established in Eisenhower's mind. He would wait for the vice president to call upon him and give him his marching orders. From Eisenhower's point of view, the call to battle that he expected did not come until much too late.[9]

There were two reasons for holding back the president. First, Nixon needed and wanted to establish his own identity as a candidate. He feared that too great an Eisenhower presence too early would allow Kennedy to label him as someone who had no program of his own but was simply relying on Ike and his coattails. Second, limiting the use of Eisenhower was an attempt to maximize his impact when he did appear late in the campaign. As a political weapon, he "would be more powerful for having been sparingly used." Nixon was correct in these calculations. Earlier and more frequent appearances by Ike would have dissipated the dramatic impact he had in the last week of the campaign.[10]

Some suspected that this reasoning was just the vice president's elaborate excuse to keep Eisenhower out of the campaign as much as possible. In this view, the unstated aim was to demonstrate that Nixon could win the election on his own without relying on the White House. Whatever the reasons, the request for Eisenhower's presence did not come until the very last minute.[11]

During the late summer and fall, the president became politically restless in Washington and Gettysburg. He had never liked JFK, whom he referred to as "Little Boy Blue," and he liked his campaign manager brother even less. Their continuing attacks on the alleged malfeasance of his administration made him angrier and angrier. At a meeting of the GOP legislative leaders in mid-August, he concluded the session with the comment, "Boy! I'm getting darned political around here!" This situation persisted through September and into October. By then, Eisenhower was annoyed by the vice president's inexplicable failure to give him the signal to commence his efforts. He was not entirely inactive as he made numerous television and speaking appearances in the first three weeks of October. In them, he attacked "fear mongering" and "misguided people" who thought the United States was becoming a second-class power. In mid-October, he made an extensive nonpolitical tour starting in Detroit and ending in Virginia on October 27. However, Nixon's call still did not come, and the president was increasingly frustrated. After the election, he told numerous individuals that he would have campaigned more for Nixon, but he "just wasn't asked." According to Barry Goldwater, Eisenhower "was sitting in Gettysburg, just jumping around like a mouse in a trap, waiting to be asked." Ike expressed his sentiments most emphatically to Earl Mazo after the election, asking the reporter: "What the hell was it, Earl? Did the s.o.b. think I was going to steal the limelight from him?" He added, "I wanted to get in there, get my gloves off."[12]

When the vice president finally called Ike and asked for his aid, there was more controversy. A hasty White House luncheon was arranged for October 31, at which time Eisenhower's schedule for the final week was agreed to. The president was unhappy because he proposed three additional campaign appearances that the vice president brushed off.[13]

Richard Nixon later explained his rejection of Ike's plan for expanded campaign appearances in the final week. According to the vice president, the night before his October 31 meeting with the president, Mamie Eisenhower made a telephone call to Pat Nixon. Mrs. Eisenhower was "distraught" and implored Mrs. Nixon to convince the vice president to avoid heavy campaigning for Ike for fear of its consequences for the president's heart. The next morning, Nixon received another call, this one from Dr. Howard Snyder, the president's private physician. Snyder told the vice president that he could not approve a heavy campaign schedule because "the strain of intense campaigning might be too much for his limited cardiac reserves." As a result of these pleas, Nixon limited his request for appearances to Eisenhower, even though the president wanted to do more. The vice president's refusal to approve an expanded campaign schedule puzzled and annoyed Ike. The moral of the story was that Nixon did not call upon Eisenhower to do more because of his concern and the concern of Mrs. Eisenhower and Dr. Snyder for Ike's health.[14]

Nixon's account of these events appeared in his memoirs published in

1978. By this time, the other participants in the event were dead or dying—Eisenhower (d. 1969), Howard Snyder (d. 1970), and Mrs. Eisenhower (d. 1979). None of the principals was left to challenge his narrative or to vouch for it. Interestingly, though, a version of Nixon's story had appeared twelve years earlier. In September 1966, political writer Ted Lewis published a column in which he told the story of the Nixon-Eisenhower lunch of October 31 in the same terms that Nixon himself used in 1978. The column emphasized the vice president's refusal to support an Eisenhower trip to Chicago in addition to those already on the schedule because of the vice president's concern for the president's health. The column ended with the assertion: "Now at last we know the truth. Nixon preferred to lose rather than jeopardize Ike's health."[15]

Old friend William E. Robinson wrote a long letter to Eisenhower bringing the story to his attention. Robinson said he was incensed at Nixon because in the aftermath of the election some people attributed the defeat to Eisenhower's inactivity. Robinson, who was present in Newport when Eisenhower made his July pledge to do whatever was asked of him, held Nixon responsible for the president's small role in the general election campaign. In Robinson's narrative, he confronted Nixon in October. He told the vice president in no uncertain terms that unless he effectively refuted the Democratic attacks on the administration and got the president to participate in the campaign, he would lose the election. According to Robinson, "not only did he [Nixon] not resent my gratuitous advice and criticism—he agreed with it and promised to correct the lapse."[16]

Eisenhower's reaction to Robinson's letter was muted. He said that the Lewis column had "certain elements of truth" and stated that he did not learn of the conversation between Nixon and Snyder until very recently. He did not endorse the thrust of the column, but neither did he deny it. Mamie and Snyder had been directly involved and not he. By this time, he and Nixon were on better terms than they had been in 1960. He may have wished to avoid any unpleasantness with his former vice president. On the other hand, Ike was never one to ignore disagreements when he thought someone was wrong or dissembling, so there was something to Nixon's account. Additional confirmation of Nixon's version came from Fred Seaton, who was present when Snyder made his appeal to the vice president.[17]

Eisenhower's health was an issue during his presidency with a heart attack in 1955, a bout with ileitis in 1956, and a stroke in 1957. His personal physician, Dr. Howard M. Snyder, was not an exceptional medical practitioner, but in the opinion of one author, he was "a supreme family doctor" and "a superb manager of the medical care" for the president. He convinced Ike to alter his behavior. The president changed his diet, exercised more regularly, and did his best to avoid outbursts of anger. In short, "Eisenhower did in the 1950s what experts are asking Americans to do today—make rational choices to protect their health because there are limits to what others can do for them."[18]

The president's health was generally good after 1957, but any intensive participation in the 1960 campaign threatened it. Infuriated by JFK and the Democrats, Ike was in the mood for a fight. This attitude produced a variety of health problems including sleeplessness, occasional serious headaches, elevated blood pressure, and skips in his heartbeat. A trip to Detroit on October 17–18 resulted in what Snyder considered a very dangerous situation. Eisenhower became enraged at a United Auto Workers leaflet that equated Republicans with the Ku Klux Klan. Eisenhower's fury translated itself into a threat to his heart. He manifested signs of high systolic blood pressure and rapid atrial fibrillation. Fortunately, Snyder was present to treat him—but his presence was a matter of luck. The doctor missed the motorcade from the White House to Andrews Air Force Base and had to follow in another car. Snyder managed to catch the flight and be with Eisenhower—but only because his car drove at 90 to 100 miles per hour to Andrews. Snyder recounted: "I made the plane all right, but had I missed it I just would not have come at all. Had this been the case, the President unquestionably would have been in extreme danger because of the episode he had with his heart action." And this was on a "nonpolitical" trip.[19]

Understandably, Mrs. Eisenhower and Dr. Snyder were concerned about the presidential health, especially after the Michigan trip. They were concerned over what might happen if the president became engaged in a round of daily campaigning with motorcades, crowds, speeches, and all the other stress that went with such an effort. They had more than sufficient reason to approach the vice president with a plea to limit Ike's campaigning.

Even with a limited campaign schedule in the last week, Eisenhower had a major impact. JFK reflected to Paul "Red" Fay that "with every word he [Eisenhower] utters, I can feel the votes leaving me. It's standing on a mound of sand with the tide running out. I tell you he is knocking our block off. . . . If the election was tomorrow I'd win easily, but six days from now it's up for grabs."[20] Of all the might-have-beens of 1960, perhaps the greatest revolves around Nixon's utilization of Eisenhower. There is a widespread belief that if the vice president had mobilized Ike even three or four days sooner, located him in the right cities, or put him on television more frequently, he probably would have emerged the victor on November 8.

The third major factor in the Nixon surge was the GOP television blitz.

Although John F. Kennedy outperformed Richard Nixon in the televised debates, the Democratic television operation was inferior to its Republican counterpart. Republican advertising on television and radio was "more pervasive and better coordinated." Democrats may have spent more money in direct payments to advertising firms for commercials on radio and TV, but the ads were badly coordinated and poorly executed. October 25 marked the beginning of the GOP TV offensive with a national telecast of a Nixon rally in Cincinnati. There were two additional national telecasts of Republican rallies in late October and early November. A live Nixon television show aired every night in the last week of the campaign. A four-hour Nixon telethon from Detroit on ABC-TV on election eve afternoon provided a grand culmination of the Republican TV effort. On the same day, the Republican campaign presented a fifteen-minute national program with Thomas E. Dewey and a final half-hour show on all three national networks, featuring Eisenhower, Nixon, and Lodge on a three-way hookup. Democratic counterprogramming was sparse and ineffective. The Nixon campaign dominated the airwaves in the last week of the presidential contest.[21]

The Republican television productions were well done and reached large audiences. Nixon's telethon on November 7 was his best use of television in the entire campaign. It attracted viewers in an estimated 20 percent of all households in the country. It allowed Nixon to come into the homes of Americans, answer their questions, and speak directly to them in a friendly, calm, and reassuring manner. Ironically, Nixon initially vetoed the show, the idea of Carroll Newton and Ted Rogers, but eventually conceded because of the demands of large donors. Exceptionally tired when he arrived at the television studio, he lashed out in anger at both stagehands and his own aides. He offered one criticism after another about the arrangements for the program, but in spite of his foul mood, the vice president performed very well. The program presented him in a very different light than had the debates. On November 7, he seemed a relaxed, sympathetic politician who was at ease talking to average Americans about their problems. It was his best television performance of the campaign, and it came on the brink of the election.[22]

Democrats were divided on Nixon's show, although most gave it grudging admiration. Theodore White conceded its effectiveness but said that it "mixed schmaltz and substance in equal proportions." He believed that the show "contributed mightily" to the Nixon surge. Ted Sorensen thought it was "insipid." Leonard Reinsch was more impressed, calling it "a slick, excellent production, albeit 'cornball' at times." John Seigenthaler considered it "very effective." Calls came in demanding that the Democratic Party answer the program, but there were no plans and no money to do so. Lawrence O'Brien believed that JFK's failure to match Nixon was a major mistake and that the closeness of the election was partly a result of the failure to offer anything comparable. On the Republican side, Herb Klein believed that the telethon "changed up to 4 percent of the vote."[23]

The Republican offensive fell short because it began too late but also because three fortuitous events offset it enough to preserve the Kennedy win. The first of these was the Martin Luther King Jr. incident and JFK's response to it. The big shift in black votes had already largely occurred. However, with the closeness of the election outcome—even if the effect was just a few tens of thousands as opposed to hundreds of thousands of votes—the episode was a benefit to the Democratic nominee at a time and in states where he needed help.

The second occurrence that aided the Democratic nominee was a late-breaking story from newspaperman Drew Pearson. At the end of October, just as the King affair was playing out, Pearson published a story that the vice president's younger brother Donald had received a $205,000 loan from Howard Hughes. The loan was supposed to finance a business venture in which Donald would be establishing eateries that would have "Nixonburgers" as their trademark product.

Pearson and other scandalmongers then and later alleged that for his money the eccentric millionaire got access to the vice president and preferential treatment in a number of areas affecting his multiplicity of business interests, most notably the Hughes Medical Institute, a tax-exempt charitable institution. Pearson was not the most credible newsman and something of a Nixon nemesis, but his allegations were well timed for maximum effect. The vice president did not handle the charges well. According to Hughes aide Robert Maheu, he offered to manage the response, but Nixon declined and decided to have his campaign take control of the explanation. It promptly botched the job and made the story even bigger. The Hughes loan did not die but enjoyed a life that extended beyond November 8. The question of the Hughes-Nixon relationship resurfaced in 1962, again in 1968, and persisted even after that. The consensus is that the allegations were rumor and innuendo. Coming as late as they did and being as complicated as they were, their impact was probably minimal. Still, in an election where mere thousands of votes made a difference, the Hughes loan story damaged the Republican candidate. The only question is, how much?[24]

If Nixon might have better handled the Drew Pearson charges, he had no control over the final incident—one that may have cost him the state of Texas. In late October, Congressman Bruce Alger and a group of Republican protestors confronted Lyndon B. Johnson and Lady Bird Johnson in the lobby of the Adolphus Hotel in Dallas. The placard-waving demonstrators were overwhelmingly middle- and upper-class white women who quickly became known as the "mink coat mob." Johnson could have made his way through the Adolphus lobby in five minutes, but he recognized the opportunity before him. LBJ proceeded to take as much time as possible, thirty minutes, as television and radio recorded the event, and newspaper reporters gleefully wrote their stories. The impression that Johnson managed to convey was that of a pair of decent citizens attempting to pass through a public accommodation and being assaulted by an unruly mob of rude Republicans.[25]

If such was LBJ's intention, he was successful beyond his wildest dreams. Hundreds of letters poured into Johnson, bemoaning the incivility to which he and Mrs. Johnson had been subjected. Overnight, LBJ, usually not a very sympathetic character, found himself the recipient of a groundswell of public support. Campaign workers were angered and infused with new energy and enthusiasm as they redoubled their efforts. The incident resonated outside the borders of the Lone Star State. Georgia senator Richard B. Russell, the most respected southern senator of his era, had not actively campaigned for a Democratic presidential candidate since 1944. He purposely spent almost all of October in Europe to avoid being involved in the 1960 contest, but he returned to the United States on October 30. Shortly thereafter, he acceded to pleas from his protégé Lyndon Johnson to come to Texas to campaign. Russell considered himself very close to Lady Bird and his decision to work for the Kennedy-Johnson ticket was a result of his outrage at the Adolphus affair. LBJ managed to convert a minor incident into a major advantage for himself and JFK in the waning days of the campaign in a very tight contest in Texas. More than a few observers believed that the ultimate Democratic victory in Texas on November 8 was a direct product of the episode in Dallas. One Johnson associate called it exaggeratedly "the greatest political error that anybody ever made" and, more reasonably, "the final thing that really clinched it for us."[26]

There were several ironies connected to the affair. Bruce Alger apparently planned the demonstration to embarrass Lyndon Johnson, but it ended up being a huge embarrassment to him, the Republican Party, and Richard Nixon. Alger was something of a firebrand. He was the lone Republican congressman in Texas in 1960 and owed his position to liberal Democrats. He had been elected because his 1954 Democratic opponent, Wallace Savage, had supported Eisenhower in the previous presidential election, and liberal Democrats were in a mood to teach him a lesson by cutting him in the midterm elections. Savage did not help his cause when he said that he did not want black votes. The upshot was that, thanks to the Democratic infighting, Bruce Alger won the election. If Democrats were pleased at making an example of Wallace Savage, they were not happy with Bruce Alger. Sam Rayburn found Alger "totally obnoxious" and refused to speak to him after the Dallas congressman said that Rayburn was OK but put party ahead of country.[27]

Alger attempted to tell his side of the Adolphus story, maintaining that the press badly distorted the facts of the matter. He even took out a full-page advertisement in the *Dallas Morning News* on November 8, but to no avail. Like so many others, he had been outmaneuvered by LBJ. The mink coat mob and Bruce Alger gave JFK and LBJ a needed lift in one of the most critical states in the Union, a state that the Democratic ticket narrowly carried on November 8. Whether the Democratic victory in Texas derived from the confrontation in Dallas is uncertain. Almost all Texans, though, seemed to agree that it was a significant factor.[28]

Another issue that did not help Nixon, contrary to conventional wisdom, was the religious question. By the time of the first presidential debate, Kennedy had gained the advantage by virtue of his performance at the Houston Ministerial Conference.[29] In Houston, he staked out a position that established himself as a strong defender of the Constitution and the separation of church and state. The event also suggested that religious prejudice motivated the Protestants who opposed him. With polling analysis in hand that showed he had everything to gain and little to lose by confronting the issue in uncompromising terms, the Kennedy campaign proceeded to do so in a fashion that manipulated religion to its advantage.

The Democratic approach identified Kennedy as a symbol of religious freedom and his opponent as a representative of religious bigotry. The nominee wisely avoided any participation in the dirty work. But he had no shortage of volunteers who were happy to hit Richard Nixon and the GOP. Bobby Kennedy, Lyndon Johnson, Harry Truman, and Adam Clayton Powell Jr. proved more than eager to leap to the attack. Robert Kennedy barnstormed through the Catskills, telling Jews that an attack on Roman Catholics could lead to an attack on them and therefore they should rally to the Democratic ticket. Lyndon Johnson, who had anti-Catholic literature available for distribution at the Democratic National Convention, now turned to throwing off slurs and innuendos about the religion of Richard Nixon. Harry Truman, campaigning through Texas, declared that the religious defamation of John F. Kennedy took place with Richard Nixon's tacit approval. In San Antonio, he told his audience, "If you vote for Nixon, you ought to go to hell." Truman was important in the South because he was a Baptist and a thirty-third degree Mason as well. Adam Clayton Powell Jr. declared the KKK was riding again and that "all the bigots will vote for Nixon and all right-thinking Christians and Jews will vote for Kennedy rather than be found in the ranks of the Klan-minded." Democrats rallied Roman Catholics behind the Democratic ticket. Simultaneously, they appealed to Jews, blacks, and liberal Protestants to join them in a crusade against intolerance.[30]

Democrats also made good use of Kennedy's Houston performance. The Houston event was edited into a half-hour program as well as one- and five-minute television spot advertisements. The latter appeared primarily in states where there was Protestant feeling against the Catholic candidate. In that use they were entirely appropriate as an attempt to educate the electorate as to Kennedy's position. The half-hour program and its use were a different story. According to the leading authority on the use of television in presidential campaigns, it aired *"disproportionately often in the fourteen states that the Bailey-Sorensen memo of 1956 had identified as states that could be swung into the Democratic column by Catholic voters."* In other words, Democrats intentionally put the Houston affair on television in heavily Catholic areas in order to incite Catholics and to mobilize them to vote for Kennedy.[31]

Meanwhile, the always reliable Joseph Alsop chimed in. Alsop, who identified Humphrey as the candidate of bigots in West Virginia, now turned his rhetoric on Nixon. Never one to avoid hyperbole, he predicted in late August that in the South "the new attack on the Roman Catholic Church will make Sen. John F. Kennedy's experience in the West Virginia primary look like an interfaith tea party." Alsop conceded that Richard Nixon had nothing to do with the anti-Catholic material but asserted that Nixon was the "intended beneficiary" and that he did not specifically repudiate those generating such literature. Nixon, like Humphrey, was an ally of religious bigots.[32]

Through all of this Nixon refused to react to the Democratic assault. Nixon abhorred religious prejudice and was especially respectful of Roman Catholicism. One of the people closest to him, Rose Mary Woods, was Catholic. One of his early political mentors was a Catholic priest, Father James Cronin. The vice president was on excellent terms with a number of the most powerful figures in the country's Catholic hierarchy, including Francis Cardinal Spellman of New York and James Francis Cardinal McIntyre of Los Angeles. In fact, Nixon probably had a better relationship with the American Catholic prelates than did John F. Kennedy. Nixon believed that he could easily have been a Catholic. He said he longed for the order and the certainty that Catholic dogma and ecclesiastical structure afforded the Catholic faithful.[33]

Beginning in September and continuing until early November, leading Republicans repeatedly informed the vice president that his Democratic opponent was having his way on the subject of religion. Bryce Harlow told the vice president that Lyndon Johnson "is talking religion at every stop, all over the country . . . and you're flat losing the campaign on religion, and that's wrong." Harlow warned Nixon that he was "being religioned right out of this campaign." At the end of the race, Peter Flanigan, executive director of Volunteers for Nixon-Lodge and a Catholic, went to the nominee and pleaded with him to do something to stop the hemorrhaging of Catholic votes from the ticket. Nixon's reply was to tell Flanigan "not to play the religious card under any circumstances whatsoever." Finally, in early November, almost on the eve of the election, Secretary of Health, Education, and Welfare Arthur Flemming prepared a draft of a speech on the religious issue calling for everyone to vote on the basis of the issues and not to be influenced by religion. Nixon rejected that, too.[34]

Then there was the curious incident with Billy Graham. The man who was the best-known Protestant evangelist in the country had met Nixon's mother in 1949 and Nixon himself in 1950–51. By 1960, Graham and Nixon were on close terms. During the year, Graham became concerned by the prospect of a Kennedy victory and a Catholic in the White House. He was convinced the Democrats were exploiting the religious issue. He urged Nixon to name Congressman Walter Judd, a former Protestant missionary, as his vice-presidential choice. Later in the campaign, Graham contacted Henry Luce with the idea of writing an article for *Life* about Nixon without openly endorsing him. Luce suggested an essay about "Richard M. Nixon— The Man." The plan was to have the piece appear in October. Graham wrote the proposed essay and submitted it to Luce. A holdup in publication, Democratic protests, and second thoughts on the part of Graham resulted in the article never being published. Throughout all of this, the vice president maintained a clear perspective on the probable negative reaction to such a piece. According to Nixon, he cautioned Graham "not to make any public endorsement of him or to associate with the campaign in any way." He told Graham that such actions would discredit Graham's ministry.[35]

Richard Nixon allowed his rival to seize the initiative and set the agenda on this critical subject. The Kennedy campaign maneuvered freely without Republican counterattacks. The Democrats handled the situation adroitly and only once found themselves in trouble, and, even then, a labor union committed the error. The misstep occurred in October, when the United Auto Workers produced a furor with a vicious political flyer urging a vote for Kennedy. The UAW publication featured the drawing of a Statue of Liberty and a hooded member of the KKK carrying a torch in one hand and a club in the other. The heading across the page read: "Which do you choose? Liberty or bigotry?" There was a backlash against this blatant attempt to identify Nixon and the GOP with the KKK. Dwight Eisenhower became angrier over this than any event in the campaign. The UAW and the Kennedy campaign realized their mistake and ignored the uproar as best they could. The clamor passed. This was the only time that Democrats or their allies were forced to retreat in their clever attacks.[36]

How does one explain Richard Nixon's unusually passive behavior as the religion issue played out in the fall campaign? His early position—that discussion of religion ought to be avoided at all costs—is understandable in terms of political advantage. After September, however, some response was needed. Yet he did nothing.[37]

Nixon offered the best explanation in *Six Crises*. There he said he resisted any statement about what his supporters called "reverse bigotry" because it would have inevitably further inflamed the issue, adding: "from a personal point of view, I could not dismiss from my mind the persistent thought, that, in fact, Kennedy was a member of a minority religion to which the presidency had been denied throughout the history of our nation and that perhaps I, as a Protestant who had never felt the strings of discrimination, could not understand his feelings—that, in short, he had every right to speak out against even possible and potential bigotry." Nixon "felt a responsibility to keep the lid on" what he called "the boiling cauldron of embittered anti-Catholicism." He wisely foresaw that if he made a late speech on religion and then won the election, his victory would be tainted by the suspicion that religious preferences had determined the outcome. Nixon concluded with the thought that "The cause of religious tolerance, which had advanced slowly and painfully for so many years would be substantially set back" if he won in that manner. It was a perceptive understanding of the issue. Nixon's refusal to play the religious card was his finest moment in the fall campaign.[38]

For this behavior, Nixon received no credit from the Kennedy camp. It saw his initial plea not to discuss the religious issue as "a shrewd political ploy." Later, it purported to detect all kinds of connections between individual Protestant clergymen who raised questions about Kennedy's religion in the White House and the Republican campaign. Of course, some individuals such as Norman Vincent Peale and Billy Graham were friends of Nixon. Democrats also alleged that Republicans conspired or cooperated with groups putting out anti-Catholic literature. It is likely that lower-level GOP officials in some locations may have attempted to manipulate the issue, but any incitement of the religious issue after September 1 benefited JFK. It was Democrats, not Republicans, who stood to gain by agitating on this subject.[39]

In addition, there was a strong suspicion in the GOP, as earlier in the Humphrey camp, that some Democratic operatives were not above sending anti-Catholic hate mail to Catholics and planting anti-Catholic literature in GOP offices in an effort to increase Catholic turnout for Kennedy. Despite the slurs on Nixon, the evidence suggests that his attitude and conduct were exemplary—and costly, since there is good reason to believe that the massaging of the religious issue was one of the keys to the Democratic triumph on November 8.

The Nixon campaign was a whirlwind of frantic activity in the final fortnight. In the last five days before the election, the candidate raced from South Carolina to Texas, Wyoming, Washington state, California, Alaska, Wisconsin, Detroit, Chicago, and finally Los Angeles as he attempted to close the gap with Kennedy while fulfilling his fifty-state pledge. Pleas that Illinois was hanging in the balance and required his presence went unheeded.

The campaign also put forward two initiatives for which it asked White House support. One was a request that Eisenhower call for publication of the health records of the presidential candidates. The second was a proposal to invite communist bloc leaders to visit the United States, while sending Eisenhower on a trip to Eastern European countries in 1961. When Nixon made the announcement on Sunday, November 6, the plan involved Herbert Hoover and Harry Truman as well as Eisenhower. These overtures met a cold reception in the White House. Eisenhower, press secretary James Hagerty, and presidential secretary Ann Whitman all found the proposals contrived and smacking of desperation. Eisenhower was sensitive about presidential health issues and refused to raise the matter. Furthermore, he had no intention of undertaking the kind of travel that Nixon proposed.[40]

And so one of the truly great presidential campaigns in United States history ended. One can nitpick at both Nixon and Kennedy, but never in the history of the country had two rivals for the presidency driven themselves harder than the Massachusetts senator and his California opponent. The campaigns may have ended on disappointing notes, but the two men deeply impressed the nation with their energy and their abilities. Never again in the twentieth century would the United States see a match between more skilled, energetic presidential candidates.

As the campaign concluded on November 7, although the candidates did not know it, they were headed into one of the closest elections of the century. In the popular vote, no other election matched it. Although the electoral vote count was not as narrow, it turned on outcomes in nineteen states in which the winning margin was less than 5 percent. Not only was there an extraordinarily close popular vote, but there were also exceptionally tight state-by-state results. With such an outcome, it is therefore interesting to examine how the candidates, their pollsters, and the major news magazines assessed the state of the presidential contest on the eve of the election.

The most accurate prediction and the least realistic view came from the Kennedy camp. John F. Kennedy, in a discussion with Rowland Evans of the *New York Herald Tribune*, laid out a highly accurate projection of where states would fall on November 8. He counted fifteen states with 187 electoral votes (New York, New Jersey, Massachusetts, Alabama, Arkansas, Georgia, Louisiana, Mississippi, Rhode Island, Connecticut, Missouri, Wisconsin, Alaska, West Virginia, and Maryland) as "securely in the Kennedy bag." Of these, two would go to Nixon (Alaska and Wisconsin), although Kennedy would lose all of Mississippi's and six of Alabama's electoral votes to unpledged electors. In the six other states with the largest electoral vote counts (Ohio, California, Pennsylvania, Texas, Michigan, and Illinois) with a total of 160 electoral votes, he felt he needed any four to win in combination with the 187 electoral votes he anticipated from the sure states. As it turned out, he won exactly four of this group (Pennsylvania, Texas, Michigan, and Illinois) with 103 electoral votes, although this was not quite enough to put him over the top, since he lost twenty-nine electoral votes that he did not expect from the first group. Kennedy believed that he had a fifty-fifty chance in Florida, North Carolina, Tennessee, Kentucky, and Nevada, and he had not written off Virginia and South Carolina. The outcomes in these states were indeed tight, and JFK won three of the seven (North Carolina, Nevada, and South Carolina). He listed other possible wins as Colorado, Arizona, Minnesota, Washington, Montana, and Delaware and won two of them (Minnesota and Delaware). Even while his aides were in the clouds dreaming of a landslide, John F. Kennedy maintained his celebrated detachment and came up with a remarkably realistic assessment of where he stood in the presidential race.[41]

If JFK was right on target, his pollster was not. Lou Harris's track record in the 1960 primary season was not good. Harris's reports at the end of the fall campaign were unrealistically positive as he seemed to be predicting an impending landslide or near landslide. According to *Newsweek*, his final projection of the popular vote had Kennedy ahead by 9 percent. He had all seven of the states with the largest electoral votes, including the two JFK would lose (California and Ohio), in the Kennedy column. In his final survey of Ohio, dated November 4 and based on polling finished by October 25, Harris declared that "Ohio appears to be solidly in the Kennedy column." He reported that "Nixon has consistently lost strength from early September through the late part of October." He correctly predicted that JFK would carry New York, Illinois, Pennsylvania, Michigan, and Texas, and he rightly noted that JFK suffered from "underexposure" in California. But the margins of victory he projected for all states were too high. There was no indication of the tight outcomes looming in Pennsylvania, Michigan, Texas, and Illinois, not to mention the defeats in Ohio and California. Curiously enough, on the one state that was safe for the Democratic nominee, New York, Harris inserted a cautionary note in his final survey. He observed that the undecided vote in the state remained high and was large enough to tip the election to the Republican.[42]

Richard M. Nixon's thoughts heading into election day are more difficult to decipher than those of his Democratic opponent. Nixon needed to maintain an optimistic public outlook, and he did. In a late *New York Herald Tribune* story, he saw himself ahead in Ohio, Pennsylvania, Texas, Illinois, and California with a total of 140 electoral votes. He argued that he would win Maine, Vermont, New Hampshire, Delaware, Virginia, Florida, South Carolina, Indiana, Iowa, Nebraska, the two Dakotas, Hawaii, Oregon, Idaho, Utah, Arizona, Wyoming, Kentucky, Tennessee, and Kansas with 147 electoral votes. He would look to Colorado, Minnesota, and Wisconsin to provide any additional needed electoral votes. Nixon proved most accurate in the second group of states, where he correctly predicted eighteen of the twenty-one, missing only on Delaware, South Carolina, and Hawaii. He was also right in two of the three states in the last category. Where he was wrong was in his estimation of the big electoral states, where he forecast victory in five and won in only two.[43]

From later comments in *Six Crises*, one can detect doubts about his prospects in Illinois, Pennsylvania, and Texas. He characterized the situation at the end as follows: "a fair chance in Pennsylvania with that state leaning to Kennedy, a better than even chance in Ohio, a fair chance in Michigan but again leaning to Kennedy, an even chance in Illinois, and both Texas and

California close but leaning to Nixon." Nixon was less confident than Kennedy and for good reason.[44]

If JFK did better than his opponent at predicting the election, the reverse was true for the two pollsters in the rival camps. Richard Nixon contended that Claude Robinson did a better job for him in 1960. The Republican candidate summed it up succinctly: "my pollster was right on the money." This conclusion may have been an exaggeration, but it was justified for Robinson's predictions on the popular vote. Robinson, throughout the campaign, had the split between the two candidates at fifty-fifty, and that was his final forecast. Robinson's record on individual states was not as accurate. Of the big seven states, he was wrong on Texas and Ohio and right on the other five. He also missed on Missouri, Hawaii, North Carolina, Nevada, Wisconsin, and Alaska, but was correct on all other states. Equally important, his projection of the Nixon vote was off by more than 4 percent in only six states (Iowa, New Hampshire, Louisiana, Alaska, Delaware, and Rhode Island).[45]

Throughout the early campaign, Robinson remained optimistic. Strangely, his most sanguine projection came in mid-October, when the Nixon campaign seemed at a low ebb. Even with the Nixon surge, Robinson grew less confident in an electoral combination that would reach the necessary 269 votes. On October 21, he produced an evaluation of the campaign as of October 14 (and the third debate) in which he put Nixon at 51 percent or better in states with 259 electoral votes. Included in these states were Illinois, Texas, and North Carolina as well as Nevada, none of which Nixon would carry in November. Robinson offered his "private forecast" on election results. It was 269 electoral votes for Nixon and 268 votes for Kennedy, not exactly an overwhelming vote of confidence.[46]

His October 28 analysis of the campaign as it stood on October 22 (and the fourth debate) had Nixon at 51 percent or better in states with 235 electoral votes. Robinson accurately pointed out that California, Texas, Ohio, and Illinois were "the key to a Nixon victory," observing that "A strong finish is needed, for several states are close to the line." He also asserted that "Nixon-Lodge can win, but the margin is very small."[47]

Robinson's final estimate of November 5 put Nixon with 51 percent or more of the popular vote in states with only 176 electoral votes. Even so, there were five misses with Missouri, Hawaii, Texas, North Carolina, and Nevada. He rated another seven states with 78 electoral votes at 50 percent, with the remaining states and their 283 electoral votes at 49 percent or less for Nixon. This was not a bright picture and represented a deterioration of the situation in mid-October. As Nixon gained in the last phase of the campaign, Robinson became more pessimistic. Robinson and Nixon may have claimed that they still thought they could win, but if they did so it was in defiance of the polling, not because of it.[48]

Outside the campaigns, the three major news magazines, *Time*, *Newsweek*, and *U.S. News & World Report*, offered their opinions on both national and state outcomes in the election. All three saw Kennedy winning. *Time* had his margin at 306 electoral votes to 149 for Nixon and 82 undecided. *Newsweek* called it 278 to 159 in favor of Kennedy with 100 undecided. *U.S. News* had Kennedy as the winner at 282 to 205 with 50 electoral votes doubtful. Of the trio, *Time* did the best job in calling the results in the big seven states with four right and *U.S. News* the worst, as it missed on five of the seven. *Newsweek* got three correct and two wrong and called the other two tossups. Overall, *Time* got thirty-three states right, even while managing somehow to omit South Dakota. *Newsweek* and *U.S. News* did almost as well, picking thirty-two and thirty-one states respectively correctly and including South Dakota. All three missed on Alaska, Ohio, Mississippi, and South Carolina. The three news magazines managed to pick between three-fifths and two-thirds of the states correctly. How impressive this performance was depends on one's viewpoint. Since the winner in nineteen states finished 5 percent or less ahead of his opponent, that number suggests picking winners was a difficult task. On the other hand, in approximately twenty states, the winner was or should have been obvious to any well-informed political observer by Labor Day.[49]

Although the projections of the news magazines were not unreasonable, they were misleading. *Time* and its companions portrayed a race in which Kennedy was widening his lead and headed for a decisive victory. The Gallup Poll indicated just the opposite trend. According to it, Kennedy's lead was shrinking and Nixon was closing fast. At the end of the debates, Gallup had Kennedy ahead 51 percent to 45 percent. In the last Gallup Poll in early November, the Kennedy margin shriveled to 49 percent to 48 percent with 3 percent undecided. With the undecided out, Gallup's final poll showed JFK at 50.5 percent and Nixon at 49.5 percent. There was an obvious contradiction between Gallup and the news magazines. The latter implicitly predicted a Kennedy sweep, perhaps even a landslide. The former predicted an election that could go either way. As it turned out, George Gallup was right, and *Time* and the other news weeklies were wrong. George Gallup predicted what the country faced on November 8, but neither of the candidates, their campaigns, the news media, or the public were ready for the reality they would encounter when election returns began to come in on November 8.[50]

9

November 8, 1960, and Its Aftermath

"I'm not discouraged—just eviscerated, lacerated and obliterated. I would have worked harder but discovered there aren't more than 24 hours to a day."
—White House aide Bryce Harlow on his reaction to the Republican defeat on November 8

On November 8, 1960, Americans went to the polls as they had not done in more than fifty years and would not do again. Voter turnout (that is, the percentage of eligible voters casting their ballots) was greater than for any of the great Roosevelt elections of 1932, 1936, and 1940, and the highest since 1908. It has not been equaled since, and now ranks as the highest voter participation in a century. Ironically, one individual who did not vote was none other than Theodore H. White, who was unable to return to New York City on November 8 and had neglected to obtain an absentee ballot. His vote would go uncast and uncounted.[1]

Until substantial returns began to come in sometime after 7:00 P.M. EST, election day was a tedious affair for the candidates, who could do nothing more than vote and wait. The waiting was nerve-racking. John F. Kennedy cast his vote in Boston, flew to Hyannis Port, and retired to the family compound, where he joined his family and some of his closest advisers like Ted Sorensen, John Bailey, and Lou Harris.[2]

Richard M. Nixon had a more adventurous day. Early in the morning he voted at his home precinct in Whittier and then decided to spend a day without the suffocating press coverage. He saw this as possibly his last chance at freedom for four years. In the vice president's words, "If we win tonight, we will not be able to escape the press or the secret service for four years." He stepped out of his limousine and into a convertible he had ordered. With military aide Don Hughes, Secret Service agent Jack Sherwood, and driver and Los Angeles detective John DiBetta, Nixon took off. He told DiBetta to escape the trailing press and Secret Service automobiles. After some evasive maneuvers, DiBetta succeeded. The four men then drove down the coast highway toward San Diego. There was an agreement that there would be no discussion of the campaign or the election, and the car radio remained off. The vice president discovered that Don Hughes had never been to Tijuana, so it was off to Tijuana, where they ate at the Old Heidelberg Restaurant. The mayor of Tijuana and the police chief joined them, and a good time was had by all. While at the restaurant, Hughes called press secretary Herb Klein to inform him of the vice president's activities. Klein was flabbergasted.

About 2:00 P.M., the four men left Tijuana for the return trip to Los Angeles, but on the way stopped at San Juan Capistrano so that Hughes could see the famous mission. In Nixon's words, he was going to take Hughes, who was "one of his favorite Catholics," to "one of my favorite Catholic places." The foursome spent more than an hour there before driving back to Los Angeles. Nixon fell asleep on the return drive, and the four men arrived at the Ambassador Hotel just before 5:00 P.M. PST. For nine hours, Nixon and friends had not spoken of the election. The episode recalled what Nixon had done eight years earlier in 1952, when he and William Rogers went to Laguna Beach, swam, and played touch football with some Marines.[3]

By the time Nixon returned to his hotel suite, it was 8:00 P.M. EST, and meaningful returns were now pouring in from the East as well as some southern and border states. The totals filtered in, but there was so much air time to fill that the television coverage inevitably dedicated itself to rehashing what had already been said numerous times, revisiting previous certitudes, and pontificating on the obvious while reiterating a vast reservoir of platitudes. Even on an exciting election night, such as November 8, 1960, there were few moments of high drama.[4]

Television network coverage on the night of November 8, 1960, possessed two striking characteristics. The first was the inept attempt to utilize computers to predict the election outcome in an effort to make network predictions seem more "scientific." In 1960, computer technology was in an early stage, and its use seemed more laughable than scientific. Almost from the outset of the telecasts on CBS, NBC, and ABC, the anchormen were reciting the prophecies emanating from the networks' computers. The computers lost credibility almost immediately as their initial predictions were wildly improbable. At 7:35 P.M., for example, the CBS computer gave Nixon a chance of accumulating as many as 479 electoral votes. In less than an hour, the CBS computer changed its mind and decided that JFK would win the election.[5]

The second attribute of the coverage was its obvious belief in a decisive Kennedy victory. The networks had prepared for a grand Kennedy triumph as the theme for the night, and when the Kennedy sweep did not materialize, the networks were poorly prepared to deal with the new reality of a long, drawn-out, state-by-state battle that carried into the next day. Initial indications favored the Democratic candidate since the early vote totals came from the Eastern time zone, where he was strongest. The television coverage assumed Kennedy would win and quickly displayed an inclination to proclaim him the victor. As early as 9:40 P.M., Eric Sevareid on CBS hinted at an announcement, saying that the computers were "pretty confident of a Kennedy victory." An hour later, he declared that "a Kennedy victory is now beyond any reasonable doubt." ABC did the same thing at 11:51 P.M. Only NBC held out, refusing to declare a winner. After midnight, though, Kennedy's popular vote lead began to shrink. The networks were forced to admit that Nixon had carried Ohio, something they had been reluctant to do, and California became doubtful, although as late as 3:00 A.M. EST, CBS was quoting Governor Pat Brown to the effect that JFK would carry California by 1 million votes. By 7:00 A.M., all three national networks had ended their continuous coverage with Kennedy the apparent victor, but without a definitive end to the election drama.

The television networks were not alone in jumping on the Kennedy bandwagon, only to have to reconsider their position later. At 12:36 A.M. on November 9, the second-edition headline of the *New York Times* proclaimed, "Kennedy Holds Wide Lead." At 1:03 A.M., the newspaper's Chicago correspondent called to say that Illinois was in the bag for JFK while his counterpart in San Francisco stated that California was safe for Kennedy: at 3:18 A.M., the late city edition went out with the banner "Kennedy Elected." Shortly thereafter, the Chicago correspondent called to say he was no longer sure of Illinois, and word came from the west coast that California was running even. At 4:47 A.M., the order went out to stop the presses, and at 7:17 A.M., an extra edition came out with the headline "Kennedy Is Apparent Victor; Lead Cut in Two Key States."[6]

As one might expect, JFK handled the night and early-morning hours gracefully. Buoyed by the good news from the East, first from Connecticut and then from Philadelphia, the Democratic camp was in a festive mood by 8:00 P.M. At 10:30 P.M., after more good tidings, a big victory seemed possible. Jacqueline Kennedy turned to her husband and said, "you're president, now." JFK replied that it was "too early yet."

Even after the Kennedy tide began to recede, he was in good enough shape in the Electoral College that it seemed only a matter of which state would put him over the top. At 3:00 A.M., four states were "at center stage," as Theodore White observed. Ahead in Michigan, Minnesota, Illinois, and California, JFK would win if any two went his way. Nixon needed all four to win—a very long shot. In Hyannis Port, they waited for Nixon to concede. The vice president did appear on television at about 3:20 A.M. and made a statement to the effect that if the current voting trends continued, John F.

Kennedy would be the winner, but the vice president did not make a formal concession. Some in the Kennedy camp were outraged, but JFK said that in Nixon's place he would not concede either. After Nixon's statement, Kennedy went home and to bed, leaving Pierre Salinger to deal with the press. He awakened next morning to news first from Theodore Sorensen and then a few minutes later from Salinger that it was over: he had won California (which turned out to be untrue), and he was president. He still had to await a formal concession from Richard Nixon, but the long election wait that carried well into Wednesday was finally over.[7]

Election night was much more painful for Richard M. Nixon. He and his family had to endure the long agony of voting returns that dripped in like water torture, and all for naught. The experience burned itself into his memory. He later recalled: "Any election night is an emotional roller coaster, but election night in 1960 was the most tantalizing and frustrating I have ever experienced." Although early victories came for him in Kentucky, Vermont, Oklahoma, and Indiana, the news was bad from the big electoral vote states. By 11:30 P.M. PST, he knew New York was in the JFK column, as was Texas, and then bad news came in from Pennsylvania. Senator Hugh Scott had told him that he could win if the Kennedy margin in Philadelphia was 200,000 or less, but the Democratic plurality there exceeded 300,000. That meant almost certain doom in Pennsylvania. With three of the big seven lost, Nixon now needed to carry at least three states from among Illinois, Michigan, Ohio, and California, and he was currently ahead in only one (Ohio), although he knew he had an excellent shot at California.[8]

Shortly thereafter, political columnist John Dreiske of the *Chicago Sun-Times* called to tell him that he would not carry Illinois. Since this state was essential to any scenario for a potential miracle victory, the vice president knew he had to consider a formal concession statement. He conferred with Len Hall, Cliff Folger, Robert Finch, Fred Seaton, and Herb Klein. Klein thought the time was right. Seaton disagreed, and Thruston Morton of the RNC and Senator Everett Dirksen were still arguing against such a statement. The result was the "if the present trend continues" statement. Later Wednesday morning, with Michigan and Minnesota definitely in the Kennedy column, Nixon did convey the official surrender. One of the men with him that night, Cliff Folger, would say, "it was one of the experiences you wouldn't care to repeat." Folger emerged with greater respect for the vice president as he, in Folger's opinion, "showed great calmness under stress when the rest of us were more excited. He had good judgment and foresaw the closeness of the contest more clearly than others." He concluded, "I never saw a man who, under trying conditions, I admired more." John F.

Kennedy handled himself very well on November 8–9, and so did Richard M. Nixon.[9]

There was a final ironic and eerie twist to the 1960 election night experience for the vice president. He underwent a very similar experience again eight years later. Election night 1968 found Nixon anxiously dealing with some of the same states from 1960. In 1968, Texas announced that "mechanical problems" were delaying final totals until the next morning. The vote in Illinois was in doubt, with Richard J. Daley holding back returns from Chicago precincts, while the Republican state organization was withholding results from downstate precincts. The 1968 election night marathon, unlike that of 1960, resolved itself in Nixon's favor.[10]

With Richard M. Nixon's formal concession on the morning of November 9, one might have thought that the election was over, but it was not. There was much more to come. To start with, there were two changes in the electoral vote count that stood at 332 for JFK and 191 for Richard Nixon on Wednesday morning.[11] The first occurred in California. On election night, almost all national news stories put the state and its thirty-two electoral votes on the Kennedy side of the ledger, perhaps influenced by the inflated claims of Pat Brown and other Democrats. As of November 10, John F. Kennedy had a lead of approximately 37,000 votes. However, there were still some 250,000 uncounted absentee ballots, and Republicans traditionally held an advantage in that category. By November 14, the Kennedy lead was down to less than 20,000. On November 15, it was under 14,000, with Los Angeles County and Orange County still to come. On November 16, Richard Nixon took the lead in California. The Republican margin increased on November 17–18, and on November 21, the final tally gave California to Nixon by more than 35,000 votes. Kennedy's total in the Electoral College shrank from 332 to 300.[12]

Democrats, especially those in California, where the claims of victory had been so strong, were upset. There was even some consideration given to challenging at least some absentee votes on technical grounds through a court action. The problem was that such legal activity could affect other states and have unforeseen consequences. Since JFK still had a surplus of thirty-one electoral votes (300 as compared to the 269 needed), even some eager to challenge the result thought better of it, and Nixon's overtime win in the Golden State held.[13]

The second shift in the Electoral College occurred in Hawaii. There the vice president had apparently won the new state by a mere 141 votes, 92,505 to 92,364. In the immediate aftermath, Hawaii Democrats were convinced the count was flawed. Led by veteran party official and lawyer Robert G.

Dodge, they pushed for a recount, which they eventually obtained. The recount started on December 13 and concluded on December 30. The final tally showed John F. Kennedy with 92,410 votes and Richard M. Nixon with 92,295. Kennedy won by 115 votes.[14]

While the results in California and Hawaii were changing, there was a good deal of post-election analysis. Most of it occurred on the GOP side since the Republicans had been the losers in the extraordinarily close election. Republican reaction took two forms. First was the inevitable second-guessing of the Nixon campaign. The second was a rapidly expanding number of allegations that the Democrats had stolen the election. Once started, these eruptions continued for months and even years afterward. All through the Republican camp there was dismay and agony for having waged such a long, hard fight only to lose it by the narrowest of margins. As Bryce Harlow recounted: "I'm not discouraged—just eviscerated, lacerated and obliterated. I would have worked harder but discovered that there aren't more than 24 hours to a day."[15]

Leading the second-guessers was none other than President Dwight D. Eisenhower. Ike did not stay up election night but went to bed at about eleven o'clock on November 8. The next day he dictated a warm letter to his vice president and took a telephone call from him. Nixon seemed to him "controlled, not downcast particularly." He told the president he still expected to win in California and Illinois and possibly Minnesota. As far as he was concerned, Nixon told Eisenhower, the president had been "magnificent." The vice president added that "basically the problem was the weakness of the Republican Party." The call concluded with Ike instructing him "to take a good rest" and saying that they could be "proud of these last eight years," and with Nixon complimenting him in turn, telling him, "You did a grand job."[16]

Nixon remembered thinking that he had never heard the president "sound more depressed." Eisenhower said that when he learned of the outcome he "felt as though I had been hit in the solar plexus with a ball bat." He began to wonder if the result would have been different if he had campaigned more extensively. Eisenhower told his secretary, Ann Whitman, that the election was a "repudiation of everything he had done for eight years." Whitman's response was representative of Eisenhower loyalists who were not enamored of the vice president and who believed that the defeat was squarely Nixon's responsibility. She believed that "the President, and the President alone, is responsible for the surprisingly good showing of the Nixon-Lodge ticket; by registration they are not entitled to it, nor are they, in my opinion by the campaign they put on."[17]

Ike did not blame himself alone. He asked Secretary of Health, Education, and Welfare Arthur Flemming: "Arthur, tell me, who was in charge of that campaign?" Flemming's reply was typical of the discontent many high-ranking Republicans felt with Nixon and his conduct of the campaign. He said: "Well, that's a little difficult to answer. There were times when it was clear that Bob Finch was in charge; at other times Len Hall seemed to be more in the driver's seat; and there were other times when Fred Seaton seemed to be [in charge]." Eisenhower's response was one of consternation: "Well, I'll never understand why I wasn't asked to participate more than I was in the campaign. There's nothing that I wanted more than to turn this position over to Dick Nixon."[18]

On November 9, Ike flew to Augusta, Georgia, for a golf vacation. On the way, he continued the second-guessing. He blamed the vice president for not asking for his advice on the campaign and for not utilizing Robert Montgomery, Ike's television adviser, who he said never would have let the vice president appear as he did in the first debate. He blamed Henry Cabot Lodge Jr. for his promise to put an African American in the cabinet and Nelson Rockefeller for refusing to take the vice presidency. He blamed himself for not campaigning more and for his "give me a week" statement. Eisenhower took Nixon's loss as a defeat for himself.[19]

Eisenhower also thought Democratic vote fraud contributed to the outcome. So did many other Republicans, who expressed this even more vociferously than did the president. This explanation—because it blamed Democrats rather than Republicans—was popular among the party faithful. Beginning on election night and proceeding almost up to December 19, when the presidential electors formally cast their ballots, Republicans mounted a sustained offensive against alleged election irregularities in a number of states.[20]

The Republican attack emerged as a genuine grassroots effort and not something directed from Washington. The main GOP assault centered on Chicago, where Republicans had been complaining about Democratic ballot manipulations for decades. Since Kennedy's margin in Illinois turned out to be a mere 8,858 votes and his plurality in Chicago had been 456,312, there was more than a little suspicion that the president-elect had emerged victorious thanks to the vote-counting genius of Mayor Richard J. Daley and his associates. On election night, Marie Suthers, the lone Republican member of the Chicago Board of Election Commissioners (BEC), charged that some ten thousand people, most of whom were Republicans, had been wrongfully removed from the voting rolls. On November 11, Frank Durham, an official of the Committee for Honest Elections, charged that the election had been stolen from Nixon and that he had never seen more "vicious" or more "fraudulent" practices in twenty-five years. On November 13, GOP Cook County chairman Francis X. Connell alleged that Democrats had pilfered 100,000 votes and with them the presidential election in Illinois. The complaining Republicans produced no documentation or other support for their allegations in any of these cases.

If Chicago produced the largest numbers of complaints and the loudest howls of protest, there was no shortage of protests from other states. Charges poured into the RNC and chairman Thruston Morton in the immediate aftermath of election day. Morton convened meetings on November 10–11 to decide on the practicality of pursuing actions against various voting irregularities. The RNC position was ambiguous. One anonymous party official seemed to offer hope for a reversal of the result, but Nixon campaign chairman Leonard Hall was pessimistic. In his view, it was too late to do anything.

Thruston Morton was in a delicate position. He could not afford to throw cold water on these fires of protest because they came from the party activists, the most loyal and most committed individuals who performed the overwhelming majority of the day-to-day work of party mobilization. For this and other reasons, he undoubtedly felt that these people were due a fair hearing, and Morton entertained serious doubts of his own about the conduct of the election in a number of states. In any event, the RNC chairman wired party leaders in eleven states, asking them to assess the vote counts in their states and to advise on whether in their opinion a recount was practical. The responses he received were generally discouraging.

These initial negative reactions did not put an end to RNC activities, especially after the absentee ballots moved California into the Nixon column after November 15. Any further changes would have put the Democratic position in imminent danger. Thus, on November 18, the RNC ordered emissaries into eight states—Illinois, Texas, Missouri, New Mexico, Nevada, South Carolina, New Jersey, and Pennsylvania—to investigate the situation and determine the feasibility of a recount. For a second time, the reports were negative, and at this point RNC activity began to decline. Morton mounted one last hurrah when in early December he undertook a highly publicized trip to Chicago, where he held a press conference at which he denounced Democratic vote fraud and announced the formation of a National Recount and Fair Elections Committee.

If RNC action slacked off after late November, various journalists and newspapers more than filled the void. The *Houston Chronicle* published three articles questioning election practices in Texas. Chicago newspapers, especially the *Chicago Tribune* and the *Chicago Daily News*, printed numerous stories about the alleged injustice perpetrated by Mayor Richard J. Daley and his minions. In addition, both newspapers supported the vote fraud claims editorially. On November 24, for example, the *Tribune* proclaimed, "It is a good guess that in an honest election Mr. Nixon would have carried Illinois by 100,000 votes." Most importantly, Earl Mazo, a political reporter for the *New York Herald Tribune* who was highly sympathetic to the vice president, authored a series of four articles that appeared nationally in early December. In explicit terms, they exposed blatant election chicanery and challenged the legitimacy of Kennedy's election. Meanwhile, Cook County Republicans also managed to stir up trouble as they pursued their version of a presidential recount in Chicago.[21]

The main enthusiasm for the crusade to right the imagined wrong of November 8 came from a few newspapers and journalists, some Cook County Republican politicians, and Thruston Morton, who genuinely believed that Nixon had been robbed. The White House showed less zeal, although President Eisenhower initially indicated some interest. The president called the attorney general to say he was "very much disturbed" about continuing allegations of fraud in the election. He wanted the federal government to exercise whatever rights and responsibilities were inherent in the situation." He "admitted" that the election was "a closed issue," but Eisenhower "felt that we owed it to the people of the United States." According to Ann Whitman, the attorney general did not feel as strongly about the matter as the president. In any case, with the vice president expressing no desire to move ahead, he dropped the idea.[22]

The standard historical view has been that Richard M. Nixon was one of those least interested in trying to pursue remedial action against alleged Democratic wrongdoing. He actively discouraged Republican efforts to challenge the outcome. He told Earl Mazo to cut short his series of articles that pointed to vote fraud as the explanation of how Kennedy had won the White House. Nixon himself promoted this interpretation of himself as the noble statesman declining to press his case for fear of the adverse consequences for the country. He painted this picture in his account of the election campaign in *Six Crises* in 1962, repeated it in his memoirs in 1978, and voiced it at the end of his life in the 1990s. He argued that any attempt to contest the election would delay the formation of the new administration, engender long-lasting bitterness in the country, and serve as a poor example to the rest of the world. Nixon declined to characterize his action as idealistic: "I wouldn't classify what I did as magnanimous or noble. . . . Responsible would be my word for it. I simply did the right thing."[23]

Nixon was capable of noble gestures and acting in the national interest, but there were also undoubtedly other factors at work. The vice president knew that the chances of upsetting the results were almost nonexistent. If he tried, he might plunge the country into a potential constitutional crisis. If he lost, as was likely, he would go down as a sore loser. Even if he had managed to oust Kennedy from his apparent victory and put himself in the White House, he would have been faced with Democratic majorities in both houses of Congress in a mood to attack him at every opportunity; it would have been next to impossible for him to govern. In short, as one of his most sympathetic biographers has noted, "Being a good loser was therefore good politics as well as good sense." Nixon was already thinking about a return to Washington. The position he took in November-December 1960 was far more likely to make such a return possible than a bitter contest to overturn the results of November 8. Finally, Nixon also took the very practical view, as he expressed it to Don Maxwell of the *Chicago Tribune*, that "The time to stop vote fraud is before and on election day and not after." There was no point in crying foul over the 1960 election. The job ahead was to prevent a recurrence of what had happened on November 8.[24]

This interpretation has had its critics. One who objected to the idea that Nixon refrained from supporting the partisan effort to undo the election was none other than Ralph de Toledano, an early Nixon supporter who later had a falling out with him. Nixon's account, according to de Toledano, had it backwards. Eisenhower did not urge a vote challenge, and Nixon did. According to Nixon's former ally, the vice president told the story to burnish his image, but, in fact, he was stoking the partisan fervor to attack Kennedy and his election.[25]

In the final analysis, de Toledano's argument fails. At first, Eisenhower did express outrage over Democratic machinations. According to Ann Whitman, no admirer of the vice president, Eisenhower did contact the attorney general about a possible investigation. There is no indication from any source other than de Toledano that the vice president ever gave encouragement to anyone working to overthrow the election. As Nixon himself said, what he did was the responsible thing, the right thing, and the best thing for the country.

Most of the post-election action occurred in the Republican camp as the party members worked off their frustrations at losing such a close election. On the Democratic side, the prevailing mood was a combination of elation at the victory, relief that the campaign was finally over, puzzlement as to why the margin was so small, and wariness as party leaders anticipated a Republican challenge. JFK, with Ken O'Donnell, Lawrence O'Brien, Mike

Feldman, Pierre Salinger, Teddy and Bobby Kennedy, and Joseph Kennedy, met on November 9 to consider the situation. They assumed a Republican challenge, particularly in Illinois, because of the noise erupting from and about that state. They were more worried about the turmoil such a challenge could provoke in the presidential transition than about the ultimate outcome. They worried that the dispute "could tie up the presidency of the United States for a period of time" and put "whoever was the winner of such a challenge in an untenable position," thinking that closely resembled Nixon's.[26]

The reports that came out of Illinois caused no great concern. Publicly Kennedy maintained confidence. In late November, he was quoted as saying, "My information is the count has been accurate." He added that he favored recounting votes whenever "they ought to be counted." By early December, John F. Kennedy was confident that the vote fraud issue was simply a matter of Republicans maneuvering for tactical advantage and that it would go away after the Electoral College voted on December 19.[27]

While confident the victory would stand, the Kennedy camp took no chances. Joseph P. Kennedy called Herbert Hoover to promote a meeting between the president-elect and his recent opponent. The idea was to bring the two together as a means to signal that Nixon accepted the election results and thereby undercut any possible challenge to the outcome. On November 13, Nixon received a call from Hoover, whom he respected, passing along the request for a meeting of the two rivals. Hoover told Nixon that "I think we are in enough trouble in the world today; some indications of national unity are not only desirable but essential." Nixon promptly called Eisenhower, who seconded Hoover's sentiments and remarked that "You [Nixon] would look like a sorehead if you didn't."[28]

The meeting took place at Nixon's hotel in Key Biscayne on November 14. According to Nixon, he and his rival talked about the election. Kennedy asked him what had been the biggest surprise for him, and the vice president replied that it had been Texas. JFK said it had been Ohio for him. According to some who got Kennedy's perspective on the meeting, Nixon did most of the talking, while Kennedy listened to him and looked at him and wondered how he had won by such a small margin.[29]

There was also a consultation between Eisenhower and Kennedy that further reinforced the reality of the Kennedy victory. Eisenhower welcomed JFK to the White House on December 6, treated him as the president-elect, and thereby placed his endorsement on the legitimacy of the Democratic election victory. That was exactly what Kennedy wanted. The president came away from the occasion with "considerable gratification." He praised

JFK's "pleasing personality, his concentrated interest, and his receptiveness." He also thought that the president-elect had conducted himself "with unusual good taste." Ike's impression of his successor was improving.[30]

There was another potential obstacle to a smooth transition that came from the Democratic side. This was the threat of independent southern presidential electors who hoped to take away electoral votes from Kennedy, and thereby increase their influence and the influence of their region by preventing a majority in the Electoral College. Contrary to predictions, a slate of independent electors had defeated Kennedy in Mississippi and won its eight electoral votes. In Alabama, only five of the eleven presidential electors elected on November 8 favored the Democratic candidate. With Kennedy's electoral vote total in late November and early December hovering at 300, or just thirty-one more than the necessary majority, and with a potential challenge emerging to the president-elect's hold on Illinois' twenty-seven electoral votes, a southern opportunity loomed. On November 18, attorney R. Lea Harris of Montgomery, Alabama, called for a meeting of southern Democratic and Republican electors for the purpose of developing a plan to elect a southern president and a Republican vice president. In the first two weeks of December, the unpledged electors from Alabama and Mississippi, along with those of a similar mind from other southern states, attempted to rally southern electors to defect from the Democratic ticket and throw the election into the House of Representatives, where presumably southern interests could make their influence felt. But with the collapse of the Republican challenge and Lyndon Johnson's behind-the-scenes maneuvering, this movement went nowhere.[31]

With the last potential challenges removed, the presidential electors met at their separate state locations and cast their ballots on December 19. The only surprise was in Oklahoma, where Republican elector Henry D. Irwin refused to support Richard Nixon and cast his vote for Senator Harry F. Byrd of Virginia. Irwin, who said he "could not stomach" Nixon, listed his occupation as "slave labor for the federal government." The status of Hawaii's electoral vote was in doubt because of the uncertainty of the outcome in that state, but otherwise the count came out as expected. Kennedy's count stood at 303 (including Hawaii), Nixon's at 222 (including Hawaii), and Byrd's at 15 (8 from Mississippi, 6 from Alabama, and 1 from Oklahoma).[32]

All that now remained was to carry out the formal acceptance and tallying of the electoral votes. The Congress met in joint session on January 6, 1961. The occasion was more interesting than usual. As presiding officer of the Senate, Vice President Richard M. Nixon was charged with presiding over the joint session that certified the victory of John F. Kennedy and his own defeat. Nixon was at his best. Before the vote, he put his arm around Sam Rayburn and congratulated the Speaker of the House on his seventy-ninth birthday. Whether Rayburn, who possessed a strong distaste for Nixon, welcomed this embrace is questionable. The official tally then began with four vote tellers—Carl Hayden and Carl Curtis from the Senate and Edna Kelly and Frances Bolton from the House. The roll of the states proceeded in alphabetical order, beginning with Alabama. With the announcement of the Alabama results, Nixon nodded to Senator Byrd and declared, "the gentleman from Virginia is now in the lead." The only minor difficulty came with Hawaii, which provided three separate certificates—one in favor of the Kennedy electors, another in favor of the Nixon electors, and a third and final one from Governor Quinn, certifying the Democratic electors. As presiding officer, Nixon ended any possible dispute by ruling in favor of the Democratic electors based on the governor's certificate. He asked if there were any objections to his ruling. There were none.[33]

At the conclusion of the roll of the states and the tallying of the electoral votes, the vice president took the opportunity to make a short speech. Nixon was capable of rising to the occasion, and this was one of his most gracious and eloquent statements. He began by noting that this was the first time in one hundred years that a presidential candidate faced the task of announcing his own defeat. He went on to say that there could not be "a more striking and eloquent example of the stability of our constitutional system," noting: "In our campaigns, no matter how hard fought they may be, no matter how close the election may turn out to be, those who lose accept the verdict and support those who win." He then extended his best wishes to JFK and LBJ as they went to work "in a cause that is bigger than any man's ambition, greater than any party. It is the cause of freedom, of justice and peace for all mankind." He concluded: "It is in that spirit that I now declare that John F. Kennedy has been elected President of the United States, and Lyndon B. Johnson, Vice-President of the United States."[34]

The vice president received a standing ovation as he declared the joint session adjourned. Sam Rayburn, from all accounts genuinely moved by Nixon's short speech, wished him well. Nixon then stepped down from the rostrum and began shaking hands with senators and representatives, Republicans and Democrats.

With the recording of the electoral votes and the proclamation of John F. Kennedy and Lyndon B. Johnson as duly elected president and vice president of the United States, the presidential election of 1960 entered history. But reinterpretation is the heart of history, and the election of 1960 is an especially fitting subject to revisit for two reasons. First, its fiftieth anniversary is here. Second, the accepted narrative of the campaign dates to 1961, as does the most-cited analysis of the election returns.[35]

Theodore White's *The Making of the President 1960* won a Pulitzer Prize and set the standard interpretation of the Kennedy-Nixon race. It emphasized Kennedy's charisma and Nixon's mistakes. White explained why Kennedy won, but evaded the equally important subject of why his victory was so narrow. If JFK was such a perfect candidate with such an efficient campaign, why was his triumph so small? Theodore H. White never came to grips with this issue and neither did other Kennedy loyalists.

White was correct that JFK waged an impressive campaign. His decision to make Lyndon B. Johnson his running mate was a masterstroke. Without LBJ, the New Englander could not have won. Johnson's presence on the ticket brought in Texas as well as the two Carolinas, probably New Mexico, and the five loyal electors in Alabama, and a total of fifty-three electoral votes. Without Johnson, the entire Kennedy position in the South could have disintegrated. Texas and the Carolinas would have voted for Nixon. Georgia and Arkansas probably would not have gone Republican, but they could have easily ended up with unpledged electors as did Mississippi and a majority of Alabama. It would have been much easier for the Massachusetts senator to make a safe choice like Symington, but he was bold enough and astute enough to recognize that the safe choice was a losing one.

With Lyndon Johnson on the ticket, the Kennedy brothers designed a simple but highly effective Electoral College strategy. Kennedy did well in the television debates and managed the issues of religion and civil rights well. For all of this, Kennedy deserves accolades.

But as good as it was, the Kennedy campaign still made mistakes. The most obvious one was the failure to pay sufficient attention to California. The most serious error was Bobby Kennedy's decision not to prepare for a final big push in the last two weeks of the campaign. This was a major mistake, especially since the Kennedy camp knew that the Republicans were preparing a television onslaught and that they could expect a series of Eisenhower speeches boosting the Republican cause.

Poor coordination between the national campaign and some state parties was another generally overlooked Kennedy failing. In the big electoral vote states, the campaign relied on state organizations and officeholders. This approach worked well in states with a powerful and efficient party organization. Certainly, there was little that Bobby Kennedy or his associates could have taught Richard J. Daley about a successful campaign. The Democratic parties in Michigan and Pennsylvania also performed very well. In Texas, it was simply a matter of allowing Lyndon Johnson to run the campaign. In these four states, Kennedy and the Democrats were in good shape thanks to powerful leaders and effective party organizations. The approach worked less well in California and Ohio, where the state parties were less efficient and faced a strong GOP.

In the South, Midwest, and West, the campaign usually dispatched an outsider to serve as state campaign coordinator. In many cases, the outsiders, unfamiliar with state and local politics, stirred up resentments. In a number of states—Florida, Missouri, and Wisconsin to mention three—the outsiders probably did more harm than good. Bobby Kennedy did not care about local and state politics. What he did care about was the election of his brother. His disdain for state and local sensitivities undermined his ultimate goal.

If the Kennedys made mistakes, so did their opponent, and he had less margin for error. Nixon's miscalculations have received more attention because he lost, and the loser in closely contested elections is always scrutinized more carefully than the winner. Agreeing to the televised debates, the fifty-state pledge, the underutilization of Eisenhower, and the failure to address the religious issue form the familiar litany of Nixon's blunders. Some of these criticisms are justified, but they are also exaggerated. Yes, Nixon agreed to the debates, but after the legislation that made the debates possible and the network invitation, he had no choice. If Nixon visited all fifty states, JFK went to forty-five. Eisenhower could have campaigned more, but Nixon was sincerely worried about the president's health, and the greater danger was Eisenhower's big push coming too soon.

The vice president received what amounted to the same number of votes that Kennedy did, so he must have done something right. In retrospect, there were two strategic decisions that Nixon got right. The first was his anticipation that the end of the campaign would be crucial. Unlike Robert Kennedy, Nixon understood that in what was likely to be a closely contested outcome, a strong end game was imperative. On this basis, Nixon planned for a surge in the two weeks before November 8 and never deviated from the plan. He wisely held back Eisenhower until then and conserved resources for a television blitz.

Nixon's second great coup was to dictate the agenda of the campaign. From the outset, he believed his best chance was to keep the campaign on foreign policy and not allow Democrats to focus national attention on domestic issues. There the Democrats had a friendly environment, where he and the GOP could not compete. Foreign policy, in contrast, worked to the advantage of Republicans, and it was Nixon's strong suit. For these reasons, he selected Henry Cabot Lodge Jr. to be his running mate. Although Lodge came in for a good deal of carping in the aftermath of the election, the early reports on him and his contributions to the campaign were highly positive. Furthermore, Lodge was something of a television star as a result of his extended appearances on national TV in the UN debates during the first half of the year. Lodge reinforced the foreign policy emphasis of the campaign and did it well.

Nixon and Lodge kept the campaign centered on foreign policy. Polls showed that the more Nixon could get the American voter to make his or her decision on the basis of which candidate would be the more effective in world affairs, better protect American interests, be more likely to preserve the peace, and be better able to counter the Soviet threat, the greater the likelihood that the vice president would emerge as the preferred candidate on November 8.[36]

In keeping the campaign on his agenda, Richard M. Nixon had two chief assistants. The first was John F. Kennedy, and the second was Nikita Khrushchev. Kennedy needed to shift public attention to domestic affairs—something easier said than done. The Democrat was more interested in international issues, and his desire to be president centered more on leading the country in its struggle with the USSR than on developing a domestic reform program. Kennedy had to convince the country that he was ready for the White House, and attempts to move the discussion away from the Cold War to various internal problems might simply increase doubts about his readiness for the White House. With Khrushchev's belligerent and boorish behavior on display in New York in September and October 1960, there was no way to deemphasize the importance of foreign policy. In the end, Kennedy went along with the Nixon agenda and allowed the campaign to rise and fall on the great foreign policy questions confronting the United States. In doing so, JFK ceded a major advantage to the vice president.

Thus, contrary to Theodore White and the conventional view of 1960, the two rival campaigns were evenly matched. The election results confirmed this. Final returns gave John F. Kennedy a miniscule popular vote advantage over Richard M. Nixon. Kennedy carried twenty-two states, thirteen of them by 5 percent or less. Nixon carried twenty-six states, six of them by 5 percent or less. Ever since 1960, these outcomes have been the subject of sharp controversy and prolonged debate.[37]

Actually, Kennedy might not have won the national popular vote. The dispute turned on Alabama, where the number of votes to which JFK was entitled was debatable. In that state, both voting machines and paper ballots gave the names of presidential electors without ever identifying the party candidates. In other words, the names of John F. Kennedy and Richard M. Nixon were nowhere to be seen on the Alabama ballot, and voters cast their ballots for electors. There was no problem on the Republican side. The leading Republican elector received 237,981 votes, and they were credited to Nixon's national total. The difficulty came on the Democratic side, where a spring primary selected five loyalist Democratic presidential electors supporting Kennedy and six unpledged electors who opposed JFK and eventually voted for Senator Harry Byrd of Virginia. Further complicating matters, the Democratic elector with the most votes was opposed to JFK.[38]

The wire services, newspapers, news magazines, and other media were not interested in this issue. They ignored the complexities of the issue and assigned Kennedy one of two totals—the 324,050 votes of the leading Democratic elector or the 318,303 votes of the highest pro-JFK elector. Thus, one can read summaries of the 1960 election results and never be aware that there were unpledged, anti-Kennedy electors in Alabama who received hundreds of thousands of votes.[39]

There is no good solution to the dilemma of how many Alabama votes to allot to JFK, but giving Kennedy credit for the 324,050 is plainly "a gross misstatement of the actual vote in the state," as the most careful student of the subject maintained. Even crediting him with the 318,303 is a distortion of the Alabama vote. The reason this debate matters is that an allocation of popular votes based on the electoral distribution would reduce Kennedy's national vote total below that of Nixon. This is admittedly an esoteric, academic issue, but it suggests Kennedy's national popular vote total is inflated. And it undermines the common assumption that John F. Kennedy received more popular votes than did Richard Nixon. In truth, no one knows which of the two men received more popular votes nationally on November 8.[40]

Aside from the closeness, the other outstanding feature of the election was its regional character. John F. Kennedy carried twenty-two states (twenty-three if one counts Alabama). Of these, three were from New England (Massachusetts, Rhode Island, and Connecticut), four were Middle Atlantic states (New York, New Jersey, Pennsylvania, and Delaware), six were former Confederate states (the Carolinas, Georgia, Louisiana, Arkansas, and Texas), two were border states (Maryland and West Virginia), and two were from the industrial Midwest (Michigan and Illinois). Half the states Kennedy carried were on the east coast. Just five Kennedy states that were not part of the Confederacy came from west of the Mississippi (Minnesota, Missouri, New Mexico, Nevada, and Hawaii).

John F. Kennedy was a regional candidate. He was young, inexperienced, and not especially well known outside the northeastern corridor of America. He was strong in New England, in the Middle Atlantic, and in the industrial Midwest. He was weak outside the big cities and suburbs. A cosmopolitan figure, the Democratic nominee was unfamiliar with, and unsympathetic to, the culture and economic interests of small-town America. As the Massachusetts senator himself proclaimed: "Where I grew up, we were taken out on a bus to see a cow." One observer of JFK remarked, "there was nothing that he [Kennedy] was less interested in than agriculture." One of the reasons he lost the vice-presidential nomination in 1956 to Estes Kefauver was that midwestern and western states went for the Tennessee senator because they distrusted Kennedy on agriculture. During the 1960 campaign, one Minnesota delegate to the Democratic National Convention said to Humphrey: "That man [Kennedy] couldn't tell a corn cob from a ukulele." Kennedy told economic adviser John Kenneth Galbraith: "I don't want to hear about agriculture from anyone but you, Ken. And I don't much want to hear about it from you either."[41]

Kennedy could not completely ignore farmers and farm states, but he would have liked to. After his first speech on agriculture, he remarked to an aide: "Did you understand anything I was saying? I sure didn't." In late September, he made his last major agricultural policy speech in South Dakota. His audience was, in the patronizing words of one of his urban aides, "a huge crowd of dour, unresponsive farmers who listened to him with all the animation of a wheat field rooted to the earthen plain." Following the speech, JFK simply said, "Well, that's over." He then uttered a four-letter expletive dismissing farmers as a concern. After his election and the appointment of Orville Freeman of Minnesota as agriculture secretary, he saw Freeman as infrequently as possible because "nothing bored him more than agriculture policy."[42]

The Massachusetts senator was able to overcome his regional limitations and win because he combined forces with another regional candidate, Lyndon B. Johnson, and because seven of the nine states with the largest numbers of electoral votes were located in sections of the country where he was strongest. Once Kennedy entered the White House, he quickly extended his reach and with his mastery of television quickly moved from a regional base to a wide national popularity.

The exceptionally tight national contest filtered its way down to the state level. Nineteen states went to the winning candidate by five points or less. The four biggest election day surprises came in Alaska, Mississippi, Ohio, and Wisconsin. Alaska was a remote state with just three electoral votes. Nobody could quite figure out what happened there, but the result was canceled out by the other new state—Hawaii—that most observers had put in the Nixon column and went for Kennedy. In Mississippi, the upset was that the unpledged elector slate defeated the loyalist slate that Senators John Stennis and James Eastland supported.[43]

Ohio and Wisconsin provided interesting examples of latent Democratic weaknesses and Republican strengths. In Ohio, Kennedy's crowds were large and loud. His failure to take the state therefore came as a rude and unpleasant shock to him, especially after Lou Harris assured him Ohio was his. Developments in both state parties affected the outcome in Ohio. On the Democratic side, there was an unpopular Democratic governor and a split in the party. There was also overconfidence from the statewide victories in 1958.[44]

On the Republican side, party chairman Ray Bliss took over and achieved something of a miracle. Although some considered Bliss overrated and possessing a distinct personality deficiency, most political observers, Democratic and Republican, saw him as a master political technician. Bliss undertook a major rebuilding operation inside the Ohio GOP and was highly successful, as the November 8 results attested. John Bailey did not think that Ohio "should have been any great surprise" because in his view Ohio was basically Republican. Richard Nixon offered a unique explanation of his win in the Buckeye State. He credited an endorsement he received from legendary Ohio State University football coach Woody Hayes, who appeared in a commercial for Nixon; in Nixon's mind, this was the key to his victory in Ohio.[45]

Nixon was comfortable in the Midwest and was able to forge a connection with the people of the states, especially outside the central cities. One Democrat reported: "What some Democrats may have overlooked is the fact that Mr. Nixon and his family are really like the people from Central Ohio. I know many people. . . . I feel these people recognized Mr. Nixon as one of their own. He seems to think like them, he acts like them, and he surely talks like them." Nixon identified with Ohioans in a way John F. Kennedy did not, and Ohioans, in turn, related well to Nixon.[46]

Wisconsin provided a similar story. Based on John F. Kennedy's performance in the Wisconsin April primary, in which he received a much larger vote than Nixon, political observers predicted Kennedy would win the state in November. But the Wisconsin Democratic Party suffered from the bitter April primary between Kennedy and Humphrey. Supporters of the two were barely on speaking terms. The Kennedy campaign sent old JFK friend Lem Billings to the state as coordinator. Billings was in a difficult position but did nothing to improve the situation.[47]

Meanwhile, the Republican Party in Wisconsin rebounded under the leadership of Claude Jaspers and others. In the September primary, the Republican turnout was higher than that for the Democrats, an indication that the April numbers were not indicative of what could be anticipated in November. Republican Catholics who cast a vote for their coreligionist in the April primary no longer had the emotional need to do so seven months later in the general election and returned to the GOP fold. On November 8, Republicans did well in the Badger State. Nixon carried Wisconsin, and Republicans won three of five state offices and six of the ten contests for the House of Representatives. Kennedy received 12,000 fewer votes than the combined total for himself and Hubert Humphrey in April.[48]

Wisconsin and Ohio are important because they suggest a more general pattern for understanding the 1960 results. The national race had an impact on state politics, but the reverse was also true. State circumstances affected the outcome of the presidential race in a given state. Richard Nixon could and did win in states where the Republican organization was strong and where Kennedy's appeal was limited. He won where the Democratic organization either did not wholeheartedly support its presidential candidate or became so divided that Nixon could sneak by even with an inferior GOP organization. Examples of this occurred in Virginia and Florida. In the former, Senator Harry F. Byrd decided that John F. Kennedy did not meet his criteria for the White House. Byrd, a staunch conservative, was not interested in the New Frontier and the philosophy underlying it. JFK and LBJ went to Byrd's Senate office to convince him that he should support the party nominee. After his visit, Kennedy was asked how far he got. His reply said all one needed to know about the likely outcome in Virginia: "I'm afraid we didn't get very far."[49]

There was no one as powerful as Senator Byrd in Florida, but the Sunshine State Democratic Party was disunited. The more moderate pro-Kennedy wing of the party, epitomized by outgoing Governor LeRoy Collins, lost control to gubernatorial nominee Farris Bryant and the more conservative faction of the party. Senator George Smathers, a boon companion of JFK, was aligned with the Bryant faction, and so was Lyndon Johnson. Figuring out what to do in Florida fell to JFK, RFK, LBJ, and Joseph Tydings from Maryland, who had been packed off to the Sunshine State to help coordinate the campaign effort. In this difficult situation, the Kennedy-Johnson ticket had the option of relying on their enthusiastic backers, who were out of power, or on Bryant and his allies, who were in power but decidedly unenthusiastic about the presidential nominee. They chose Bryant. The upshot was that the party regulars effectively froze out the most energetic Kennedy backers and spent the greater part of the campaign doing little. Thanks to their effort, or lack thereof, Richard Nixon emerged victorious in the Sunshine State.[50]

Nixon needed four of the seven states with the largest blocs of electoral votes, although he might have won with three plus two other states such as Minnesota and Missouri each with ten to fifteen electors. (Nixon did not carry either of these states, nor did he carry North Carolina, which also fit this description.) From the outset, the odds were against the Republican candidate. Nixon faced an almost insurmountable hurdle in New York. A strong GOP organization existed, but it was dedicated to Nelson Rockefeller and not Richard Nixon, and Rockefeller had small interest in a Nixon victory. In addition, Kennedy was highly popular in New York, and the large Roman Catholic population there rallied to him. While Nixon was comfortable in a state like Ohio or Wisconsin and Kennedy uncomfortable, the situation was reversed in the Empire State, where Kennedy was in his element and Nixon was out of place. Even if the New York Democratic Party was something of a snake pit with venomous competition between party regulars and reformers, Kennedy's advantage was so great in the Empire State that he was never in trouble.

The other two states in which Nixon was at a significant disadvantage were Pennsylvania and Michigan. Both were industrial states with slumping economies and powerful Democratic state organizations. In Pennsylvania, Governor David Lawrence and Congressman William Green, the two most powerful figures in the Quaker State, worked effectively for the Democratic ticket. Nixon was less fortunate. From the outset of the campaign, rumors circulated that the Philadelphia GOP was not committed to his candidacy. The two key figures were former sheriff Austin Meehan and city party chairman Wilbur Hamilton. Both, according to political operatives, were beholden to Democratic interests. Meehan was in the Democratic-controlled construction business, and Hamilton had insurance contracts from the city. Both were susceptible to Democratic pressure, and the election results out of Philadelphia and its suburbs did not suggest they put up much resistance. Kennedy was strong in the Philadelphia area and Pittsburgh. Those strengths combined with the Republican organizational weakness were enough to allow the Democratic candidate to prevail by more than 116,000 votes.[51]

Michigan was another difficult state for Nixon. Democrats controlled the governorship and both U.S. Senate seats. Organized labor, chiefly in the form of the United Auto Workers (UAW), exerted more influence than in any state in the country. Kennedy's defense of Walter Reuther during earlier Senate hearings earned him labor support. With the governor, the UAW, and a powerful state party organization on his side and considerable personal appeal to the white ethnic and African-American populations of Detroit and its environs, JFK held a superior position from the beginning. Without a Republican organization of the size and strength of either Ohio or Illinois, and with Kennedy generally well regarded in the state, Nixon made a strong but losing fight and fell short by almost 67,000 votes. As in Pennsylvania, the industrial economic doldrums afflicting the country harmed the Republican candidate. In Michigan and Pennsylvania, Richard Nixon paid the political price for the Eisenhower administration's refusal to stimulate the economy in 1959 and 1960. The combination of organizational weakness and economic problems defeated the vice president in these two states.

With his chances less than fifty-fifty in New York, Pennsylvania, and Michigan, Nixon needed the four other large states—California, Ohio, Illinois, and Texas. He won two, but the failure in the other two doomed his White House hopes. Nixon held the upper hand in California and Ohio. Although the Democrats controlled most state offices and occupied all four Senate seats, the GOP had strong state organizations. In addition, the Democratic governors were unpopular and the Democratic Party badly divided. California was Nixon's native state. Ohio was a state with a long Republican tradition. It was unsurprising that both went Republican on November 8.

Illinois was like Ohio—a midwestern state with a powerful GOP organization that strongly supported the vice president, who was popular in the state. Republicans controlled most state offices and one of the two U.S. Senate seats. There was, however, one important difference between the two states. In Ohio, political conditions worked in favor of the vice president. In Illinois, they created a highly unfavorable environment for him in 1960. The great negative was the presence of Governor William G. Stratton, who had served two terms and was bidding for an unprecedented third term. Tainted with scandal and on bad terms with many Republican politicians, the governor was unpopular. Even Eisenhower, not one usually given to political maneuvering, was well aware of the Illinois situation and Stratton's drag on the ticket. Ike reported that he had heard repeated criticisms of Stratton, including assertions that the governor was "down the drain." Eisenhower thought Stratton a good governor but someone who was "a one-man show," "secretive," and "a little Napoleon." Nixon also found himself associated with a lackluster U.S. Senate candidate, Samuel Witwer, who was challenging popular incumbent Paul Douglas. Of the statewide GOP candidates, only Secretary of State Charles Carpentier was a strong vote-getter, but he could not offset the liabilities of Stratton and Witwer. An extremely weak state ticket and the dissension within Republican ranks defeated Nixon in Illinois.[52]

As the Illinois GOP self-destructed, Mayor Richard J. Daley carefully and effectively built the foundation for a Democratic victory. In January, he came up with the perfect candidate for governor, Judge Otto Kerner, son-in-law of Anton Cermak, the founder of the modern Chicago Democratic Party organization. Kerner had an impeccable record with no independent tendencies, and he was a Protestant. Kerner's religious affiliation was important because it meant that, with the nomination of John F. Kennedy, Democrats could present a balanced ticket to the people of Illinois. The selection of Kerner provided an indication that Daley planned to support Kennedy six months before his announcement. In addition, an important local race for Cook County state's attorney was critical to the Chicago Democratic Party and further inspiration for a maximum effort on November 8.[53]

Thus, Richard M. Nixon found himself trapped by circumstances in Illinois. With the Illinois GOP badly divided, Nixon ran on a ticket with an unpopular and scandal-tainted gubernatorial candidate and an underwhelming senatorial candidate. He faced an energized Democratic Party eager to turn out to vote for John F. Kennedy and a Chicago Democratic Party that was desperate to win a critical local race. In different circumstances, Richard Nixon would have carried Illinois in 1960. But the disadvantages he faced on November 8, 1960, were too great, and he failed by 8,858 votes out of 4,757,409. The loss of Illinois doomed the vice president. Without that key state, there was no plausible scenario by which he could reach the White House.

Even if he had carried Illinois, Nixon still needed Texas.[54] Nixon was sanguine about his prospects in the Lone Star State. There were reasons for his optimism. Through September and October, Claude Robinson told the vice president he was ahead. Robinson apparently based his assurances on the respected Belden Poll that indicated a small but clear and steady preference for Nixon. Nevertheless, Robinson and Nixon should never have counted upon Texas. Republicans held no statewide offices and no seats in the state legislature. Except in a few counties, there was no effective GOP organization.[55]

In any case, Lyndon Johnson was not about to tolerate a loss in his state.

Although there were parts of the state antagonistic to Kennedy, there were sections, especially in south Texas, highly favorable to him. Kennedy's campaign energized Mexican Americans. With a powerful political machine at their disposal and virtually no organized Republican opposition, Democrats could do whatever they pleased with the election returns. The Adolphus Hotel incident provided whatever additional boost the Kennedy-Johnson ticket needed to win, and it did so by more than 46,000 votes. The story in Texas, as in Illinois, was one of might-have-beens. The election turned on Illinois and Texas. Nixon needed both, and he got neither.[56]

John F. Kennedy had triumphed, but his triumph was an extraordinarily narrow one. Immediately, Democrats, Republicans, and nonpartisan analysts attempted to explain why Kennedy had won, why Nixon had lost, and why Kennedy's margin was so unimpressive. For anyone who carefully and dispassionately examined 1960, the explanations for Kennedy's victory and Nixon's strong showing were natural and logical. For many loyalists on both sides, though, such assessments were too antiseptic and too impersonal. In the aftermath of the election, partisans preferred more conspiratorial interpretations that illuminated events in terms of their understandings of good and evil. For emotional reasons as well as motivations involving self-interest, party leaders now moved to fashion election legends that satisfied their souls and psyches as well as their political interests.

10

The Myths of 1960

"Only a practitioner of religious prejudice could ignore the unmistakable evidence that Kennedy was its chief victim in the 1960 campaign."
—Theodore C. Sorensen

"Mr. President . . . with a little luck and the help of a few close friends, you're going to carry Illinois."
—Richard J. Daley to John F. Kennedy on election night, according to Ben Bradlee

"The election was stolen from Richard Nixon in Illinois in 1960. . . . [T]here are many who, like me, believe Richard Nixon defeated John Kennedy in Illinois by at least 100,000 votes in 1960."
—William Harrison Fetridge, head of Midwest Volunteers for Nixon-Lodge, on the presidential election outcome in Illinois

"White had cast Nixon as the villain, as in a novel."
—Theodore H. White on *The Making of the President 1960* as a novel with Nixon as the villain

While the election was over, the controversy concerning it was just beginning. Historians, political scientists, politicians, and interested citizens began trying to make sense of what had happened. Inevitably, these interpretations were more about satisfying the practical and psychological needs of the interpreter than anything else. The explanations made their way into the national consciousness, where they have continued to shape the popular perception of the election for a half century.

On the Democratic side, the key question was not how and why John F. Kennedy won the election: that was taken for granted. For Democrats, the issue was why he won by such a narrow margin. Did he not wage a far superior campaign? Was he not a far superior candidate? How could the repulsive Richard Nixon have come so close to defeating the Democratic hero?

The obvious answer was that Kennedy ran against a strong Republican candidate supported by a popular incumbent president. Kennedy's rival put on a good effort of his own. This prosaic reality, though, was hardly worthy of Camelot. So Democrats dispensed with the obvious and moved on to formulate a legend to explain why Kennedy did not win by the decisive margin they thought that he deserved. Their myth was simple and straightforward. Religious prejudice unfairly deprived John F. Kennedy of his mandate. According to Democratic politicians, various Kennedy courtiers, and some scholars, religious prejudice cost the Democrat between 1 and 3 million votes, with some estimates even higher. Thus, religious bigotry and only religious bigotry prevented November 8 from turning out the way it should have. Even the most recent scholarly accounts of 1960 have uncritically accepted the bigotry explanation for the election results. There has been no serious reexamination of this thesis since the original analyses of the early 1960s.[1]

Any political myth has roots in reality, and this one is no exception. In 1960, even if most Protestant and Catholic Americans lived in relative harmony, a tidal wave of religious literature was generated during the course of the year, most of it unreasonable or scurrilous. The conventional wisdom over the past half century has held that the Democratic nominee's faith was a negative, not a positive, in the election and that it cost him a significant number of votes. This judgment is the crux of the answer that most Democrats supplied to the great riddle of 1960—if JFK was such a splendid candidate and his opponent so odious, how is it that the Democratic hero won so narrowly? There was no need to criticize Kennedy or his campaign aides or Democratic leaders in the states or give any credit to Richard Nixon and the GOP. It was simply a matter of religious intolerance. With that conclusion, all need for thought or analysis disappeared.

In politics, though, it is always wise to look beneath the surface for an explanation of why individuals say and do things. Three distinct groups advanced the argument that JFK's religion had cost him a large number of votes. The first were the Kennedy acolytes, who possessed an overwhelming emotional investment in the candidate and his campaign. Utterly astounded when he did not win decisively against a man they considered an impossibly loathsome alternative, they were incapable, for psychological reasons, of admitting that the Kennedy campaign made serious mistakes or that Nixon and his aides were their equals or near equals. They seized upon religion reflexively and used it to explain everything. Among this group were Theodore Sorensen, Kenneth O'Donnell, and others. To Sorensen, Kennedy was the "chief victim" of religious prejudice in 1960 and "only a practitioner of religious prejudice could ignore the unmistakable evidence" to that effect. In other words, not only did bigots prevent a massive Kennedy victory, but the only ones who would deny that conclusion were bigots themselves. That Sorensen took this position was deliciously ironic since he was the one in

1956 to author the famous memorandum arguing that Democrats should nominate JFK as vice president because as a Catholic he would attract votes that a Protestant would not. Sorensen suffered no apparent embarrassment in moving from his position that Kennedy would gain votes by virtue of his religion in 1956 to complaining that he had lost votes because of his religion after 1960. In O'Donnell's view, JFK lost 10 million votes because he was Roman Catholic. According to O'Donnell, "John Kennedy, if he were Stu Symington, would've beaten Nixon by 20 million votes."[2]

The second group that resorted to religion for their explanation of the election results included various campaign aides and Democratic politicians. These individuals possessed a distinct, practical self-interest in the religious interpretation. Democrats expected a decisive win. When they did not get it, someone or something had to take the blame. From the standpoint of the Kennedy aides and Democratic bosses, it was far better to credit the election results to religious bigotry than to scrutinize their own performances. In other words, bigots were a convenient scapegoat.

Chief among such advocates was Lou Harris. The pollster had predicted a big Kennedy win in the popular vote and an equally convincing triumph in the Electoral College. He was wrong on both counts. Harris's projection of a nine-point popular vote margin turned to ashes. So did his forecast of JFK carrying Ohio and California and a number of other states. Even before election day, Harris contended that religion was at the bottom of why Kennedy was losing certain states. He saw prejudice as the basis of almost any Nixon lead. He even attributed it to why the vice president was ahead in Kansas. There he found "rampant religious bigotry" without which Kennedy would be ahead. JFK and Joseph P. Kennedy had paid very large sums of money to Harris for his work, which turned out to be not very accurate on November 8. Lou Harris had a huge stake in promoting the idea that religious prejudice had massively skewed the election results. His argument that religion was the central cause of Kennedy's underperformance in the popular and electoral vote must be understood in the light of his vested interest in this theory.[3]

Other individuals with a vested interest in a religious explanation of the vote were Democratic politicians like Ohio governor Michael DiSalle and California governor Pat Brown. The Democratic nominee expected to carry those two states and did not. Obviously, an explanation was in order. It was far easier to blame anti-Catholic votes in central and southern Ohio and in the Central Valley of California for the losses in those two states than to confess organizational and other failures. The same thing could be said for states such as Wisconsin and Maine. In the latter, Senator Edmund Muskie declared that an additional 60,000 voters went to the polls in 1960 as compared to 1956. According to Muskie, "Every one of those 60 to 70,000 additional votes appears to have been cast against Jack [Kennedy] on the basis of the religious issue." Democrats from losing states in 1960 welcomed Lou Harris's theory as a means of escaping responsibility. The religious explanation suited them just fine.[4]

Happily for Harris, DiSalle, Brown, and other Democrats on the hot seat for their less than scintillating performance in November, a scholarly analysis appeared in June 1961 that supported their position. Professor Philip E. Converse and others of the Survey Research Center at the University of Michigan produced an article in the *American Political Science Review* that presented preliminary conclusions based on the examination of voter data. The study concluded that John F. Kennedy had indeed lost votes as a consequence of his religion. According to the SRC, Kennedy "did not in any sense exceed the 'normal' vote expectations . . . rather, he fell visibly below these expectations."[5]

Central to this argument was the establishment of a baseline vote that a generic Democratic candidate could expect to achieve. After a description of calculations that utilized the turnout rates across seven categories of party identifiers, the Michigan scholars asserted that in "the normal presidential election" with short-term political forces in equilibrium and favoring neither party, one could expect the Democratic proportion of the two-party popular vote "to fall in the vicinity of 53–54 percent." Although dressed up in mathematical language, this conclusion was little more than an educated guess.[6]

After evaluation of the short-term forces of 1960, the authors decided that John F. Kennedy's vote was down 2.2 percent because the gains JFK received from Catholic voters who supported him were outweighed by losses from Protestant Democrats and independents who voted against him. With a turnout of almost 69 million voters, this meant JFK lost approximately 1.5 million votes to the religious issue and without its presence would have won by more than 3 million votes. Ever since the publication of this article in 1961, it has been accepted as the truth on the subject and continues to be cited after the passage of almost five decades.[7]

Surprisingly, scholars have been unwilling to revisit the premises underlying the Michigan survey, specifically the proposition that the baseline vote for a Democratic candidate in 1960 was 53–54 percent of the two-party vote. In retrospect, this calculation was clearly wrong. Beginning in 1948 and proceeding through 1996, only one Democratic presidential candidate reached the allegedly "normal" level. That was Lyndon Johnson in

1964, one of the most abnormal election years of the post-1945 era. So, there was no "normal" 53–54 percent Democratic vote in presidential elections in 1960. In other words, there is no good reason to think that John F. Kennedy should have received any more votes than he did and therefore no basis for contending that his religion degraded his popular vote total. The chief scholarly argument that Kennedy was hurt by his religion is no longer credible, no matter how many eminent scholars continue to cite it.[8]

What Democrats, pollsters, and social scientists failed to understand was that John F. Kennedy's religion was an asset rather than a liability. The great Roosevelt coalition that brought Democrats five consecutive victories from 1932 through 1948 was fraying around the edges. The South was increasingly unreliable, and the Catholic vote in the North was moving away from its Democratic loyalties. Nixon, with his sympathy to Catholic concerns, understanding of the conservative Catholic mentality, and good relations with the American Catholic hierarchy, was poised to make major inroads on the Catholic vote. That is one of the major reasons he would have easily defeated Johnson, Stevenson, or Symington, none of whom had much appeal to Catholics.[9]

Some observers cited the fact that Kennedy ran behind Democratic congressional candidates as an indication that his religion hurt him. These statistics are both irrelevant and unpersuasive. Polling clearly demonstrated that voter behavior was different at the presidential level. The vote in congressional elections reflected the dominant Democratic Party identification and the belief that Democrats were best for America on domestic issues. In the vote for president, party identification meant less and the primary concerns for voters were the issues of war and peace. In such an environment, Republican presidential candidates inevitably performed better than in congressional races.

In addition, with the Democratic domination of Congress, Democrats were more often the incumbents. Therefore, Democratic candidates were usually better known than their opponents. They were also more influential in Congress because of the Democratic majority. In congressional races, the typical Democratic candidate possessed a marked advantage against the normal Republican challenger. In presidential contests, Republicans were at least the equals of their Democratic rivals. After FDR and Truman, Democratic presidential candidates stopped running even with or ahead of congressional Democrats. Eisenhower was unusually popular, and Adlai Stevenson was a poor candidate, but the pattern established in the 1950s was no aberration. Democrats in races for the House of Representatives outperformed their presidential candidates not only in 1960 but in every four-year election of the 1960s, the 1970s, and 1980s with the exception of 1964. That John F. Kennedy ran behind his party's congressional candidates in 1960 was not unusual and requires no conspiracy theories to explain.

Religion remains one of the great conundrums of 1960. It involved two great paradoxes. The first was the intensity of religious feeling but the lack of a decisive impact. This issue inflamed people like no other subject in 1960. Protestants voted overwhelmingly for Nixon, and Catholics even more overwhelmingly for Kennedy. Yet, there is no good evidence that religion affected the final totals in the national popular vote. Thousands opposed Kennedy because of his religion, but just as many thousands were willing to vote for him because of it.

The other great paradox was that as ferocious as the feelings were on the issue, they did not significantly affect the Kennedy presidency. One can assume that hate mail poured into the White House and various kooks fulminated about the imminent papal takeover of the country. Yet in spite of the obsession over religion in 1960, it largely disappeared after inauguration day. The Kennedy presidency stirred passions, but they were passions over racial tensions and foreign policy issues such as Cuba and Vietnam. In the 1960s, the United States plunged into a decade of bitter partisanship, radical right- and left-wing protest, and domestic violence, but almost none of it had anything to do with religion.

Just as Democrats invented their version of 1960 by formulating a myth that religious intolerance took away votes from John F. Kennedy and prevented a glorious victory, Republicans were hard at work as well. In the Republican case, the task was to confront the outcome of the election and explain the defeat. As previously noted, two main schools of Republican thought emerged about their narrow loss. The first blamed Richard Nixon for his conduct of the campaign. The second attributed the defeat to Democratic vote fraud. The second school prevailed, and vote fraud became the most popular GOP interpretation of why the election was lost. Quickly it became the great Republican myth of 1960, which lives on fifty years later in a different century.[10]

As with the Democratic complaints about bigotry, the Republican protests about vote fraud were plausible. Certain areas of the country were notorious for voting irregularities. Some southern states had a well-earned reputation for being willing to manipulate election returns to achieve the desired results. Republicans and Democrats knew in 1960 that in a close election, Lyndon B. Johnson would do whatever it took to ensure the election came out the right way. LBJ stole elections in college and stole the Senate election of 1948. In that year, according to Robert Caro, he and his henchmen stole tens of thousands of votes, and when they were not enough, he stole some more. In 1960, he was fully capable of repeating this performance, if necessary, to make himself vice president.[11]

The other major center of vote chicanery could be found in the large cities of the Northeast and Midwest, where Democratic bosses controlled vast blocs of votes. Although the big-city machines in 1960 were not what they had been, the Chicago Democratic Party of Mayor Richard J. Daley remained a model of efficiency when it came to getting out the vote and making sure that it came out correctly. If LBJ possessed an overwhelmingly strong incentive to make sure votes were counted in a favorable fashion, so did Mayor Daley, who had a critical local election at stake on November 8.

Republicans were no angels themselves. In the late nineteenth century, they pilfered as many votes as Democrats. By 1960, though, the GOP capability to stuff ballot boxes had seriously declined. The party controlled none of the largest cities of the country and few states. Democrats, on the other hand, dominated America's largest cities, virtually all of the South, and most of the border states. In these locations, the Republican Party was so weak that Democrats could do whatever they pleased. It was not that Republicans were more virtuous than Democrats. Democrats simply had more power and more opportunity to fix elections in 1960.

In spite of the predictions of a close outcome and the dangers of potential ballot manipulation, the Republican Party was unprepared for what it encountered on election night. With preliminary results showing losses in twelve states by less than 5 percent(six of them by fewer than 10,000 votes) and with reports of voting irregularities pouring in, especially from Illinois and Texas, it was natural for Republicans to become convinced (or to convince themselves) that they had been swindled. In the following weeks, months, and years, it became an article of faith for the Republican rank-and-file as well as the party hierarchy that the election had been stolen. There is no doubt that this was a sincerely held belief on the part of reasonable men, not just party hacks or the true believers. As Nixon friend Pat Hillings put it to the vice president, "I believe you would be our President today if the election had not been stolen from us in certain places such as Illinois and Texas." Robert Finch believed that Nixon was "counted out."[12]

Even Democrats contributed to this view. Theodore H. White conceded in a later book that the Californian had a legitimate grievance when it came to vote fraud in 1960, especially in Illinois and Texas. Then there was the famous statement from Chicago on election night. Originally, it appeared in Ben Bradlee's book *Conversations with Kennedy*. Bradlee quoted Daley as telling the candidate on that night, "Mr. President . . . with a little luck and the help of a few close friends, you're going to carry Illinois." Republicans leaped upon this statement as prima facie proof that Daley was engaged in stealing votes. Ever since the quotation appeared, Bradlee has been attempting to explain his way out of the plain meaning of Daley's statement. Bradlee did qualify the quotation with an immediate reference to an unnamed Nixon staff member who allegedly determined that "Republicans could well have stolen as many votes in southern Illinois as Daley might have stolen in Cook Country." Needless to say, Republicans omitted this quotation in their diatribes. In a later book, Bradlee said of the Daley quotation: "I don't know what the hell Daley meant. If it was Irish humor, it seems particularly inappropriate, not to say dumb." He then repeated his story that upon further investigation Republicans decided that they probably stole as many votes in the southern part of the state as Daley had in Cook County. None of this was very persuasive, and Bradlee undoubtedly wished he had never used the original declaration by Daley.[13]

Embellishing on this theme, John F. Kennedy Jr. even came to Chicago in 1996 and said in a speech, "In the 1940s my grandfather bought the [Chicago] Merchandise Mart, and in the 1970s my family bought the Apparel Center, and of course in the 1960 election my family bought 20,000 votes in Cook County." Even if Bradlee did not, the Kennedys seemed to find the subject of vote fraud amusing.[14]

Inevitably, Richard Nixon and his family absorbed and embraced the idea that he had been cheated out of the presidency. Nixon himself made this clear in his 1962 treatment of the election in Six Crises. Pat Nixon thought vote fraud had cost her husband the election, as did their two daughters, Tricia and Julie. Late in life, Nixon recalled in a more humorous vein that "Mrs. Nixon still says we should order a recount." When Tricia and Julie Nixon received checks as Christmas presents in 1960, they insisted that the money be sent to the Chicago recount effort.[15]

The individual, though, who did more than anyone else to engrave the vote fraud story in history was the reporter Earl Mazo. The national political correspondent for the New York Herald Tribune, Mazo was an influential pro-Nixon journalist whose columns appeared in the Washington Post and the Chicago Sun-Times, among other newspapers; his reach extended far and wide. In early December, Mazo wrote four articles denouncing what he described as massive fraud, especially in Texas and Illinois.[16]

Mazo's series caused something of a sensation. His findings were preserved for posterity first in Nixon's account in Six Crises that quoted from the articles and then again from a friendly biography published in 1968, as Nixon prepared to make his second presidential bid.[17] From these narratives, the Mazo-Nixon version of miscounts infiltrated into countless books and articles about 1960, where it became the conventional wisdom, at least in Republican and independent circles.

Inevitably, one has to ask, What is the evidence for massive fraud? How well do the GOP allegations hold up, especially in Illinois? There were other states, most notably Nevada, South Carolina, New Mexico, and Missouri, about which Republicans had questions, but because of their prominence, the case for vote fraud rises or falls on Texas and especially Illinois. In Texas, Kennedy's plurality was substantial at 46,257 votes and the election records sketchy. In contrast, in Illinois, the final margin was much smaller (8,858 votes out of 4,757,404) and the stakes higher at twenty-seven electoral votes. With more extensive documentation, Illinois was the best test case for vote fraud in 1960.

The documentation concerning voting irregularities in Chicago came from three main sources. The first was a discovery recount of November-December 1960 that centered on the Cook County state's attorney race but also touched the presidential contest. The second was an official recount of the local election in February-March 1961. The final source was the report of the special prosecutor, issued in April 1961.

The two recounts showed that Democrats had likely stolen tens of thousands of votes. But they stole most of them in the state's attorney's election and not in the presidential contest. Republican lawyers and party officials were surprised when they were able to look at the paper ballots in more than six hundred Chicago precincts. What they found did not match their expectations. There were some indications of minor Democratic pilfering but no strong evidence of massive fraud in the presidential returns.

The other implication of the recounts was that the Republican cause was hopeless from the start. The GOP precinct organization was in a shambles in much of the city, and Republicans had almost no way of knowing what had gone on in hundreds of precincts. The mechanics of voting in Chicago further contributed to the Republican inability to produce strong evidence of chicanery. Of the city's 3,771 precincts, 634 used paper ballots and 3,137 had voting machines. Although Republicans could demonstrate significant irregularities in the paper-ballot precincts, they could not do the same in voting-machine precincts. There the lack of any paper trail made it impossible to challenge the recorded vote—and voting-machine precincts constituted more than 80 percent of the precincts in Chicago. In other words, the Republican attempt to prove widespread vote thievery was doomed from the beginning. Chicago Democrats had stolen votes, but Republicans could not prove they had stolen the election.

There were two confirmations of this judgment. The first came from an independent investigation in Chicago. The vote fraud charges created such a political stink that Judge Richard Austin appointed a special prosecutor to investigate the election irregularities. The special prosecutor was Morris J. Wexler, a prominent thirty-four-year-old Chicago attorney. A man of impeccable professional reputation, Wexler was a registered Democrat but was not under the thumb of the organization. Wexler set about his task with the aim of creating what he called an election audit. His goal was not to track down vote thieves but to provide a list of alleged irregularities, investigate them, and provide a public accounting for what he found. With a strong, able, but small staff, Wexler set about his business.

On April 13, 1961, Wexler issued a report that examined alleged irregularities under six categories: voting-machine miscounts, paper-ballot miscounts, suspect voters, unqualified voters, improper influence of voters, and miscellaneous irregularities. The Special Prosecutor's Report (SPR) ran to some 220 pages and made neither Republicans nor Democrats happy. The former were exasperated by Wexler's unwillingness to pass judgment on the conduct of the election. The latter were furious over his suggestion that there were serious errors in the tallying of paper ballots. Later they became even unhappier when Wexler indicted more than six hundred election judges for contempt on the basis that they did not carry out the election laws.

In the end, the SPR is the best, most dispassionate, most nonpartisan assessment of the conduct of the election in Chicago on November 8, 1960. It had its limitations since it was based solely on the allegations made to it. Wexler and his staff made no attempt to develop new evidence on their own. Although the SPR took no stand on whether irregularities had affected the election outcome, implicitly it upheld the legitimacy of the outcome.[18]

Republicans sincerely believed they had been cheated in Illinois and in Texas, but they did not prove their case. As with Democratic complaints about religious prejudice, there were underlying motivations that bear examination. The charges of voting irregularities provided convenient excuses why the national campaign and state organizations had lost. Charges of vote fraud enabled Republicans to say that they had won but that the deserved victory had been stolen from them. This explanation was more satisfying than looking inward for an explanation of why they had failed in various states. For any number of party officials, the vote fraud issue deflected blame and was therefore most welcome.

The allegations possessed the additional benefit of creating an issue that incited the party faithful, raised money, generated publicity, and cast

Democrats in a most unfavorable light. Vote fraud mobilized the party rank-and-file. Republicans successfully exploited this issue in Chicago and in Illinois for more than a decade. In 1968, the party launched a massive poll-watching effort that helped Nixon carry the state. If Republicans thought that Democrats had treated them unfairly in 1960, both the state party and the national party profited from the abuse throughout the next decade.

Also rejecting Republican vote fraud claims was the Illinois State Electoral Board (SEB), the official state body responsible for certifying election results. It met on December 14, 1960. Republicans had a four-to-one majority on the board with Governor William Stratton, Secretary of State Charles Carpentier, Attorney General William Guild, and State Auditor Elbert Smith and only a lone Democrat, State Treasurer Joseph Lohman. The Republican majority had the power to do something about what many Republican loyalists considered an illegitimate election. Cook County GOP chairman Francis X. Connell and party attorney George Dapples appeared before the SEB and made emotional appeals to the members not to certify the state electoral votes to John F. Kennedy, based on what they claimed was overwhelming evidence of vote fraud. Examined closely, the arguments of Connell and Dapples provided a good deal more heat than light. They made sweeping charges but offered almost no specific supporting evidence for their assertions.

The four Republicans on the SEB were caught in the middle between partisan demands and the lack of substantive evidence to support the allegations. To refuse to certify the election would have been a truly radical step, and the GOP quartet was not about to do that, especially on the basis of flimsy arguments advanced on December 14. So these Republican office-holders who actually had the power to do something about vote fraud in the state that appeared to be the most affected by it rejected the opportunity and voted unanimously to certify the electoral votes of Illinois to John F. Kennedy. They politely commended Connell and Dapples for their efforts, but stated that they could not refuse to certify unless they saw overwhelming evidence that the election had been stolen—and no such evidence had been presented. Even the *Chicago Tribune*, one of the leading advocates for the proposition that Democrats had hijacked the election, conceded that the SEB could not have acted otherwise. For all the GOP bloviating about a stolen election, the refusal of Republican officials to act demonstrated the inherent weakness in the Republican case. Leveling charges was easy; proving them was hard. And being willing to act on them was even more difficult. Republicans were happy and eager to make charges, but unable or unwilling to proceed further.[19]

With the casting of the electoral votes on December 19, 1960, any hopes Republicans might have harbored of upsetting John F. Kennedy's election ended. But neither the casting of the electoral votes in December, nor the counting of the votes and the proclamation that John F. Kennedy was duly elected president in January, nor even JFK's inauguration later in January laid the 1960 election fraud issue to rest. Republicans continued to publicize it through the 1960s and beyond.

In many ways, the Republican vote fraud legend resembled the Democratic religious prejudice myth. In both instances, there was an element of truth to the partisan claims. There were voters who cast their ballots against John F. Kennedy because he was a Roman Catholic, just as there were election officials who stole votes from Richard Nixon. In both cases, there were psychological reasons for the partisan beliefs. The belief in religious prejudice allowed Democrats to see themselves as enlightened individuals fighting the good fight for democracy, equality, and religious freedom. The Republican focus on vote fraud permitted the party faithful to view themselves as the party of good government and the upholder of clean, honest elections. On both sides, there were also self-interested reasons for subscribing to what became the party orthodoxy.

The two myths were also comparable in that at their core they were untrue. Thousands of voters undoubtedly cast their ballots on a religious basis, but there is no convincing evidence that John F. Kennedy was denied a sweeping victory because of this influence on voting. Similarly, Richard Nixon may have had thousands of votes stolen from him in Illinois, Texas, and other states, but Republicans never produced persuasive evidence that Nixon's losses to Democratic shenanigans cost him the election. In the end, it was easier to believe in an emotionally comforting legend than it was to confront the messy reality of close elections.

A third myth was the biggest and most potent one of all. This was Theodore H. White's portrayal of the candidates and the campaign in what became the master narrative of 1960. In 1959, White decided to write a book about the 1960 campaign. It would not be the usual history, but a story with a hero, and "it would be written as a novel is written."[20] It would be the account of a protagonist who confronted and overcame great challenges. Long before November 8, White found his hero in John F. Kennedy and his villain in Richard M. Nixon. His novelistic needs, supplemented by his attraction to Kennedy and his distaste for Nixon, dictated his characterizations. Kennedy was "young, rich, heroic, witty, well read—and handsome." He was also "cool," "elegant," "immaculate," "humorous," and "a joy to be with." He exuded charisma. He exercised "control" that was "precise, taut, disciplined." He made "command decisions." His campaign "purred" with "virtuoso performances."[21] White's book celebrated the American presidential election process and the presidency itself as well as John F. Kennedy. In romanticizing the presidency, White further contributed to the elevation of JFK.

In contrast to Kennedy as hero, Nixon became the villain—but he was a small villain more offstage than on. White dedicated more than three times the number of pages to Kennedy and the Democrats than to Nixon and the GOP. And on the Republican side, White seemed more interested in Nelson Rockefeller than Nixon. For the period before the national convention, the author devoted much more attention and many more pages to the New York governor than to the man who would become the presidential nominee. White clearly saw Rocky as more capable, more dynamic, and possessed of better ideas. His attitude toward Nixon was disdainful. The vice president might have been a villain, but he was a not very impressive one.[22]

Literary needs also shaped the narrative. The plot required events that validated the hero. It allowed no recounting of weakness or of less than noble actions on his part. Thus, nowhere in White's chronicle could a reader find a mention of the missile gap hoax, the debate over Quemoy and Matsu, or Kennedy's manipulation of the Cuban issue. The Luce journalist sanitized the Kennedy response to the Martin Luther King Jr. incident. White's account of the election was moving and captured the magic of the Kennedy appeal, but it was a peculiar kind of history. It was devoid of the inconvenient details that did not fit the characters and the plot. It was therefore less true to the record than it could have been or should have been.

As he composed his paean of praise to JFK and his effort, White came to identify himself with the Kennedy campaign. His growing friendship with the candidate inevitably limited his ability to criticize the man, and the author made no effort to maintain any independence. He became one of the Kennedy retinue and sought out Kennedy approval for his work. He circulated the manuscript for *The Making of the President 1960* to Robert F. Kennedy, Pierre Salinger, Lou Harris, and Ken O'Donnell, among others and accepted suggestions from them as to what material should be included and excluded. The Kennedys and their aides decided what was history and what was not.

This combination of a novelistic conception of history and the author's ingratiation with the Kennedy campaign produced what amounted to the first installment of the Camelot myth. So, White helped create the legend of Kennedy's Camelot—"a magic moment in American history, when gallant men danced with beautiful women, when great deeds were done, when artists, writers, and poets met at the White House, and the barbarians beyond the walls held back." White confessed that the "magic Camelot of John F. Kennedy never existed" and that seeing the Kennedy administration as Camelot is "a misreading of history."[23] He also admitted that he had willingly participated in its creation. Whatever his later regrets, and they do not appear to be many, White's version of 1960 was a spectacular success personally, financially, and professionally. It established him as the preeminent popular authority on presidential elections.

So mesmerized were journalists and historians that no one pointed to the obvious flaw in his interpretation. If JFK's charisma was so great, how was it that his opponent received just as many votes? If the Kennedy campaign was so magnificent and the Nixon campaign so error-prone, why did Nixon almost win? These were dangerous questions with even more dangerous answers. White never dared to come to grips with these issues because addressing them honestly would undermine the unity and integrity of his story. The logical answers (after one dismissed the religious red herring) were that Kennedy was not as captivating as White suggested and Nixon's campaign was not so wretched. But with such responses the White thesis unravels, and so do the accounts of the Kennedy courtiers. Given these unsettling implications, it is unsurprising that most writers have preferred to ignore such inconvenient truths and embrace the standard White thesis.

Fifty years later, a reconsideration of 1960 is in order. Any realistic understanding of the election must include a willingness to lay aside the myths that dominate the subject. This means discarding the notion that John Kennedy's religion prevented him from winning a decisive victory and the idea that vote fraud kept Richard Nixon out of the White House. Most importantly, it means that one must abandon the eloquent hagiography of Theodore White, give more credit to Richard M. Nixon, and rediscover the realities of John F. Kennedy's close victory. Such history may not be as elegant and dramatic as the Camelot legend, but it is a fairer and more accurate representation of what happened in 1960.

Appendix. Votes for President, 1960, by State and Party

1960 Census Population	State	Electoral Vote Rep.	Electoral Vote Dem.	Total Vote	Republican	Democratic	Other	Plurality		Total Vote Rep.	Total Vote Dem.	Major Vote Rep.	Major Vote Dem.
3,266,740	Alabama		5*	570,225	237,981	324,050	8,194	86,069	D	41.7%	56.8%	42.3%	57.7%
226,167	Alaska	3		60,762	30,953	29,809	–	1,144	R	50.9%	49.1%	50.9%	49.1%
1,302,161	Arizona	4		398,491	221,241	176,781	469	44,460	R	55.5%	44.4%	55.6%	44.4%
1,786,272	Arkansas		8	428,509	184,508	215,049	28,952	30,541	D	43.1%	50.2%	46.2%	53.8%
15,717,204	California	32		6,506,578	3,259,722	3,224,099	22,757	35,623	R	50.1%	49.6%	50.3%	49.7%
1,753,947	Colorado	6		736,236	402,242	330,629	3,365	71,613	R	54.6%	44.9%	54.9%	45.1%
2,535,234	Connecticut		8	1,222,883	565,813	657,055	15	91,242	D	46.3%	53.7%	46.3%	53.7%
446,292	Delaware		3	196,683	96,373	99,590	720	3,217	D	49.0%	50.6%	49.2%	50.8%
4,951,560	Florida	10		1,544,176	795,476	748,700	–	46,776	R	51.5%	49.5%	51.5%	48.5%
3,943,116	Georgia		12	733,349	274,472	458,638	239	184,166	D	37.4%	62.5%	37.4%	62.6%
632,772	Hawaii		3	184,705	92,295	92,410	–	115	D	50.0%	50.0%	50.0%	50.0%
667,191	Idaho	4		300,450	161,597	138,853	–	22,744	R	53.8%	46.2%	53.8%	46.2%
10,081,158	Illinois		27	4,757,409	2,368,988	2,377,846	10,575	8,858	D	49.8%	50.0%	49.9%	50.1%
4,662,498	Indiana	13		2,135,360	1,175,120	952,358	7,882	222,762	R	55.0%	44.6%	55.2%	44.8%
2,757,537	Iowa	10		1,273,810	722,381	550,565	864	171,816	R	56.7%	43.2%	56.7%	43.3%
2,178,611	Kansas	8		928,825	561,474	363,213	4,138	198,261	R	60.4%	39.1%	60.7%	39.3%
3,038,156	Kentucky	10		1,124,462	602,607	521,855	–	80,752	R	53.6%	46.4%	53.6%	46.4%
3,257,022	Louisiana		10	807,891	230,980	407,339	169,572	176,359	D	28.6%	50.4%	36.2%	63.8%
969,265	Maine	5		421,767	240,608	181,159	–	59,449	R	57.0%	43.0%	57.0%	43.0%
3,100,689	Maryland		9	1,055,349	489,538	565,808	3	76,270	D	46.4%	53.6%	46.4%	53.6%
5,148,578	Massachusetts		16	2,469,480	976,750	1,487,174	5,556	510,424	D	39.6%	60.2%	39.6%	60.4%
7,823,194	Michigan		20	3,318,097	1,620,428	1,687,269	10,400	66,841	D	48.8%	50.9%	49.0%	51.0%
3,413,864	Minnesota		11	1,541,887	757,915	779,933	4,039	22,018	D	49.2%	50.6%	49.3%	50.7%
2,178,141	Mississippi	*		298,171	73,561	108,362	116,248	7,886	U	24.7%	36.3%	40.4%	59.6%
4,319,813	Missouri		13	1,934,422	962,221	972,201	–	9,980	D	49.7%	50.3%	49.7%	50.3%
674,767	Montana	4		277,579	141,841	134,891	847	6,950	R	51.1%	48.6%	51.3%	48.7%
1,411,330	Nebraska	6		613,095	380,553	232,542	–	148,011	R	62.1%	37.9%	62.1%	37.9%
285,278	Nevada		3	107,267	52,387	54,880	–	2,493	D	48.8%	51.2%	48.8%	51.2%
606,921	New Hampshire	4		295,761	157,989	137,772	–	20,217	R	53.4%	46.6%	53.4%	46.6%
6,066,782	New Jersey		16	2,773,111	1,363,324	1,385,415	24,372	22,091	D	49.2%	50.0%	49.6%	50.4%
951,023	New Mexico		4	311,107	153,733	156,027	1,347	2,294	D	49.4%	50.2%	49.6%	50.4%
16,782,304	New York		45	7,291,079	3,446,419	3,840,085	14,575	393,666	D	47.3%	52.5%	47.4%	52.6%
4,556,155	North Carolina		14	1,368,556	655,420	713,136	–	57,716	D	47.9%	52.1%	47.9%	52.1%
632,446	North Dakota	4		278,431	154,310	123,963	158	30,347	R	55.4%	44.5%	55.5%	44.5%
9,706,397	Ohio	25		4,161,859	2,217,611	1,944,248	–	273,363	R	53.3%	46.7%	53.3%	46.7%
2,328,284	Oklahoma	7*		903,150	533,039	370,111	–	162,928	R	59.0%	41.0%	59.0%	41.0%
1,768,687	Oregon	6		776,421	408,060	367,402	959	40,658	R	52.6%	47.3%	52.6%	47.4%
11,319,366	Pennsylvania		32	5,006,541	2,439,956	2,556,282	10,303	116,326	D	48.7%	51.1%	48.8%	51.2%
859,488	Rhode Island		4	405,534	146,502	258,032	–	110,530	D	36.4%	63.6%	36.4%	63.6%
2,382,594	South Carolina		8	386,688	188,558	198,129	1	9,571	D	48.8%	51.2%	48.8%	51.2%
680,514	South Dakota	4		306,487	178,417	128,070	–	50,347	R	58.2%	41.8%	58.2%	41.8%
3,567,089	Tennessee	11		1,051,792	556,577	481,453	13,762	75,124	R	52.9%	45.8%	53.6%	46.4%
9,579,677	Texas		24	2,311,084	1,121,310	1,167,567	22,207	46,257	D	48.5%	50.5%	49.0%	51.0%
890,627	Utah	4		374,709	205,361	169,248	100	36,113	R	54.8%	45.2%	54.8%	45.2%
389,881	Vermont	3		167,324	98,131	69,186	7	28,945	R	58.6%	41.3%	58.6%	41.4%
3,966,949	Virginia	12		771,449	404,521	362,327	4,601	42,194	R	52.4%	47.0%	52.8%	47.2%
2,853,214	Washington	9		1,241,572	629,273	599,298	13,001	29,975	R	50.7%	48.3%	51.2%	48.8%
1,860,421	West Virginia		8	837,781	395,995	441,786	–	45,791	D	47.3%	52.7%	47.3%	52.7%
3,951,777	Wisconsin	12		1,729,082	895,175	830,805	3,102	64,370	R	51.8%	48.0%	51.9%	48.1%
330,066	Wyoming	3		140,782	77,451	63,331	–	14,120	R	55.0%	45.0%	55.0%	45.0%
179,323,175	TOTAL	219*	303*	68,838,218	34,108,157	34,226,731	503,330	118,574	D	49.5%	49.7%	49.9%	50.1%

Source: *America Votes 5: A Handbook of Contemporary American Election Statistics*, ed. Richard M. Scammon, p. 1.
* Senator Harry F. Byrd of Virginia received six electoral votes from Alabama, eight from Mississippi, and one from Oklahoma.

Notes

Abbreviations

ACW	Ann C. Whitman (Dwight D. Eisenhower's secretary)
AES	Adlai E. Stevenson
AWF	Ann Whitman File (Dwight D. Eisenhower Library)
CA	*Chicago's American*
CDN	*Chicago Daily News*
CST	*Chicago Sun-Times*
CT	*Chicago Tribune*
DDE	Dwight D. Eisenhower
DDEL	Dwight D. Eisenhower Library
GC	General Correspondence
JFK	John F. Kennedy
JFKL	John F. Kennedy Library
LAT	*Los Angeles Times*
LBJ	Lyndon B. Johnson
LBJL	Lyndon B. Johnson Library
MJ	*Milwaukee Journal*
NARA-LN	National Archives and Records Administration—Laguna Niguel
NYDN	*New York Daily News*
NYHT	*New York Herald Tribune*
NYP	*New York Post*
NYT	*New York Times*
NYTM	*New York Times Magazine*
OHI	Oral History Interview
PPP	Pre-Presidential Papers
RFK	Robert F. Kennedy
RFKP	Robert F. Kennedy Papers
RMN	Richard M. Nixon
RMNL	Richard M. Nixon Library
RSP	Richard Scammon Papers (at John F. Kennedy Library)
SEP	*Saturday Evening Post*
SPF	Senate Political Files (at Lyndon B. Johnson Library)
TSP	Theodore Sorensen Papers (at John F. Kennedy Library)
WP	*Washington Post*
WSJ	*Wall Street Journal*

Introduction

1. See Ambrose, *Nixon*, 607. The most recent accounts of the election are Donaldson, *First Modern Campaign*; Pietrusza, *1960—LBJ vs. JFK vs. Nixon*; Rorabaugh, *The Real Making of the President*; and Gifford, *The Center Cannot Hold*. All of these new works continue to subscribe implicitly or explicitly to White's thesis.

Chapter 1. National Party Politics in the 1950s

1. The election statistics cited here and subsequently in this chapter are from Rusk, ed., *A Statistical History of the American Electorate*. Table 4–4, p. 134, provides popular vote percentages for presidential candidates. Table 5–3, pp. 215–16, gives the breakdown of membership in the House of Representatives by party; table 6–2, p. 377, does the same thing for the Senate. Table 5–5, p. 220, provides the Democratic percentage of the total raw popular vote in the country for the House of Representatives. Table 7–2, pp. 442–43, gives the results of gubernatorial elections in a given election year. Unless otherwise noted, all subsequent election results come from these tables.

2. With forty-eight states in the Union, there were forty-eight governors, ninety-six senators, and 435 members of the House of Representatives. To the extent the preceding figures do not add up to these numbers, the differences are accounted for by officeholders who bore a different party identification and by vacancies.

3. Ladd, *Transformations*, 291–92.

4. On 1948, see Donaldson, *Truman Defeats Dewey*; and Gullan, *The Upset That Wasn't*.

5. Gallup, ed., *Gallup Poll*, June 13, 1951 (poll conducted May 19–24, 1951), 2:989; ibid., January 12, 1953 (poll conducted December 6–11, 1952), 2:1114.

6. For the Eisenhower revival, see especially Greenstein, *Hidden-Hand Presidency*; and Ambrose, *Eisenhower*. Both books appeared in the 1980s and were representative of a revisionism that significantly elevated Eisenhower's standing. For the Schlesinger article, see Schlesinger, "Our Presidents." Schlesinger rejoiced in Ike's low ranking (see Schlesinger, *Journals, 1952–2000*, 162, 278). For a sense of the academic milieu in which the anti-Eisenhower spirit flourished, see Jumonville, *Henry Steele Commager*; and Schlesinger, *Journals, 1952–2000*. Schlesinger and company, though, were largely out of touch with reality. Schlesinger thought Stevenson was going to win in 1952. In 1972, he was of the opinion that that year's presidential election would be "very close" (see Schlesinger, *Journals, 1952–2000*, 19–22, 362).

7. See, for example, Neustadt, *Presidential Power*; and Rossiter, *The American Presidency*.

8. Alexander, *Holding the Line*, xv–xvi. See also Reichard, *Politics as Usual*. Reichard is more complimentary of Eisenhower.

9. On Eisenhower and the press, see Halberstam, *Fifties*, 702–4; The Reminiscences of Charles Roberts, November 20, 1972, p. 7, in the Oral History Collection of Columbia University. Fletcher Knebel took a poll of reporters on the Eisenhower

campaign train in 1952 and found them two to one for Stevenson (see The Reminiscences of Edward Folliard, September 1, 1967, p. 19, in the Oral History Collection of Columbia University). For the Eisenhower quote on Alsop, see Ambrose, *Eisenhower*, 563. On Lippmann and Stevenson, see Steel, *Walter Lippmann*, 480–84, 502, 506.

10. Ambrose, *Eisenhower*, 26–28.

11. For an exposition of Eisenhower's core values and his decision-making process, see Snead, *Gaither Committee*, 15–42.

12. The low point came in late 1958, when his approval sank to 52 percent with 30 percent disapproval. By early 1960, Eisenhower's approval rating had rebounded to 64 percent with 22 percent disapproving (see Gallup, ed., *Gallup Poll*, November 26, 1958 [poll conducted November 7–12, 1958], 3:1579; ibid., April 8, 1960 [poll conducted March 30–April 4, 1960], 3:1661).

13. Ladd, *Transformations*, 27, 233–35, 262–65; Sundquist, *Dynamics*, 228–29.

14. Brownell, *Advising Ike*, 126; Ambrose, *Eisenhower*, 118; Ambrose, *Nixon*, 548.

15. Sundquist, *Dynamics*, 287; Ambrose, *Nixon*, 484; Brownell, *Advising Ike*, 302.

16. I. Morgan, *Eisenhower versus "The Spenders,"* 99–100; I. Morgan, *Deficit Government*, 80–85; Sloan, *Eisenhower*, 143–51.

17. *NYT*, June 7, 1959, November 14, 1959.

18. Gallup, ed., *Gallup Poll*, November 26, 1958 (poll conducted November 7–12, 1958), 2:1579.

19. On the California intrigue featuring Nixon, Knowland, Knight, and Earl Warren, see Montgomery and Johnson, *One Step*, 105–23, 162–65, 189–201, 228–60.

20. *NYT*, November 2, 1958.

21. On the 1958 elections, see Ambrose, *Eisenhower*, 487–89; Ambrose, *Nixon*, 483–504; *NYT*, November 6, 1958; Montgomery and Johnson, *One Step*, 233–60, and Nixon, *RN*, 220. The Republican disadvantage increased with the admission of Alaska and Hawaii as states. Alaska joined the Union in January 1959 with one Democratic representative and two Democratic senators. Hawaii was admitted in August 1959 with one Democratic representative, one Democratic senator, and one Republican senator. With the addition of the two states, the count in the House of Representatives became 284–153. In the Senate, it became 66–34 (see Scammon, ed., *America Votes—4*, 18–23, 90–94).

22. On legislative numbers, see *The Book of the States, 1960–1961*, 37.

23. Alexander, *Holding the Line*, 243

24. On the Eisenhower comeback, see Ambrose, *Eisenhower*, 511–80; and Alexander, *Holding the Line*, 244–62. On Eisenhower's improved health, see Lasby, *Eisenhower's Heart Attack*, 253–62.

25. See Gallup, ed., *Gallup Poll*, December 7, 1958 (poll conducted November 7–12, 1958), 2:1581; ibid., November 22, 1959 (poll conducted November 12–17, 1959), 3:1642; ibid., November 25, 1959 (poll conducted November 12–17, 1959), 3:1642.

26. See Caro, *Master of the Senate*, 840–41; and Evans and Novak, *Lyndon B. Johnson*, 196–220.

27. On Khrushchev, see W. Taubman, *Khrushchev*; Beschloss, *MAYDAY*; Beschloss, *Crisis Years*; Fursenko and Naftali, *Khrushchev's Cold War*; and Ulam, *The Rivals*.

28. Fursenko and Naftali, *Khrushchev's Cold War*, 40–41; Beschloss, *MAYDAY*, 149–50; I. Morgan, *Eisenhower versus the "Spenders,"* 131. On the "bomber gap," see Prados, *Soviet Estimate*, 38–50; and Barrett, *CIA and Congress*, 234–50.

29. The literature on the missile gap is extensive. For a sampling of work on the subject, see Roman, *Eisenhower and the Missle Gap*; Prados, *Soviet Estimate*, 65–66, 70–95, 111–20; Snead, *Gaither Committee*, 169–77, 180–81; Barrett, *CIA and Congress*, 262–73, 301–13, 323–30, 356–74; P. Taubman, *Secret Empire*, 270–80, 296–97, 323–24; Bottome, *Missile Gap*, 115–45; and Preble, *Kennedy and the Missile Gap*, 10–11, 44–45, 56–59, 72–73, 80–81, 86–87, 96–97, 106–9, 154–57.

30. On the missile gap coalition, see McDougall, *Heavens and the Earth*, 218–19; and Fursenko and Naftali, *Khrushchev's Cold War*, 258.

31. On Symington, see McFarland, *Cold War Strategist*, 59–63, 69–72, 77–80, 85–96; and Olson, *Symington*, 335–37, 350–51, 364–66. There was little respect for Symington. When he was being considered as a vice-presidential nominee, two of the chief journalist allies of the Democrats, Joe Alsop and Philip Graham of the *Washington Post*, argued strongly against the choice of Symington because they did not consider him smart enough to be one heartbeat away from the presidency.

32. *NYT*, February 5, 1960.

33. *NYT*, November 14, 1959, September 1, 1959.

34. On Alsop, see J. Alsop, *I've Seen the Best of It*; Yoder, *Joe Alsop's Cold War*; and Merry, *Taking on the World*.

35. Stewart Alsop, "How Can We Catch Up?" *SEP*, December 14, 1957, 26ff., and "Our Gamble with Destiny," *SEP*, May 16, 1959, 116–17; Thomas R. Phillips, "The Growing Missile Gap," *Reporter*, January 8, 1959, 11; Joseph Alsop, "After Ike the Deluge," *WP*, October 7, 1959.

36. Ambrose, *Eisenhower*, 560–63; Beschloss, *MAYDAY*, 154.

37. Beschloss, *MAYDAY*, 154; Roman, *Eisenhower and the Missile Gap*, 34–35. On Allen Dulles and the missile gap, see Grose, *Gentleman Spy*, 473–74, 507; P. Taubman, *Secret Empire*, 273, 275, 296–97; and Helgerson, *Getting to Know the President*, chap. 3, pp. 5–6. By 1960, Eisenhower was completely fed up with the CIA and its performance and believed it required a massive restructuring (see Weiner, *Legacy of Ashes*, 166–67).

38. On the Gaither Report, see Snead, *Gaither Committee*.

39. Ibid., 120–28.

40. Two other privately done studies, one by the Rockefeller Foundation and one from Johns Hopkins University, also registered doubts about U.S. defense policy (see Bottome, *Missile Gap*, 47–48; and Snead, *Gaither Committee*, 110–13).

41. Gallup, ed., *Gallup Poll*, February 10, 1960 (poll conducted December 10–12,

1959), 3:1634; Bottome, *Missile Gap*, 238–39; Zaloga, *The Kremlin's Nuclear Sword*, 48–50; Ambrose, *Ike's Spies*, 276–78.

42. See Roman, *Eisenhower and the Missile Gap*, 45, for the limits of the U-2 intelligence. For the Democratic reaction to the revelation that there was no missile gap and their refusal to admit their error, see Preble, *Kennedy and the Missile Gap*, 153–57; Theodore Sorensen OHI, March 24, 1964, JFKL, pp. 12–13; Stuart Symington OHI, September 4, 1964, JFKL, pp. 1–2; Symington, "Where the Missile Gap Went," *Reporter*, February 15, 1961, 21–23; and Sorensen, *Counselor*, 188–89. See also Gaddis, *We Now Know*, 254–60.

43. Parmet, *JFK*, 10.

Chapter 2. Kennedy and Nixon before 1960

1. Reeves, *President Kennedy*, 19.

2. The last Gallup Poll on Kennedy of November 10, 1963, had him at 59 percent approval and 28 percent disapproval. The poll was conducted October 11–16 (see Gallup, ed., *Gallup Poll*, 3:1850). Gallup also showed Kennedy well ahead of his prospective opponents in trial heats for the 1964 presidential election. He led Rockefeller by thirty-one points, Nixon by twenty-one, and Barry Goldwater by sixteen (see Gallup, ed., *Gallup Poll*, 3:1836, 1841, 1845; see also Piereson, *Camelot and the Cultural Revolution*, 27–29). For examples of the emotional reaction to the assassination of JFK, see the memorandum by Elspeth Huxley at the conclusion of the Joseph Alsop OHI, June 23, 1964, JFKL. It describes how Alsop and Maxwell Taylor were reduced to tears at their recollection of the Kennedy assassination.

3. White, "For President Kennedy an Epilogue," *Life*, December 6, 1963, 158–59. See White, *In Search of History*, 520–25; Hoffman, *Theodore H. White*, 1–3; and Piereson, *Camelot and the Cultural Revolution*, 58–61, 83–87, 184–89. According to one account, Jacqueline Kennedy was dismayed by the character of Lee Harvey Oswald. She remarked that JFK "didn't even have the satisfaction of being killed for civil rights. . . . [I]t had to be some silly little communist" (see Manchester, *Death of a President*, 407; and Piereson, *Camelot and the Cultural Revolution*, 59). *Camelot* was a popular Broadway musical of the early 1960s, the songs from which Jacqueline Kennedy told White that she and the president enjoyed listening to on their record player. Whether this assertion was true is a matter of debate. Interestingly, the one individual who confirmed JFK's love of the music from *Camelot* was none other than Judith Campbell Exner (see Exner, *My Story*, 220).

4. For Sorensen's list of Kennedy's vices and imperfections, see Sorensen, *Kennedy*, 28–29. The classic example of the nature of Kennedy court history is Arthur Schlesinger's analysis of the meaning of the Bay of Pigs. According to him: "It was a horribly expensive lesson; but it was well learned. . . . [N]o one can doubt that failure in Cuba in 1961 contributed to success in Cuba in 1962." In Schlesinger's world, the Bay of Pigs was actually good because it prepared the administration to be successful in the missile crisis (see Schlesinger, *Thousand Days*, 297).

The best works on JFK are Joan Blair and Clay Blair, *The Search for JFK*; Parmet, *Jack: The Struggles of John F. Kennedy* and *JFK: The Presidency of John F. Kennedy*; N. Hamilton, *JFK: Reckless Youth*; and Reeves, *President Kennedy*. Of these, only the work of Hamilton had the support of the Kennedy family. That initial endorsement quickly vanished, and a major controversy developed when Hamilton's portrayal of JFK's life to 1947 did not meet Kennedy family approval. On the controversy over the Hamilton book, see *NYT*, December 3, 1992, and January 22, 1993. More recently, Robert Dallek, *An Unfinished Life: John F. Kennedy, 1917–1963*, has provided the most complete one-volume study of JFK, one that is highly sympathetic and was completed with Kennedy family support.

5. For Theodore Sorensen's vision of what might have been had JFK lived, see Sorensen, *Counselor*, 351–52.

6. John Fitzgerald Kennedy was the second son. The other children were: Joseph Jr. (b. 1915, d. 1944), Rosemary (b. 1918, d. 2005), Kathleen (b. 1920, d. 1948), Eunice (b. 1921, d. 2009), Patricia (b. 1924, d. 2006), Robert Francis (b. 1925, d. 1968), Jean (b. 1928), and Edward Moore (b. 1932, d. 2009).

7. On Joseph P. Kennedy, see R. Whalen, *Founding Father*; Koskoff, *Joseph P. Kennedy*; Schwarz, *Joseph P. Kennedy*; S. Hersh, *Dark Side*; and Kessler, *Sins of the Father*.

8. On Joseph P. Kennedy as ambassador and his relationship with FDR, see Beschloss, *Kennedy and Roosevelt*; and Doris Kearns Goodwin, *Fitzgeralds and the Kennedys*, 512–89. Felix Frankfurter OHI, June 10, 1964, JFKL, p. 5.

9. On Joseph P. Kennedy's wealth, see Smith, "The Fifty-Million Dollar Man." See also *NYT*, October 28, 1957.

10. Bradlee, *Good Life*, 167–70; N. Hamilton, *JFK*, 115; S. Hersh, *Dark Side*, 16–18.

11. Burner, *John F. Kennedy*, 14; N. Hamilton, *JFK*, 108, 163.

12. On JFK and sex, see N. Hamilton, *JFK*; Giglio, *Presidency of John F. Kennedy*, 10, 267–71, 308–9; Reeves, *President Kennedy*, 110, 288–92, 678–79, 689, 707; and S. Hersh, *Dark Side*. Nigel Hamilton's characterization of JFK as a "reckless youth" is especially appropriate in light of his affair with Inga Arvad. "Inga Binga," as JFK liked to call her, was regarded as a possible German spy. His consorting with her while he was with the Office of Naval Intelligence was extraordinarily risky. While Hamilton has portrayed JFK's reckless sexual behavior before 1947, Seymour Hersh has provided a convincing account of the same chronic behavior for 1960–63. In this period, Kennedy became involved with a mistress of the leading Chicago mobster as well as with a possible East German spy. In 1962, J. Edgar Hoover paid JFK a visit and explained the dangers of his liaison with Judith Campbell Exner, who was the mistress of Sam Giancana. If Hoover made any impression, it did not prevent JFK from involving himself with Ellen Rometsch, the possible East German spy (see R. Powers, *Secrecy and Power*, 359–60; and S. Hersh, *Dark Side*, 13–34, 222–46, 294–325, 387–90, 398–406; see also Exner, *My Story*).

13. Baker, *Wheeling and Dealing*, 78; Caro, *Master of the Senate*. For a good picture

of Georgetown society and its avant-garde attitudes toward sex in the 1950s and 1960s, see Burleigh, *Very Private Woman*, 134–35, 183–220.

14. Bradlee, *Good Life*, 216–17; Brinkley, *David Brinkley*, 141–42.

15. S. Hersh, *Dark Side*, 32–33.

16. On JFK's health and especially the Addison's disease, the most complete treatment is Dallek, *Unfinished Life*, 73–81, 100–105, 123, 152–53, 195–96. See also Blair and Blair, *Search for JFK*, 560–79; Reeves, *President Kennedy*, 24, 42–44, 242–43, 668–69; N. Hamilton, *JFK*, 809–12; Ferrell, *Ill-Advised*, 151–56; Gilbert, *Mortal Presidency*, 145–70; and Parmet, *Jack*, 191–92.

17. Dallek, *Unfinished Life*, 197–98, 212. Dallek was granted unprecedented access to Kennedy's medical records.

18. Reeves, *President Kennedy*, 44.

19. For representative samples of the denials, misrepresentations, and rationalizations, see Salinger, *With Kennedy*, 40–41; Galbraith, *Life*, 373; Sorensen, *Kennedy*, 38–39; and Schlesinger, *Journals, 1952–2000*, 58. See also Gore Vidal, "Coached by Camelot," *New Yorker*, December 1, 1997, 84–92. Vidal says that JFK called him and asked him to talk to Richard Rovere, who was writing an article for *Esquire*, to tell Rovere that he (JFK) did not have Addison's.

20. N. Hamilton, *JFK*, 504.

21. For JFK's naval service and the story of *PT-109*, see N. Hamilton, *JFK*, 497–633; and Blair and Blair, *Search for JFK*, 209–80, 586–87. The Blairs were less impressed than Hamilton with Kennedy's performance.

22. Albert J. Zack OHI, November 28, 1967, JFKL, p. 1; *NYT*, October 12, 1959.

23. N. Hamilton, *JFK*, 796–97.

24. George Smathers OHI, Interview III, Tape 2, July 10, 1964, JFKL, p. 3.

25. Giglio, *Presidency of John F. Kennedy*, 7; Bart Lytton OHI, June 8, 1966, JFKL, p. 42.

26. *NYT*, April 19, 1959.

27. For personal observations of Kennedy's style, see Schlesinger, *Thousand Days*, 114–16; Sorensen, *Kennedy*, 13–14; Clifford, *Counsel*, 303–4; Galbraith, *Life*, 373; and Bradlee, *Good Life*, 236.

28. Reeves, *President Kennedy*, 19; S. Hersh, *Dark Side*, 30–31.

29. Reeves, *President Kennedy*, 477–78; Bradlee, *Good Life*, 237–38.

30. Felix Frankfurter OHI, June 10, 1964, JFKL, pp. 19–20; Hardeman and Bacon, *Rayburn*, 434, 445; D. B. Hardeman OHI, January 3, 1970, DDEL, p. 107.

31. Charles Spalding OHI by John F. Stewart, March 14, 1968, JFKL, p. 32. The Three-I League was a low minor league far removed from major league baseball. Giglio, *Presidency of John F. Kennedy*, 8–9; Parmet, *Jack*, 145–52.

32. Charles Spalding OHI, March 14, 1968, JFKL, pp. 32–33; J. Alsop, *I've Seen the Best of It*, 411.

33. See Thomas, *Robert Kennedy*, 59–64; R. Martin, *Ballots*, 176; Dallek, *Unfinished Life*, 157–76; and T. Whalen, *Kennedy versus Lodge*.

34. On the 1956 Democratic convention, see R. Martin, *Ballots*, 373–455.

35. Heymann, *RFK*, 115; Thomas, *Robert Kennedy*, 74. Stevenson, for his part, developed a hearty distaste for the Kennedys, especially Bobby.

36. Ken O'Donnell OHI, July 23, 1969, JFKL, vol. 1, p. 9.

37. Rowland Evans Jr. OHI, January 7, 1966, JFKL, pp. 42–43. See also Joseph Alsop OHI, June 23, 1964, JFKL, p. 49; Robert Nathan OHI, June 9, 1967, JFKL, p. 19.

38. Parmet, *Jack*, 408–14; Land, "John F. Kennedy's Southern Strategy, 1956–1960."

39. Parmet, *Jack*, 513–14; Schaffer, *Chester Bowles*, 167–72; Galbraith, *Life*, 373.

40. The historical literature on Richard M. Nixon is large. There have been several major examinations of Nixon as well as innumerable shorter works that offer insights. The most complete biography is Stephen Ambrose, *Nixon* (1987–91) in three volumes. Herbert Parmet's *Richard Nixon and His America* (1990) is a good one-volume biography. Two important works that deal with Richard Nixon's early years are Roger Morris, *Richard Milhous Nixon: The Rise of an American Politician* (1990), and Irwin F. Gellman, *The Contender Richard Nixon: The Congress Years, 1946–1952* (1999). One should note that although Morris and Gellman provide the best coverage of Nixon's early years, they are bitterly opposed on some points. Morris is strongest on the period before 1946, while Gellman offers the best account of Nixon between 1946 and 1952. A penetrating study that focuses on the Nixon presidency but also treats his pre-presidential career is Richard Reeves, *President Nixon: Alone in the White House* (2001). Needless to say, the literature on Nixon extends far beyond these works and cannot be summarized in a note. There are also, of course, numerous hatchet jobs on Nixon, none of them of any great value except to raise the important question of how and why Nixon managed to arouse such hatred—a hatred that existed long before the Watergate scandal.

41. The Reminiscences of Kevin McCann, December 21, 1966, p. 41, in the Oral History Collection of Columbia University; The Reminiscences of Henry Roemer McPhee, December 4, 1970, p. 52, in the Oral History Collection of Columbia University; Harlow, "The Man and the Political Leader," in Thompson, ed., *Nixon Presidency*, 7; Evans and Novak, *Nixon*, 9.

42. Sidey, "Perspectives on Richard Nixon," in Friedman and Levantrosser, eds., *Richard M. Nixon*, 9; Small, *Presidency of Richard Nixon*, 2; Reeves, *President Nixon*, 12. For a comparison of theories about Nixon's personality, see Haldeman, *Ends of Power*, 62.

43. Haldeman, *Ends of Power*, 70–71; Humes, *Confessions*, 125; Robert E. Cushman OHI, March 4, 1977, DDEL, p. 9. Nixon told Cushman, "You do the hiring and firing . . . just don't make anybody unhappy." Obviously, the observations of Haldeman and John Ehrlichman must be regarded with caution because of the falling out between them and Nixon during the Watergate affair, but because of their closeness to Nixon, their comments do offer insight.

44. The Reminiscences of Edward P. Morgan, September 12, 1967, p. 52, in the Oral History Collection of Columbia University; Haldeman, *Ends of Power*, 69, 70; Sidey, "The Man and Foreign Policy," in Thompson, ed., *Nixon Presidency*, 305.

45. Ehrlichman, *Witness to Power*, 67; Dickerson, *Among Those Present*, 200.

46. Ambrose, *Eisenhower*, 601; Bradlee, *Conversations with Kennedy*, 32; Rovere, *Final Reports*, 145.

47. White, *Making of the President*, 299–300. See also Reston, *Deadline*, 406.

48. Morris, *Richard Milhous Nixon*, 166–67; RMN to Robert Collins, January 19, 1961, RMN PPP, GC, Box 163 (Robert Collins File), RMNL*; RMN to Herb Kaplow, February 21, 1961, RMN PPP, GC, Box 396, RMNL*; Ambrose, *Nixon*, 42–43; Reeves, *President Nixon*, 314. RMNL materials marked with an asterisk were originally viewed at the National Archives site in Laguna Niguel, California, where they were located until 2006. All Nixon's pre-presidential papers have been transferred from Laguna Niguel to the RMNL in Yorba Linda.

49. Sidey, "The Man and Foreign Policy," in Thompson, ed., *Nixon Presidency*, 301; Harlow, "The Man and the Political Leader," in Thompson, ed., *Nixon Presidency*, 10.

50. For Richard Nixon's early years, 1913–40, see Morris, *Richard Milhous Nixon*, 1–203; Ambrose, *Nixon*, 21–104; Parmet, *Richard Nixon*, 30–88; and Black, *Richard M. Nixon*, 1–74. Nixon's brothers were Harold (b. 1909, d. 1933), Francis Donald (b. 1914, d. 1987), Arthur (b. 1918, d. 1925), and Edward (b. 1930). For the latest inside view of the Nixon family, see the account of Nixon's youngest brother, Edward, in Nixon and Olson, *The Nixons*.

51. Morris, *Richard Milhous Nixon*, 98–99; Black, *Richard M. Nixon*, 70–71.

52. See Small, *Presidency of Richard M. Nixon*, 7; Morris, *Richard Milhous Nixon*, 246–54; Ambrose, *Nixon*, 105–16.

53. See Morris, *Richard Milhous Nixon*, 257–866; Gellman, *Contender*.

54. For the conventional view of 1946 and 1950, see Morris, *Richard Milhous Nixon*, 206–38, 515–621; and Mitchell, *Tricky Dick*. For the heterodox view and a strong rebuttal to Morris and Mitchell, see Gellman, *Contender*. Gellman has successfully debunked the Nixon demonology for 1946 and 1950 and become the standard on Nixon's controversial campaigns against Voorhis and Douglas. On 1952, see Morris, *Richard Milhous Nixon*, 737–866; Ambrose, *Nixon*, 271–300; and Parmet, *Richard Nixon*, 225–61. See also Harlow, "The Man and the Political Leader," in Thompson, ed., *Nixon Presidency*, 5.

55. Morris, *Richard Milhous Nixon*, 861–62; S. Alsop, *Nixon & Rockefeller*, 147. On Rayburn's attitude toward Nixon, see Dulaney and Phillips, eds., *Speak, Mister Speaker*, 257–58, 264, 279, 343, 353, 414, 417.

56. McCullough, *Truman*, 909; Ambrose, *Nixon*, 501; D. B. Hardeman OHI, Interview II, March 12, 1969, LBJL, pp. 21, 22; Parmet, *JFK*, 15.

57. Nixon, *RN*, 110; RMN to Mrs. S. E. Bartley, November 16, 1961, RMN PPP, Sam Rayburn Correspondence, Box 22, RMNL; Crowley, *Nixon off the Record*, 13.

58. Summers, *Arrogance of Power*, 59–80; S. Alsop, *Nixon & Rockefeller*, 29; Cronkite, *Reporter's Life*, 187; Elizabeth Gatov OHI, 1978, JFKL, p. 101.

59. Ambrose, *Nixon*, 300.

60. The Reminiscences of Robert Donovan, January 3, 1968, DDEL, p. 20, in the

Oral History Collection of Columbia University; Krock, *Memoirs,* 304–5; Ambrose, *Nixon,* 371–77.

61. Ambrose, *Eisenhower,* 292–326.

62. The work that most thoroughly explores the Kennedy-Nixon relationship is Matthews, *Kennedy & Nixon.* See also Nixon-Kennedy correspondence in RMNL, specifically RMN to Judge Samuel E. Whitaker, December 31, 1953; Jacqueline Kennedy to RMN, December 5, 1954; JFK to RMN, n.d. (but certainly 1952); Jacqueline Kennedy to RMN, January 8, 1958. In 1971, Nixon had Jacqueline Kennedy and her two children for a private visit to the White House. See also Chalmers Roberts OHI, November 8, 1977, JFKL, p. 29, for JFK's positive assessment of Nixon and his abilities in May 1958.

63. On Nixon's continuing admiration for JFK, see Manchester, *Death of a President,* 447. On the Kennedy-Nixon relationship in 1960, see Matthews, *Kennedy & Nixon,* 127–91. There is no doubt that during 1960 Kennedy developed a disdain for Nixon (see Schlesinger, *Journals, 1952–2000,* 87; Bradlee, *Conversations with Kennedy,* 32). However, before 1960, the Democrat got along quite well with the California Republican. After 1959, though, Kennedy mythology and Nixon demonization demanded that the earlier good relations be consigned to oblivion, and so they have in most accounts.

Chapter 3. John F. Kennedy and the Democratic Nomination

1. *NYT,* September 24, 1959; Sorensen, *Kennedy,* 98.

2. *NYT,* February 1, 1960; Charles McWhorter to RMN, April 3, 1959, RMN PPP, GC, Box 145 (Marquis Childs File), RMNL.*

3. *Guide to U.S. Elections,* 5th ed., 1:353–55, 356–57.

4. *NYT,* November 24, 1959, March 6, 1960; *NYDN,* May 5, 1960, May 14, 1960; Eleanor Roosevelt, "My Day," *Capital Times,* April 7, 1960.

5. Gallup, ed., *Gallup Poll,* 3:1590, 1601, 1607, 1613, 1617, 1622–23, 1630, 1640, 1645, 1651, 1656.

6. White, *Making of the President,* 135–37; Parmet, *Jack,* 507–8; Terry Sanford OHI, July 27, 1970, JFKL, p. 8; Teno Roncalio OHI, December 20, 1965, JFKL, p. 32.

7. "An Analysis of a Trial Pairing of Vice President Richard M. Nixon vs. Senator John F. Kennedy for the Presidency of the United States," October 1957, JFK PPP, Box 819, Harris: A Trial Pairing, JFKL; Louis Harris, "A Proposal for Survey Research in 1959," December 29, 1958, TSP, Box 25, Sorensen Campaign Memos (Folder 1), JFKL; "A Study of Presidential Preferences in Nebraska," April 1959, JFK PPP, Box 816, Harris: Presidential Preferences in Nebraska, April 1959, JFKL.

8. Sorensen, *Kennedy,* 131; K. O'Donnell, *Johnny,* 148–51; "A Study of Presidential Preferences in Ohio," April 1959, TSP, Box 2, JFKL.

9. Ed Reingold, "Kennedy in Ohio," Clark Clifford Papers, Microfilm Roll 1, JFKL; Michael V. DiSalle OHI, February 4, 1969, LBJL, p. 3.

10. K. O'Donnell, *Johnny*, 148–52; Schlesinger, *Robert Kennedy*, 194; John Bailey OHI, April 10, 1964, JFKL, pp. 19–21; Heymann, *RFK*, 146; DiSalle, *Second Choice*, 197–200; *NYT*, January 6, 1960; William H. Hessler, "How Kennedy Took Ohio," *Reporter*, March 3, 1960, 21–22. Senator Wayne Morse was unhappy because he planned to be the favorite son candidate from Oregon.

11. Memorandum for Senator Kennedy, January 7, 1960, JFK PPP, Box 934, Illinois—Personnel, September 3–October 26, 1959, JFKL.

12. Sorensen, *Kennedy*, 133; Patrick J. Lucey OHI, August 1, 1964, JFKL, pp. 14–15; Joseph Alsop, "Kennedy's Dilemma," *NYHT*, January 13, 1960; Pat Lucey to Theodore Sorensen, December 22, 1959, TSP, Box 27, Correspondence, 1959–1960, Wisconsin (Folder 1), JFKL.

13. "The Catholic Vote in 1952 and 1956," Arthur M. Schlesinger Jr. Papers, Box W-8, JFKL; Claude Robinson to Nixon, Hall, Finch, October 21, 1960, "Campaign Evaluation as of October 14, 1960 (Third Debate)," RMN PPP, Presidential Debates Preparations, Box 61, RMNL; W. Thompson, *History of Wisconsin*, 686–87; "A Study of Preferences for President in Wisconsin," April 1959, JFK PPP, Box 819, Harris, JFKL; "A Study of the Presidential Primary Election in Wisconsin in the Prospective Contest for the Democratic Nomination," December 1959, RSP, Box 1, JFKL; James Reston, "Madison, Wisconsin," *NYT*, March 2, 1960, January 22, 1960.

14. James B. Brennan OHI, December 9, 1965, JFKL, p. 17.

15. W. Thompson, *History of Wisconsin*, 682–84; Ivan Nestingen OHI, March 3, 1966, JFKL, p. 10.

16. William J. Riggins OHI, December 6, 1965, JFKL, p. 11; Sorensen, *Kennedy*, 136; Cyrus Rice OHI, December 7, 1965, JFKL, p. 10; Ivan Nestingen OHI, March 3, 1966, JFKL, p. 14; Ira Kapstein OHI, December 15, 1965, JFKL, p. 11; *Capital Times*, March 31, 1960.

17. *MJ*, March 24 and 25, 1960.

18. Ibid., March 19 and 21, 1960.

19. Humphrey, *Education*, 207.

20. Ibid., 208–9.

21. Pierre Salinger OHI, July 19, 1965, JFKL, p. 55; Salinger, *With Kennedy*, 33; *Time*, March 7, 1960, 15; *Newsweek*, March 28, 1960, 35; Bradlee, *Conversations with Kennedy*, 16–17.

22. *MJ*, March 19 and 20, 1960; *NYHT*, March 19, 1960.

23. Silvestri, "John F. Kennedy," 37; Humphrey, *Education*, 209; see *Capital Times*, March 31, 1960, April 1, 1960; *MJ*, March 31, 1960, April 1 and 2, 1960; *WP*, April 1, 1960.

24. Norman Clapp OHI, n.d., JFKL, p. 2; Ivan Nestingen OHI, March 3, 1966, JFKL, p. 4; Peter Dugal OHI, January 14, 1966, JFKL, p. 25; *MJ*, March 19 and 20, 1960.

25. The Wisconsin results were as follows:

DISTRICT	HUMPHREY	KENNEDY	KENNEDY PERCENTAGE
First	34,345	46,386	57.5
Second	53,149	50,878	48.9
Third	35,785	27,764	43.7
Fourth	41,780	89,562	68.2
Fifth	49,240	65,790	57.2
Sixth	27,234	44,307	61.9
Seventh	30,163	36,278	54.6
Eighth	23,104	59,211	71.9
Ninth	39,610	28,054	41.5
Tenth	32,343	27,794	46.2
TOTAL	366,753	476,024	56.5

Source: M. G. Toepel and H. Rupert Theobald, *The Wisconsin Blue Book, 1962*, 753–56. http://digital.library.wisc.edu/1711/dl/WI.

26. See "A Special Report on the 3rd and 9th Congressional Districts of Wisconsin," January 1960, RFKP, Box 45 (Harris), JFKL; "A State-Wide Survey of Preferences in the Democratic Presidential Primary in Wisconsin," February 23, 1960, RFKP, Box 45 (Harris), JFKL; "A Study of the Democratic Primary Election for President in Wisconsin in the Third, Ninth, and Seventh Congressional Districts," March 7, 1960, RFKP, Box 45 (Harris), JFKL.

27. Salinger, *P.S.*, 73; Salinger, *With Kennedy*, 33–34.

28. Transcript, "What Happened in Wisconsin," CBS-TV, April 5, 1960, 11:15–12:00 midnight EST, RFK Papers, Pre-Administration Political Files, Box 50, State Files: Wisconsin Primary, Miscellaneous, December 31, 1958–April 30, 1960, JFKL; Hilty, *Robert Kennedy*, 141; Thomas, *Robert Kennedy*, 93; Cronkite, *Reporter's Life*, 185–86.

29. *NYT*, April 6, 1960; *WP*, April 6, 1960.

30. *NYT*, April 7, 1960; James Reston, "Wisconsin Wins Again," *NYT*, April 7, 1960; *Time*, April 18, 1960, 17; *Capital Times*, April 7, 1960.

31. W. Thompson, *History of Wisconsin*, 686–92.

32. *NYHT*, April 8, 1960.

33. White, *Making of the President*, 97; Sorensen, *Kennedy*, 139; *MJ*, January 31, 1960; Patrick J. Lucey OHI, August 1, 1964, JFKL, pp. 18–20.

34. White, *Making of the President*, 96–97; W. Thompson, *History of Wisconsin*, 692–93.

35. White, *Making of the President*, 96.

36. The best account of the West Virginia primary is Fleming, *Kennedy vs. Humphrey*.

37. "A Study of Voter Attitude in West Virginia on Presidential Preferences," January 1960, RSP, Box 2, JFKL.

38. See White, *Making of the President*, 101, 109. The first entry gives the 60–40 difference, and the second gives the 64–36. These later polls, though, did *not* cover

the entire state but just Kanawha County (Charleston). They therefore did not survey the same group of voters as the first one that gave Kennedy a big lead. The problem is that, to my knowledge, we do not have available to us other statewide polls from April and May. Nevertheless, White and others have treated subsequent polls as if they were precisely comparable to the first one. Ken O'Donnell claims that Harris had Humphrey ahead 70–30 (see K. O'Donnell, *Johnny*, 160–61, 170; see also Fleming, *Kennedy vs. Humphrey*, 28–29).

Something was obviously amiss with the wildly gyrating polls. According to Harris and White, JFK started with a 70–30 lead, fell to a 36–64 or 40–60 deficit (at least in Kanawha County), and finally won the primary with a 61–39 margin. These numbers are irreconcilable. No one can dispute the final result of 61–39, so suspicion must fall on either the preliminary Harris poll or the ones conducted in April and May. Insofar as White and Harris attempted to reconcile these wildly different numbers, they did so on the basis that West Virginians were not aware of Kennedy's religion at the time of the first poll but did know about it by mid-April. As the West Virginia campaign continued, Harris showed mounting Kennedy strength. By primary day, JFK had forged ahead, according to White and Harris, 52–48. Even that figure does not explain the final 61–39 margin.

Available accounts agree that Kennedy did gain momentum in the course of the primary. The big question was: Where did he stand at the outset? Did he begin at 36 percent or 40 percent, as suggested by Harris and White, or was the starting point higher? On May 10, John F. Kennedy carried 61 percent of the vote in West Virginia and 52 percent in Kanawha County. If one accepts the mid-April Harris poll showing JFK at 40 percent in Kanawha County as valid and assumes the differential for the state vote remained constant, this would mean that at the time Kennedy was running at 40 percent in Kanawha, he was at approximately 49 percent in West Virginia. In other words, the race was even, and it is highly likely that he was never as far behind as imagined by Lou Harris, members of the press, and almost all chroniclers of the West Virginia primary.

39. White, *Making of the President*, 99. On slating, see Fleming, *Kennedy vs. Humphrey*, 86–100, 119–22, 153–55.

40. John Bailey OHI, April 10, 1964, JFKL, p. 71; *NYT*, May 6, 1960.

41. Meeting Re West Virginia Primary—April 8, 1960, RFK Papers, Pre-Administration Political Files, Box 39, Memos: RFK Incoming, January 1960–August 1960, JFKL; Fleming, *Kennedy vs. Humphrey*, 10; Chalmers M. Roberts OHI, November 8, 1977, JFKL, p. 34; Roberts, *First Rough Draft*, 176. There is much disagreement as to whether religion was an important factor in West Virginia in 1960. See the dozens of OHIs in the JFKL from West Virginians for the widely differing opinions. The April 8 meeting noted above is usually portrayed as one in which West Virginians told RFK that the reason his brother was behind in the state was because of his religion. A reading of the minutes of the meeting does not support that assertion. When asked, the great majority reported that religion was not a major problem in their counties.

42. Fleming, *Kennedy vs. Humphrey*, 34–40; Joseph Alsop, "The Folks of Slab

Fork," *NYHT*, April 15, 1960; Alsop, "The People Speak," *NYHT*, April 18, 1960; Alsop, "The Figures Speak," *NYHT*, April 20, 1960.

43. S. Hersh, *Dark Side*, 90–101; *NYT*, April 26 and 27, 1960; Humphrey, *Education*, 217–18. Hersh emphasizes Kennedy money and vote buying but tends to discount the importance of organized crime in the West Virginia primary. For his part, Theodore H. White claims that although the Kennedy campaign was buying votes, so were the Humphrey supporters (see White, *In Search of History*, 465–66).

44. *NYT*, May 7, 1960; Fleming, *Kennedy vs. Humphrey*, 50–52; R. Goodwin, *Remembering America*, 88; Schlesinger, *Robert Kennedy*, 201; Charles Spalding OHI, March 24, 1968, JFKL, p. 57; Humphrey, *Education*, 475; Rowland Evans Jr. OHI, January 7, 1966, JFKL, pp. 40–42; McCarthy, *Up 'Til Now*, 135–36; Rorabaugh, *Real Making of the President*, 54. Ben Bradlee said that JFK told him that he ought to look into the war records of Edward McCormack of Massachusetts, a longtime Kennedy antagonist, and Nelson Rockefeller (Bradlee, *Conversations with Kennedy*, 74–75). In 1961, when JFK tried to make FDR Jr. secretary of the navy, Secretary of Defense Robert McNamara rejected FDR Jr. on the grounds he was a drunk and a womanizer (Reeves, *President Kennedy*, 28–29).

45. That Kennedy won on his own merits is one of the central conclusions of Fleming (see Fleming, *Kennedy vs. Humphrey*, 107–18, 151–60; see also *WP*, May 31, 1960; and Humphrey, *Education*, 218). For a contrary opinion that there was massive fraud that affected the primary, see S. Hersh, *Dark Side*, 93–99. Larry O'Brien says the total Kennedy outlay in West Virginia was $100,000 (see O'Brien, *No Final Victories*, 69). O'Brien's claim is simply not credible. On the Kennedy spending, see S. Hersh, *Dark Side*, 93–99; and Loughry, *Don't Buy Another Vote*, 3–27. For the perspective of a West Virginia political boss, see Chafin and Sherwood, *Just Good Politics*, 114–50. See also Peters, *Tilting at Windmills*, 99–111.

46. Fleming, *Kennedy vs. Humphrey*, 63–67; *NYHT*, April 27, 1960; *WSJ*, May 3, 1960; *WP*, May 5, 1960; *NYT*, May 9, 1960.

47. Joseph Alsop, "Off Chance for Kennedy," *NYHT*, May 6, 1960; Mildred Jeffrey OHI, January 25, 1970, JFKL, p. 20; Pierre Salinger OHI, July 19, 1965, JFKL, p. 60; Lawrence O'Brien OHI, September 18, 1985, I, p. 27; K. O'Donnell, *Johnny*, 170.

48. Charles G. Peters Jr. OHI, October 24, 1964, JFKL, p. 12.

49. Walter Spolar OHI, June 9, 1966, JFKL, p. 5; "Report of Larry King on trip to Wyoming, May 6–10, 1960," May 13, 1960, SPF, Box 135, Johnson for President File, 1959–1960 (Wyoming—Political information File), LBJL. On the weakness of the Johnson campaign effort, see McPherson, *Political Education*, 171–78.

50. Larry Jones to Larry Blackmon, "Information on Western States for Irvin Hoff," March 24, 1960, SPF, Box 146, Johnson for President HQ, General Files, 1959–60 (Western States Contacts), LBJL.

51. Bob Kennedy to Steve Smith, May 25, 1960, Pre-Administration Political Files, Box 39, Memos, RFK Outgoing, May 1960–September 1960, RFKP, JFKL. For unknown reasons, RFK's count omitted Alaska and Montana.

52. For the situation in Pennsylvania, see David L. Lawrence OHI, January 26,

1966, JFKL, pp. 4–10, 23; Joseph S. Clark OHI, December 16, 1965, JFKL, pp. 40–46.

53. *NYT*, March 3, 1960; K. O'Donnell, *Johnny*, 103. For the most complete study of the California situation, see Bunzel and Lee, *California Democratic Delegation*. On Pat Brown, JFK, the California delegation and the national convention, see Rarick, *California Rising*, 180–86, 189–204.

54. Frederick G. Dutton OHI, May 3, 1965, JFKL, pp. 18–20; Bart Lytton OHI, June 8, 1966, JFKL, pp. 5–6. For Pat Brown's perspective, see the two oral history interviews in the JFKL; and Rarick, *California Rising*, 191–204.

55. Edmund G. Brown OHI by Joe B. Frantz, February 20, 1969, JFKL, p. 11; Marks to Blundell, Memo, June 23, 1960, SPF, Box 192, National Citizens Committee (Blundell File, Confidential), LBJL.

56. Bradlee, *Good Life*, 209–10; Bradlee, *Conversations with Kennedy*, 30.

57. India Edwards OHI, February 4, 1969, LBJL, pp. 23–25; *NYT*, July 5, 1960. In response to the charges concerning JFK's health, Robert Kennedy denied that his brother had Addison's. Two Kennedy doctors issued a statement in June declaring the candidate's health was "excellent." Of course, LBJ had his own health problems, deriving from a 1955 heart attack. He carried a laminated copy of a cardiogram with him to show people that he was fit (see Dickerson, *Among Those Present*, 37).

58. David L. Lawrence OHI, June 26, 1966, JFKL, pp. 5, 6, 10; Weber, *Don't Call Me Boss*, 357–64; R. Goodwin, *Remembering America*, 77; K. O'Donnell, *Johnny*, 176–77; O'Neill, *Man of the House*, 90–91; Hugh Sidey OHI, April 7, 1964, JFKL, p. 19.

59. Hugh Sidey OHI, April 7, 1964, JFKL, p. 19; Schlesinger, *Robert F. Kennedy*, 206; Joseph D. Tydings OHI, September 30, 1965, JFKL, p. 14; White, *Making of the President*, 201–3.

60. For the complete vote on the first ballot, see *Guide to U.S. Elections*, 1:648. This source contains a small error. It shows 3 Alabama votes for JFK, not the 3.5 he received. This mistake is in the third (1994), fourth (2001), and fifth (2005) editions, but not in the first (1975) and second (1985) editions, which get the Alabama vote right.

61. Theodore White argues that to have stopped Kennedy, his opponents needed to hold him "substantially below 700 votes" on the first ballot (see White, *Making of the President*, 159).

62. Douglas, *Fullness*, 257; Memorandum, June 22, 1960, SPF, Box 255, Political Files, 1959–1960 (Memoranda), LBJL; Joseph D. Tydings OHI, September 30, 1965, JFKL, pp. 14–15; Guthman and Shulman, *Robert Kennedy*, 21; Douglass Cater, "A Tide in the Affairs of John F. Kennedy," *Reporter*, August 4, 1960, 16; Stewart L. Udall OHI, January 12, 1970, JFKL, pp. 23–24.

63. K. O'Donnell, *Johnny*, 180, 185; John Bailey OHI, April 10, 1964, JFKL, pp. 40, 41. In Alabama, one source asserts that Kennedy had fourteen votes but told Patterson to provide just three on the first ballot and then jump to fourteen on the second ballot to show JFK momentum (see Land, "John F. Kennedy's Southern Strategy," 56–57). For the situation in New Jersey, see Frank Thompson OHI,

March 10, 1965, JFKL. Thompson claims that Meyner had a promise that he would be recognized to switch New Jersey's votes to JFK at the end of the first ballot but never got it.

64. There are numerous incompatible accounts of the selection of Johnson as vice president. For a sampling, see Schlesinger, *Thousand Days*, 39–59; Schlesinger, *Robert F. Kennedy*, 206–11; Parmet, *JFK*, 21–30; Guthman and Schulman, *Robert Kennedy*, 21–24; O'Neill, *Man of the House*, 94–95; White, *Making of the President*, 172–74; Dallek, *Lone Star Rising*, 578–81; Witcover, *Crapshoot*, 147–63; R. Goodwin, *Remembering America*, 101; Hardeman and Bacon, *Rayburn*, 435–44; K. Graham, *Personal History*, 257–67; Hilty, *Robert Kennedy*, 156–65; Shesol, *Mutual Contempt*, 42–47; Dallek, *Unfinished Life*, 269–74. For the latest attempt to unravel the mystery, see Rorabaugh, *Real Making of the President*, 82–91.

65. Hugh Sidey OHI, April 7, 1964, JFKL, p. 24; Reeves, *President Kennedy*, 118–19; Bradlee, *Conversations with Kennedy*, 31.

66. Steel, *Night*, 109; Thomas, *Robert Kennedy*, 96; Dallek, *Lone Star Rising*, 559; Shesol, *Mutual Contempt*, 10; Baker, *Wheeling and Dealing*, 118; Booth Mooney OHI, April 8, 1969, LBJL, p. 33; Guthman and Shulman, *Robert Kennedy*, 26. RFK's famous remark about LBJ dates to 1965, but the attitude that it bespoke was already well established in 1960.

67. On LBJ's thinking, see Dallek, *Lone Star Rising*, 577–78; Evans and Novak, *Lyndon B. Johnson*, 281–88; Gilbert, *Mortal Presidency*, 188; McPherson, *Political Education*, 178–79; Harry McPherson OHI, December 5, 1968, LBJL, p. 3; George E. Reedy to LBJ, June 14, 1960, U.S. Senate Papers, 1949–1961, Box 427, Office Files of George Reedy, Reedy: 1960 Convention, Los Angeles, LBJL; Robert Baskin OHI, March 16, 1974, LBJL, p. 20.

68. Shesol, *Mutual Contempt*, 44–45; Richard L. Lyons, "Kennedy Set to Offer Johnson Second Place," *WP*, July 12, 1960.

69. Humphrey, *Education*, 474; McFarland, *Cold War Strategist*, 109–11; Clifford, *Counsel*, 316–19; Dickerson, *Among Those Present*, 43–49; Parmet, *JFK*, 22–31; Stossel, *Sarge*, 151–55; Kaufman, *Henry M. Jackson*, 120–23; Krock, *Memoirs*, 362. LBJ said that JFK told him afterward that Freeman would have been the choice after him (see Evans and Novak, *Lyndon B. Johnson*, 280).

70. Stossel, *Sarge*, 151–55.

71. RFK denied his father had anything to do with the Johnson decision, but he made several statements about the vice-presidential choice that were untrue. Therefore, one must be careful in crediting elements of his account that were not corroborated by others (see Schlesinger, *Robert F. Kennedy*, 211). For the case that JPK was a factor, see B. Hersh, *Bobby and J. Edgar*, 11–15, 203; D. Goodwin, *Fitzgeralds and the Kennedys*, 802; DiSalle, *Second Choice*, 205; and Kessler, *Sins of the Father*, 383.

72. Baker, *Wheeling and Dealing*, 123–30; Herman Talmadge OHI, July 17, 1969, LBJL, p. 11; Evans and Novak, *Lyndon B. Johnson*, 287; Hardeman and Bacon, *Rayburn*, 435–44.

73. Bryant, *Bystander*, 149–51; Charles Bartlett OHI, May 6, 1969, LBJL, pp. 35–36.

74. Evans and Novak, *Lyndon B. Johnson*, 283–86; White, *Making of the President 1964*, 407–15; Dallek, *Unfinished Life*, 270–75.

75. One author argues that JFK was permitting RFK to run around trying to get LBJ to withdraw as a way of allowing his brother and others to exhaust their dislike of Johnson (see Hilty, *Robert Kennedy*, 164–65).

76. White, *Making of the President*, 175–77; Joseph Sharkey OHI, November 1, 1967, JFKL, p. 48; Dallek, *Lone Star Rising*, 581–82.

77. Stewart Udall OHI, April 18, 1969, LBJL, p. 11.

78. Schlesinger, *Thousand Days*, 60; Parmet, *JFK*, 31; Reinsch, *Getting Elected*, 125; Savage, *JFK, LBJ*, 69; White, *Making of the President*, 177; Matthews, *Kennedy & Nixon*, 134–35; JKG to JFK, Galbraith Papers, Box 74, Correspondence with JFK, January 16, 1959–December 30, 1960, JFKL; Galbraith, *Letters to Kennedy*, 10–12.

79. Reeves, *President Kennedy*, 432; Fite, *Richard B. Russell*, 377; Parmet, *JFK*, 34.

Chapter 4. Richard M. Nixon and the Republican Nomination

1. S. Alsop, *Nixon & Rockefeller*, 79–80; Perlstein, *Before the Storm*, 55; Persico, *Imperial Rockefeller*, 36–37.

2. *NYT*, September 12, 1959, September 14, 1959; *WP*, December 19, 1959; *NYT*, December 20, 1959; White, *Making of the President*, 81–88; Gifford, *The Center Cannot Hold*, 22–40.

3. Memo, Charles McWhorter to RMN, August 27, 1959, RMN PPP, GC, Box 636 (James Reston File), RMNL*; *NYT*, October 10, 1959, November 26, 1959.

4. The Reminiscences of Robert Merriam, March 3, 1969, p. 139, in the Oral History Collection of Columbia University; Ambrose, *Nixon*, 502; Collier and Horowitz, *Rockefellers*, 339.

5. Ehrlichman, *Witness to Power*, 20–21; *Portland Sunday Telegram*, January 17, 1960; Aitken, *Nixon*, 267; White, *Making of the President*, 74–75.

6. *NYT*, November 29, 1959; Perlstein, *Before the Storm*, 60; White, *Making of the President*, 75–77; Persico, *Imperial Rockefeller*, 40–41; Claude Robinson to RMN, June 1960, RMN PPP, GC, Box 647 (Claude Robinson File), RMNL.*

7. Ambrose, *Nixon*, 520–28.

8. Gallup, ed., *Gallup Poll*, January 23, 1959 (poll conducted January 7–12, 1959), 3:1588; ibid., December 16, 1959 (poll conducted November 12–17, 1959), 3:1645; "A Survey of Democratic Presidential Prospects in New York State," February 1960, RSP, Box 2, JFKL.

9. *NYT*, December 27, 1959.

10. Nixon, *Six Crises*, 332; The Reminiscences of Robert Finch, June 19, 1967, p. 27, in the Oral History Collection of Columbia University.

11. Donovan, *Confidential Secretary*, 165; Ambrose, *Eisenhower*, 559; Memcon, DDE Presidential Papers, AWF, AW Diary Series, Box 11, May 4, 1960, DDEL.

12. John Reagan McCrary to DDE, April 1, 1960, DDE Presidential Papers, AWF, Name Series, Box 10, DDE Politics, 1960—Nixon Campaign, DDEL.

13. Ambrose, *Eisenhower*, 593–94; Ambrose, *Nixon*, 548.

14. Vidal, *Palimpsest*, 361.

15. Humes, *Confessions*, 109; Trohan, *Political Animals*, 291–92; Brownell, *Advising Ike*, 301, 302.

16. Ambrose, *Eisenhower*, 319–25, 560; The Reminiscences of Milton Eisenhower, September 6, 1967, p. 47, in the Oral History Collection of Columbia University; Beschloss, *MAYDAY*, 113–14; Ambrose, *Nixon*, 511–13. In October 1960, Eisenhower observed that if Nixon had taken the position of secretary of defense, he would have been in a stronger position in his bid for the presidency than he was (ACW Diary, 10–4–60, DDE Presidential Papers, AWF, AW Diary Series, Box 11, DDEL).

17. The Reminiscences of Robert Finch, June 19, 1967, p. 59, in the Oral History Collection of Columbia University; Crowley, *Nixon off the Record*, 15, 16.

18. Ambrose, *Nixon*, 547, 548–49. As little as Eisenhower thought of Kennedy and Johnson, he had a lower opinion of Bobby Kennedy.

19. DDE to Oveta Culp Hobby, May 9, 1960, DDE Presidential Papers, AWF, DDE Diary Series, Box 49, DDE Dictation, May 1960, DDEL.

20. *WP*, April 8, 1960, May 26, 1960; *NYT*, May 26, 1960; ACW to DDE, June 9, 1960, DDE Presidential Papers, AWF, ACW Diary Series, Box 11, ACW Diary—June 1960, DDEL; Memcon DDE to NAR, June 11, 1960, DDE Presidential Papers, AWF, DDE Diary Series, Box 50, Telephone Calls—June 1960, DDEL; Gifford, *The Center Cannot Hold*, 41–52.

21. For Alsop's January columns and stories, see *NYHT*, January 1, 25, 26, 27, 28, 29, and 31, 1960.

22. *NYT*, February 18, 20, and 22, 1960, March 1, 1960. Allen Dulles was not helping matters with his speeches about growing Soviet missile capabilities and with his ineffectual congressional testimony. On Dulles, see Helgerson, *Getting to Know the President*, chap. 3, p. 5; and Grose, *Gentleman Spy*, 473–74. For the true situation, see Roman, *Eisenhower and the Missile Gap*, 38–41, 45–46. The truth of the missile balance in 1960 was not easy to see, but there was substantial reason to believe that there was no gap. However, the final confirmation of Eisenhower's view did not come until 1961.

23. White, *Making of the President*, 115–18; Ambrose, *Eisenhower*, 569–79; Thomas, *Very Best Men*, 165–72, 216–20.

24. Nixon, *Six Crises*, 333; Evans and Novak, *Nixon in the White House*, 13; Morgan, "Eisenhower and the Balanced Budget," in Warshaw, ed., *Reexamining the Eisenhower Presidency*, 128; I. Morgan, *Eisenhower versus "The Spenders,"* 160–66, 180.

25. Walter Lippmann, "A Satisfied Nation," *NYHT*, January 21, 1960; Nixon, *RN*, 215.

26. *NYT*, June 29, 1960, July 20, 1960; White, *Making of the President*, 181, 191–96.

27. White, *Making of the President*, 196–98; Nixon, *Six Crises*, 337–39; Klein, *Making It Perfectly Clear*, 99–102; The Reminiscences of Robert Merriam, March 3,

1969, pp. 135–38, in the Oral History Collection of Columbia University; Robert Merriam Papers, Box 1, Republican Party Platform, July 1960, DDEL.

28. White, *Making of the President*, 198–201; William E. Robinson Diary, Visit at Newport, Rhode Island, July 18–25, 1960, William E. Robinson Papers, Box 4, Eisenhower, July 1960–December 1960, DDEL; Report of Conversation of the President with the Vice President, Newport, July 24, 1960, DDE Presidential Papers, AWF, DDE Diary Series, Box 51, Telephone Calls—July 1960, DDEL; D. Eisenhower, *Waging Peace*, 595–96; Ambrose, *Nixon*, 551–52. The final platform language on defense was: "The United States can and must provide whatever is necessary to insure its own security. . . . To provide more would be wasteful. To provide less would be catastrophic" (Ambrose, *Nixon*, 552).

29. *NYT*, July 30, 1960; White, *Making of the President*, 200–201.

30. Ambrose, *Nixon*, 551–53; The Reminiscences of Robert Finch, June 19, 1967, p. 41, in the Oral History Collection of Columbia University.

31. Perlstein, *Before the Storm*, 80–82, 87–93.

32. Ibid., 94–95; Goldwater, *With No Apologies*, 101–4, 109–17; Critchlow, *Conservative Ascendancy*, 48–52. According to Critchlow, Brent Bozell, not Goldwater, wrote *Conscience of a Conservative*, and it is questionable whether Goldwater even read the manuscript before it appeared in print.

33. "Voting Intentions Regarding Presidential and Vice-Presidential Candidates among California Voters as of July 1960," RMN PPP, Campaign 1960, Polls, Series 71, Box 2, RMNL.

34. DDE–Gabe Hauge Telephone Conversation, ACW Memcon, July 19, 1960, AWF, DDE Diary Series, Box 51, Telephone Calls—July 1960, DDEL; Ambrose, *Nixon*, 547.

35. Nixon, *RN*, 215.

36. Nixon, *Six Crises*, 341–42; Nixon, *RN*, 216.

37. The Reminiscences of Robert Finch, June 19, 1967, pp. 43–44, in the Oral History Collection of Columbia University; Ambrose, *Nixon*, 553–54; White, *Making of the President*, 206. The best contemporary newspaper account is Carleton Kent and Joseph Albright, "Why Leaders Picked Lodge," *CST*, July 29, 1960.

38. Arthur Burns to RMN, July 29, 1960, RMN PPP, GC, Box 115, RMNL.*

39. Gallup, ed., *Gallup Poll*, July 6, 1960 (poll conducted June 16–21, 1960), 3:1675–76; ibid., August 17, 1960 (poll conducted July 30–August 4, 1960), 3:1681.

Chapter 5. The General Election Campaign, July 28–September 25

1. White, Making of the President, 263.

2. Evans and Novak, *Lyndon B. Johnson*, 263–64; White, *Making of the President*, 249; Bryce Harlow, Memo for the Record of Meeting between DDE and Sam Rayburn, May 10, 1960, DDE Presidential Papers, AWF, DDE Diary Series, Box 50, Staff Notes, DDEL; Official White House Transcript of President's Press and Radio Conference #191, September 7, 1960, DDE Presidential Papers, AWF, Press Conference Series, Box 10, Press & Radio Conference, DDEL; *Time*, September 5, 1960, 12.

3. White, *Making of the President*, 249–51; McCullough, *Truman*, 974–75; John Sharon OHI, November 7, 1967, JFKL, pp. 29, 31; "1960 Political Speeches Given by Former President Harry S. Truman, David H. Stowe Papers, Box 1, Correspondence and Itinerary re Campaign Trips of President Truman, September–November 1960, JFKL; *NYT*, August 21, 1960; Lash, *Eleanor*, 296–300.

4. Dallek, *Unfinished Life*, 276–79; White, *Making of the President*, 246–47.

5. Savage, *JFK, LBJ*, 76; White, *Making of the President*, 296–99; Sorensen, *Counselor*, 181. Lest one think that the Kennedy campaign was one big, happy family, there were some fierce rivalries (see R. Goodwin, *Remembering America*, 138–39; Schlesinger, *Journals, 1952–2000*, 226–27).

6. Buford Ellington OHI, October 2, 1970, LBJL, p. 35; Dallek, *Lone Star Rising*, 583; Dickerson, *Among Those Present*, 56.

7. Wofford, *Of Kennedys and Kings*, 38; S. Hersh, *Dark Side*, 142–47; Hewitt, *Tell Me a Story*, 98–99.

8. Parmet, *JFK*, 10.

9. *Time*, July 11, 1960, 19–23; ibid., July 25, 1960, 59.

10. Hoffman, *Theodore H. White*, 150; Bradlee, *Conversations with Kennedy*, 18–19.

11. Bradlee, *Conversations with Kennedy*, 19–20, 48; Reeves, *President Kennedy*, 279–80; Laura Knebel OHI, December 8, 1965, JFKL, pp. 2–3. On regrets, see Roberts, *First Rough Draft*, 180; Reston, *Deadline*, 290; and Fletcher Knebel OHI, May 1, 1977, JFKL, pp. 13–16, 20–21.

12. Reeves, *President Kennedy*, 280; Hugh Sidey OHI, April 7, 1965, p. 35; Sidey, "The President's Voracious Reading Habits." The story said JFK could read "at least 1,200 words per minute and sometimes more than that." As an example of how the invented story of Kennedy's reading prowess became accepted historical fact, in Manchester, *Death of a President*, 67, the author has JFK "speed reading at twelve hundred words a minute" diplomatic cables and intelligence reports as he flew to Texas on November 21, 1963.

13. Bradlee, *Good Life*, 266–71. In fairness, it should be noted that Mary Meyer was Bradlee's sister-in-law. Bradlee regarded the diary as a private family matter.

14. Hoffmann, *Theodore H. White*, 140. There is a continuing tendency to overrate Robert Kennedy as campaign manager (see Rorabaugh, *Real Making of the President*, 157, 200).

15. Schlesinger, *Robert Kennedy*, 193; Hilty, *Robert Kennedy*, 147; Jamieson, *Packaging the Presidency*, 162; Peter Lisagor OHI, April 22, 1966, p. 35.

16. White, *Making of the President*, 255, 258–59; Silvestri, "John F. Kennedy," 145–47, 152–53; Powell, "An Analytical and Comparative Study," 208–14.

17. Gallup, ed., *Gallup Poll*, August 17, 1960 (poll conducted July 30–August 4, 1960), 3:1681; ibid., September 14, 1960 (poll conducted August 25–30, 1960, 3:1683; ibid., September 25, 1960 (poll conducted September 9–14, 1960), 3:1685–86.

18. "Kennedy before Labor Day," Simulactics Report #2, August 25, 1960, DNC,

1960 Campaign, Box 212, JFKL. See also Casey, *Making of a Catholic President*, 161–62.

19. *NYHT*, September 8, 1960. On the Peale affair, see Carty, *A Catholic in the White House?* 58–61; Balmer, *God in the White House*, 25–31. For Peale's side of the story, see George, *God's Salesman*, 190–220. For the most recent account, see Casey, *The Making of a Catholic President*, 143–44. Casey is a conspiracy theorist who alleges that Nixon had secret agents working with Protestant groups to undermine and discredit Kennedy (see Casey, *The Making of a Catholic President*, 93–150).

20. Dallek, *Unfinished Life*, 282–84.

21. Kemper, "John F. Kennedy before the Greater Houston Ministerial Association," 167; Matthews, *Kennedy & Nixon*, 142–44.

22. Leonard Hall & Robert Finch, Memorandum, August 16, 1960, James P. Mitchell Papers, Box 192, 1960 Politics—August (Folder 2), DDEL.

23. *NYDN*, September 15, 1960; Ambrose, *Nixon*, 569; Powell, "An Analytical and Comparative Study," 230–70.

24. Ambrose, *Nixon*, 576–77; *NYDN*, September 15, 1960. For an overview of the Nixon campaign staff, see White, *Breach of Faith*, 80–85, 92–96.

25. White, *Making of the President*, 266–67; Nixon, *Six Crises*, 345.

26. Nixon, *Six Crises*, 344, 345; Ambrose, *Nixon*, 560; White, *Making of the President*, 266–67; *WP*, August 17, 1960; *NYDN*, October 25, 1960.

27. William Ewald OHI, December 16, 1977, pp. 28–29, DDEL; James Shepley OHI, August 23, 1967, p. 34, DDEL; Ambrose, *Nixon*, 557; Jamieson, *Packaging the Presidency*, 151; S. Alsop, *Nixon & Rockefeller*, 172; Earl H. Blaik to RMN, July 31, 1960, RMN PPP, GC, Box 86, RMNL.* See also Earl Blaik to James D. Hughes, August 26, 1960, in which Blaik reiterated his concerns and told Hughes that he is in the best position "to determine when the Vice President is pushing himself too much" and urges him to "stand up and so state the fact." There is a note by Nixon on Blaik's letter to him telling Rose Mary Woods that she ought to read Blaik's letters and adding, "He would have made a helluva good campaign manager!"

28. Ehrlichman, *Witness to Power*, 24, 27; Ambrose, *Nixon*, 556–57; Klein, *Making It Perfectly Clear*, 12; White, *Making of the President*, 313; The Reminiscences of Robert Finch, June 19, 1967, p. 64, in the Oral History Collection of Columbia University; Garment, *Crazy Rhythm*, 117; Jamieson, *Packaging the Presidency*, 151; James D. Hughes to RMN, October 7, 1962, RMN PPP, GC, Box 360, NARA, LN; William Ewald OHI, December 16, 1977, p. 31, DDEL. In 1968, some of Nixon's aides resisted coming back to his campaign until they were assured that he would not repeat the pattern of 1960. Nixon did learn from 1960, and there were some significant differences in his campaign organization in 1968 (see Rosen, *Strong Man*, 42).

29. Klein, *Making It Perfectly Clear*, 12; Len Hall to RMN, November 20, 1961, RMN PPP, GC, Box 313, RMNL.* For the latest critique of Nixon's management of the 1960 campaign, see Rorabaugh, *Real Making of the President*, 117–19.

30. On Nixon's relationship with the *LA Times*, Chandler, and Palmer, see Morris, *Richard Milhous Nixon*; Gellman, *Contender*; and McDougal, *Privileged Son*, 88–89,

141, 176–77, 193, 206, 227–28. On the situation in Illinois, see William Rentschler to Robert H. Finch, November 5, 1960, RMN PPP, Box 627, RMNL.* In the letter, Rentschler asserted that "virtually every newspaper in Illinois has endorsed Nixon."

31. Harlow, "The Man and the Political Leader," in Thompson, ed., *Nixon Presidency*, 10–11.

32. Ehrlichman, *Witness to Power*, 271.

33. White, *Making of the President*, 299–301. For Nixon's speeches on the toy train and the pony in Tuscola and Mattoon, Illinois, see *Freedom of Communication: Final Report of the Committee on Commerce*, United States Senate, pt. 2, *The Speeches, Remarks, Press Conferences, and Study Papers of Richard M. Nixon, August 1 through November 7, 1960*, 830–31, 839.

34. Lungren, *Healing Richard Nixon*, 65; Aitken, *Nixon*, 287.

35. Sarah McClendon to LBJ, September 25, 1960, SPF, Box 89, Election Subject Files, 1959–1960, VP—Recommendations—September, File 1, LBJL; Joe Lastelic to LBJ, n.d., LBJ Papers, SPF, Box 207, VP Campaign, Travel File, Campaign Trip, October 24–29, Calif., Wash., Mont., Utah, Okla, LBJL; George E. Reedy to LBJ, September 23, 1960, LBJ Papers SPF, Box 263, Political Files, 1959–1960—Press, LBJL; Klein, *Making It Perfectly Clear*, 87–93; Sidey, "The Man and Foreign Policy," in Thompson, ed., *Nixon Presidency*, 302, 305. To be fair, Hugh Sidey and Tom Wicker later expressed regrets about the unprofessional coverage of Nixon in 1960.

Meade Alcorn told me in 1974 that one of the members of the debate panel for the first televised debate was overheard in a telephone conversation conveying information about the likely questions. He did not identify the individual. The action probably made little, if any, difference in the debate. The incident is more significant for the press attitude that it symbolized. It is interesting that before the second, third, and fourth debates the transcripts record a statement by the moderator to the effect that the candidates had no knowledge of the questions that would be asked. There was no such statement prior to the first debate.

36. Ambrose, "Comparing and Contrasting Ike and Dick," in Friedman and Levantrosser, eds., *Richard M. Nixon*, 15.

37. See Official White House Transcript of President Eisenhower's Press and Radio Conference #190, August 24, 1960, DDE Presidential Papers, AWF, Press Conference Series, Box 10, DDEL. See also The Reminiscences of Robert Merriam, January 13, 1969, pp. 45–46, in the Oral History Collection of Columbia University.

38. The Reminiscences of Nathan Twining, August 17, 1967, pp. 170–71, in the Oral History Collection of Columbia University; The Reminiscences of James Hagerty, Interview 7, April 17, 1965, p. 520, in the Oral History Collection of Columbia University; Ambrose, *Nixon*, 599–601; The Reminiscences of Merriman Smith, January 3, 1968, p. 44, in the Oral History Collection of Columbia University. In 1962, Eisenhower gave a speech in San Francisco in which he laid out in detail Nixon's role in the administration. Unfortunately, it was two years too late, but

it was what Eisenhower could have and should have said in 1960 (see DDE Speech, October 8, 1962, RMN PPP, DDE Speeches/Statements, Aug. 1952–1962, RMNL).

39. *NYT*, August 21, 1960; *NYHT*, August 21, 1960.

40. Gallup, ed., *Gallup Poll*, September 25, 1960 (poll conducted September 9–14, 1960), 3:1685–86.

Chapter 6. The General Election Campaign, September 26–October 21

1. Edgerton, *Columbia History*, 198–201; Manchester, *Glory*, 850–52; Baughman, *Same Time, Same Station*, 146–49, 296–98; Frank, *Thin Air*, 128–34. Kennedy aide Richard Goodwin was one of the prosecuting attorneys in the quiz-show scandal (see R. Goodwin, *Remembering America*, 43–65).

2. White, *Making of the President*, 279–83; Barnouw, *History of Broadcasting*, 161–62.

3. On Eisenhower's attitude, see The Reminiscences of Walter Thayer, April 28, 1967, pp. 50–52, in the Oral History Collection of Columbia University; A. J. Goodpaster, Memcon DDE and John Diefenbaker, October 1, 1960, DDE Pres. Papers, AWF, DDE Diary Series, Box 53, Staff Notes—September 1960, DDEL. For Nixon's thoughts, see Nixon, *Six Crises*, 348, 384–85.

4. See Klein, *Making It Perfectly Clear*, 103; Nixon, *Six Crises*, 348; Nixon, *RN*, 217–18.

5. White, *Making of the President*, 178; J. Leonard Reinsch OHI, January 5, 1966, JFKL, p. 10. Victor Lasky denied that this ever happened. He said Nixon was not at home but at a small dinner party where he watched Kennedy's speech but said nothing about the candidate's performance (Victor Lasky to RMN, October 11, 1961, RMN PPP, GC, Box 813, Theodore White File, RMNL*). In fact, there is no evidence outside of White's and Reinsch's anecdotal accounts that this event ever occurred or that Nixon ever made the alleged statement. The incident is another example of how those allied to JFK fabricated episodes to make their case for the superiority of the Kennedy campaign and the inferiority of his rival's.

6. The Reminiscences of J. Clifford Folger, January 25, 1968, p. 22, in the Oral History Collection of Columbia University.

7. The Reminiscences of Robert Merriam, January 13, 1969, pp. 107–8, in the Oral History Collection of Columbia University. This is a plausible story, and Merriam had no vested interest in inventing it, but I was unable to confirm it in the records of the legislative leaders' conference meetings in the Eisenhower Library in Abilene, Kansas.

8. Claude Robinson to RMN, August 1, 1960, RMN PPP, GC, Box 247, Claude Robinson File, RMNL.*

9. "Nineteen Sixty—A Study in Political Change," RMN PPP, GC, Box 361, Bob Humphreys File, RMNL*; News Summary, July 1, 1960, RMN PPP, Campaign 1960, News Summaries, Series 69/1, Box 142, RMNL.

10. Claude Robinson to RMN, September 1, 1960, RMN PPP, GC, Box 647, RMNL.*

11. "Political Behavior Report #6: Public Opinion and Richard Nixon," February 1960, Belknap, 1960, RFKP, Pre-Administration Political Files, Box 39, Memos: RFK Incoming, January 1960–August 1960, JFKL.

12. Reinsch, *Getting Elected*, 134.

13. Matthews, *Kennedy & Nixon*, 148; Halberstam, *Fifties*, 731; The Reminiscences of Edward Folliard, September 7, 1967, p. 42, in the Oral History Collection of Columbia University; The Reminiscences of Howard K. Smith, January 19, 1967, p. 31, in the Oral History Collection of Columbia University; Bradlee, *Good Life*, 211; R. Goodwin, *Remembering America*, 115.

14. There are numerous accounts of what happened or did not happen, many of them contradicting each other (see White, *Making of the President*, 283–90; Hewitt, *Tell Me a Story*, 67–70; Collier and Horowitz, *Kennedys*, 244–46; and Nixon, *Six Crises*, 363–64). For the views of Ted Rogers, who was Nixon's television adviser, see his long letter on the subject (Ted Rogers to RMN, September 5, 1961, p. 7, RMN PPP, GC, Box 649, Ted Rogers File, RMNL*).

15. Parmet, *Eisenhower*, 137; Jamieson, *Packaging the Presidency*, 151.

16. Ted Rogers to RMN, September 5, 1961, p. 7, RMN PPP, GC, Box 649, Ted Rogers File, RMNL.*

17. *NYDN*, September 28, 1960; *LAT*, September 27, 1960; *WP*, September 27 and 28, 1960; *NYHT*, September 28, 1960.

18. Ambrose, *Nixon*, 575; Dickerson, *Among Those Present*, 56; Merry, *Taking on the World*, 355; The Reminiscences of Howard K. Smith, January 19, 1967, p. 31, in the Oral History Collection of Columbia University.

19. K. O'Donnell, *Johnny*, 211–12; *NYT*, September 28, 1960; White, *Making of the President*, 291.

20. Nixon, *Six Crises*, 366, 367; The Reminiscences of James Hagerty, Interview 2, January 31, 1968, p. 124, in the Oral History Collection of Columbia University.

21. Julius Klein to RMN, September 27, 1960, RMN PPP, GC, Box 300 (George Grassmuck File), RMNL*; The Reminiscences of James Hagerty, Interview 2, January 31, 1968, p. 124, in the Oral History Collection of Columbia University; Memo on Lodge Reaction to First Debate, September 27, 1960, RMN PPP, GC, Box 457, HCL File, RMNL.*

22. Memo on Telephone Conversation between DDE and RMN, September 25, 1960, DDE Presidential Papers, AWF, DDE Diary Series, Box 52, Telephone Calls—September 1960, DDEL.

23. Claude Robinson Note, September 28, 1960, RMN PPP, Series 45, Box 1, RMNL*; Claude Robinson to Nixon, Hall, Finch, October 1, 1960, RMN PPP, GC, Box 647, Robinson File, RMNL.*

24. Nixon, *Six Crises*, 368; Memo on Lodge Reaction to First Debate, September 27, 1960, RMN PPP, GC, Box 457, HCL File, RMNL*; Frank, *Thin Air*, 167.

25. *NYT*, October 8, 1960; "An Analysis of the Second Kennedy-Nixon Debate," October 11, 1960, RSP, Box 2, JFKL; "An Analysis of the Third Kennedy-Nixon

Debate," October 19, 1960, RSP, Box 2, JFKL; Claude Robinson to Nixon, Hall, Finch, October 13, 1960, "Campaign Evaluation as of October 7, 1960 (Second Debate)," RMN PPP, Campaign 1960, Presidential Debates Preparations, Box 61, RMNL; Claude Robinson to Nixon, Hall, Finch, October 21, 1960, "Campaign Evaluation as of October 14, 1960 (Third Debate)," RMN PPP, Campaign 1960, Presidential Debates, Box 61, RMNL. Robinson pronounced debate three a clear Nixon victory, while Harris characterized it as a standoff.

26. Ambrose, *Nixon*, 588; *NYHT*, October 17, 1960; Nixon, *RN*, 220; Nixon, *Six Crises*, 375; Matthews, *Kennedy & Nixon*, 158–63.

27. David Riesman to Louis Harris, John Kenneth Galbraith Papers, Box 74, GC, September 6, 1960–November 29, 1960, JFKL.

28. Fursenko and Naftali, *Khrushchev's Cold War*, 320–21; Ambrose, *Ike's Spies*, 311–12; Thomas, *Very Best Men*, 208; Ambrose, *Nixon*, 550.

29. For the Kennedy statement of October 20, 1960, see www.jfklink.com/speeches/jfk/Oct60/jfk201060cuba.html.

30. R. Goodwin, *Remembering America*, 124–26; Parmet, *JFK*, 48–49.

31. Nixon, *Six Crises*, 382. In March 1962, the dispute broke into the open upon publication of Nixon's book *Six Crises*. In it, the former vice president alleged that Kennedy knew about the CIA operation as a result of briefings from then CIA director Allen Dulles. Dulles denied the accuracy of Nixon's assertions and tried to pass off the controversy as "an honest misunderstanding." Dulles maintained that his briefings "were intelligence briefings on the world situation; they did not cover our own government's plans or programs for action overt or covert." However, in a telephone conversation, according to Nixon, the current DCI, John McCone, "categorically" informed him that "Dulles had told him that he had told Kennedy about the covert operation." McCone added that Senator George Smathers had also informed him that Kennedy knew about the CIA activity (see *NYT*, March 21, 1962; and Memcon of telephone conversation between RMN and John McCone, March 20, 1962, DDE Post Presidential Papers, Special Names Series, Box 14, Nixon, Richard M., 1962, DDEL; see also Victor Lasky to Harvey Wheeler, August 15, 1962; and Harvey Wheeler to Victor Lasky, August 20, 1962, RMN PPP, GC, Box 440, Victor Lasky 1960 File, RMNL*).

32. Parmet, *JFK*, 47–49; Ambrose, *Nixon*, 592; Roberts, *First Rough Draft*, 186. On the continuing controversy over what Dulles did and did not tell Kennedy, see Helgerson, *Getting to Know the President*, 3–5; Kornbluh, ed., *Bay of Pigs Declassified*, 273–74; Weiner, *Legacy of Ashes*, 165, 291; and Grose, *Gentleman Spy*, 508–9.

33. Burleigh, *Very Private Woman*, 105–6, 118; Thomas, *Very Best Men*, 389; Bissell, *Reflections of a Cold Warrior*, 159–160; S. Hersh, *Dark Side*, 157–175. Kennedy's knowledge of what the administration was up to in Cuba was obviously limited or he would have known by the time of the fourth debate that there was no possibility of a military operation in October or early November.

34. S. Hersh, *Dark Side*, 175–78; Trest and Dodd, *Wings of Denial*, 16–22. When the Bay of Pigs invasion took place, airmen from the Alabama National Guard participated in the operation. Four of them were killed. When informed of the

Alabama National Guard participation and the apparent death of the four men, RFK remarked: "This better not be another Francis Gary Powers. . . . Those Americans better be dead" (see Thomas, *Robert Kennedy*, 124).

35. J. Edgar Hoover to RMN, November 2, 1960, RMN PPP, J. Edgar Hoover Correspondence, Box 19, RMNL; Telephone Calls—Tues. Oct. 25, RFK Papers, Pre-Administration Political Files, Box 34, Cuba as a Campaign Issue, October 6–27, 1960, JFKL.

36. Ambrose, *Nixon*, 592.

37. Ibid., 592–93; Black, *Richard M. Nixon*, 413; Nixon, *RN*, 221.

38. Schlesinger, *Thousand Days*, 74; *NYT*, October 3, 1960; *NYHT*, October 5, 7, and 9, 1960.

39. *NYHT*, October 2, 1960; *WP*, October 15, 1960; Robert Waldron OHI, January 28, 1976, Interview 1, LBJL, p. 15; Robert Baskin OHI, March 16, 1974, LBJL, p. 21.

40. Reedy, *Lyndon B. Johnson*, 54–55. The best account of the campaign in the South, the independent elector movement, and LBJ's effort is Rorabaugh, *Real Making of the President*, 123–39. See also Novotny, "John F. Kennedy, the 1960 Election, and Georgia's Unpledged Electors in the Electoral College."

41. *NYHT*, October 9, 1960. In late October, Eisenhower said, "I do not understand what has happened in New York State" (see DDE to Barry T. Leithead, October 29, 1960, #1689, Galambos and Van Ee, eds., *Papers of Dwight David Eisenhower*, 21:2143–44).

42. Haldeman, *Ends of Power*, 66; James D. Hughes to RMN, October 7, 1962, RMN PPP, GC, Box 360, RMNL.*

43. For a representative comment by a Nixon loyalist who thought his candidate was losing, see John Reagan McCrary to DDE, October 11, 1960, DDE Presidential Papers, White House Central Files, Office Files, Box 713, Republican Presidential Campaign, Folder 14, DDEL. For a sample of the differing views on Lodge and his campaign, see *Newsweek*, September 19, 1960, 39; *NYT*, October 6 and 10, 1960; Tom Wicker OHI, June 16, 1970, LBJL, p. 10.

44. Claude Robinson to Nixon, Hall, Finch, October 13, 1960, "Campaign Evaluation as of October 7, 1960 (Second Debate)," RMN PPP, Campaign 1960, Presidential Debates Preparations, Box 61, RMNL; Claude Robinson to Nixon, Hall, Finch, October 21, 1960, "Campaign Evaluation as of October 14, 1960 (Third Debate)," RMNL; Gallup, ed., *Gallup Poll*, October 12, 1960 (poll conducted September 28–October 2, 1960), 3:1687; ibid., October 26, 1960 (poll conducted October 18–23, 1960), 3:1688.

45. Nixon always maintained that the impact of the debates was minimal. To support this view, he compared the Gallup Poll before the first debate with JFK at 51 percent and him at 49 percent and the last poll before the election that put Kennedy at 50.5 percent and him at 49.5 percent. Nixon interpreted these figures to mean the debates really changed nothing. Of course, the fallacy was that one does not know what the final poll would have been without any debates (see Nixon, *RN*, 221).

Chapter 7. Civil Rights and the General Election Campaign

1. Attwood, *Reds and the Blacks*, 6–7.

2. The common term contemporary in 1960 for African Americans was "Negroes." To be consistent with current usage, I have used "African Americans" and "blacks" in this book.

3. On island communities, see Wiebe, *Search for Order*; Reeves, *President Kennedy*, 62.

4. George Smathers OHI, Interview 3, III, Tape 1, July 10, 1964, JFKL, p. 7; Bryant, *Bystander*, 15–17, 34–42; Sorensen, *Kennedy*, 49; Harris Wofford OHI, November 29, 1965, JFKL, pp. 10–11. Richard Reeves notes that Kennedy was uncomfortable with Harry Truman's casual and frequent use of the "n" word. LBJ also employed it liberally.

5. Paul Douglas OHI, June 6, 1964, JFKL, pp. 9–11; Joseph Rauh OHI, December 23, 1965, JFKL, p. 15; Parmet, *Jack*, 408–14.

6. Bryant, *Bystander*, 64–65; Evans and Novak, *Lyndon B. Johnson*, 133–40; Caro, *Master of the Senate*; Charles McWhorter to RMN, "Clarence Mitchell—NAACP," March 8, 1960, RMN PPP, GC, Box 521 (Clarence Mitchell File), RMNL.*

7. Roy Wilkins in a difficult decision supported the 1957 final bill because "A start toward our goal . . . would be better than standing still" (see Wilkins, *Standing Fast*, 245; see also Bryant, *Bystander*, 64–79; Wofford, *Kennedys and Kings*, 46; Sorensen to Pat Lucey, March 19, 1960, TSP, Correspondence, 1959–60, Box 26, Wisconsin [Folder 2], JFKL; Marjorie Lawson OHI, October 25, 1965, JFKL, p. 6; Sorensen, *Kennedy*, 49–50; Dallek, *Unfinished Life*, 216–18).

8. Branch, *Parting the Waters*, 277, 312–13; Bryant, *Bystander*, 103–6.

9. Kennedy, *Profiles in Courage*, 107–30, 197–98. On Kennedy's southern strategy, see Land, "John F. Kennedy's Southern Strategy, 1956–1960."

10. Bryant, *Bystander*, 88–90.

11. Ibid., 90–91; Brauer, *John F. Kennedy*, 341.

12. Bryant, *Bystander*, 111, 127–28; Marjorie Lawson OHI, October 25, 1965, JFKL, p. 10; Patrick Lucey OHI, August 1, 1964, pp. 26–27, JFKL; Branch, *Parting the Waters*, 306–7.

13. Carson, ed., *Papers of Martin Luther King, Jr.*, 5:478–80; Branch, *Parting the Waters*, 314; Thomas, *Robert Kennedy*, 128; Bryant, *Bystander*, 133; Garrow, *Bearing the Cross*, 142; Steel, *Night*, 158.

14. Wofford, *Kennedys and Kings*, 47–48, 51–52; Bryant, *Bystander*, 132–37, 143–45.

15. Bryant, *Bystander*, 149.

16. *WP*, July 11, 1960; Anthony Shriver, "Kennedy's Call to King," JFKL, p. 37; Bryant, *Bystander*, 145, 149–52; Herbert Tucker OHI, March 9, 1967, p. 23.

17. On Eisenhower's attitudes, see Theodore M. Hesburgh OHI, March 27, 1966, JFKL, p. 10; E. Frederic Morrow OHI, February 23, 1977, DDEL, pp. 16–21, 34; Branch, *Parting the Waters*, 213, 687; Wilkins, *Standing Fast*, 212, 222, 233–36, 243–46, 255–58, 278. According to Branch, JFK was "completely relaxed" at social

gatherings with blacks in "stark" contrast with Eisenhower. Wilkins concurs. E. Frederic Morrow believed that Eisenhower was "neither intellectually nor emotionally disposed to combat segregation in general" (see E. F. Morrow, *Way Down South*, 121).

18. Ambrose, *Eisenhower*, 126; Nichols, *Matter of Justice*, 26–46; Lawson, *Black Ballots*, 142–43; E. Frederic Morrow OHI, February 23, 1977, DDEL, pp. 62–63.

19. Branch, *Parting the Waters*, 180–81, 323; E. Frederic Morrow OHI, February 23, 1977, DDEL, p. 41; E. F. Morrow, *Forty Years*, 77–100, 168–78, 210–17, 221–23; Siciliano, *Walking on Sand*, 155–70.

20. E. F. Morrow, *Forty Years*, 104–5, 178–84, 189–90. Morrow had a high regard for Adams. After Adams's departure, Jerry Persons became chief of staff. Persons was a congenial Alabaman but much less sympathetic to civil rights (see Siciliano, *Walking on Sand*, 171–73).

21. Ambrose, *Nixon*, 614–15.

22. Nichols, *Matter of Justice*, 36–38; DDE to RMN, August 15, 1953, RMN PPP, Series 207 (Appearances), Box 13, RMNL*; RMN Broadcast, October 23, 1955, RMN PPP, Series 207, Box 40, File 7, RMNL*; Television Script for April 22, 1956, RMN PPP, Series 207, Box 51, File 9, RMNL*; Minority Community Resources Conference January 1958, RMN PPP, Series 207, Box 76, File 4, RMNL.*

23. *Chicago Defender*, August 17, 1957; Clarence Mitchell to RMN, July 6, 1959, RMN PPP, Box 521 (Clarence Mitchell File), RMNL*; *NYT*, June 21, 1960. Morrow had a high opinion of Nixon in the 1950s. According to him, the vice president believed that blacks should not be relegated to and insulated in positions in minority affairs and ambassadorships in African countries (see E. F. Morrow, *Forty Years*, 185–88).

24. Branch, *Parting the Waters*, 199, 214, 219–20; RMN Handwritten Notes, June 13, 1957, RMN PPP, MLK Correspondence, Box 22, RMNL; Garrow, *Bearing the Cross*, 90–91, 117; Carson, ed., *Papers of Martin Luther King, Jr.*, 4:204, 224, 262–64, 277, 482–83, 500; 5:197. In contrast, John F. Kennedy does not even appear in the index of volume 4.

25. Garrow, *Bearing the Cross*, 118–19; MLK to RMN, August 30, 1957, RMN PPP, MLK Correspondence, RMNL, Box 22.

26. Falkner, *Great Time Coming*, 261; Rampersad, *Jackie Robinson*, 261, 324. On the Robinson-Nixon relationship in the later 1950s, see Long, ed., *First Class Citizenship*, 26–28, 32–34, 35–39, 43, 48–50, 51–52.

27. Falkner, *Great Time Coming*, 269–70; Rampersad, *Jackie Robinson*, 341, 343. On Robinson and Nixon in 1960, see Long, ed., *First Class Citizenship*, 89–90, 91–92, 94–95, 97–101.

28. Rampersad, *Jackie Robinson*, 343–44; *Capital Times*, April 1, 1960; *NYP*, February 22, 1960, March 16, 1960, April 8, 1960, May 23, 1960, and August 26, 1960.

29. Falkner, *Great Time Coming*, 278; Allen, *Jackie Robinson*, 219; Bryant, *Bystander*, 135–36; Branch, *Parting the Waters*, 306–8; Rampersad, *Jackie Robinson*, 345. On the Robinson-JFK relationship in 1960, see Long, ed., *First Class Citizenship*,

95–96, 107–8; and Robinson, *I Never Had It Made*, 137–38. Peter Lisagor of the *Chicago Daily News* reported in May 1961 that Robinson had had a change of heart about the Kennedys, but that was an exaggeration. Robinson said he had no regrets over supporting Nixon in 1960. In 1968, Robinson favored Hubert Humphrey over Robert F. Kennedy (see Long, ed., *First Class Citizenship*, 128–29, 178–79). Robinson paid a price for his stand. He lost his column in the liberal *New York Post* and came under heavy criticism for his support of Nixon (see Rampersad, *Jackie Robinson*, 352–53; Falkner, *Long Time Coming*, 281–82; Long, ed., *First Class Citizenship*, 116–17).

30. Untitled memorandum, RFKP, Pre-Administration Political Files, Box 34, Campaign Strategy, October 1960–November 1960, JFKL; Manning, *William L. Dawson*, 128–36.

31. Of the six black wards, five (all except the Twenty-fourth) were under the control of Congressman William L. Dawson, the most powerful black politician in Chicago. On Dawson and Chicago, see Manning, *William L. Dawson*; Beito and Beito, *Black Maverick*, 174–87.

32. On Stevenson's lack of support for civil rights and weakness among black voters, see Manning, *William L. Dawson*, 124–26, 128–35.

33. Bryant, *Bystander*, 172. The Kennedy campaign also relied on black sports stars and celebrities (see Manning, *William L. Dawson*, 146).

34. Bryant, *Bystander*, 166, 176–78. On the support for the African students and Kennedy's use of Africa, see Meriwether, "Worth a Lot of Negro Votes."

35. "Kennedy and Nixon on Civil Rights: Some Comparisons," SPF, Box 261, Political Files, 1959–1960 (Issues), LBJL; George Reedy Statement on Nixon, October 6, 1960, Senate Political Files, Box 268, LBJL; Lawson, *Black Ballots*, 243–44; Heymann, *RFK*, 177.

36. *WP*, August 4, 1960; Wofford, *Kennedys and Kings*, 313; Stossel, *Sarge*, 156–58; Branch, *Parting the Waters*, 341.

37. For infighting in the CRS, see Marjorie Lawson OHI, October 25, 1965, JFKL; Herbert Tucker OHI, March 9, 1967, JFKL; Harris Wofford OHI, May 22, 1968, JFKL; Branch, *Parting the Waters*, 341–42; Shriver, "Kennedy Call to King," JFKL, pp. 81–82.

38. Branch, *Parting the Waters*, 342; Louis Martin OHI, May 14, 1969, LBJL; Wofford, *Kennedys and Kings*, 60.

39. Branch, *Parting the Waters*, 341–44, 347; Stossel, *Sarge*, 160–61; Wofford, *Kennedys and Kings*, 60; John Seigenthaler OHI, July 22, 1964, JFKL, pp. 119–21. On the black press, see Ritchie, *Reporting from Washington*, 28–46.

40. Hilty, *Robert Kennedy*, 169–70; Branch, *Parting the Waters*, 342–43. On the bad relations between the Kennedys and Dawson, see Manning, *William L. Dawson*, 144–47. However, after his election JFK offered to nominate Dawson as postmaster general. Dawson declined.

41. C. Hamilton, *Adam Clayton Powell, Jr.*, 336–37; Branch, *Parting the Waters*, 343.

42. Shriver, "Kennedy's Call to King, JFKL, pp. 16–18; Aitken, *Nixon*, 282.

43. Bryant, *Bystander*, 163–66.

44. Bob Haldeman to Finch and Klein, January 13, 1960, RMN PPP, Series 207, Box 122, File 29, RMNL*; William E. Robinson to RMN, August 29, 1960, GC, Box 649, RMNL*; Russell Kirk to Charley [McWhorter?], October 22, 1960, RMN PPP, GC, Box 414, RMNL*; Gifford, *The Center Cannot Hold*, 76–86.

45. Lawson, *Black Ballots*, 254; Bryce Harlow, Memo for the Record of Meeting among DDE, RMN, Thruston Morton, Genl. Persons, et al., December 28, 1960, DDE Presidential Papers, AWF, DDE Diary Series, Box 55, Staff Notes—December 1960, DDEL; Claude Robinson to Nixon, Hall, Finch, October 21, 1960, "Campaign Evaluation as of October 14, 1960," p. 12, RMN PPP, Presidential Debates Preparations, Box 61, RMNL.

46. For the shift in black votes in Pennsylvania, for example, see "A Study of the Presidential Election in Pennsylvania," Wave II, October 12, 1960, RSP, Box 1, JFKL. Harris showed Kennedy moving from a 58 percent to 42 percent advantage in September to a 66 percent to 34 percent advantage in October. There is an ongoing debate on whether the critical shift in the black vote took place before the Martin Luther King Jr. incident or as a result of it.

47. Branch, *Parting the Waters*, 344–49; Wofford, *Kennedys and Kings*, 12–13. On June 24, 1960, Martin Luther King Jr. had written to Chester Bowles that he "had very little enthusiasm for Mr. Kennedy when he first announced his candidacy." However, when King discovered that Kennedy had asked Bowles to serve as a foreign policy advisor, his mind "immediately changed." "I said to myself, 'If Chester Bowles is Mr. Kennedy's advisor, he must be thinking right on the major issues'" (Carson, ed., *Papers of Martin Luther King, Jr.*, 5:480).

48. Wofford, *Kennedys and Kings*, 14–15; Bryant, *Bystander*, 180–82.

49. See White, *Making of the President*, 321–23; Dallek, *Unfinished Life*, 292–93; Wofford, *Kennedys and Kings*, 14–22; Stossel, *Sarge*, 162–68; Bryant, *Bystander*, 180–86; Branch, *Parting the Waters*, 354–72; Carson, ed., *Papers of Martin Luther King, Jr.*, 5:522–36; Parmet, *JFK*, 55–56. The most comprehensive examination of the historiography of the subject may be found in Kuhn, "There's a Footnote to History!"

50. Reeves, *President Kennedy*, 62. Harris Wofford had Chester Bowles call Coretta Scott King to offer assurances that everything possible was being done to free her husband. As it happened, Bowles was with Adlai Stevenson at the time and attempted to get Stevenson to talk to Mrs. King. Stevenson refused to do so (see Branch, *Parting the Waters*, 360).

51. Shriver, "Kennedy Call to King," JFKL, pp. 32–33; Wofford, *Kennedys and Kings*, 19; Stossel, *Sarge*, 162–68.

52. Henderson, *Ernest Vandiver*, 122–25; Kuhn, "There's a Footnote to History," 589–92; J. Ernest Vandiver OHI, May 22, 1967, JFKL, pp. 25–28, 68–70; RFK OHI, December 4, 1964, JFKL, pp. 347–48; Thomas, *Robert Kennedy*, 102–4. For the Camelot version of RFK's call, see White, *Making of the President*, 385–87;

and Schlesinger, *Thousand Days*, 74. Even non-Camelot historians, though, have adopted the legend of Robert Kennedy's call to Judge Mitchell as historical reality (see, for example, Thomas, *Robert F. Kennedy*, 102–4; and Branch, *Parting the Waters*, 366–67). The White-Schlesinger account of the Martin Luther King Jr. incident is a classic example of Kennedy court history. It romanticized and sanitized the story while leaving out the grubby political details.

53. White, *Making of the President*, 323; *Pittsburgh Courier*, November 5, 1960. See Carson, ed., *Papers of Martin Luther King, Jr.*, 5:535–37, 540–41, 544–53, for statements he made and interviews he gave after his release through November 6.

54. Shriver, "Kennedy Call to King," JFKL, 22–25; White, *Making of the President*, 323; Wofford, *Kennedys and Kings*, 23–24. For a replication of the famous pamphlet, see Carson, ed., *Papers of Martin Luther King, Jr.*, 5:538–39. The claims of Wofford, Shriver, and others that they produced a million or more copies of the "blue bomb" seem exaggerated. Given the proximity of election day, the logistics of producing, shipping, and handing out so many leaflets, and the necessity to maintain a low profile, it seems unlikely that such numbers were actually printed and distributed. The story of the "blue bomb" illustrates another aspect of Kennedy court history: the tendency to self-congratulation. The Kennedy people liked to think of themselves as the best and the brightest. They were convinced that they were much smarter and more enlightened and that they consistently outwitted the less imaginative Republicans.

55. E. Frederic Morrow, OHI by Dr. Thomas Soapes, February 23, 1977, DDEL, pp. 8, 54; The Reminiscences of E. Frederic Morrow, April 15, 1968, pp. 140–41, in the Oral History Collection of Columbia University. Afterward, Morrow blamed Nixon's staff, not the vice president, noting, "It was his advisors rather than Nixon who did me in" (see E. F. Morrow, *Forty Years*, 208). On Robinson, Nixon, and the King incident, see Robinson, *I Never Had It Made*, 135–40; Long, ed., *First Class Citizenship*, 114–15; and Gifford, *The Center Cannot Hold*, 86–87. In spite of his disappointment over Nixon's conduct in 1960, Robinson remained on friendly terms with him in 1961 and 1962. With the rise of Barry Goldwater and Nixon's willingness to support him in 1964, Robinson's attitude soured. In 1968, Robinson backed Nelson Rockefeller and then Hubert Humphrey. He said he was "terribly disappointed" when Nixon won. Still, Robinson attended a dinner of black businessmen for Nixon's reelection campaign in 1972. In his last letter to Robinson in September 1972, Nixon told him he had put him on his all-time baseball team. Robinson died in October 1972 (see Robinson, *I Never Had It Made*, 235–41; and Long, ed., *First Class Citizenship*, 123–24, 140–41, 157–58, 166–68, 282–86, 312–13, 317–18).

56. Nixon, *Six Crises*, 390–91; Telegrams, RMN PPP, MLK Correspondence, Box 22, RMNL; White, *Making of the President*, 315; GG [George Grassmuck?] to RH Finch, November 15, 1960, RMN PPP, MLK Correspondence, RMNL; *Pittsburgh Courier*, November 26, 1960.

Chapter 8. The Final Days of the General Election Campaign, October 22–November 7

1. White, *Making of the President*, 319–20.

2. *NYHT*, October 31, 1960; *NYDN*, October 17, 21, 24, 26, 28, and 31, 1960; White, *Making of the President*, 319.

3. Salinger, *With Kennedy*, 50; R. Goodwin, *Remembering America*, 128; Sorensen, *Kennedy*, 209; Roger Tubby to RFK, "Memorandum on Democratic National Committee Campaign Operations," December 13, 1960, JFK PPP, Box 1045, DNC, Interoffice Memoranda, JFKL.

4. Schlesinger, *Thousand Days* 74; Mildred Jeffrey OHI, January 25, 1970, JFKL, p. 53; R. Goodwin, *Remembering America*, 130.

5. Adlai E. Stevenson to Lady Barbara Jackson, October 28, 1960, Johnson, ed., *Papers of Adlai E. Stevenson*, 7:573; Bowles, *Promises*, 297; *NYHT*, November 2, 1960; "Memorandum on the Last 9 Days of Campaign," n.d., RFKP, Pre-Administration Political Files, Box 43, Political Miscellany, October 7–November 5, 1960, and undated, JFKL; *Newsweek*, November 14, 1960, 21; Sorensen, *Kennedy*, 221.

6. White, *Making of the President*, 301; Nixon, *Six Crises*, 390.

7. White, *Making of the President*, 320.

8. Ibid., 310.

9. Ibid., 309; The Reminiscences of Meade Alcorn, June 5, 1967, p. 158, in the Oral History Collection of Columbia University.

10. The Reminiscences of Walter Thayer, April 28, 1967, pp. 20–21, in the Oral History Collection of Columbia University; Nixon, *RN*, 221.

11. White, *Making of the President*, 309; The Reminiscences of Robert Merriam, January 13, 1969, pp. 47–48, in the Oral History Collection of Columbia University; The Reminiscences of L. Richard Guylay, March 2, 1967, pp. 56–57, in the Oral History Collection of Columbia University; The Reminiscences of Milton Eisenhower, September 6, 1967, pp. 43–45, in the Oral History Collection of Columbia University.

12. *NYT*, October 11, 16, 17, 19, and 21, 1960; The Reminiscences of Thomas B. Curtis, October 23, 1972, p. 44, in the Oral History Collection of Columbia University; The Reminiscences of Barry Goldwater, June 15, 1967, p. 24, in the Oral History Collection of Columbia University; The Reminiscences of Earl Mazo, November 23, 1971, p. 11, in the Oral History Collection of Columbia University. While Eisenhower bemoaned Nixon's failure to call on him for more campaigning, very occasionally he would admit to his physical limitations. In a late October response to a plea to campaign in upper New York State, the president noted there was a problem of "mere physical endurance" and that "Many people seem to forget that I am seventy years old." He added that he might be available for a day but that "would call down Mamie's wrath" (see DDE to Barry T. Leithead, October 29, 1960, #1689, in Galambos and Van Ee, eds., *Papers of Dwight David Eisenhower*, 21:2144).

13. White, *Making of the President*, 309; Ambrose, *Eisenhower*, 602.

14. Nixon, *RN*, 222. See also Ambrose, *Eisenhower*, 602.

15. Wicker, *One of Us*, 243; Ted Lewis, "Capitol Stuff," *NYDN*, September 8, 1966.

16. William E. Robinson to DDE, September 13, 1966, DDE Post Presidential Papers, Special Names Series, Box 17, Robinson, William E., 1963–66 (Folder 1), DDEL.

17. DDE to William E. Robinson, September 21, 1966, DDE Post Presidential Papers, Special Names Series, Box 17, Robinson, William E., 1963–66 (Folder 1), DDEL; Jamieson, *Packaging the Presidency*, 148.

18. Lasby, *Eisenhower's Heart Attack*, 281, 330–31. See also Ferrell, *Ill-Advised*, 53–150; Gilbert, *Mortal Presidency*, 80–132.

19. Gilbert, *Mortal Presidency*, 114–16; Lasby, *Eisenhower's Heart Attack*, 284–87. For Snyder's records of his treatment of Eisenhower, see Howard M. Snyder Papers, DDEL. For the Detroit incident, see General Snyder's Progress Reports for October 17–18, 1960, Howard M. Snyder Papers, Box 10, Medical Diary re DDE, September 1–December 31, 1960 (Folder 2), DDEL; and Thomas Mattingly, "Dwight D. Eisenhower Diseases of the Cardiovascular System" (Part Three), 12 November 1955 to 21 January 1961, Thomas W. Mattingly Papers, Box 1, Cardiovascular System—Part Three, DDEL.

20. Fay, *Pleasure of His Company*, 65.

21. White, *Making of the President*, 311–12; Savage, *JFK, LBJ*, 85; Jamieson, *Packaging the Presidency*, 153.

22. *WP*, November 8, 1960; Evans and Novak, *Nixon*, 5; Jamieson, *Packaging the Presidency*, 153.

23. White, *Making of the President*, 373–74; Reinsch, *Getting Elected*, 157; Sorensen, *Kennedy*, 209; John Seigenthaler OHI, February 21, 1966, JFKL, pp. 166–170; Savage, *JFK, LBJ*, 323; Klein, *Making It Perfectly Clear*, 61.

24. Ambrose, *Nixon*, 597–600; Maheu and Hack, *Next to Hughes*, 83–85, 117–19, 204–18; Summers, *Arrogance of Power*, 154–58; Hack, *Hughes*, 241, 268, 302, 311–16.

25. Dallek, *Lone Star Rising*, 587–88.

26. LBJ Papers, SPF, Box 248, Bulk mail, 1960—Dallas Incident, LBJL; Elizabeth Carpenter OHI, Interview 1, December 3, 1968, LBJL, p. 33; Murray Watson, Field Report, November 10, 1960, LBJ Papers SPF, Box 215, JFK-LBJ Democratic Campaign, Field Reports (File 1), LBJL; Charles Boatner OHI, December 16, 1968, LBJL; Cecil Burney OHI, November 26, 1968, LBJL, p. 42; General Carl Phinney OHI, October 11, 1968, LBJL, pp. 17–20; Fite, *Richard B. Russell, Jr.*, 377–79. See also Rorabaugh, *Real Making of the President*, 135, 137.

27. For Rayburn's long antagonism toward Alger, see Dulaney and Phillips, eds., *Speak, Mister Speaker*, 259, 275, 349, 353, 420, 444.

28. Sundquist, *Dynamics*, 293; Hardeman and Bacon, *Rayburn*, 417; Bruce Alger to RMN, November 11, 1961, RMN PPP, GC, Box 26, RMNL.*

29. See the discussion of this event in chapter 5.

30. Thomas, *Robert Kennedy*, 105; Matthews, *Kennedy & Nixon*, 143; Edith Green

OHI, August 23, 1985, LBJL, p. 13; Carty, *Catholic in the White House?*, 90, 91–92; Clark Clifford to JFK, July 19, 1960, Clifford Papers, Roll 1, JFKL.

31. Jamieson, *Packaging the Presidency*, 134; emphasis in the original.

32. *WP*, August 29, 1960; *NYHT*, September 14, 1960, October 26, 1960.

33. On Nixon's religious attitudes, see Colson, *Born Again*, 64, 179–80, 183–84.

34. Dallek, *Lone Star Rising*, 586; Aitken, *Nixon*, 280; Nixon, *Six Crises*, 396.

35. Billy Graham to RMN, September 24, 1960, October 17, 1960, November 2, 1960, RMN PPP, GC, Box 299, RMNL*; B. Graham, *Just As I Am*, 392–93, 445; Ambrose, *Nixon*, 546–47, 602–3; Miller, *Billy Graham*, 74–84; Nixon, *Six Crises*, 393–94. Billy Graham did write an article that appeared in *Life* just before the election, but it was a general piece that urged Americans to get out and vote. In it, he mentioned neither Nixon nor Kennedy by name (see Billy Graham, "We Are Electing a President of the World," *Life*, November 7, 1960, 109–10).

36. See David Lawrence, "U.A.W. Paper Denounced for Raising Bigotry Issue," *NYHT*, October 19, 1960.

37. Ambrose, *Nixon*, 545.

38. Nixon, *Six Crises*, 367–68.

39. For Democratic attitudes, see James Wine OHI, January 26, 1967, JFKL; *NYT*, October 25, 1960; Parmet, *JFK*, 41–42; Willard Edwards to RMN, RMN PPP, Box 226, RMNL.* For the latest Democratic conspiracy theory on Nixon's exploitation of the religious issue, see Casey, *Making of a Catholic President*, 83, 99–150.

40. Ambrose, *Nixon*, 601–2.

41. Rowland Evans, "How Kennedy Thinks He Can Win Election," *NYHT*, October 31, 1960.

42. "A Study of the Presidential Election in Ohio," Wave III, November 4, 1960, RSP, Box 1, JFKL; "A Study of the Presidential Election in Pennsylvania," Wave III, November 3, 1960, RSP, Box 2, JFKL; "A Study of the Presidential Election in California," Wave III, October 31, 1960, RSP, Box 1, JFKL; "A Survey of the Presidential Election in New York," Wave III, November 4, 1960, RSP, Box 1, JFKL; "A Survey of the Presidential Election in Texas," Wave III, RFK Papers, Poll #830: The Presidential Election in Texas, III, November 3, 1960, JFKL; "A Survey of the Presidential Election in Illinois," Wave III, November 2, 19–60, RSP, Box 1, JFKL. There is one caveat that must be attached to this analysis. The Harris polls available in the John F. Kennedy Library do not include any late polling that Harris did for Kennedy. For example, the poll cited in *Newsweek* is not there, as far as I could tell. In addition, there are no late polls from key states. It is conceivable that Harris did show some tightening of some state races at the end.

43. *NYHT*, October 30, 1960.

44. Nixon, *Six Crises*, 410–11.

45. Claude Robinson to Nixon, Hall, Finch, November 10, 1960, "Variations between Our Vote Estimates and the Election," RMN PPP, Series 258, Box 1, RMNL.*

46. Claude Robinson to Nixon, Hall, Finch, October 21, 1960, "Campaign Eval-

uation as of October 14, 1960 (Third Debate)," RMN PPP, Presidential Debates Preparations, Box 61, RMNL.

47. Claude Robinson to Nixon, Hall, Finch, October 28, 1960, "Campaign Evaluation as of October 22, 1960 (Fourth Debate)," RMN PPP, Presidential Debates Preparations, Box 61, RMNL.

48. Claude Robinson to Nixon, Hall, Finch, November 10, 1960, "Variations between Our Vote Estimates and the Election," RMN PPP, Series 258, Box 1, RMNL.* The November 5 estimates are contained in the November 10 document. I did not find the November 5 estimates as a separate document.

49. *Time*, November 7, 1960, 24–25; *Newsweek*, November 7, 1960, 40–45; *US-NWR*, November 7, 1960, 38–53.

50. See Gallup, ed., *Gallup Poll*, November 4, 1960 (poll conducted October 18–23, 1960), 3:1689; ibid., November 7, 1960 (poll conducted October 30–November 4, 1960), 3:1690. It is possible that the disparity between *Time* et al. and the Gallup Poll can be reconciled. Gallup's final poll caught the final Nixon surge. *Time* and the other news magazines did not because of their publication deadlines.

Chapter 9. November 8, 1960, and Its Aftermath

1. Hoffman, *Theodore H. White*, 143.

2. For a description of how John F. Kennedy spent election day, see White, *Making of the President*, 4–30.

3. Nixon, *Six Crises*, 407–9; Don Hughes Memorandum, January 28, 1961, RMN PPP, Series 258, Box 1, RMNL*; Klein, *Making It Perfectly Clear*, 51–52; Aitken, *Nixon*, 289.

4. Some television executives were not enamored of election coverage. Reuven Frank of NBC-TV said: "election night is a TV show about adding. . . . We showed numbers and more numbers." He also noted that "The urge to use pointless gimmicks is irresistible" (see Frank, *Thin Air*, 161–62).

5. This analysis of television network coverage is based on CML, "Election Night Coverage: American Broadcasting Company-TV," "Election Night Coverage: Columbia Broadcasting System-TV," and "Election Night Coverage: National Broadcasting Company-TV." All three documents are found in RMN, PPP Series 258, Box 1, RMNL.*

6. Reston, *Deadline*, 289.

7. White, *Making of the President*, 18–25, 345–49; Sorensen, *Kennedy*, 212.

8. Nixon, *Six Crises*, 411–12.

9. Ibid., 415–17; The Reminiscences of Robert Finch, June 19, 1967, p. 67, in the Oral History Collection of Columbia University; The Reminiscences of J. Clifford Folger, January 25, 1968, p. 22, in the Oral History Collection of Columbia University.

10. Price, *With Nixon*, 36–37. The similarities between 1960 and 1968 are striking. In 1960, Nixon carried twenty-six states. In 1968, he won twenty-four of the

twenty-six from 1960, losing only Washington and Maine. In 1968, he added North and South Carolina, Illinois, New Jersey, Nevada, and Missouri.

11. There were a total of 537 electoral votes. However, Mississippi and its 8 electoral votes went to a slate of independent electors as did 6 from Alabama.

12. See *LAT*, November 11–22, 1960.

13. Harold Leventhal to RFK, "California Situation," December 7, 1960, RFKP, Pre-Administration Political Files, Box 39, 1960 Camp & Transition, Memos: K–L, JFKL.

14. The narrative of the Hawaii recount may be found in A. A. Smyser, "How Kennedy Won 1960 Recount in Hawaii," *Honolulu Star-Bulletin*, June 8, 1963. See also Ronald B. Jamieson Papers, JFKL. Jamieson was the judge who heard the Hawaii recount case.

15. Bryce Harlow to Victor Emanuel, November 16, 1960, AWF, Campaign Series, Box 4, 1960 Election, DDEL.

16. DDE to RMN, November 9, 1960, DDE Presidential Papers, AWF, DDE Diary Series, Box 54, DDE Dictation—Nov. 1960, DDEL; ACW Diary, November 9, 1960, DDE Presidential Papers, AWF, DDE Diary Series, Box 54, Diary—Nov. 1960, DDEL.

17. Eisenhower, *Waging Peace*, 601–2, 652–53; ACW Diary, November 9, 1960, DDE Presidential Papers, DDE Diary Series, Box 54, Diary—Nov. 1960.

18. Dr. Arthur S. Flemming OHI, June 3, 1988, DDEL, p. 41.

19. Ambrose, *Eisenhower*, 604.

20. The following narrative is based on my earlier book (see Kallina, *Courthouse over White House*, 96–144).

21. *Chicago Tribune*, November 24, 1960. See *Houston Chronicle* for November 22, 23, and 24 for an examination of alleged Texas irregularities. The *Chronicle* afforded continuing coverage of Republican complaints about the conduct of the election until the dismissal of a GOP legal suit on December 12. Other newspapers such as the *Dallas Morning News* also provided widespread publicity for the Republican case. For Earl Mazo's articles, see *NYHT* for December 4–7, 1960. Mazo's articles appeared in a number of other newspapers and thereby achieved national exposure. For the situation in Chicago, see Kallina, *Courthouse*, 109–12, 119–20, 121–25.

22. ACW Diary, November 30, 1960, DDE Presidential Papers, DDE Diary Series, Box 54, Diary—Nov. 1960, DDEL; Ambrose, *Eisenhower*, 604.

23. Mazo and Hess, *Nixon*, 249–50; Nixon, *Six Crises*, 446–47; Nixon, *RN*, 224; Crowley, *Nixon off the Record*, 30; Aitken, *Nixon*, 292.

24. Aitken, *Nixon*, 292; RMN to W. D. Maxwell, December 30, 1960, RMN PPP, GC, Box 484, RMNL.*

25. Brodie, *Richard Nixon*, 433; Summers, *Arrogance of Power*, 217–18.

26. Pierre Salinger OHI, July 19, 1965, JFKL, p. 103.

27. *WP*, November 29, 1960; Harold Leventhal to RFK, December 5, 1960, "Status of Illinois Recount," RFKP, Pre-Administration Political Files, Box 39, 1960 Campaign & Transition, Memos: K–L, JFKL; *WP*, November 2, 1960.

28. Nixon, *Six Crises*, 436–38.

29. Bradlee, *Conversations with Kennedy*, 32; Matthews, *Kennedy & Nixon*, 187–88.

30. Eisenhower, *Waging Peace*, 603. It is possible to make too much of the rapprochement between Eisenhower and Kennedy. Although Ike's opinion of the president-elect might have improved, it had no other way to go. In early January, Eisenhower showed his distrust of the incoming administration with comments about Kennedy's appointments in the State Department. He called it a "menagerie" consisting of "one individual who is no less than a crackpot, another noted for his indecisiveness, and still another of demonstrated stupidity, and, finally one famous only for his ability to break the treasury of a great state" (see DDE to Robert Winship Woodruff, January 3, 1961, #1757, Galambos and Van Ee, eds., *Papers of Dwight David Eisenhower*, 21:2231).

31. *NYHT*, November 20, 1960; *CST*, November 19, 1960; Peirce, *People's President*, 106; Novotny, "John F. Kennedy, the 1960 Election, and Georgia's Unpledged Electors in the Electoral College," 382–90, 394–96.

32. Peirce, *People's President*, 107–8, 124.

33. Ibid., 18.

34. Mazo and Hess, *Nixon*, 250.

35. Converse et al., "Stability and Change in 1960: A Reinstating Election," 269–80.

36. All Gallup Polls gave Nixon and the GOP a distinct advantage when it came to questions such as who would better keep the United States out of World War III and who would do a better job of protecting American interests (see Gallup Polls for May 29 [3:1669], June 10 [3:1672], and September 7 [3:1683]). In the same way, all Gallup Polls gave Kennedy and the Democrats a decisive lead on questions like which party would better keep the country prosperous (see poll for July 15 [3:1676]). In addition, the big Democratic advantage on the matter of which party people would like to see control Congress should be read as a question about which one would best deal with domestic issues.

37. As Theodore H. White pointed out, there is no official popular vote count for presidential elections. One can find different versions of Kennedy's margin of victory. The two most common numbers mentioned are 112,803 and 118,574. The difference derives from what vote one assigns Kennedy in Alabama (see White, *Making of the President*, 462–63; Scammon, ed., *America Votes 5*, 1). The confusion can be seen in *Guide to U.S. Elections*, which produced one JFK popular vote total for Alabama and nationally in the first and second editions (1976, 1985) and then different numbers in the third, fourth, and fifth editions (1994, 2001, 2005). See also Rusk, ed., *Statistical History of the American Electorate*, table 4–58, p. 192.

38. For this and the following discussion of Alabama, see Peirce, *People's President*, 100–107, 348–49; *Congressional Quarterly Weekly Report*, February 17, 1961, 285–88; Rorabaugh, *Real Making of the President*, 125–26; and Gaines, "Popular Myths about Popular Vote–Electoral College Splits," 71–75. Gaines provides the most recent and the clearest explanation of how the Alabama Democratic slate came into existence. Democrats knew that if they fielded two slates, as they did

in Mississippi, Nixon would probably carry the state so they put forward just one slate made up of both independent and loyalist electors selected in the party primary. The leading Alabama Kennedy elector finished with 318,303. Some analysts credited Kennedy with this vote. Others gave him the 324,050 votes of the leading Alabama elector, who was unpledged and anti-Kennedy.

39. Peirce, *People's President*, 102–3.

40. Ibid., 9, 102–3. If Alabama's popular votes are allocated in proportion to the electoral vote, then JFK receives five-elevenths, or 147,295, of the Democratic Party state total. If this number is then applied to the national count, Kennedy's national plurality disappears, and Nixon emerges as the popular vote winner in the country by slightly more than 58,000 votes (see Peirce, *People's President*, 103–4).

41. Galbraith, *Life*, 356, 357; Donald M. Wilson OHI, January 14, 1972, JFKL, p. 38; Humphrey, *Education*, 232; Witcover, *Crapshoot,* 141–42.

42. R. Goodwin, *Remembering America*, 119–20; Reeves, *President Kennedy*, 277; Giglio, *Presidency of John F. Kennedy*, 36.

43. One explanation of what happened in Mississippi involves a film of Harry Belafonte in Harlem endorsing JFK. The film was made available to those in the country who thought they could make effective use of it. One of the names on the list was Michigan governor G. Mennen Williams. Apparently, the film was mistakenly shipped to Representative John Bell Williams, an ardent segregationist from Mississippi. Without viewing the film, Democrats put it on Mississippi television immediately after Senator John Stennis endorsed JFK over statewide TV. Needless to say, this was one television program that did not help Kennedy's cause (see Heymann, *RFK*, 176; and John Seigenthaler OHI, February 21, 1966, JFKL, pp. 197–200).

44. "Summary of Investigation of Reports from All Sections of Ohio as to Election Results—Nov. 8, 1960," Pierre Salinger Papers, Box 9, Election, 1960, JFKL.

45. John Seigenthaler OHI, February 21, 1966, JFKL, p. 223; John Bailey OHI, April 10, 1964, JFKL, pp. 84–85; ACW note on conversation with Bryce Harlow, May 26, 1961, DDE Post-Presidential Papers, Special Name Series, Box 6, Harlow, Bryce—1961 (Folder 6), DDEL; Wicker, *One of Us*, 254–55. Nixon would later deliver one of the eulogies at Woody Hayes's funeral in 1987.

46. "Summary of Investigation of Reports from All Sections of Ohio as to Election Results—Nov. 8, 1960," Pierre Salinger Papers, Box 9, Election, 1960, JFKL.

47. James W. Symington OHI, January 18, 1968, JFKL, p. 7; James B. Brennan OHI, December 9, 1965, JFKL, p. 16; John Seigenthaler OHI, February 21, 1966, JFKL, pp. 215–16.

48. W. Thompson, *History of Wisconsin*, 694–99.

49. J. Lindsay Almond OHI, February 5, 1969, JFKL, p. 23. See also Sweeney, "Whispers in the Golden Silence"; and Rorabaugh, *Real Making of the President*, 137–38.

50. *NYT*, August 24, 1960, p. 17; Joe Tydings to JFK, RFK, "Report on Florida," August 11, 1960, DNC Papers, 1960 Campaign, Box 129, Florida, August 11–October 25, 1960, JFKL; LeRoy Collins OHI, November 2, 1965, pp. 26–29, 36, JFKL; J.

Millard Tawes OHI, March 1, 1968, JFKL, p. 14; Joseph D. Tydings OHI, September 30, 1965, JFKL, pp. 16–17; C. Farris Bryant OHI, March 5, 1971, LBJL, pp. 5–6; John V. Russell to JFK, September 1960, JFK PPP, Box 978, Florida Political, P-SC, JFKL.

51. *Philadelphia Inquirer*, November 21, 1960; RMN PPP, Series 207, Box 139, File 24, RMNL.* See also Madonna, *Pivotal Pennsylvania*, 45–53.

52. DDE to RMN, October 1, 1960, DDE Presidential Papers, AWF, Administrative Series, Box 28, Richard M. Nixon, 1958–61 (Folder 1), DDEL. On Stratton and 1960, see Kenney, *Political Passage*, 168–79. Stratton's biographer concludes: "in a real sense, Richard Nixon was a victim of Stratton's insistence on running for governor in 1960" (Kenney, *Political Passage*, 178). One observer believed that Charles Carpentier could have successfully challenged Stratton in the Republican primary and then won the general election. With Carpentier as the GOP gubernatorial candidate, Nixon would very likely have carried Illinois. A biographer of Paul Douglas refers to Witwer as "a nondescript attorney from Chicago with almost no political experience and less name recognition" (see Biles, *Crusading Liberal*, 149). Douglas said he spent more time in 1960 campaigning for Kennedy than for himself.

53. On the Chicago political situation in 1960, see Royko, *Boss*, 97–121; O'Connor, *Clout*, 145–62; Kallina, *Courthouse*, 21–61.

54. Illinois and Texas with their combined 51 electoral votes added to Nixon's total of 219 would have given him 270 electoral votes.

55. There were 181 Democrats in the state legislature and no Republicans. In November, Republicans mounted campaigns in just six of twenty-two congressional districts. One candidate (Bruce Alger) won, and only two others got as much as 25 percent of the vote (see Scammon, ed., *America Votes 4*, 401–2).

56. Claude Robinson to Nixon, Hall, Finch, November 10, 1960, "Variations between Our Vote Estimates and the Election," RMN PPP, Series 258, Box 1, RMNL.* There is more than one way to explain Nixon's loss in Texas. It is interesting that the thirteen South Texas counties plus Bexar County (San Antonio) that provided LBJ's margin of victory in the 1948 Senate contest were also decisive in 1960. Kennedy-Johnson carried these fourteen counties by slightly more than 51,000 votes. A less conspiratorial view is that Republican strength in the larger counties just did not hold up in 1960 for whatever reasons. In 1956, Eisenhower carried fourteen of the largest sixteen counties. In 1960, Nixon carried just six of them. Especially notable was Harris County (Houston), where Nixon suffered a net loss of more than 41,000 votes from 1956 (see Scammon, ed., *America Votes 2*, 393–97; and *America Votes 4*, 391–95).

Chapter 10. The Myths of 1960

1. The most important scholarly analysis that posited the religious explanation is Converse et al., "Stability and Change in 1960: A Reinstating Election." See also Pool et al., *Candidates, Issues, and Strategies*. For recent works that continue to accept uncritically the religious explanation, see Dallek, *Unfinished Life*, 296;

Reichard, *Politics as Usual*, 177; and Donaldson, *First Modern Campaign*, 156–57. Dallek and Reichard rely on Converse et al., while Donaldson cites Pool et al. Carty, *A Catholic in the White House?* cites both Converse et al. and Pool et al. W. J. Rorabaugh departs from this conventional wisdom (see Rorabaugh, *Real Making of the President*, 181–82).

2. Sorensen, *Kennedy Legacy*, 66; R. Martin, *Seeds of Destruction*, 275. A 20 million vote margin would have translated into approximately 44.5 million for JFK with 64.5 percent of the popular vote and 24.5 million for Nixon. It would have been the biggest victory in American history. Popular vote totals for presidential elections are available back to 1828. The highest recorded percentage is LBJ's 61.1 percent in 1964. The biggest margin was Nixon's 18 million advantage over George McGovern in 1972.

3. Lou Harris, "A Brief Analysis of the 1960 Presidential Election," RSP, Box 1, JFKL; "A Study of the Presidential Election in Kansas," October 13, 1960, JFKL.

4. DiSalle, *Second Choice*, 213–15; Edmund S. Muskie OHI, January 4, 1966, JFKL, pp. 29–30.

5. Converse et al., "Stability and Change in 1960," 273. The SRC data for its voter surveys are available at the University of Michigan. See also Campbell et al., *Survey Research Center 1960 American National Election Study* (SRC Study 440—ICPR Study 7216).

6. Converse et al., "Stability and Change in 1960," 274.

7. See Dallek, *Unfinished Life*, 296. A second study appeared three years later, in 1964, and reached similar conclusions. The second analysis came from the Simulactics group that had worked for John F. Kennedy in 1960. Its examination decided that John F. Kennedy would have received an additional 1.5 million votes without the presence of the religious issue, although JFK's Catholicism may have helped the Democratic nominee in the Electoral College because of the concentration of Catholic votes in large northeastern and midwestern states with big numbers of electoral votes (see Pool et al., *Candidates, Issues, and Strategies*). Donaldson, *First Modern Campaign*, 156–57, cites Pool as the basis for his conclusion that Kennedy lost votes because of his religion.

8. Obviously, Democratic candidates failed to achieve that level in 1952, 1956, 1968, 1972, 1976, 1980, 1984, and 1988 as well as 1960. It can be argued that Bill Clinton did attain it in 1992 and 1996, when his proportion of the total popular was below 50 percent because of the presence of a strong third-party candidate (Ross Perot). In 1992 and 1996, Clinton did achieve more than 52 percent of the two-party vote, as did Harry Truman in 1948. It is questionable, though, how valid the two-party vote figure is in an election like 1992 or 1996 or 1948. When a candidate receives less than 50 percent of the popular vote and still wins, the candidate is a minority president, like it or not. Of Democratic presidential candidates from FDR through Bill Clinton, only Lyndon Johnson in 1964 and Jimmy Carter in 1976 managed to obtain more than 50 percent of the vote. Ironically, if Democratic presidential candidates had difficulty reaching the 53 percent plateau after

1945, Republicans did it more easily. Five times between 1945 and 1996, the GOP candidate achieved or exceeded this level—in 1952, 1956, 1972, 1984, and 1988.

9. There is disagreement over the Catholic vote. According to Gallup, Eisenhower won 44 percent of the Catholic vote in 1952 and 49 percent in 1956, but Nixon won just 22 percent in 1960. Gallup reported that 62 percent of Catholics who voted Republican in 1956 voted Democratic in 1960 (see RNC Research Division, "The 1960 Elections," p. 11, DDE Presidential Papers, AWF, Campaign Series, Box 4, 1960 Elections, DDEL; see also Gallup, ed., *Gallup Poll*, 3:1692–94). Other estimates put Nixon's share of the Catholic vote under 20 percent (see Lopatto, *Religion and the Presidential Election*, 53–61, 80–93; and Kellstedt and Noll, "Religion, Voting for President, and Party Identification, 1948–1964," 360–63). Lopatto, and Kellstedt and Noll suggest that the nomination of Kennedy helped stop the movement of Catholic voters to vote Republican in presidential elections.

10. Recent biographers of Nixon tend to provide a partial endorsement for the proposition that he lost the election because of voting irregularities (see Ambrose, *Nixon*, 606, 608; and Black, *Richard Nixon*, 420). Rosen, *Strong Man*, 32, says Nixon loss was "very likely the result of voter fraud in swing states." Reichard, *Politics as Usual*, 177, is equivocal. Donaldson, *First Modern Campaign*, 150–51, 184–85, is still more doubtful.

11. Caro, *Master of the Senate*, 115–16. For the complete story of 1948, see Caro, *Means of Ascent*, 303–402. For a more favorable view of LBJ and 1948, see Dallek, *Lone Star Rising*, 298–348.

12. Pat Hillings to RMN, December 21, 1960, RMN PPP, GC, Box 341, RMNL*; The Reminiscences of Robert Finch, June 19, 1967, pp. 66–67, in the Oral History Collection of Columbia University. For other expressions of Republican belief in a stolen election, see Ed Derwinski to RMN, May 22, 1961, RMN PPP, GC, Box 212, RMNL*; James Scott Kemper to DDE, December 2, 1960, DDE Presidential Papers, White House Central Files, Office File, Box 698, Elections & Voting (Folder 5), DDEL; Price, *With Nixon*, 38–41; Les Arends to RMN, November 16, 1960, RMN PPP, GC, Box 49, RMNL.*

13. White, *Breach of Faith*, 70–71; Bradlee, *Conversations with Kennedy*, 33; Bradlee, *Good Life*, 213. Democrats and their apologists like to claim either that there was no vote fraud (Lawrence O'Brien), or that Republicans stole just as many or more votes in Illinois than they did (see O'Brien, *No Final Victories*, 96–97; Sorensen, *Counselor*, 195; Ciconne, *Daley*, 11; Sullivan, *Legend*, 122). Sullivan was later press secretary to Mayor Daley. Bradlee's claim that an unnamed Republican looked into the situation and found that Republicans had stolen as many votes downstate as Democrats had in Chicago is not credible. To my knowledge, no one has produced a single documented example of Republican vote fraud in Illinois in 1960.

There is no agreement, nor is there likely to be, as to exactly what took place in Chicago on election night. For differing theories on Daley's actions and strategy, see Royko, *Boss*, 118–20; O'Connor, *Clout*, 154–62; Fetridge, *With Warm Regards*, 53–58; and E. Kennedy, *Himself*, 184–86. Fetridge was convinced an honest count would have shown Nixon carrying the state by 100,000 votes. Kennedy almost certainly would have gained votes outside of Cook County in any statewide recount, but it is well to remember that there were also corrupt Democratic downstate counties. Most prominent was St. Clair County (East St. Louis), which produced the third-highest margin of any Illinois county.

Finally, of course, there were stories that Sam Giancana and organized crime in Chicago were instrumental in Kennedy's victory in Illinois. Supposedly, Giancana supported JFK because of the entreaties of Joseph P. Kennedy and Frank Sinatra. Giancana liked to brag that he had elected JFK, but his claims are unconvincing (see Brashler, *The Don*, 195–97; and S. Hersh, *Dark Side*, 131–54; see also O'Connor, *Clout*, 158). O'Connor maintains that the two leading Chicago wards controlled by organized crime, the First and the Twenty-eighth, produced smaller than expected Democratic majorities. There is no reason to think that the influence of organized crime on the election was significant. The most recent exploration of the vote fraud issue in Chicago is Greenberg, "Was Nixon Robbed?" but it is misleading in suggesting there was little vote fraud in 1960. Democrats committed a massive amount of vote fraud in Chicago in 1960. However, most of it seemed to focus on a local race and Republicans never produced convincing evidence that it affected the outcome of the presidential contest in Illinois.

14. Merriner, *Mr. Chairman*, 83.

15. Nixon, *Six Crises*, 438–39, 445–46; Julie Nixon Eisenhower, *Pat Nixon*, 196–201; Crowley, *Nixon off the Record*, 30.

16. For Mazo's articles, see *NYHT*, December 4–7, 1960. Mazo's charges as put forward in 1968 were more extensive than those published in December 1960.

17. Mazo and Hess, *Nixon*.

18. A copy of the Special Prosecutor's Report may be found in the archives of the Chicago Historical Society. The CHS also possesses the most complete set of poll watchers' reports from the Joint Civic Committee on Elections for the election of November 8, 1960. Wexler's report largely demolished accusations lodged by the Chicago newspapers and by Earl Mazo concerning voting irregularities. In the most blatant example, the *Chicago Tribune* reported that Beatrice Murphy of 4737 S. Woodlawn was a ghost voter because her address was a vacant lot. The special prosecutor's staff was able to show that Ms. Murphy was no ghost, but a legal voter who lived at 4734 S. Woodlawn. A mistake in the address led to a hasty conclusion that was untrue.

Wexler also eroded the credibility of Earl Mazo, his reports, and his sources. Based on the SPR and city voting records, it is possible to check seven claims made by Mazo in his December 6, 1960, article in the *New York Herald Tribune*. What the examination revealed was that in six of the seven cases, Mazo was mistaken. For example, in the Fourth Ward, Thirty-first Precinct (4/31), Mazo reported that a deceased individual and someone who had moved out of the precinct had cast ballots. The SPR showed these two persons to be husband and wife, who had been alive and well at their listed address for three years. In 27/26 and 27/27, Mazo alleged overcasts (that is, more votes cast than applications to vote). The record of the official returns in the Chicago Municipal Reference Library for 27/26 showed 283 applications to vote with 265 as the highest total vote in any race. In 27/27, applications to vote came to 407, and the highest vote was 393. In retrospect, it appears that Mazo's problems seemed to rest with his sources. His information came primarily from the Committee on Honest Elections. This group was highly partisan and unreliable. Unfortunately for Earl Mazo, he became a victim of his sources.

For the ambiguities inherent in vote fraud allegations, see the classic case of 2/50 and the analysis of Ernest Tucker and Norman Glubok, "50th of the 2d—Fraud amid the Rubble?" *CA*, December 4, 1960. See also Kallina, *Courthouse*, 112–13, 186–87; Kallina, "Was Nixon Cheated in 1960?" 138–40.

19. Kallina, *Courthouse*, 138–44; *CT*, December 15, 1960.

20. White, *In Search of History*, 454.

21. Ibid., 453–55, 461, 462; White, *Making of the President*, 21, 52, 157, 323, 324; Hoffman, *Theodore H. White*, 107–15.

22. White believed Nixon had "all the magnetism of a boiled turkey" (see Hoffman, *Theodore H. White*, 142). It should be noted that White's opinion of Nixon improved in *The Making of the President 1968* and *The Making of the President 1972*.

23. White, *In Search of History*, 524–25. According to White, Jacqueline Kennedy thought that "Camelot, heroes, fairy tales, legends, were what history was all about."

Sources

This book is based on research in the archives of the John F. Kennedy Library (Boston, Massachusetts), the Dwight D. Eisenhower Library (Abilene, Kansas), the Lyndon B. Johnson Library (Austin, Texas), and the Richard M. Nixon Library (Yorba Linda, California). Until recently, the great majority of Nixon's papers for the prepresidential period were located at the National Archives and Records Administration site in Laguna Niguel, California. These have been transferred to the Richard M. Nixon Library in Yorba Linda, where I saw most of the Nixon Pre-Presidential Papers. In the notes, I have identified with an asterisk all Nixon papers viewed at Laguna Niguel but now at Yorba Linda. My research at these presidential libraries concentrated on 1959–60, although in the case of the Eisenhower and Nixon Libraries, there were valuable materials that dated to 1961–62.

I also looked at the following newspapers for all or part of 1960: *Capital Times* (Madison, Wisconsin), *Chicago Daily News, Chicago Defender, Chicago Sun-Times, Chicago Tribune, Chicago's American, Los Angeles Times, Milwaukee Journal, New York Daily News, New York Herald Tribune, New York Post, New York Times,* and *Washington Post.*

In addition to the archives in the presidential libraries and the newspapers, I made use of the following material:

Articles, Theses, and Dissertations

Converse, Philip E., Angus Campbell, Warren E. Miller, and Donald E. Stokes. "Stability and Change in 1960: A Reinstating Election." *American Political Science Review* 55, no. 2 (June 1961): 269–80.

Gaines, Brian J. "Popular Myths about Popular Vote–Electoral College Splits." *PS: Political Science and Politics* 34, no. 1 (March 2001): 70–75.

Gifford, Laura Jane. "'Dixie Is No Longer in the Bag': South Carolina and the Election of 1960." *Journal of Policy History* 19, no. 2 (Spring 2007): 207–33.

Greenberg, David. "Was Nixon Robbed? The Legend of the Stolen 1960 Presidential Election." *Slate,* October 16, 2000.

Hersh, Seymour. "May and Zelikow Confidential." *Diplomatic History* 22, no. 4 (Fall 1998): 654–61.

Kallina, Edmund F., Jr. "Was the 1960 Presidential Election Stolen? The Case of Illinois." *Presidential Studies Quarterly* 15 (Winter 1985): 113–18.

————. "Was Nixon Cheated in 1960? Tracing the Vote Fraud Legend." *Journalism Quarterly* 62, no. 1 (Spring 1985): 138–40.

Kellstedt, Lyman, and Mark Noll. "Religion, Voting for President, and Party Identification, 1948–1964," in Noll, ed., *Religion and American Politics: From the Colonial Period to the 1980s.* New York: Oxford University Press, 1990.

Kemper, Diane A. "John F. Kennedy before the Greater Houston Ministerial Association, September 12, 1960: The Religious Issue." Ph.D. diss., Michigan State University, 1968.

Kuhn, Clifford M. "'There's a Footnote to History!': Memory and the History of Martin Luther King's October 1960 Arrest and Its Aftermath." *Journal of American History* 84, no. 2 (September 1997): 583–95.

Land, Guy Paul. "John F. Kennedy's Southern Strategy, 1956–1960." *North Carolina Historical Review* 56, no. 1 (January 1979): 41–63.

————. "Mississippi Republicanism and the 1960 Presidential Election." *Journal of Mississippi History* 40, no. 1 (February 1978): 33–48.

May, Ernest R., and Philip D. Zelikow. "Camelot Confidential." *Diplomatic History* 22, no. 4 (Fall 1998): 642–53.

Melton, Thomas R. "The 1960 Presidential Election in Georgia." Ph.D. diss., University of Mississippi, 1985.

Meriwether, James H. "'Worth a Lot of Negro Votes': Black Voters, Africa, and the 1960 Presidential Campaign." *Journal of American History* 95, no. 3 (December 2008): 737–63.

Novotny, Patrick. "John F. Kennedy, the 1960 Election and Georgia's Unpledged Electors in the Electoral College." *Georgia Historical Quarterly* 88, no. 3 (Fall 2004): 375–97.

Powell, James G. "An Analytical and Comparative Study of the Persuasion of Kennedy and Nixon in the 1960 Campaign." Ph.D. diss., University of Wisconsin, 1963.

Schlesinger, Arthur M., Jr. "Our Presidents: A Ranking by Seventy-Five Historians." *New York Times Magazine*, July 29, 1962.

Sidey, Hugh. "The President's Voracious Reading Habits." *Life*, March 17, 1961, 55–56, 59–60.

Silvestri, Vito N. "John F. Kennedy: His Speaking in the Wisconsin and West Virginia Primaries of 1960." Ph.D. diss., Indiana University, 1966.

Smith, Philip. "The Fifty-Million Dollar Man." *Fortune*, November 1957, 176–80, 226–38.

Sweeney, James R. "Whispers in the Golden Silence: Harry F. Byrd, Sr., John F. Kennedy, and Virginia Democrats in the 1960 Presidential Election." *Virginia Magazine of History and Biography* 99, no. 1 (January 1991): 3–44.

Traffas, Joan. "The 'Viva Kennedy' Clubs in South Texas." Master's thesis, North Texas State University, 1972.

White, Theodore H. "For President Kennedy an Epilogue." *Life*, December 6, 1963, 158–59.

Books and Other Secondary Materials

Aitken, Jonathan. *Nixon: A Life*. Washington, D.C.: Regnery, 1993.

Alexander, Charles C. *Holding the Line: The Eisenhower Era, 1952–1961*. Bloomington: Indiana University Press, 1975.

Allen, Maury. *Jackie Robinson: A Life Remembered*. New York: Franklin Watts, 1987.

Alsop, Joseph P. *I've Seen the Best of It*. With Adam Platt. New York: Norton, 1992.

Alsop, Stewart. *Nixon & Rockefeller: A Double Portrait*. Garden City: Doubleday, 1960.

Ambrose, Stephen. *Eisenhower: The President*. New York: Simon and Schuster, 1984.

———. *Ike's Spies: Eisenhower and the Espionage Establishment*. With Richard H. Immerman. Jackson: University Press of Mississippi, 1999.

———. *Nixon: The Triumph of a Politician, 1962–1972*. New York: Simon and Schuster, 1989.

Anderson, Jack. *Peace, War, and Politics: An Eyewitness Account*. With Daryl Gibson. New York: Tom Doherty Associates, 1999.

Attwood, William. *The Reds and the Blacks: A Personal Adventure*. New York: Harper and Row, 1967.

Baker, Bobby. *Wheeling and Dealing: Confessions of a Capitol Hill Operator*. New York: Norton, 1978.

Balmer, Randall. *God in the White House, a History: How Faith Shaped the Presidency from John F. Kennedy to George W. Bush*. New York: HarperCollins, 2008.

Barnouw, Erik. *A History of Broadcasting in the United States: The Image Empire*. New York: Oxford University Press, 1970.

Barrett, David M. *The CIA and Congress: The Untold Story from Truman to Kennedy*. Lawrence: University Press of Kansas, 2003.

Baughman, James L. *Same Time, Same Station: Creating American Television, 1948–1961*. Baltimore: Johns Hopkins University Press, 2007.

Beito, David, and Linda Royster Beito. *Black Maverick: T.R.M. Howard's Fight for Civil Rights and Economic Power*. Urbana: University of Illinois Press, 2009.

Bergquist, Laura, and Stanley Tetrick. *A Very Special President*. New York: McGraw-Hill, 1965.

Beschloss, Michael. *The Crisis Years: Kennedy and Khrushchev, 1960–1963*. New York: Edward Burlingame Books, 1991.

———. *Kennedy and Roosevelt: The Uneasy Alliance*. New York: Norton, 1980.

———. *MAYDAY: Eisenhower, Khrushchev and the U-2 Affair*. New York: Harper and Row, 1986.

Biles, Roger. *Crusading Liberal: Paul H. Douglas of Illinois*. DeKalb: Northern Illinois University Press, 2002.

———. *Richard J. Daley: Politics, Race, and the Governing of Chicago*. DeKalb: Northern Illinois University Press, 1995.

Bill, James A. *George Ball: Behind the Scenes in U.S. Foreign Policy*. New Haven: Yale University Press, 1997.

Bissell, Richard M., Jr. *Reflections of a Cold Warrior: From Yalta to the Bay of Pigs*. With Jonathan E. Lewis and Frances T. Pudlo. New Haven: Yale University Press, 1996.

Black, Conrad. *Richard M. Nixon: A Life in Full*. New York: Public Affairs, 2007.

Blair, Joan, and Clay Blair Jr. *The Search for JFK*. New York: Berkeley, 1976.

The Book of the States, 1960–1961. Chicago: Council of State Governments, 1960.

Bottome, Edgar M. *The Missile Gap: A Study of the Formulation of Military and Political Policy*. Rutherford, N.J.: Fairleigh Dickinson Press, 1971.

Bowles, Chester. *Promises to Keep: My Years in Public Life, 1941–1969*. New York: Harper and Row, 1971.

Bradlee, Benjamin. *Conversations with Kennedy*. New York: Norton, 1975.

———. *A Good Life: Newspapering and Other Adventures*. New York: Simon and Schuster, 1995.

Branch, Taylor. *Parting the Waters: America in the King Years, 1954–1963*. New York: Simon and Schuster, 1988.

Brashler, William. *The Don: The Life and Death of Sam Giancana*. New York: Harper and Row, 1977.

Brauer, Carl M. *John F. Kennedy and the Second Reconstruction*. New York: Columbia University Press, 1977.

———. *Presidential Transitions: Eisenhower through Reagan*. New York: Oxford University Press, 1986.

Brinkley, David. *Brinkley's Beat: People, Places and Events That Shaped My Time*. New York: Knopf, 2003.

———. *David Brinkley: 11 Presidents, 4 Wars, 22 Political Conventions, 1 Moon Landing, 3 Assassinations, 2,000 Weeks of News and Other Stuff on Television and 18 Years of Growing Up in North Carolina*. New York: Knopf, 1995.

Brodie, Fawn M. *Richard Nixon: The Shaping of His Character*. New York: Norton, 1981.

Brownell, Herbert. *Advising Ike: The Memoirs of Attorney General Herbert Brownell*. With John P. Burke. Lawrence: University Press of Kansas, 1993.

Bruno, Jerry, and Jeff Greenfield. *The Advance Man*. New York: William Morrow, 1971.

Bryant, Nick. *The Bystander: John F. Kennedy and the Struggle for Black Equality*. New York: Basic Books, 2006.

Bunzel, John H., and Eugene C. Lee. *The California Democratic Delegation of 1960*. The Inter-University Case Program, #67. University of Alabama, 1962.

Burleigh, Nina. *A Very Private Woman: The Life and Unsolved Murder of Presidential Mistress Mary Meyer*. New York: Bantam Books, 1998.

Burner, David. *John F. Kennedy and a New Generation*. Glenview, Ill.: Scott Foresman, 1988.

Burns, James MacGregor. *John Kennedy: A Political Profile*. New York: Harcourt, Brace, Jovanovich, 1960.

———. *Running Alone: Presidential Leadership from JFK to Bush II: Why It Has Failed and How We Can Fix It*. New York: Basic Books, 2006.

Campbell, Tracy. *Deliver the Vote: A History of Election Fraud, an American Political Tradition, 1742–2004*. New York: Carroll and Graf, 2005.

Caro, Robert A. *The Years of Lyndon Johnson: Master of the Senate*. New York: Knopf, 2002.

———. *The Years of Lyndon Johnson: Means of Ascent*. New York: Knopf, 1990.

Carson, Clayborne, ed. *The Papers of Martin Luther King, Jr.* Vols. 4 and 5. Berkeley and Los Angeles: University of California Press, 2000, 2005.

Carty, Thomas J. *A Catholic in the White House?: Religion, Politics, and John F. Kennedy's Presidential Campaign*. New York: Palgrave Macmillan, 2004.

Casey, Shaun A. *The Making of a Catholic President: Kennedy vs. Nixon 1960*. New York: Oxford University Press, 2009.

Chafin, Raymond, and Topper Sherwood. *Just Good Politics: The Life of Raymond Chafin, Appalachian Boss*. Pittsburgh: University of Pittsburgh Press, 1994.

Childs, Marquis. *Eisenhower: Captive Hero: A Critical Study of the General and the President*. New York: Harcourt Brace, 1958.

———. *Witness to Power*. New York: McGraw-Hill, 1975.

Ciccone, F. Richard. *Daley: Power and Presidential Politics*. Chicago: Contemporary Books, 1996.

Clifford, Clark. *Counsel to the President: A Memoir*. With Richard Holbrooke. New York: Random House, 1991.

Clowse, Barbara Barksdale. *Ralph McGill: A Biography*. Macon, Ga.: Mercer University Press, 1998.

Cohen, Adam, and Elizabeth Taylor. *American Pharaoh, Mayor Richard J. Daley: His Battle for Chicago and the Nation*. Boston: Little, Brown, 2000.

Collier, Peter, and David Horowitz. *The Kennedys: An American Drama*. New York: Summit Books, 1984.

———. *The Rockefellers: An American Dynasty*. New York: Holt, Rinehart and Winston, 1976.

Colson, Charles. *Born Again*. Old Tappan, N.J.: Chosen Books, 1976.

Critchlow, Donald T. *The Conservative Ascendancy: How the GOP Right Made History*. Cambridge: Harvard University Press, 2007.

Cronkite, Walter. *A Reporter's Life*. New York: Knopf, 1996.

Crowley, Monica. *Nixon in Winter*. New York: Random House, 1998.

———. *Nixon off the Record*. New York: Random House, 1996.

Dallek, Robert. *Lone Star Rising: Lyndon Johnson and His Times, 1908–1960*. New York: Oxford University Press, 1991.

———. *An Unfinished Life: John F. Kennedy, 1917–1963*. Boston: Little, Brown, 2003.

David, Paul T., ed. *The Presidential Election and Transition, 1960–1961*. Washington: Brookings Institution, 1961.

DeLoach, Cartha. *Hoover's FBI: The Inside Story by Hoover's Trusted Lieutenant*. Washington: Regnery, 1995.

deToledano, Ralph. *One Man Alone: Richard Nixon*. New York: Funk and Wagnalls, 1969.

Dickerson, Nancy. *Among Those Present: A Reporter's Twenty-Five Years in Washington*. New York: Random House, 1976.

DiSalle, Michael V. *Second Choice*. New York: Hawthorn Books, 1966.

Divine, Robert. *The Sputnik Challenge: Eisenhower's Response to the Soviet Satellite*. New York: Oxford University Press, 1993.

Dobbs, Ricky F. *Yellow Dogs and Republicans: Allan Shivers and Texas Two-Party Politics*. College Station: Texas A&M University Press, 2005.

Donaldson, Gary A. *The First Modern Campaign: Kennedy, Nixon, and the Election of 1960*. Lanham, Md.: Rowman and Littlefield, 2007.

———. *Truman Defeats Dewey*. Lexington: University Press of Kentucky, 1999.

Donovan, Robert J. *Confidential Secretary: Ann Whitman's 20 Years with Eisenhower and Rockefeller*. New York: Dutton, 1988.

Douglas, Paul H. *In the Fullness of Time: The Memoirs of Paul H. Douglas*. New York: Harcourt Brace Jovanovich, 1971.

Dulaney, H. G., and Edward Hake Phillips, eds. *Speak, Mister Speaker*. Bonham, Tex.: Sam Rayburn Foundation, 1978.

Edgerton, Gary R. *The Columbia History of American Television*. New York: Columbia University Press, 2007.

Ehrlichman, John. *Witness to Power: The Nixon Years*. New York: Simon and Schuster, 1982.

Eisenhower, Dwight D. *The White House Years: Waging Peace, 1956–1961*. Garden City: Doubleday, 1965.

Eisenhower, Julie Nixon. *Pat Nixon: The Untold Story*. New York: Simon and Schuster, 1986.

Eisenhower, Milton. *The President Is Calling*. Garden City: Doubleday, 1974.

Eisenhower, Susan. *Mrs. Ike: Memories and Reflections on the Life of Mamie Eisenhower*. New York: Farrar, Straus and Giroux, 1996.

Erie, Steven P. *Rainbow's End: Irish-Americans and the Dilemmas of Urban Machine Politics, 1840–1985*. Berkeley and Los Angeles: University of California Press, 1988.

Evans, Rowland, and Robert Novak. *Lyndon B. Johnson: The Exercise of Power*. New York: New American Library, 1966.

———. *Nixon in the White House: The Frustration of Power*. New York: Random House, 1971.

Ewald, William H. *Eisenhower the President: Crucial Days, 1951–1960*. Englewood Cliffs, N.J.: Prentice Hall, 1981.

Exner, Judith. *My Story*. New York: Grove Press, 1977.

Falkner, David. *Great Time Coming: The Life of Jackie Robinson, from Baseball to Birmingham*. New York: Simon and Schuster, 1995.

Fay, Paul B., Jr. *The Pleasure of His Company*. New York: Harper and Row, 1966.

Ferrell, Robert H. *Ill-Advised: Presidential Health and Public Trust*. Columbia: University of Missouri Press, 1992.

Fetridge, William Harrison. *With Warm Regards: A Reminiscence.* Chicago: Dartnell, 1976.

Fite, Gilbert C. *Richard B. Russell, Jr., Senator from Georgia.* Chapel Hill: University of North Carolina Press, 1991.

Fleming, Dan B., Jr. *Kennedy vs. Humphrey, West Virginia, 1960: The Pivotal Battle for the Democratic Presidential Nomination.* Jefferson, N.C.: McFarland, 1992.

Fontenay, Charles. *Estes Kefauver: A Biography.* Knoxville: University of Tennessee Press, 1980.

Frank, Reuven. *Into Thin Air: The Brief, Wonderful Life of Network News.* New York: Simon and Schuster, 1991.

Freedom of Communication: Final Report of the Committee on Commerce, United States Senate. Pt. 1, *The Speeches, Remarks, Press Conferences, and Study Papers of John F. Kennedy, August 1 through November 7, 1960.*

————. Pt. 2, *The Speeches, Remarks, Press Conferences, and Study Papers of Richard M. Nixon, August 1 through November 7, 1960.*

Friedman, Leon, and William F. Levantrosser, eds. *Richard M. Nixon: Politician, President, Administrator.* Westport, Conn.: Greenwood, 1991.

Fursenko, Aleksandr, and Timothy Naftali. *Khrushchev's Cold War: The Inside Story of an American Adversary.* New York: Norton, 2006.

————. *"One Hell of a Gamble": Khrushchev, Castro, and Kennedy, 1958–1964.* New York: Norton, 1997.

Gabler, Neal. *Winchell: Gossip, Power, and the Culture of Celebrity.* New York: Knopf, 1994.

Gaddis, John Lewis. *We Now Know: Rethinking Cold War History.* New York: Oxford University Press, 1997.

Galambos, Louis, and Daun Van Ee, eds. *The Papers of Dwight D. Eisenhower.* Vol. 21. Baltimore: Johns Hopkins University Press, 2001.

Galbraith, John Kenneth. *Ambassador's Journal: A Personal Account of the Kennedy Years.* Boston: Houghton Mifflin, 1969.

————. *Letters to Kennedy.* Edited by James Goodman. Cambridge: Harvard University Press, 1998.

————. *A Life in Our Times: A Memoir.* Boston: Houghton Mifflin, 1981.

Gallup, George, ed. *The Gallup Poll: Public Opinion, 1935–1971.* 3 vols. New York: Random House, 1972.

Garment, Leonard. *Crazy Rhythm: My Journey from Brooklyn, Jazz and Wall Street to Nixon's White House, Watergate, and Beyond.* New York: Random House, 1997.

Garrow, David J. *Bearing the Cross: Martin Luther King, Jr. and the Southern Christian Leadership Conference.* New York: Random House, 1986.

Gellman, Irwin. *The Contender Richard Nixon: The Congress Years, 1946–1952.* New York: Free Press, 1999.

Gentry, Curt. *J. Edgar Hoover: The Man and the Secrets.* New York: Norton, 1991.

George, Carol V. R. *God's Salesman: Norman Vincent Peale & the Power of Positive Thinking.* New York: Oxford University Press, 1993.

Gifford, Laura Jane. *The Center Cannot Hold: The 1960 Presidential Election and the Rise of Modern Conservatism*. DeKalb: Northern Illinois University Press, 2009.

Giglio, James N. *The Presidency of John F. Kennedy*. Lawrence: University of Kansas Press, 1991.

Gilbert Robert E. *The Mortal Presidency: Illness and Anguish in the White House*. New York: Basic Books, 1992.

Goldwater, Barry M. *With No Apologies: The Personal and Political Memoirs of United States Senator Barry M. Goldwater*. New York: Morrow, 1979.

Goodwin, Doris Kearns. *The Fitzgeralds and the Kennedys*. New York: Simon and Schuster, 1987.

Goodwin, Richard N. *Remembering America: A Voice from the Sixties*. Boston: Little, Brown, 1988.

Gorman, Joseph Bruce. *Kefauver: A Political Biography*. New York: Oxford University Press, 1971.

Graham, Billy. *Just as I Am: The Autobiography of Billy Graham*. New York: Harper-Collins, 1997.

Graham, Katherine. *Personal History*. New York: Knopf, 1997.

Greenberg, David. *Nixon's Shadow: The History of an Image*. New York: Norton, 2003.

Greenstein, Fred. *The Hidden-Hand Presidency: Eisenhower as Leader*. New York: Basic Books, 1982.

Grimshaw, William J. *Bitter Fruit: Black Politics and the Chicago Machine, 1931–1991*. Chicago: University of Chicago Press, 1992.

Grose, Peter. *Gentleman Spy: The Life of Allen Dulles*. New York: Houghton Mifflin, 1994.

Guide to U.S. Elections. 5th ed. Washington: Congressional Quarterly Press, 2005.

Gullan, Howard I. *The Upset That Wasn't: Harry S Truman and the Crucial Election of 1948*. Chicago: Ivan R. Dee, 1998.

Guthman, Edwin O., and Jeffrey Shulman. *Robert Kennedy in His Own Words: The Unpublished Recollections of the Kennedy Years*. New York: Bantam Books, 1988.

Hack, Richard. *Hughes: The Private Diaries, Memos and Letters*. Beverly Hills: New Millennium Press, 2001.

Halberstam, David. *The Fifties*. New York: Villard Books, 1993.

Haldeman, H. R. *The Ends of Power*. With Joseph Dimona. New York: New York Times Books, 1978.

Hamby, Alonzo. *Liberalism and Its Challengers: FDR to Reagan*. New York: Oxford University Press, 1985.

———. *Man of the People: A Life of Harry S. Truman*. New York: Oxford University Press, 1995.

Hamilton, Charles. *Adam Clayton Powell, Jr.: The Political Biography of an American Dilemma*. New York: Atheneum, 1991.

Hamilton, Nigel. *JFK: Reckless Youth*. New York: Random House, 1992.

Hardeman, D. B., and Donald C. Bacon. *Rayburn: A Biography*. Austin: Texas Monthly Press, 1987.

Heinemann, Ronald L. *Harry Byrd of Virginia*. Charlottesville: University Press of Virginia, 1996.

Helgerson, John L. *Getting to Know the President: CIA Briefings of Presidential Candidates, 1952–1992*. Washington: Center for the Study of Intelligence, CIA, 1996.

Henderson, Harold P. *Ernest Vandiver: Governor of Georgia*. Athens: University of Georgia Press, 2000.

Herken, Gregg. *Counsels of War*. New York: Knopf, 1985.

Hersh, Burton. *Bobby and J. Edgar: The Historic Faceoff between the Kennedys and J. Edgar Hoover That Transformed America*. New York: Carroll and Graf, 2007.

Hersh, Seymour. *The Dark Side of Camelot*. Boston: Little, Brown, 1997.

Hewitt, Don. *Tell Me a Story: Fifty Years and 60 Minutes in Television*. New York: Public Affairs, 2001.

Heymann, C. David. *RFK: A Candid Biography of Robert F. Kennedy*. New York: Dutton, 1998.

Hilty, James W. *Robert Kennedy: Brother Protector*. Philadelphia: Temple University Press, 1997.

Hoffman, Joyce. *Theodore H. White and Journalism as Illusion*. Columbia: University of Missouri Press, 1995.

Humes, James C. *Confessions of a White House Ghostwriter*. Washington: Regnery, 1997.

Humphrey, Hubert H. *The Education of a Public Man: My Life in Politics*. Garden City: Doubleday, 1976.

Jamieson, Kathleen Hall. *Packaging the Presidency: A History and Criticism of Presidential Campaign Advertising*. 3rd ed. New York: Oxford University Press, 1996.

Johnson, Walter, ed. *The Papers of Adlai Stevenson*. Vol. 7. Boston: Little, Brown, 1977.

Jones, Howard. *The Bay of Pigs*. New York: Oxford University Press, 2008.

Jumonville, Neil. *Henry Steele Commager: Midcentury Liberalism and the History of the Present*. Chapel Hill: University of North Carolina Press, 1999.

Kaiser, David. *American Tragedy: Kennedy, Johnson, and the Origins of the Vietnam War*. Cambridge: Harvard University Press, 2000.

Kallina, Edmund F., Jr. *Courthouse over White House: Chicago and the Presidential Election of 1960*. Orlando: University of Central Florida Press, 1988.

Kaufman, Robert G. *Henry M. Jackson: A Life in Politics*. Seattle: University of Washington Press, 2000.

Kennedy, Eugene C. *Himself: The Life and Times of Mayor Richard J. Daley*. New York: Viking Press, 1978.

Kennedy, John F. *Profiles in Courage*. New York: Pocket Books, 1957.

Kenney, David. *A Political Passage: The Career of Stratton of Illinois*. Carbondale: Southern Illinois University Press, 1990.

Kessler, Ronald. *The Sins of the Father: Joseph P. Kennedy and the Dynasty He Founded*. New York: Warner Books, 1996.

Klein, Herbert G. *Making It Perfectly Clear*. Garden City: Doubleday, 1980.

Kornbluh, Peter, ed. *Bay of Pigs Declassified: The Secret CIA Report on the Invasion of Cuba*. New York: New Press, 1998.

Koskoff, David S. *Joseph P. Kennedy: A Life and Times*. Englewood Cliffs, N.J.: Prentice Hall, 1974.

Kotlowski, Dean J. *Nixon's Civil Rights: Politics, Principle, and Policy*. Cambridge: Harvard University Press, 2001.

Kraus, Sidney. *The Great Debates: Background—Perspective—Effects*. Bloomington: Indiana University Press, 1962.

Krock, Arthur. *Memoirs: Sixty Years on the Firing Line*. New York: Funk and Wagnalls, 1968.

Ladd, Everett Carll, Jr. *Transformations of the American Party System: Political Coalitions from the New Deal to the 1970s*. With Charles D. Hadley. 2nd ed. New York: Norton, 1978.

Lasby, Clarence G. *Eisenhower's Heart Attack: How Ike Beat Heart Disease and Held on to the Presidency*. Lawrence: University Press of Kansas, 1997.

Lash, Joseph P. *Eleanor: The Years Alone*. New York: Norton, 1972.

Lasky, Victor. *It Didn't Start with Watergate*. New York: Dial Press, 1977.

Lawson, Stephen F. *Black Ballots: Voting Rights in the South, 1944–1969*. New York: Columbia University Press, 1976.

Leuchtenberg, William. *In the Shadow of FDR: From Harry Truman to Ronald Reagan*. Ithaca, N.Y.: Cornell University Press, 1983.

Lodge, Henry Cabot. *The Storm Has Many Eyes: A Personal Narrative*. New York: Norton, 1973.

Long, Michael G., ed. *First Class Citizenship: The Civil Rights Letters of Jackie Robinson*. New York: Henry Holt, 2007.

Lopatto, Paul. *Religion and the Presidential Election*. New York: Praeger, 1985.

Loughry, Dr. Allen H., II. *Don't Buy Another Vote, I Won't Pay for a Landslide: The Sordid and Continuing History of Political Corruption in West Virginia*. Parsons, W.V.: McClain Printing, 2006.

Lubell, Samuel. *The Future of American Politics*. 3rd rev. ed. New York: Harper and Row, 1965.

Lungren, John C. *Healing Richard Nixon: A Doctor's Memoir*. Lexington: University Press of Kentucky, 2003.

Madonna, G. Terry. *Pivotal Pennsylvania: Presidential Politics from FDR to the Twenty-first Century*. Mansfield, Pa.: Pennsylvania Historical Association, 2008.

Maheu, Robert, and Richard Hack. *Next to Hughes: Behind the Power and Tragic Downfall of Howard Hughes by His Closest Advisor*. New York: HarperCollins, 1992.

Mahoney, Richard D. *Sons & Brothers: The Days of Jack and Bobby Kennedy*. New York: Arcade, 1999.

Manchester, William. *Controversy and Other Essays in Journalism, 1950–1975*. Boston: Little, Brown, 1976.

———. *The Death of a President*. New York: Harper and Row, 1967.

————. *The Glory and the Dream: A Narrative History of America, 1932–1972*. Boston: Little, Brown, 1974.

Manning, Christopher. *William L. Dawson and the Limits of Black Electoral Leadership*. DeKalb: Northern Illinois University Press, 2009.

Marlin, George. *The American Catholic Voter: 200 Years of Political Impact*. South Bend: St. Augustine's Press, 2004.

Martin, John Bartlow. *Adlai Stevenson and the World*. Garden City: Doubleday, 1977.

————. *Adlai Stevenson of Illinois*. Garden City: Doubleday, 1976.

Martin, Ralph G. *Ballots and Bandwagons*. Chicago: Rand McNally, 1964.

————. *Seeds of Destruction: Joe Kennedy and His Sons*. New York: G. P. Putnam's Sons, 1995.

Martin, William. *A Prophet with Honor: The Billy Graham Story*. New York: William Morrow, 1991.

Matthews, Christopher. *Kennedy & Nixon: The Rivalry That Shaped Postwar America*. New York: Simon and Schuster, 1996.

Mazo, Earl, and Stephen Hess. *Richard Nixon: A Political Portrait*. New York: Popular Library, 1968.

McCarthy, Eugene. *Up 'Til Now: A Memoir*. New York: Harcourt, Brace, Jovanovich, 1987.

McCullough, David. *Truman*. New York: Simon and Schuster, 1992.

McDougal, Dennis. *Privileged Son: Otis Chandler and the Rise and Fall of the L.A. Times Dynasty*. New York: Perseus, 2001.

McDougall, Walter A. *The Heavens and the Earth: A Political History of the Space Age*. New York: Basic Books, 1985.

McFarland, Linda. *Cold War Strategist: Stuart Symington and the Search for National Security*. Westport, Conn.: Praeger, 2001.

McKeever, Porter. *Adlai Stevenson: His Life and Legacy*. New York: William Morrow, 1989.

McLendon, Sarah. *My Eight Presidents*. New York: Wyden Books, 1978.

McPherson, Harry. *A Political Education: A Washington Memoir*. Austin: University of Texas Press, 1995.

Merriner, James L. *Mr. Chairman: Power in Dan Rostenkowski's America*. Carbondale: Southern Illinois University Press, 1999.

Merry, Robert W. *Taking on the World: Joseph and Stewart Alsop—Guardians of the American Century*. New York: Viking Press, 1996.

Metz, Robert. *CBS: Reflections in a Bloodshot Eye*. Chicago: Playboy Press, 1975.

Miller, Steven P. *Billy Graham and the Rise of the Republican South*. Philadelphia: University of Pennsylvania Press, 2009.

Mitchell, Greg. *Tricky Dick and the Pink Lady: Richard Nixon vs. Helen Gahagan Douglas: Sexual Politics and the Red Scare, 1950*. New York: Random House, 1998.

Montgomery, Gayle, and James W. Johnson. *One Step from the White House: The Rise and Fall of Senator William F. Knowland*. Berkeley and Los Angeles: University of California Press, 1998.

Morgan, Anne Hodges. *Robert S. Kerr: The Senate Years*. Norman: University of Oklahoma Press, 1977.

Morgan, Iwan W. *Deficit Government: Taxing and Spending in Modern America*. Chicago: Ivan R. Dee, 1995.

———. *Eisenhower versus "The Spenders": The Eisenhower Administration, the Democrats and the Budget, 1953–1960*. New York: St. Martin's Press, 1990.

Morris, Roger. *Richard Milhous Nixon: The Rise of an American Politician*. New York: Henry Holt, 1990.

Morrow, E. Frederic. *Forty Years a Guinea Pig*. New York: Pilgrim Press, 1980.

———. *Way Down South Up North*. Philadelphia: United Church Press, 1973.

Morrow, Lance. *The Best Year of Their Lives: Kennedy, Johnson, and Nixon in 1948, Learning the Secrets of Power*. New York: Basic Books, 2005.

Neustadt, Richard E. *Presidential Power: The Politics of Leadership*. New York: Wiley, 1960.

Newman, John M. *JFK and Vietnam: Deception, Intrigue and the Struggle for Power*. New York: Warner Books, 1992.

Nichols, David A. *A Matter of Justice: Eisenhower and the Beginning of the Civil Rights Revolution*. New York: Simon and Schuster, 2007.

Nixon, Ed, and Karen Olson. *The Nixons: A Family Portrait*. Bothell, Wash.: Book Publishers Network, 2009.

Nixon, Richard M. *RN: The Memoirs of Richard Nixon*. New York: Grosset and Dunlap, 1978.

———. *Six Crises*. Garden City: Doubleday, 1962.

Noll, Mark A., ed. *Religion and American Politics: From the Colonial Period to the 1980s*. New York: Oxford University Press, 1990.

Novak, Robert D. *The Prince of Darkness: 50 Years of Reporting in Washington*. New York: Crown, Forum, 2007.

O'Brien, Lawrence F. *No Final Victories: A Life in Politics—from John F. Kennedy to Watergate*. Garden City: Doubleday, 1974.

O'Connor, Len. *Clout: Mayor Daley and His City*. Chicago: Regnery, 1975.

O'Donnell, Helen. *A Common Good: The Friendship of Robert F. Kennedy and Kenneth P. O'Donnell*. New York: William Morrow, 2008.

O'Donnell, Kenneth P. *"Johnny, We Hardly Knew Ye": Memories of John Fitzgerald Kennedy*. With David F. Powers and Joe McCarthy. Boston: Little, Brown, 1972.

Olson, James C. *Stuart Symington: A Life*. Columbia: University of Missouri Press, 2003.

O'Neill, Tip. *Man of the House: The Life and Political Memoirs of Tip O'Neill*. With William Novak. New York: Random House, 1987.

Parmet, Herbert S. *Eisenhower and the American Crusades*. New York: Macmillan, 1972.

———. *Jack: The Struggles of John F. Kennedy*. New York: Dial Press, 1980.

———. *JFK: The Presidency of John F. Kennedy*. New York: Dial Press, 1983.

———. *Richard Nixon and His America*. New York: Konecky and Konecky, 1990.

Peirce, Neal R. *The People's President: The Electoral College in American History and the Direct-Vote Alternative*. New York: Simon and Schuster, 1968.

Perlstein, Rick. *Before the Storm: Barry Goldwater and the Unmaking of the American Consensus*. New York: Hill and Wang, 2001.

Persico, Joseph E. *The Imperial Rockefeller: A Biography of Nelson A. Rockefeller*. New York: Simon and Schuster, 1982.

Peters, Charles. *Tilting at Windmills: An Autobiography*. Reading, Mass.: Addison-Wesley, 1988.

Phillips, Kevin P. *The Emerging Republican Majority*. New Rochelle, N.Y.: Arlington House, 1969.

Piereson, James. *Camelot and the Cultural Revolution: How the Assassination of John F. Kennedy Shattered American Liberalism*. New York: Encounter Books, 2007.

Pietrusza, David. *1960—LBJ vs. JFK vs. Nixon: The Epic Campaign That Forged Three Presidencies*. New York: Union Square Press, 2008.

Poen, Monte M. *Strictly Personal and Confidential: The Letters Harry Truman Never Mailed*. Boston: Little, Brown, 1982.

Pool, Ithiel de Sola, Robert P. Abelson, and Samuel L. Popkin, *Candidates, Issues, and Strategies: A Computer Simulation of the 1960 Presidential Election*. Cambridge: MIT Press, 1964.

Powers, Richard Gid. *Secrecy and Power: The Life of J. Edgar Hoover*. New York: Free Press, 1987.

Powers, Thomas. *Intelligence Wars: America's Secret History from Hitler to al-Qaeda*. New York: New York Review of Books, 2002.

———. *The Man Who Kept the Secrets: Richard Helms and the CIA*. New York: Knopf, 1999.

Prados, John. *The Soviet Estimate: U.S. Intelligence Analysis and Russian Military Strength*. Princeton, N.J.: Princeton University Press, 1982.

Preble, Christopher. *John F. Kennedy and the Missile Gap*. DeKalb: Northern Illinois University Press, 2004.

Price, Raymond. *With Nixon*. New York: Viking Press, 1977.

Rae, Nicol C. *The Decline and Fall of the Liberal Republicans from 1952 to the Present*. New York: Oxford University Press, 1989.

Rampersad, Arnold. *Jackie Robinson: A Biography*. New York: Knopf, 1997.

Rarick, Ethan. *California Rising: The Life and Times of Pat Brown*. Berkeley and Los Angeles: University of California Press, 2005.

Reedy, George. *Lyndon B. Johnson: A Memoir*. New York: Andrews and McMeel, 1982.

Reeves, Richard. *President Kennedy: A Profile of Power*. New York: Simon and Schuster, 1993.

———. *President Nixon: Alone in the White House*. New York: Simon and Schuster, 2001.

Reichard, Gary. *Politics as Usual: The Age of Truman and Eisenhower*. 2nd ed. Wheeling, Ill.: Harlan Davidson, 2004.

Reinsch, J. Leonard. *Getting Elected: From Radio and Roosevelt to Television and Reagan*. New York: Hippocrene Books, 1988.

Rentschler, Bill. *Goldwater: A Tribute to a Twentieth-Century Political Icon*. Chicago: Contemporary Books, 2000.

Reston, James. *Deadline: A Memoir*. New York: Random House, 1991.

Richelson, Jeffrey. *The Wizards of Langley: Inside the CIA's Directorate of Science and Technology*. Cambridge, Mass.: Westview Press, 2001.

Ritchie, Donald A. *Reporting from Washington: The History of the Washington Press Corps*. New York: Oxford University Press, 2005.

Roberts, Chalmers M. *First Rough Draft: A Journalist's Journal of Our Times*. New York: Praeger, 1973.

Robinson, Jackie, as told to Alfred Duckett. *I Never Had It Made: An Autobiography*. Hopewell, N.J.: Ecco Press, 1995.

Roemer, William F., Jr. *Roemer: Man Against the Mob*. New York: Donald I. Fine, 1989.

Roman, Peter J. *Eisenhower and the Missile Gap*. Ithaca, N.Y.: Cornell University Press, 1995.

Rorabaugh, W. J. *The Real Making of the President: Kennedy, Nixon, and the 1960 Election*. Lawrence: University Press of Kansas, 2009.

Rosen, James. *The Strong Man: John Mitchell and the Secrets of Watergate*. New York: Doubleday, 2008.

Rossiter, Clinton. *The American Presidency*. 2nd ed. New York: Harcourt, Brace, 1960.

Rovere, Richard. *Final Reports: Personal Reflections on Politics and History in Our Time*. Garden City: Doubleday, 1984.

Royko, Mike. *Boss: Richard J. Daley of Chicago*. New York: Dutton, 1971.

Rusk, Jerrold G., ed. *A Statistical History of the American Electorate*. Washington, D.C.: Congressional Quarterly Press, 2001.

Russo, Gus. *The Outfit: The Role of Chicago's Underworld in the Shaping of Modern America*. New York: Bloomsbury, 2001.

Safire, William. *Before the Fall: An Inside View of the Pre-Watergate White House*. New York: Doubleday, 1975.

Salinger, Pierre. *P.S.: A Memoir*. New York: St. Martin's Press, 1995.

——. *With Kennedy*. Garden City: Doubleday, 1966.

Savage, Sean J. *JFK, LBJ, and the Democratic Party*. Albany: State University of New York Press, 2004.

Scammon, Richard M., ed. *America Votes: A Handbook of Contemporary Election Statistics*. Vol. 2. New York: Macmillan, 1958.

——. *America Votes—4: A Handbook of Contemporary Election Statistics*. Pittsburgh: University of Pittsburgh Press, 1962.

——. *America Votes—5: A Handbook of Contemporary Election Statistics*. Pittsburgh: University of Pittsburgh Press, 1964.

Schaffer, Howard B. *Chester Bowles: New Dealer in the Cold War*. Cambridge: Harvard University Press, 1993.

Schlesinger, Arthur M., Jr. *The Imperial Presidency*. Boston: Houghton Mifflin, 1973.

———. *Journals, 1952–2000*. New York: Penguin Press, 2007.

———. *Robert Kennedy and His Times*. Boston: Houghton Mifflin, 1978.

———. *A Thousand Days: John F. Kennedy in the White House*. Boston: Houghton Mifflin, 1965.

Schwarz, Ted. *Joseph P. Kennedy: The Mogul, the Mob, the Statesman, and the Making of an American Myth*. Hoboken, N.J.: Wiley, 2003.

Shesol, Jeff. *Mutual Contempt: Lyndon Johnson, Robert Kennedy, and the Feud That Defined a Decade*. New York: Norton, 1997.

Siciliano, Rocco C. *Walking on Sand: The Story of an Immigrant Son and the Forgotten Art of Public Service*. With Drew M. Ross. Salt Lake City: University of Utah Press, 2004.

Sidey, Hugh. *John F. Kennedy, President*. New York: Atheneum, 1963.

Slayton, Robert A. *Empire Statesman: The Rise and Redemption of Al Smith*. New York: Free Press, 2001.

Sloan, John W. *Eisenhower and the Management of Prosperity*. Lawrence: University Press of Kansas, 1991.

Small, Melvin. *The Presidency of Richard Nixon*. Lawrence: University Press of Kansas, 1999.

Snead, David C. *The Gaither Committee, Eisenhower, and the Cold War*. Columbus: Ohio State University Press, 1999.

Sorensen, Theodore C. *Counselor: A Life at the Edge of History*. New York: Harper, 2008.

———. *Kennedy*. New York: Harper and Row, 1965.

———. *The Kennedy Legacy*. New York: Macmillan, 1969.

Steel, Ronald. *In Love with Night: The American Romance with Robert Kennedy*. New York: Simon and Schuster, 2000.

———. *Walter Lippmann and the American Century*. Boston: Little, Brown, 1980.

Steinberg, Alfred. *Sam Rayburn: A Biography*. New York: Hawthorn Books, 1975.

Stossel, Scott. *Sarge: The Life and Times of Sargent Shriver*. Washington: Smithsonian Books, 2004.

Sullivan, Frank. *Legend: The Only Inside Story about Mayor Richard J. Daley*. Chicago: Bonus Books, 1989.

Sullivan, William C. *The Bureau: My Thirty Years in Hoover's FBI*. With Bill Brown. New York: Norton, 1979.

Summers, Anthony. *The Arrogance of Power: The Secret World of Richard Nixon*. With Robbyn Swan. New York: Viking Press, 2000.

———. *Sinatra: The Life*. New York: Knopf, 2005.

Sundquist, James L. *Dynamics of the Party System: Alignment and Realignment of Political Parties in the United States*. Rev. ed. Washington: Brookings Institution, 1983.

Talbot, David. *Brothers: The Hidden History of the Kennedy Years*. New York: Free Press, 2007.

Taubman, Philip. *Secret Empire: Eisenhower, the CIA, and the Hidden Story of America's Space Espionage*. New York: Simon and Schuster, 2003.

Taubman, William. *Khrushchev: The Man and His Era*. New York: Norton, 2003.

Thomas, Evan. *Robert Kennedy: His Life*. New York: Simon and Schuster, 2000.

———. *The Very Best Men—Four Who Dared: The Early Years of the CIA*. New York: Simon and Schuster, 1995.

Thompson, Kenneth W., ed. *The Nixon Presidency: Twenty-two Intimate Perspectives of Richard M. Nixon*. Lanham, Md.: University Press of America, 1987.

Thompson, William F. *The History of Wisconsin: Continuity and Change, 1940–1965*. Madison: State Historical Society of Wisconsin, 1988.

Trest, Warren, and Don Dodd. *Wings of Denial: The Alabama Air National Guard's Covert Role at the Bay of Pigs*. Montgomery: New South Books, 2001.

Trohan, Walter. *Political Animals: Memoirs of a Sentimental Cynic*. Garden City: Doubleday, 1975.

Ulam, Adam. *The Rivals: America and Russia since World War II*. New York: Viking Press, 1971.

Vidal, Gore. *Homage to Daniel Shays: Collected Essays, 1952–1972*. New York: Random House, 1972.

———. *Palimpsest: A Memoir*. New York: Random House, 1995.

Warshaw, Shirley Anne, ed. *Reexamining the Eisenhower Presidency*. Westport, Conn.: Greenwood Press, 1993.

Watson, Mary Ann. *The Expanding Vista: American Television in the Kennedy Years*. New York: Oxford University Press, 1990.

Weber, Michael P. *Don't Call Me Boss: David L. Lawrence, Pittsburgh's Renaissance Mayor*. Pittsburgh: University of Pittsburgh Press, 1988.

Weeks, O. Douglas. *Texas in the 1960 Presidential Election*. Austin: Institute of Public Affairs, University of Texas, 1961.

Weiner, Tim. *Legacy of Ashes: The History of the CIA*. New York: Doubleday, 2007.

Whalen, Richard J. *The Founding Father: The Story of Joseph P. Kennedy*. New York: New American Library, 1964.

Whalen, Thomas J. *Kennedy versus Lodge: The 1952 Massachusetts Senate Race*. Boston: Northeastern University Press, 2000.

White, Theodore H. *America in Search of Itself: The Making of the President, 1956–1980*. New York: Harper and Row, 1982.

———. *Breach of Faith: The Fall of Richard Nixon*. New York: Atheneum, 1975.

———. *In Search of History: A Personal Adventure*. New York: Harper and Row, 1978.

———. *The Making of the President 1960*. New York: Atheneum, 1961.

———. *The Making of the President 1964*. New York: Atheneum, 1965.

Wicker, Tom. *One of Us: Richard Nixon and the American Dream*. New York: Random House, 1991.

Wiebe, Robert. *The Search for Order, 1877–1920*. New York: Hill and Wang, 1967.

Wilkins, Roy. *Standing Fast: The Autobiography of Roy Wilkins*. With Tom Matthews. New York: Viking Press, 1982.

Witcover, Jules. *Crapshoot: Rolling the Dice on the Vice Presidency*. New York: Crown, 1992.

Wofford, Harris. *Of Kennedys and Kings: Making Sense of the Sixties*. New York: Farrar, Straus and Giroux, 1980.

Wyden, Peter. *Bay of Pigs: The Untold Story*. New York: Simon and Schuster, 1979.

Yoder, Edwin M., Jr. *Joe Alsop's Cold War: A Study of Journalistic Influence and Intrigue*. Chapel Hill: University of North Carolina Press, 1995.

Zaloga, Stephen J. *The Kremlin's Nuclear Sword: The Rise and Fall of Russia's Strategic Nuclear Forces, 1945–2000*. Washington, D.C.: Smithsonian Institution Press, 2002.

Index

ABC-TV, 165, 178, 179
Abernathy, Ralph, 143, 154–55
Abram, Morris, 152
Acheson, Dean, 45, 46
Adams, Sherman, 15, 142, 244n20
Addison's disease, 31–32, 70, 72, 75
Adolphus Hotel, 167–68, 200
African Americans, 6, 133, 146, 169; and
    Eisenhower, 108, 141–42, 151; and JFK,
    30, 37–38, 135–36, 138, 139, 152, 157;
    and Nixon, 108–9, 135–36, 140–46,
    151, 157
Alabama: and Democratic presidential
    nomination, 69, 70, 74, 231n63; and
    election results, 188, 190, 253–54n37,
    254n40; in presidential election cam-
    paign, 115, 173, 192–93
Alabama Air National Guard, 129–30,
    241–42n34
Alaska, 70, 173, 175, 176, 194–95, 219n21
Alcorn, Meade, 83–84, 238n35
Alexander, Charles, 9
Alger, Bruce, 166–68
Alphand, Hervé, 130
Alsop, Joseph: Eisenhower's opinion of,
    10; and JFK health, 35; and missile gap,
    20, 22, 88–90; and presidential debates,
    123; in presidential election campaign,
    131, 159–60, 169; on Symington,
    220n31; and vice-presidential nomina-
    tion, 76; and West Virginia primary,
    65, 66
Alsop, Stewart, 20, 46, 110
Ambrose, Stephen, 2, 22, 88, 130, 142
American Political Science Review, 204
Amsterdam News, 149

Anderson, Robert, 13, 14, 87, 90, 142
Arizona, 68, 173, 174
Arkansas, 173, 190, 193
Arthur, Chester, 9
Arvad, Inga, 222n12
Austin, Richard, 210

Bailey, John, 54, 63, 78, 99, 177, 195
Baker, Bobby, 27, 76, 77, 132
Ball, George, 130
Barnett, Ross, 124
Bartlett, Charles, 25, 78, 102
Bassett, James, 107, 133
Bayley, Ed, 56
Bay of Pigs, 221n4, 241–42n34
Becker, William, 112
Behrens, Earl, 112
Belafonte, Harry, 139, 149, 254n43
Belden Poll, 199
Benson, Ezra Taft, 14
Billings, Lem, 196
Bissell, Richard, 129
Blacks. *See* African Americans
Blaik, Earl, 110, 237n27
Bliss, Ray, 195
Bolton, Frances, 189
Bowles, Chester, 38, 49, 152, 159, 246n47,
    246n50
Bozell, Brent, 235n32
Bradlee, Benjamin: as author of *Conversa-
    tions with Kennedy*, 207–8; and JFK, 34,
    97, 101–3, 230n44, 236n13; and Nixon,
    40, 122; on vote fraud, 207–8, 257n13
Bricker, John, 13
Brinkley, David, 30
Brown, Pat, 52, 70–71, 72, 179, 181, 203–4

Brownell, Herbert, 87, 91, 142
Brunt, A. W., 69
Bryant, Farris, 196
Buckley, Charles, 52
Burleigh, Nina, 29
Burns, Arthur, 39, 89–90
Butler, Paul, 17, 50
Byrd, Harry F., 188, 189, 193, 196
Byrd, Robert, 65

Calhoun, John, 138
California: and Democratic presidential
    nomination, 68, 69, 70–71, 72, 73; on
    election day 1960 and after, 179, 180,
    181–82, 184, 190, 203; in 1958 elec-
    tions, 15; in 1960 presidential election
    campaign, 98–99, 103, 108, 133, 158,
    159, 173, 174, 175, 191
Camelot, 1, 26, 27, 154, 201, 213–216,
    221n2
Capital Times, 55, 58, 59
Caro, Robert, 206–7
Carpentier, Charles, 199, 211, 255n52
Carter, Jimmy, 256n8
Casey, Shaun, 237n19
Castro, Fidel, 127–30
Catholics, 205, 206; in presidential elec-
    tion campaign, 100, 104–6, 168–72,
    202, 257n9; in West Virginia, 64; in
    Wisconsin, 54–55, 57–60, 64, 196
CBS-TV, 59, 142, 178, 179
Central Intelligence Agency (CIA), 15, 18,
    21, 129, 220n37, 241n31
Cermak, Anton, 199
Chamberlain, Neville, 28, 72
Chandler, Norman, 111
Checkers speech, 107, 119, 122
Chicago, 37, 92–96, 142, 183–86, 207–17,
    257–58n13
Chicago Daily News, 111, 185
Chicago Defender, 143, 149
Chicago Sun-Times, 180, 208
Chicago Tribune, 111, 185, 186, 211,
    258n18
Chock Full O'Nuts, 144, 145
Christie, Sidney, 63

CIA. *See* Central Intelligence Agency
Civil Rights Act of 1957, 137, 143, 145
Civil Rights Section, 147, 148, 149–50, 155
Clifford, Clark, 76–77
Clinton, William J., 256n8
Cold War, 1, 14–15, 16, 17, 192
Collins, LeRoy, 196
Collins, Robert, 41
Colorado, 68, 69, 173, 174
Committee for Honest Elections, 183,
    259n18
Connell, Francis, 184, 211
Connecticut, 173, 179, 193
Conscience of a Conservative (Goldwater),
    93, 235n32
Conversations with Kennedy (Bradlee),
    207–8
Corbett, Billy, 41
Corcoran, Thomas, 76, 77
Cronkite, Walter, 46, 59
Cronin, James, 169
Crotty, Peter, 52
Cuba, 1, 127–30, 206, 213, 241n31,
    241n33
Curtis, Carl, 189
Cushing, Cardinal Richard, 65

Dallas Morning News, 168
Dapples, George, 211
Daley, Richard: and Democratic presiden-
    tial nomination, 52, 71, 72, and Demo-
    cratic vice-presidential nomination, 76,
    78; and presidential election campaign,
    190, 199; and vote fraud, 181, 183,
    207–8, 257–58n13
Dawson, William, 79, 138, 147, 148, 149,
    150, 156, 245n31, 245n40
Debates. See Presidential debates
Delaware, 69, 173, 174,175, 193
Democratic Advisory Council, 17
Democratic National Committee, 17, 98,
    99, 149, 155
Democratic National Convention: 1956,
    36; 1960, 49, 61, 71–80, 168, 194
Democratic Party: 6–7, 11–12, 24, 50,
    104–5, 139, 147, 151; of California, 71;

of Chicago and Cook County, 199, 207; of Florida, 196; of Georgia, 154; of New York, 197; of Wisconsin, 61, 145

Depression. *See* Great Depression

DeSapio, Carmine, 52, 74, 76, 78, 159

De Toledano, Ralph, 186

Dewey, Thomas, 7, 8, 44, 159, 165

DiBetta, John, 177

Dirksen, Everett, 180

DiSalle, Michael, 52, 53–54, 71, 78, 203–4

Docking, George, 72, 73

Dodge, Robert, 181–82

Douglas, Helen Gahagan, 44, 45, 111, 121, 225n54

Douglas, Paul, 199, 255n52

Dreiske, John, 180

Drummond, Roscoe, 111

Dubinsky, David, 79

Dulles, Allen, 15, 21, 128–29, 234n22, 241n21

Dulles, John Foster, 16, 45, 82, 87, 126

Durham, Frank, 183

Eastland, John, 195

Edwards, Willard, 111

Ehrlichman, John, 111, 224n40

Eisenhower, Dwight David: and African Americans, 108, 141–42, 151–52, 156, 243–44n17; character and intellect, 8–9; on election day 1960 and after, 182–83, 185–86, 187–88, 248n12; health of, 162–64; and JFK, 86, 88, 161, 253n30; on Knowland, 4, 13; and LBJ, 86, 88; and missile gap, 17, 20–24, 89; and Nixon, 46–47, 84, 85–88, 161–64; popularity, 11, 205; and presidential election campaign of 1952, 8; and presidential election campaign of 1960, 98, 109, 118, 125, 126, 160–65, 171, 172, 191, 198; and Republican Party, 13–14; and Rockefeller, 85–86, 92, 94; on spending, 10.–11

Eisenhower, Mamie, 162–64

Eisenhower, Milton, 13, 86–87

Elections

—Congressional: of 1928, 4; of 1930, 4; of 1932, 5, 7; of 1934, 7; of 1936, 5, 7; of 1938, 6, 7; of 1942, 5, 6, 7; of 1944, 5, 6, 7; of 1946, 6, 7, 12; of 1948, 7, 12; of 1952, 11, 12; of 1956, 11, 12; of 1958, 14–16, 24, 49, 81–82

—Presidential: of 1916, 1; of 1928, 4; of 1932, 5, 7; of 1936, 5, 7; of 1940, 5, 7; of 1944, 5, 7; of 1948, 7, 12, 97; of 1952, 8, 9, 11, 12, 13, 256–57n8; of 1956, 11, 12, 13, 36–37, 149, 256–57n8; of 1964, 205, 206, 256n8; of 1968, 12, 181, 256n8; of 1972, 12, 256–57n8; of 1976, 1, 118, 256n8; of 1980, 256n8; of 1984, 256–57n8; of 1988, 256–57n8; 1992, 256n8; of 1996, 256n8

Electoral College, 1, 5, 108–9, 181–82, 187–88, 190, 203

Evans, Rowland, 37, 102, 173

Evjue, William, 55–56

Ewald, William, 110

Exner, Judith Campbell, 221n3, 222n12

Faubus, Orval, 37

Fay, Paul, 31, 164

FBI. *See* Federal Bureau of Investigation

FCC. *See* Federal Communications Commission

Federal Bureau of Investigation (FBI), 43, 130

Federal Communications Commission (FCC), 59, 117

Feldman, Mike, 186–87

Fetridge, William, 201, 257–58n13

Finch, Robert, 39, 85, 97, 107, 180, 183, 207

Flanigan, Peter, 170

Flemming, Arthur, 170, 183

Florida, 173, 174, 191, 196–97

Folger, J. Clifford, 180

Folliard, Edward, 122

Fonda, Henry, 43

Ford, Gerald R., 94

Fortune, 28

Frank, Reuven, 126, 251n4

Frankfurter, Felix, 28, 34

Freeman, Orville, 60, 76, 194, 232n69

Gaither Committee, 21–22

Gaither, H. Rowan, 21

Galbraith, John Kenneth, 79, 102, 194

Gallup, George, 176

Gallup Polls: Democratic presidential nomination, 51; Eisenhower approval, 11, 15; JFK approval, 221n2; JFK v. Nixon, 16, 96, 104, 116, 133–34, 158, 176, 242n45, 253n36, 257n9; missile gap, 22; Nixon v. Rockefeller, 85; Truman approval, 7–8

Gates, Thomas, 21

Gellman, Irwin, 224n40, 225n54

Georgia, 115–16, 153–57, 173, 190, 193

Giancana, Sam, 222n12, 258n13

Goldberg, Arthur, 78

Goldwater, Barry, 5, 77–78, 81, 113, 162, 247n55; and *Conscience of a Conservative*, 93, 235n32; and Republican national convention, 92, 93, 95, 96

Goodwin, Richard, 122, 128–29, 159, 239n1

GOP. *See* Republican Party

Graham, Billy, 170, 171, 250n35

Graham, Philip, 76, 78, 129, 220n31

Great Depression, 4, 6, 33, 42

Green, William, 72, 78, 197

Grey, Zane, 87

Gruenther, Al, 87

Guild, William, 211

Guylay, L. Richard, 107

Hagerty, James, 10, 124, 125, 156, 172

Haldeman, H. R., 39–40, 41, 107, 110, 133, 224n40

Hall, Leonard: and Eisenhower, 13; and 1960 presidential election campaign 107, 110–11, 151, 180, 184, 247n55; and 1960 presidential nomination, 83–84

Halleck, Charles, 119

Hamilton, Nigel, 33, 38, 222n4, 222n12

Hamilton, Wilbur, 197

Harlow, Bryce, 39, 41–42, 111, 113, 170, 177, 182

Harriman, Averell, 49, 82

Harris, Louis: on election day 1960 and

after, 177, 203–4, 213; polls for JFK for presidential nomination, 51, 53; in presidential election campaign, 99, 126, 127, 158, 160, 173–74, 195, 250n42; West Virginia primary polls, 62, 66, 228–29n38; Wisconsin primary polls, 55, 58

Harrison, Benjamin, 9

Hartke, Vance, 73

Hartsfield, William, 152–53, 156

Hauge, Gabriel, 94

Hawaii: admitted to the Union, 219n21; on election day 1960 and after, 181–82, 188, 189, 193, 195; in 1960 presidential election campaign, 174, 175

Hayden, Carl, 189

Hays, Wayne, 53

Hays, Woody, 195

Heaney, Gerald, 57

Herblock, 124

Hersh, Seymour, 222n12, 230n43

Hess, Rudolf, 46

Herter, Christian, 127

Hillings, Pat, 207

Hiss, Alger, 7, 44, 45, 46, 81

Hobby, Oveta Culp, 13, 88

Hoffa, James, 56, 57

Holding the Line (Alexander), 9

Hoover, Herbert, 4, 172m, 187

Hoover, J. Edgar, 130, 222n12

House of Representatives, 4–7, 13, 15, 188, 196, 205–6, 219n21

Houston Chronicle, 184

Houston Ministerial Association, 98, 104, 105–6, 168

Hughes, Don, 107, 133, 177

Hughes, Howard, 166

Humphrey, George, 82

Humphrey, Hubert H.: and JFK, 38, 194; and missile gap, 19; as presidential candidate in 1960, 49, 51, 54, 145; as presidential candidate in 1968, 247n55; on vice presidential nomination, 76; in West Virginia primary, 61–67, 169; in Wisconsin primary, 54–61, 139, 196

Hyannis Port, 98, 179

Intercontinental Ballistic Missile (ICBM), 17–22

ICBM. *See* Intercontinental Ballistic Missile

Idaho, 174

Illinois: and Democratic presidential nomination, 67, 68, 70; on election day 1960 and after, 179, 180, 181, 182, 184, 187, 207–11, 255n52; in 1960 presidential campaign, 98, 108, 133, 173, 174, 175, 193; in 1968 presidential election campaign, 252n10

Illinois State Electoral Board, 211

Indiana, 73, 174, 180

Intercontinental Ballistic Missile. *See* ICBM

Iowa, 174, 175

Irwin, Henry, 188

Jackson, Henry "Scoop", 19, 76

Jamieson, Kathleen, 103

Jaspers, Claude, 196

Jeffrey, Mildred, 159

Jenner, William, 13

Jet, 149

Johnson, Andrew, 9, 138

Johnson, Ed, 69

Johnson, Lady Bird (Claudia), 75–76, 77, 167–68

Johnson, Lester, 55

Johnson, Lyndon: and African Americans, 243n4; and civil rights, 139, 140; Eisenhower's opinion of, 83, 88; and JFK, 38; and missile gap, 19; as presidential candidate in 1960, 49, 51, 53, 61, 65, 68, 72; and presidential debates, 123; in presidential election of 1964, 204–5, 256n8; and religious issue, 168, 170; as Senate majority leader, 16–17, 81, 137; and sex, 29; as vice-presidential candidate in presidential election, 95, 99–100, 108, 116, 131–32, 147–48, 150, 157, 167–68, 170, 199–200; and vice-presidential nomination, 74–79, 91, 95, 190; and vote fraud, 206–7

Jones, Ray, 150

Judd, Walter, 94, 170

Justice Department, 156

Kanawha County, W.Va., 62, 229n38

Kansas, 73, 174, 203

Kaplow, Herbert, 41

Kastenmeier, Robert, 55

Kefauver, Estes, 36, 38, 50, 51, 53, 136, 194

Kelly, Edna, 189

Kennedy, Edward (JFK's brother), 187

Kennedy, Jacqueline Bouvier (JFK's spouse): and Camelot, 1, 26, 221n3, 259n23; on election day 1960, 179; on LBJ, 75, 78; marriage to JFK, 36; in Wisconsin primary, 56

Kennedy, John F. (JFK): and African Americans, 135–40, 145–57; character, 29–33; and Cuba, 127–31; and Democratic national convention of 1960, 71–80; and Eisenhower, 86, 88, 161, 253n30; on election day 1960 and after, 177, 179–80, 186–88, 190–91; and end of presidential campaign, 158–60, 164, 172; and Gallup Poll, 16, 51, 96, 104, 116, 133–34, 158, 176, 221n2, 242n45, 253n36; health, 30–32, 35, 75, 231n57; and Joseph P. Kennedy, 29–32; and Martin Luther King Jr., 139–40, 152–54; and LBJ, 75–79; life before 1960, 29–38; and missile gap, 19, 89; and Nixon, 47–48, 226n62; as presidential candidate, 100–101, 190–92; and presidential debates, 117–31; and presidential election results, 192–98; and press, 101–2, 111–13; and *PT-109*, 32 and religion, 57–60, 64–65, 104–6, 168–71, 202–5; and sex, 29–30, 222n12; and vice-presidential choice, 75–79, 91, 94; and West Virginia primary, 61–67; and Wisconsin primary, 54–61; and World War II, 32–33

Kennedy, John F., Jr. (JFK's son), 208

Kennedy, Joseph P. (JFK's father): early years, 27–28; on election day 1960 and after, 186, 187; and family, 28–30; and

Kennedy, Joseph P.—*continued*
FDR, 27–28; Hubert Humphrey on, 56; and JFK, 29–33, 35; and Nixon, 47; and presidential election campaign, 100, 151, 203, 258n13; stroke, 29; and vice-presidential nomination, 74, 77, 79, 80; and West Virginia primary, 65

Kennedy, Joseph P., Jr. (JFK's brother), 29, 33, 64

Kennedy, Kathleen (JFK's sister), 29

Kennedy & Nixon (Matthews), 2

Kennedy, Robert F. (JFK's brother): and African Americans, 139–40, 145, 148–57; and Bay of Pigs, 241–42n34; as campaign manager, 35, 52, 53, 99, 103, 160, 168, 190–91; and civil rights, 138, 139, 140; and Walter Cronkite, 59; death, 26; and Democratic convention, 69–80; and Michael DiSalle, 53–54; on election day 1960 and after, 187, 213;and LBJ, 99; and Martin Luther King Jr. arrest, 153–55, 158; and vice-presidential nomination, 75–79; and West Virginia primary, 64–67, 228–29n38

Kennedy, Rose (JFK's mother), 29, 56

Kennedy, Rosemary (JFK's sister), 29

Kentucky, 69, 70, 173, 174, 180

Kerner, Otto, 199

Kerr, Robert, 69, 75, 77

Khrushchev, Nikita: and Eisenhower, 15, 17, 18, 24; and Nixon, 47, 84; and 1960 presidential election campaign, 89, 128, 192

King, Coretta Scott, 153, 155, 156, 157, 158, 246n50

King, Martin Luther, Jr.: arrest and release, 152–58, 166, 213; and JFK, 135, 138, 139, 147, 152,-54, 157; and Nixon, 143, 144, 155–57

King, Martin Luther, Sr., 135, 155

Kirk, Grayson, 59

Kissinger, Henry, 41

Klein, Herbert, 113, 118, 166, 178, 180

Klein, Julius, 125

Knebel, Fletcher, 218n9

Knight, Goodwin, 15

Knowland, William, 4, 13, 15, 81, 86

Kraft, Polly, 34

Krock, Arthur, 111, 136

Lanphier, T. G., 19

Lasky, Victor, 239n5

Lausche, Frank, 53, 123

Lawford, Patricia Kennedy, 101

Lawrence, David, 52, 70, 71, 72, 76, 78, 79, 197

Lawrence, William, 112–13

Lawson, Belford, 138

Lawson, Marjorie, 138, 147, 148

Lehman, Herbert, 52

LeMay, Curtis (general), 18

Lewis, Ted, 163

Liberals, 17, 37, 38, 45, 51, 55, 80, 137, 139

Life (magazine), 20, 39, 102, 170, 250n35

Lippmann, Walter, 9, 10, 90

Lisagor, Peter, 103, 245n29

Lodge, Henry Cabot, Jr.: as choice as vice-presidential nominee, 94–95; in 1960 presidential election campaign, 112, 125–26, 133, 183, 192; in 1952 Senate election campaign, 35–36, 136

Lohman, Joseph, 211

Look (magazine), 86

Los Angeles Times, 111, 123

Louisiana, 173, 175, 193

Loveless, Herschel, 72

Luce, Henry, 102, 170

Lucey, Patrick, 54, 55

Maheu, Robert, 166

Maine, 5, 174, 203–4, 252n10

Making of the President 1960, The (White), 1, 26, 190, 213–16

Mansfield, Mike, 68

Marshall Plan, 7, 8, 44

Martin, Louis, 135, 147, 148–49, 150, 151, 153–55

Martin, William McChesney, 14

Maryland, 173, 193

Massachusetts, 98, 108, 173, 193

Matsu, 126, 127, 213

Matthews, Christopher, 2

Maxwell, Don, 186
Mazo, Earl, 111, 162, 185, 208–9, 258–59n18
McCarthy, Eugene, 65, 72, 95
McCarthy, Joseph, 13, 37, 46, 55, 60, 81
McClellan, John, 37
McClendon, Sarah, 112, 114
McCone, John, 21, 241n21
McCrary, Tex, 86
McDonough, Robert, 63
McElroy, Neil, 21
McGee, Gale, 68–69
McGrory, Mary, 112
McIntyre, Cardinal James Francis, 169
McMillin, Miles, 55
McNamara, Robert, 230n44
Meehan, Austin, 197
Merriam, Robert, 107, 114, 119–20, 239n5
Meyer, Mary, 102, 236n13
Meyner, Robert, 52, 69, 70, 72, 73, 74, 232n63
Michigan: and Democratic presidential nomination, 68, 70; and election day 1960 and after, 180; in 1960 presidential election campaign, 98, 108, 173, 179, 190, 193, 197–98
Michigan Chronicle, 149
Miller, Ray, 53
Milwaukee Journal, 56, 57–58
Minnesota, 69, 173, 174, 179, 180, 182, 193, 197
Missile gap, 17–24, 90, 91, 213, 234n22
Mississippi, 173, 176, 188, 194–95, 254n43
Missouri, 173, 184, 191, 193, 197, 209, 252n10
Mitchell, Clarence, 137, 140, 143
Mitchell, James, 94
Mitchell, Oscar, 153–55, 156
Mohr, Charles, 114, 115
Montana, 68, 70, 73
Montgomery, Robert, 124, 183
Morgan, Edward, 40
Morris, Roger, 224n40
Morrow, E. Frederic, 142, 155–56, 243n17, 244n20, 247n55
Morse, Wayne, 54, 227n10

Morton, Thruston, 94, 107, 180, 184, 185
Mundt, Karl, 13
Murrow, Edward R., 9–10
Muskie, Edmund, 203

National Association for the Advancement of Colored People (NAACP), 137, 138, 139, 142, 145, 148, 156
NAACP. See National Association for the Advancement of Colored People
National Conference of Citizens for Religious Freedom, 105
National Conference on Constitutional Rights, 147, 148, 151
National Recount and Fair Elections Committee, 184
NATO. See North Atlantic Treaty Organization
NBC-TV, 113, 121, 178, 179
Nebraska, 51, 55, 67, 174
Nelson, Gaylord, 55, 56
Nevada, 68, 173, 175, 184, 193, 209, 252n10
Newark Times, 113
New Deal, 4, 5, 6, 8, 10, 13, 27, 44, 82, 108
New Frontier, 79
New Hampshire, 50, 52, 54, 67, 83, 84, 174, 175
New Jersey: and Democratic presidential nomination, 68, 73–74; in 1960 presidential election campaign, 98, 108, 173, 184, 193; in 1968 presidential election campaign, 252n10
New Mexico, 69, 184, 190, 193, 209
New Republic, The (magazine), 20
Newsweek (magazine), 20, 40, 57, 71, 160, 174, 176
Newton, Carroll, 107, 165
New York: and Democratic presidential nomination, 68, 70; in 1960 presidential election campaign, 98, 108, 132, 159, 173, 180, 193, 197
New York Daily News, 123, 158
New York Herald Tribune, 20, 66, 158, 173, 174, 185, 208
New York Post, 145

New York Times: on Democratic presidential nomination, 50; on JFK, 34; on missile gap, 20; on 1958 elections, 15; on 1960 presidential election campaign, 111, 112; on 1960 election night, 179; on Nixon, 84; on Rockefeller, 83; and West Virginia primary, 66; and Wisconsin primary, 59

Nitze, Paul, 21

Nixon, Arthur (RMN's brother), 42

Nixon, Donald (RMN's brother), 166

Nixon, Frank (RMN's father), 42

Nixon, Hannah (RMN's mother), 42

Nixon, Harold (RMN's brother), 42

Nixon, Julie (RMN's daughter), 208

Nixon, Pat (RMN's spouse), 43, 107, 208

Nixon, Richard Milhous (RMN): and African Americans, 108–9, 135–36, 140–46, 151, 157; as campaigner, 107–110, 251–52n10; and campaign strategy, 107–9, 160–66, 191–92; character, 38–42; and civil rights, 142–44; and Cuba, 127–31, 241n31, 244n23, 247n55; and Eisenhower, 46–47, 84, 85–88, 161–64; on election day 1960 and after, 177–78, 180–82, 185–89; and election results, 193, 195–200; and end of presidential campaign, 160–66, 172–76; and Gallup Polls, 16, 85, 96, 104, 116, 133–34, 158, 176, 242n45, 253n36, 257n9; and JFK, 47–48, 226n62, 226n63; and Martin Luther King Jr., 143–44, 155–57; life before 1960, 38–48, 110; and missile gap, 21; and presidential debates, 117–31; and press, 111–14; and religious issue, 106, 168–72, 257n9; and Republican national convention of 1960, 91–96; and Republican Party, 81–82, 84; and Jackie Robinson, 144–45, 155–57; and Rockefeller, 83, 91–92, 94; *Six Crises*, 171, 174, 185, 208, 241n21 and vice-presidential choice, 81, 94–95

Nixon, Tricia (RMN's daughter), 208

North Atlantic Treaty Organization (NATO), 7, 8, 44

North Carolina: and Democratic presidential nomination, 69, 70; in 1960 presidential election campaign, 115, 173, 175, 190, 193, 197; in 1968 presidential election campaign, 252n10

North Dakota, 174

Notre Dame University, 100

O'Brien, Lawrence: and Democratic presidential nomination, 66; in 1960 presidential election campaign, 99, 101, 158, 166, 186, 230n45, 257n9; and RFK, 37

O'Connell, Daniel, 52

O'Donnell, Kenneth: and Democratic presidential nomination, 54, 66; and election day 1960 and after, 186, 202–3, 213; in 1960 presidential election campaign, 99, 101, 148, 153, 159; and RFK, 37, 54; and vice-presidential nomination, 78; and West Virginia primary, 66

Ohio: and Democratic presidential nomination, 53–54, 67, 73; on election day 1960 and after, 179, 180, 187, 203; and 1958 elections, 15; in 1960 presidential election campaign, 98, 108, 133, 160, 173, 174, 175, 176, 191, 194–95, 197–98

Oklahoma, 68, 180, 188

O'Neill, Thomas "Tip", 77

Oregon, 52, 69, 73, 103, 174

Oswald, Lee Harvey, 221n3

Palmer, Kyle, 111

Parmet, Herbert, 24, 100, 129

Patterson, John: and Cuba, 129–30; and Democratic convention, 231n63; and JFK, 38, 56, 74, 137–39, 145

Peale, Norman Vincent, 105, 171

Pearson, Drew, 166

Pennsylvania: and Democratic presidential nomination, 68, 70; on election day 1960 and after, 180, 184; in 1960 presidential election campaign, 98, 108, 173, 174, 190, 193, 197–98

Percy, Charles, 91

Perot, Ross, 256n8

Persons, Jerry, 156, 244n20

Pittsburgh Courier, 149

Potter, Philip, 112, 113
Powell, Adam Clayton, Jr., 79, 138, 149, 150, 156, 168–69
Prendergast, Michael, 52, 78, 159
Presidential debates, 116–131, 134
President's Committee on Government Contracts, 142
Primaries, 49–50; Illinois, 67, Indiana, 67; Maryland, 67; Massachusetts, 67; Nebraska, 67; New Hampshire, 51, 54, 67; Oregon, 67; Pennsylvania, 67; West Virginia, 61–67, 103; Wisconsin, 53, 54, 56–61, 67, 103
Profiles in Courage (Kennedy), 38, 50, 138
Protestants: in presidential election campaign, 104–6, 168–70, 202, 206; in West Virginia primary, 64; in Wisconsin primary, 57, 59, 60, 64
Proxmire, William, 55
PT-109 (boat), 32

Quemoy, 126, 127, 213
Quinn, William, 189

Randolph, A. Philip, 150
Rayburn, Sam: and Bruce Alger, 168; and JFK, 34–35, 75; and Nixon, 45–46, 189; and Adam Clayton Powell Jr., 150; as Speaker of the House, 16–17, 98; and vice-presidential nomination, 75, 77, 78
Reagan, Ronald, 44, 113–14
Rebozo, Bebe, 40
Reconstruction, 138, 148, 157
Reedy, George, 132, 148
Reeves, Frank, 147, 148, 149
Reeves, Richard, 34, 136
Reinsch, Leonard, 99, 117, 121, 165, 239n5
Religious issue: in presidential election campaign, 104–6, 168–70, 191, 202–6; in West Virginia primary, 62–67; in Wisconsin primary, 57–61, 63, 64
Republican National Committee, 13, 84, 107
Republican National Convention, 91–97
Republican Party (GOP): in 1930s and

1940s, 4–5, 44; in 1950s, 8, 11–16, 24, 44; in 1960, 81–82, 91–97, 151, 160, 182, 196, 207
Reston, James, 59, 126, 129
Reuss, Henry, 55
Reuther, Walter, 78, 198
Reynolds, John, 55
Rhee, Syngman, 89
Rhode Island, 173, 175, 193
Riesman, David, 127
Robinson, Claude: and Nixon, 107; and polls for 1960 presidential election, 90, 91, 120, 133, 151–52, 175–76, 199; and presidential debates, 117, 120, 125, 126
Robinson, Jackie, 139, 144–45, 146, 155–56, 244–45n29
Robinson, William, 163
Rockefeller, Nelson: and Eisenhower, 85–86, 88, 94; and JFK, 230n44; and missile gap, 20–21; and Nixon, 83, 90–94; and presidential election campaign, 108, 183, 197; and presidential nomination, 81–85, 88–93; and Theodore White, 213
Rogers, Ted, 107, 122, 123, 165
Rogers, William, 178
Rometsch, Ellen, 222n12
Roncalio, Teno, 68
Roosevelt, Eleanor, 52, 80, 98, 151
Roosevelt, Franklin Delano, 4–7, 10–12, 27–28, 79, 108, 131, 142, 151, 205
Roosevelt, Franklin D., Jr., 63, 65, 67, 230n44
Roosevelt, James, 27
Roper, Elmo, 59
Rose, Alex, 78
Ross, Edmund, 138
Rovere, Richard, 40–41, 223n19
Rowe, James, 68, 99
Russell, Richard, 80, 154, 167
Russell, Robert, 154, 156
Rustin, Bayard, 144, 150

Salinger, Pierre, 66, 99, 103, 153, 180, 187, 213
Salisbury, Harrison, 112
San Francisco Chronicle, 112

Thomas, George, 136

Thousand Days, A (Schlesinger), 26

Thurmond, Strom, 7, 12

Till, Emmett, 142

Time (magazine): and Democratic convention, 71; and JFK, 38, 101; and missile gap, 20; and presidential election campaign, 98, 114, 176; and Wisconsin primary, 57, 59

Treaty of Fifth Avenue, 92, 93

Trohan, Walter, 87

Truman, Harry: and African Americans, 142, 243n4; approval ratings, 7–8; conception of presidency, 10–11; and JFK, 80, 98; and Nixon, 45–46; and presidential election of 1948, 7, 12, 97, 256n8; and presidential election of 1960, 168–69, 172

Twenty-One (television program), 117

Twining, Nathan, 18

Tydings, Joseph, 196

UAW. *See* United Auto Workers

Udall, Stewart, 68, 73–74

United Auto Workers (UAW), 164, 171, 198

U.S. News & World Report (magazine), 20, 176

Utah, 174

U-2, 23, 89

Vandiver, Ernest, 154–56

Van Doren, Charles, 117

Van Dyke, Jerry, 69

Vanocur, Sander, 113

Vermont, 5, 174, 180

Vidal, Gore, 223n19

Virginia, 173, 174, 196

Voorhis, Jerry, 43, 44, 45, 111, 121, 225n54

Vote fraud, 183–187, 206–12, 214, 257–58n13, 259n18

Wagner, Robert, 78

Wallace, Henry, 7, 12

Wall Street Journal, 66

Washington Post, 20, 66, 76, 123, 208

Watergate, 5, 38, 224n40

Watson, Thomas, 59

West Virginia, 61–67, 103, 173, 193

Wexler, Morris, 210

White, Byron, 68, 148

White, Theodore: and Camelot, 1, 26, 154; on election day 1960 and after, 177, 179, 201, 207; and JFK, 3, 97, 101–2; and *Making of the President 1960*, 1, 26, 190, 212–14; on Nixon, 39, 41, 92, 259n22; and presidential election campaign, 103, 110, 112, 116, 118–19, 124, 154, 158, 160–61, 165, 192, 239n5; and West Virginia primary, 63, 228–29n38, 230n43; and Wisconsin primary, 61

Whitman, Ann, 13, 40, 172, 182, 185, 186

Wicker, Tom, 112, 238n35

Wiebe, Robert, 135

Wilkie, Wendell, 8

Wilkins, Roy, 79, 138, 139, 143, 145

Williams, G. Mennen, 49, 52, 254n43

Williams, John Bell, 254n43

Wilson, Charles, 82

Wilson, Lyle, 111

Wilson, Richard, 111

Wilson, Woodrow, 10–11

Wisconsin: April primary, 33, 54–64, 145; presidential election results, 173, 174, 175, 191, 195–96, 197, 203

Witwer, Samuel, 199, 255n52

Wofford, Harris: and Kennedy presidential campaign, 100, 136, 138, 140, 146–52, 154–55, 157, 246n50, 247n54; and Martin Luther King Jr. arrest and release, 152, 154, 155–57

Woods, Rose Mary, 107, 113, 124, 169, 237n27

Wyoming, 68, 73, 174

Edmund F. Kallina Jr. is professor of history at the University of Central Florida. He is the author of *Claude Kirk and the Politics of Confrontation* (UPF, 1993) and *Courthouse over White House: Chicago and the Presidential Election of 1960* (UPF, 1988).